REMEMBERING NAYE
AND THE GRAY BULL ENGIRO

African Storytellers of the Karamoja Plateau and the Plains of Turkana

The Jie people of northern Uganda and the Turkana of northern Kenya have a genesis myth about Nayeche, a Jie woman who followed the footprints of a gray bull across the waterless plateau and who founded a "cradle land" in the plains of Turkana. In *Remembering Nayeche and the Gray Bull Engiro*, Mustafa Kemal Mirzeler shows how the poetic journey of Nayeche and the gray bull Engiro and their metaphorical return during the Jie harvest rituals gives rise to stories, imagery, and the articulation of ethnic and individual identities.

Since the 1990s, Mirzeler has traveled to East Africa to apprentice with storytellers. *Remembering Nayeche and the Gray Bull Engiro* is an account both of his experience listening to these storytellers and of how oral tradition continues to evolve in the modern world. Mirzeler's work contributes significantly to the anthropology of storytelling, the study of myth and memory, and the use of oral tradition in historical studies.

(Anthropological Horizons)

MUSTAFA KEMAL MIRZELER is an associate professor in the Department of English at Western Michigan University.

Anthropological Horizons

Editor: Michael Lambek, University of Toronto

This series, begun in 1991, focuses on theoretically informed ethnographic works addressing issues of mind and body, knowledge and power, equality and inequality, the individual and the collective. Interdisciplinary in its perspective, the series makes a unique contribution in several other academic disciplines: women's studies, history, philosophy, psychology, political science, and sociology.

For a list of the books published in this series see p. 367

Remembering Nayeche and the Gray Bull Engiro

African Storytellers of the Karamoja Plateau and the Plains of Turkana

MUSTAFA KEMAL MIRZELER

UNIVERSITY OF TORONTO PRESS
Toronto Buffalo London

ISBN 978-1-4426-4866-1 (cloth)
ISBN 978-1-4426-2631-7 (paper)

Library and Archives Canada Cataloguing in Publication

Mirzeler, Mustafa Kemal, author
Remembering Nayeche and the gray bull Engiro : African storytellers of the
Karamoja Plateau and the Plains of Turkana/Mustafa Kemal Mirzeler.

Includes bibliographical references and index.
ISBN 978-1-4426-4866-1 (bound). – ISBN 978-1-4426-2631-7 (pbk.)

1. Jie (African people) – Folklore.   2. Jie (African people) – Social life and
customs.   3. Storytelling – Uganda – Kotido District.   4. Ethnology –
Uganda – Kotido District.   I. Title.

GR356.52.J53M57 2014   398.2089'965   C2013-908304-9

University of Toronto Press acknowledges the financial assistance to its
publishing program of the Canada Council for the Arts and the Ontario Arts
Council.

Canada Council   Conseil des Arts
for the Arts   du Canada

ONTARIO ARTS COUNCIL
CONSEIL DES ARTS DE L'ONTARIO
50 YEARS OF ONTARIO GOVERNMENT SUPPORT OF THE ARTS
50 ANS DE SOUTIEN DU GOUVERNEMENT DE L'ONTARIO AUX ARTS

University of Toronto Press acknowledges the financial support of the
Government of Canada through the Canada Book Fund for its publishing
activities.

Contents

Illustrations

Preface and Acknowledgments

This book took form through a multitude of inquiries and discussions, both in the field and in academic settings. It started in cold library rooms, in offices of various academics, and in my solitary contemplation on the shores of Lake Mendota on the University of Wisconsin–Madison campus. My discussions with colleagues, students, and others who have heard or read the various parts of this book have each contributed in their own unique ways to its creation.

I am indebted to friends at the University of Wisconsin–Madison, John Loud and Geoff Bradshaw, who listened to me about my experiences of working with African storytellers. The late Neil Whitehead, David Henige, and Jan Vansina heard, read, and commented on various chapters of this book. My research would perhaps not have been possible had I not consulted with Professor Crawford Young during that cold snowy winter morning in his office. I will always remember his kind spirit, wisdom, and humanity. His memory lives in every page of this book.

At the University of Wisconsin–Madison, I also want to thank Aili Tripp for her kindness and support and for facilitating my successful contact in Kampala, which was necessary in obtaining research clearance.

During the last phase of writing this book, I returned to Kampala and Najie Uganda, in 2010 and 2011, where I met with Lodoch and Sister Camilla Roach, who both were integral and indispensable to this project. My grateful thanks also to my esteemed colleagues Dyan Mazurana and Sandra Gray and Western Michigan University for making my journeys to Uganda possible.

In addition there are a number of individuals whose work, critique, and wisdom have been invaluable. I would like to recognize and thank

P.H. Gulliver and Pamela Gulliver, the principal anthropologists of the Turkana and Jie people, for sharing their knowledge and memories of their fieldwork experiences with me; Elizabeth Marshall-Thomas for hosting me in her home and generously sharing her memories and experiences of working in Karamoja Plateau and Turkana land; Professor James Barber and June Barber for hosting me in their home and sharing their memories and experiences of working many years in Karamoja Plateau during the late colonial era; Paul Spencer for sharing his memories of working around Lake Turkana among the Elmolo people and around Mount Kulal; Sister Camilla Roach who has shared many of the experiences in the field with me and who has heard most of the arguments put forward in this book. I am grateful to Father Cisternino, Father Anthony Barrett, Neal Sobania, Aneesa Kassam, Rada Dyson-Hudson and Neville Dyson-Hudson, Sandra Gray, David Eaton, Mary Sundal, Elizabeth Stites, and Michael Lokuruka for generously sharing their expert knowledge of the region. I am grateful to my esteemed colleagues Lisa Gabbert, Beverly Stoeltje, Michael Jindra, and Allen Webb for their encouragement in the publication of this book. Mary Sundal, David Henige, Richard Bauman, John Saillant, and Jan Vansina, all read the book and their interventions greatly improved its quality. Endless theoretical discussions with late Robert Collins, Neil Whitehead, and others have shaped my thinking about the contemporary predicament of Karimojong communities. The anonymous reviewers at University of Toronto Press read the entire manuscript twice, at least, and offered suggestions and insights that helped focus the book, contributing immensely to its readability. Douglas Hildebrand has been a very encouraging and understanding editor. His suggestions were invaluable to the theoretical focus of the book.

Over the years, I presented portions of this book at various universities and conferences. Specifically, I am grateful to Lawrence Robbins at Michigan State University; Dorothy Noyes, Margaret Mills, and Ray Cashman at Ohio State University; and the literature faculty and students at the University of Notre Dame. I am grateful to Professor Guenther Schlee and various staff members at the Max Planck Institute in Halle Saale, Germany; and faculty and staff at the Makerere Institute of Social Research, Kampala, Uganda. Material was also presented at the annual meeting of the American Folklore Association, the American Anthropological Association, the African Studies Association, and the Baku State University in Azerbaijan.

In Karamoja Plateau and Turkana land, I have many people to thank, and I apologize to anyone I do not name. For being generous in sharing very important information about the Jie and the Turkana oral tradition, I thank the following storytellers: Lodoch, Logwee, Rianaro, the late Lokapilan, Nakapor and Nadul, and Paul Longoli, Joseph Lodungokol, Napau, Ekeno, Sebastian Lakarsante, and many others. I am grateful to the governments of Kenya and Uganda for allowing me to do this research. I thank the Social Science Research Council, and the John D. and Catherine T. MacArthur Foundation for their generous funds, which made it possible for me to conduct two years of research from 1994 to 1995 and from 1996 to 1997. My subsequent research projects have been funded by the National Endowment for the Humanities, the Wenner-Gren Foundation, and Western Michigan University. At Western Michigan University I would like to thank Provost Green, Dean Enyedi, Dr Ltynski, Dr Kohler, Dr Hodge, Dr Bush, and Dr Utz for their generous financial and administrative support. It would not have been possible for me to get my book edited for publication without their support. I am especially grateful to Richard Utz, my former chair, for providing an opportunity for me to share parts of this book with my colleagues at Western Michigan University. I am also grateful to my colleague John Saillant, of the Departments of English and History, for consulting on my manuscript. The technical assistance of Gwen A. Little and J. Glatz at Western Michigan University is gratefully acknowledged.

Finally, this book would not have been completed without the support of my family. Mumbi and David have grown up with this project, listening to the stories I collected from Africa and to my stories about the African storytellers I worked with. Finally I must acknowledge the greatest support of all in the person of my treasured wife and life partner. Her insight and inspiration were constant and comforting. Singlehandedly she took care of our family while I was conducting my many months of fieldwork in Kenya and Uganda. This book is more hers than it is mine. And now it is yours.

Maps

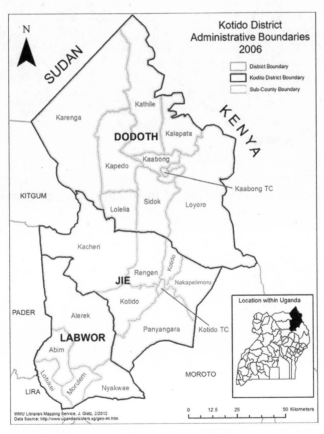

1: Map of Kotido District Administrative Boundaries
(northern Uganda)

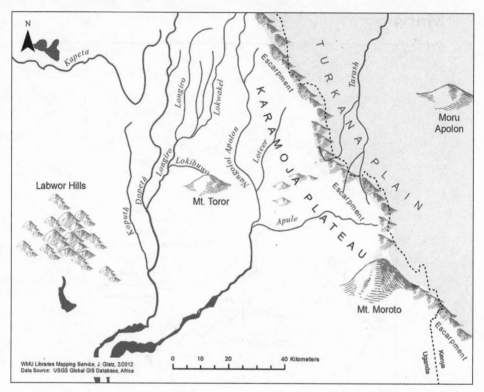

2: Map of Karamoja Plateau and the Plains of Turkana (northern Uganda and Kenya)

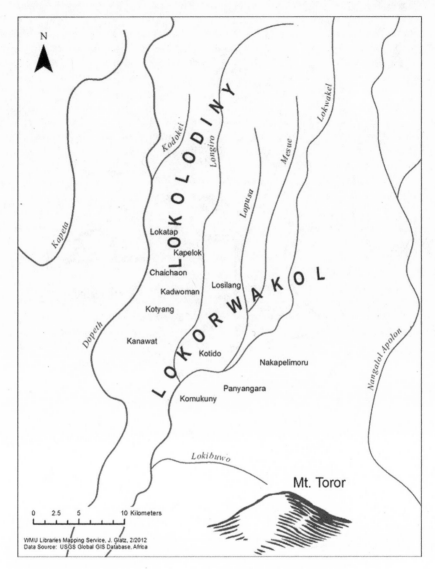

3: Map of Lokalodiny and Lokorwakol territorial divisions in Najie (Kotido District)

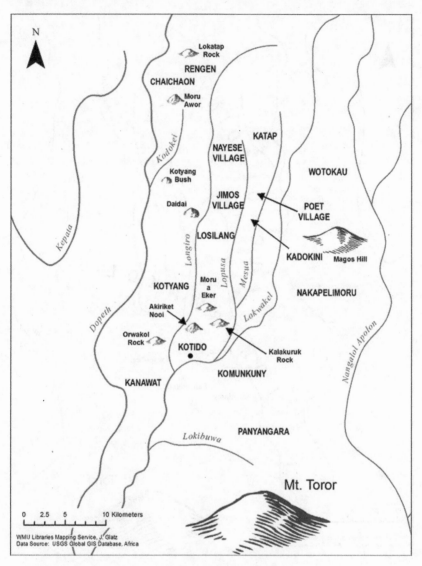

4: Map of rivers and villages in Najie (Kotido District)

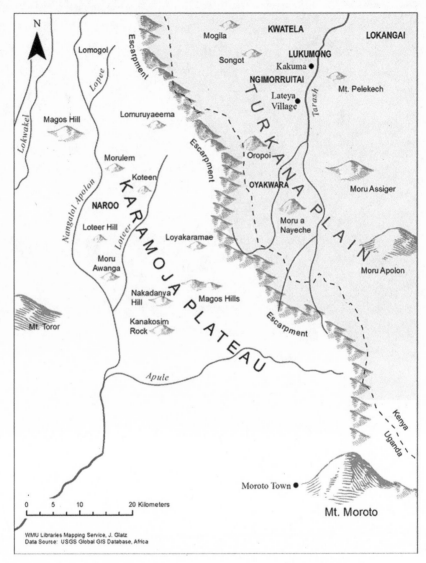

5: Map of Jie and Turkana grazing area (northern Uganda and Kenya)

A Note on Languages and Personal Names

Jie and Turkana Languages

Since my work relies heavily on translated materials, particularly those involving the transcription and translation of autobiographical narratives and stories, it is important to give detailed information about my competence in the Jie and the Turkana languages and to describe my editorial work. Before I first began my research in Najie, I had already independently studied Turkana, a Nilotic language closely related to Jie, for a year at the University of Wisconsin, Madison. This was followed by two months of an intensive Turkana language course at the Makioki Language Institute in Nairobi, Kenya. In addition, I had the opportunity to practice the Turkana language for eight months along the shores of Lake Turkana, and on the banks of the Tarash River in the Turkana District of Kenya. By the time I came to Najie, I had enough grammatical proficiency and sufficient vocabulary in Turkana to communicate with people and to follow discussions in a rudimentary way. In addition, a few months before the completion of my fieldwork in Najie, I found myself communicating adequately, if haltingly, in the Jie language.

I recorded all the stories and autobiographical materials as told to me, and translated them with the assistance of my local fieldwork assistants, Joseph Lodungokol, Paul Longoli, and Philip Lowokor. In addition, Lodoch also volunteered to assist me in translating his autobiographical narratives and other stories. Whenever passages or sections from his narratives were not clear, he dictated them to me and I wrote them down. All my tape recordings and handwritten dictations from my research are still extant in 2013, the year in which I am composing this volume.

The difficulties of translation are evident to anyone who attempts such a challenging task. Those difficulties become even greater when one tries to transcribe and translate from an oral to a written form. It was especially challenging to translate the subtleties of the voices of storytellers, who constantly adjust speech and tone to articulate and convey the complex meanings to their words in front of different audiences. Within these limitations and difficulties, I have sought to keep my translations as close to the original performances as possible. My fieldwork assistants provided me with countless invaluable insights into the historical traditions as we translated them together. They are all my friends and my teachers, and they are present in many ways in all parts of this work.

The Jie language does not yet have a codified spelling or written form. To follow some fairly standard spellings and pronunciations, I have used the recommendations and suggestions of my Jie friends, Lodoch, Joseph Lodungokol, Joseph Longok, and others. It is difficult to create a standardized tonal transliteration for this language for English-speaking audiences, particularly when Turkish and Kurdish languages are my mother tongues; hence, my hearing of other languages is inevitably affected by these two languages. One thing I have done is to use the "ch" sound, as in "achieve," for the sound found in such names as Nayeche or Lodoch, as both I and my Jie friends find the c-h spelling to be an appropriate way of producing the sound in written and spoken form. Hence I spell Nayeche with a "ch," instead of Nayece without the "h," as some other observers might have done, and Acholi instead of Acoli. In addition, I use "ng" at the beginning of a word to form the plural. This syllable is pronounced like the ng in "thong" or in "song." The sound "ng" is common both to Jie and Turkana languages.

I use the actual names of most of the storytellers in this book to give them the credit they deserve for their stories (historical traditions, popularly known biographies, and folktales). I obtained their permission to do this following the guidelines provided by the American Folklore Society. For other people I use pseudonyms, with the exception of those who are my friends, such as Lodoch, Joseph Lodungokol, Rianaro, Urien, Logwee, and Nakapor, or well-known Jie and Turkana prophets and public figures.

Personal Names

Barber, James: a British colonial officer, lived in Moroto, Karamoja, conducted extensive research in Karimojong history and published prolifically

Barber, June: married to James Barber, lived in Moroto, Karamoja, in the 1950s

Dyson-Hudson, Neville: principal anthropologist of the Karimojong Cluster

Dyson-Hudson, Rada: principal anthropologist of the Karimojong Cluster

Gulliver, P.H.: British anthropologist, first studied the Jie and the Turkana people

Gulliver, P.A.: British anthropologist, married to P.H. Gulliver, worked in Jie land and Turkana land together with P.H. Gulliver

Ekeno: Turkana storyteller

Lamphear, John: American historian, wrote on the oral traditions of the Jie and the Turkana people

Lodoch: Jie storyteller

Lodiny: ancestral hero of the Lodiny people

Locholo: Turkana storyteller

Lotum: Jie firemaker, Nakapor's father

Logwee: Jie storyteller in Jimos village, Rianaro's daughter

Lokapelan: storyteller from Toroi village

Loriang: great Jie war leader, esteemed ancestral figure, lived in the late 1800s and early 1900s

Lokerio: Turkana prophet, supposed to have parted Lake Turkana and to have brought camels to the Turkana people

Lokopelan: Turkana prophet, dreamed of the coming of the white people

Lokwii: Jie leader, elected in 1996 to the Parliament of Uganda

Marshall Thomas, E.: American travel writer and anthropologist, lived in Dodoth land, wrote about the Dodos people

Nacham: founder of the Kacheri community

Nadul: Nakapor's eldest wife

Napau: Turkana diviner, traditional doctor, and storyteller

Napeyo: Lodoch's wife

Nayeche: heroine of the Turkana origin story

Orwakol: ancestral hero of the Orwakol clan of the Jie

Rianaro: Jie storyteller from Jimos village

Tufnell, H.M.: British colonial officer, toured Karamoja in early 1900s, reported the presence of firearms in the region

Urien: Jie storyteller, Rianaro's brother

REMEMBERING NAYECHE
AND THE GRAY BULL ENGIRO

African Storytellers of the Karamoja Plateau
and the Plains of Turkana

Introduction

Ethnography of Oral Tradition

Some of my fondest memories of graduate school at the University of Wisconsin–Madison are of Harold Scheub's African Storyteller class. For an audience of five hundred students in Bascom Hall, Scheub performed African stories, drawing from the fantasy images of Xhosa tradition. These fantastic traditional images were at the heart of Scheub's lectures and performances. It was here that I was inspired to study African oral tradition.

As I watched Scheub perform these enthralling stories during the course of his lectures, I began over the course of the semester, to feel an increasing sense of resonance and connection with these tales. I came to understand them as a symbolic repetition of certain experiences similar to those of my childhood, when I listened to the master storytellers of the villages on the slopes of Taurus Mountain in southeastern Turkey.

Perhaps what fascinated me most about this African Storyteller class was the juxtaposition, in my mind, of a professor, in modern apparel, telling stories to students of science and literature at a modern American university, set beside Kurdish and Turkish storytellers, in traditional clothes, narrating stories and epics to children in dimly lit rooms or to adults in mud-plastered coffee houses. The physical and social contrast of Scheub with the Kurdish and Turkish storytellers created both discordance and correspondence. When I mentioned that I wanted to study African oral tradition, one professor recommended that I should study Kurdish culture and people and do native anthropology rather than studying African oral traditions. But I was fascinated by African oral traditions and continued to read African stories and myths, in

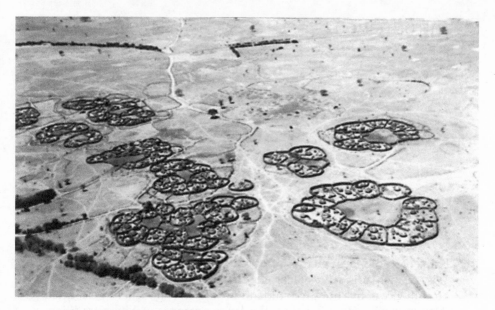

Figure 0.1: Najie. Author photo (Kotido District)

addition to my regular readings on ethnography and anthropological theory. Reading and studying African oral traditions became yet another graduate school experience, and more and more I found myself immersed in this fascinating, colorful field.

About two years after the African Storyteller class, I found myself in northern Kenya. Again, I was listening to stories; this time beside a dry river bed along the lava-strewn shores of Lake Turkana, listening to a story of a young woman named Nayeche, who had come from Najie, on the Karamoja Plateau, following the footprints of a lost gray bull named Engiro. Here, according to the tale, she had settled, by the headwaters of Tarash River in the desert plains of Turkana land, and, here, she gave birth to Turkana society.

After many nights of participating in storytelling performances and listening to the story of Nayeche and of many others, I began asking myself to what extent is the journey of Nayeche and the lost bull a key cultural event in this society? To what extent is this story different from – and the same as – for example, the story of the gray wolf, in Turkish oral tradition, that led the Turkish people from the Altay Mountains to the Central Asian steppes and finally to the shores of the Mediterranean Sea?

A year spent in Turkana land, collecting stories and historical traditions about the journey of Nayeche and the gray bull Engiro, gave me insight into the significance of oral tradition in the lives of these people in this vast dry zone. This led me to realize that to understand the meaning of origin in Turkana oral tradition I had to live in Najie, the home of the gray bull and Nayeche.

Najie is a part of the great Karamoja Plateau in northern Uganda that slopes east toward northern Kenya, where it drops sharply and gives way to the great Turkana plains (see map 2). As an ecological zone, Najie is characterized by thin vegetation and a dry, hot climate. From September to May, in the long dry season, the whole of Najie bakes in the heat of the sun, and the arid earth of Najie becomes a dust crust. When the hot wind blows, scorching dusty sands envelop the thirsty plateau, and Najie becomes barren and waterless. All water sources dry up except for a few wells near the Longiro River. Some people say that if it were not for the wells of the Longiro River, there might be no life whatsoever in Najie. For the Jie storytellers, the Longiro River is the sap of life, not only because of its dry-season wells, but also because its muddy water attracted the gray bull Engiro, the progenitor of all the Jie cattle. The Jie storytellers describe how Orwakol, the first firemaker and the founder of Jie society, captured the gray bull Engiro while it drank at the Longiro River. The gray bull Engiro later went missing during a long dry season. During this season, according to the storytellers, the sun became very hot and parched the land, drying up the wells, killing the cattle, and burning all the vegetation.

It was during this long hot dry season that Nayeche, the daughter of Orwakol, followed the footprints of the gray bull Engiro, thinking that the gray bull Engiro must have smelled the water and the grass. Hungry and thirsty, Nayeche had wandered forlornly over the waterless plateau. After passing Nakapelimoru, she crossed Nangalol Apolon. The great river was dry, but the footprints of the gray bull Engiro were there. It is there, in the dry course of Nangalol Apolon, that Nayeche's footprints became mixed with the footprints of the gray bull Engiro.
    When Nayeche reached the Koteen Hill, there were some wild fruits, which she gathered and ate. That night, Nayeche slept on the hill, and in the morning she continued her journey, following the footprints of the gray bull Engiro, as she descended from the plateau to the plains. She continued walking until she reached the headwaters of the Tarash

River in the plains. The Tarash River was also dry, but Nayeche continued to think that the gray bull Engiro must have smelled the water.

In the dry riverbed, when Nayeche reached a bushy place, she noticed a well with water in it and said to herself, "This is the water that the gray bull Engiro must have smelled. This is the water that the gray bull must have left for me." After Nayeche drank the water, she walked into the bush and climbed up the hill and made a fire there in the evening. When the gray bull Engiro smelled the fire, he also climbed the hill and slept next to Nayeche. In the morning, Nayeche noticed that the bush was teeming with wild fruits, and she said to herself, "I will stay here and gather some wild fruits. The gray bull Engiro is also here."

Nayeche stayed in the bush with the gray bull Engiro. In the mornings, when the gray bull Engiro went to graze in the bush, Nayeche went and gathered wild fruits and dried them on the rocks of the hill. In the evenings, she made a fire and cooked wild fruits and ate them as the gray bull Engiro watched her.

This is how Nayeche lived for many years, until one day a few young Jie men came to the upper Tarash River looking for pasture. They saw Nayeche as she gathered wild fruits and recognizing her they said to her, "Are you not Nayeche?" "Yes I am," she replied. After spending some time at the hill, the young men asked Nayeche to return with them to Najie but she refused. Pointing to the dried wild fruits on the rocks of the hill, Nayeche told them, "These are my wild fruits and this is my hill, where I sleep. This place is now my home."

After spending more time at the hill, the young Jie men realized that the place had plenty of wild fruits, good grass, and plenty of water. The young men spoke among themselves, saying, "This place is good. Why don't we bring our wives and children and settle here?" The young men went back to Najie, and they told the Jie people about Nayeche and the gray bull Engiro and about the hill with the green grass and its teeming wild fruits. Upon hearing this, many young men followed them, bringing their wives and children and their few emaciated cattle. They settled in the bush around the hill. The gray bull Engiro consorted with their cattle and their cattle multiplied. Many years later, Nayeche died and the Jie people buried her near the hill, and they named the hill Moru a Nayeche (the Hill of Nayeche) and they called themselves Turkana.

P.H. Gulliver, a British anthropologist, recorded a version of the Nayeche oral tradition[1] in 1948, and he published a brief summary in 1952.

Gulliver interpreted this oral tradition as an account, on the one hand, of the segmentation, societal dispersal, and amalgamation of the Jie and the Turkana people and, on the other hand, as a political charter enabling these two communities to form alliances against their common enemies (Gulliver 1952a, 6).

Working within the tropes of the early anthropological models of agnatic principles and segmentary processes, John Lamphear, an American historian, furthered Gulliver's (1952a) hypothesis and interpreted the Nayeche oral tradition extensively in terms of its historical message. The rationale underlying Lamphear's interpretation of the Nayeche oral tradition is that origin myths, such as that of Nayeche, contain clear historical messages about the past. In this respect, the Nayeche oral tradition contains a "clear message" about the "acquisition of Zebu cattle" (Lamphear 1988, 32), followed by the increasing warfare and militarization of the Turkana pastoralist communities in the eighteenth and nineteenth centuries in East Africa. Once he identified the message as such, Lamphear attempted to corroborate the arrival of Nayeche and the gray bull Engiro in the upper Tarash River region in the 1720s (Lamphear 1976, 36, 91–3).

Althouth Lamphear's thesis makes an important contrbution to Jie and the Turkana oral history, his conclusion about the images of the Nayeche and the gray bull Engiro oral tradition is not the only possible interpretation. My research introduced me to a world of the Jie and the Turkana storytellers, for whom the Nayeche and the gray bull Engiro story was more than a historical event or chronology. For example, my experiences among the Jie and the Turkana people have shown me that the local people do not recall information beyond three generations. And, as Gulliver (1952a, 5) points out, the Jie people do not themselves date events.

I will address Lamphear's historical reconstruction and chronology in the conclusion; but I found that in the world of the storytellers the story of the gray bull Engiro, and in many of the other oral traditions, the passion of the storytellers was for the telling of the story – the performance. The Jie and the Turkana storytellers whom I interviewed were never interested in discovering the chronology of the actual event of Nayeche's journey or any other event of the 1720s. Their interest lay in the memory of how and where Nayeche traveled on the desolate plateau. They would raise their questions regarding the journey of Nayeche and the gray bull Engiro during dispute mediations and in various performances of oral tradition.

The Jie and the Turkana people do not have a word for history as it is understood in the West; the closest term is *eemut*, or *ngiemuto*, in plural (literally, "story-history"). The *eemut* encompasses all forms of oral narratives including the Nayeche and the gray bull Engiro tradition, covering myth, legends, folktales, memories, and anecdotes. Although the Jie and the Turkana distinguish between historical and fictional *eemut*, both classes of narratives abound in fantasy images. The Jie and the Turkana histories are a part of local discourse, always presented in story form and filled with folklore themes. Discourse analysis can clearly illuminate the intrusion of oral legends of family conflict episodes into the purported history of clan and tribal origin. The images of *ngiemuto* are distilled from people's historical experiences and they center around the great themes in their culture.

In a work much like this one, Karin Barber (1991) persuasively argues that performance of oral tradition as discourse shapes collective memory and identity. For Barber, oral tradition refers to those aspects of memory that exist outside of history as a discourse, yet they are entangled with history. Barber (1991, 2007) recognizes therein some valuable evidence of attitude and discourse as well the fragments of history in oral traditions. Like Barber's work, this book is not a reconstruction of history. Instead, what follows is an exploration of how Nayeche and the gray bull Engiro are remembered through various performances of oral tradition and how this remembering is entangled with discourses of identity and biography. As well, this book moves in a different direction from Barber's. My concern is not oral tradition as historical evidence, but rather the cultural and political contexts in which the images of the past are constructed through remembering. The story of Nayeche and the gray bull Engiro references not only the past, but pressing social and political concerns of the moment of its remembering.

Although my argument will become clear in the following chapters, let me begin with this idea – the story of Nayeche and the gray bull Engiro in the oral tradition associates memory with the current concerns of the Jie and the Turkana people. The primary importance of the story of Nayeche and gray bull Engiro's journey lies not in the remembering of the 1720s or other distant times, but in the lessons that narrated memories impart. What remembering Nayeche and the gray bull Engiro does is call for action. Invoking the remembered story informs the present. One of my arguments in this book is that we cannot understand the importance of historical traditions such as Nayeche and the gray bull Engiro without considering their relationship to present concerns. The Jie and the Turkana storytellers often recall and invoke the images of their oral traditions as they deal with their present challenges. As such, oral tradition provides the Jie and Turkana storytellers with symbols and values from the past that help resolve present problems. For example, when Apamulele, the Turkana storyteller, negotiated the peace between the feuding Jie and Turkana (chapter 5), he did so by poetically presenting Nayeche and the gray bull Engiro's journey on the waterless plateau.

My conversations with storytellers regarding the interplay of history and memory confirm the symbolic importance of the story of Nayeche in the context of political organization and interethnic relationship between the Jie and the Turkana communities as well as in situations created by colonialism and modern state-building. There are some parallels between these communities' use of oral tradition to define social and political relations in the present context and other peoples, such as the people of Okuku (Barber 1991), of Kaluli (Schieffeling 1976 [2005]), of Tiv (Bohannon 1953), of Luapula (Cunnison 1951), of Kalapola (Basso 1995), and of Merina (Bloch 1986). In chapter 1, I illustrate this point when I discuss Ugandan efforts to modernize and to build a nation-state, both leading the Jie, previously agropastoralists, with strong traditions of animal husbandry, into agricultural production. While this trend may have appeared to be productive, creative, and progressive, in fact the modernization[2] has been uneven and brutally forceful. Through the upheavals involved in economic and political change, storytellers have articulated a critical perspective, in poetically inflected forms, against the forces of modernization and the nation-state. The storytellers have crafted counter-narratives with moral principles shaped by ancient oral traditions like that of Nayeche and the gray bull Engiro. Through these counter-narratives, the storytellers make sense of rapidly changing conditions and seek to steer their society.

The story of Nayeche and the gray bull Engiro, as well as other Jie and Turkana oral traditions, are enmeshed not only with present social and political relations, but also with multiple cultural practices, vocabularies, biographies, and historical experiences. Thus, the performances of historical traditions of the Jie and of the Turkana people from the upper Tarash River region are artistically creative, and they reflect biographical and political reality. For the Jie and the Turkana people, to construct a historical tradition is to construct oneself as a vulnerable person living in an arid environment who shares a destiny with others who are also vulnerable. Past vulnerabilities (to a dry environment) have

informed a response by storytellers to present vulnerabilities (to economic and political changes). This lends critical insight into the art of
historical tradition as discourse in the Jie and in the Turkana society: to
tell a story of the past is to offer a suggestion for today. It is for these
reasons that I use the terms "practice" and "discourse" interchangeably
in describing the Jie and the Turkana oral traditions.

The notion of discourse has become prominent in the past 30 years.
This notion specifies ways in which language, culture, emotion, and
social actions are united and it encompasses the way this unity enables
the members of the society to express themselves through their cultural
themes. My usage of the notion of discourse resonates with L. Abu-
Lughod's articulation of the term, which she sometimes refers to as sentiments or ideology that people can use to express themselves and feel
those experiences at the same time (Abu-Lughod 1986, 255–8 [also cited
by Kratz 1994, 38]). In this respect, the Jie and the Turkana historical
traditions represent a set of values and ideals of personhood that inform
deeply felt individual experiences of feeling vulnerable and dependent.
Hence the historical traditions communicate moral responsibility for
people to share resources. It is perhaps for this reason, according to
Nakapor, the late Jie firemaker, that people use the word *akoro* (hunger)
when they encounter one another or to greet each other (chapter 2).
Survival in an unpredictable environment forms the dominant ideology of the Jie and of the Turkana culture.

Walking along the banks of the Longiro and of the Tarash River and
participating in the performances of historical traditions have shown
me how the storytellers bring together the aura of tradition, the specificity of place, and the collective memory as they poetically unfold the
narrative of the capturing of the gray bull Engiro on the banks of the
Longiro River and the journey of Nayeche on the waterless plateau.
Culturally specific memories of Nayeche and Engiro, disguised and entangled in the workings of the performances, are spatially embedded in
the waterless plateau and in the magnificent sites of Moru a Nayeche
and of the Tarash River.

The journey of Nayeche and gray bull Engiro, as it is imagined, remembered, and narrated involves descriptions and actual places. The
memory of the journey and the places through which Nayeche traveled
are not only artfully constructed but they are also collectively imagined.
Slyomovics (1998) reminds us how Halbwachs (1950, 53) is concerned
with the ways in which past is collectively represented and narrated
over time. The images of collective memories are preserved within the

spatial configuration of society, providing members with a sense of permanence and stability. In a similar work, Connerton (1989, 1–3) argues that members of society presuppose a collective memory inscribed in the narratives that convey ideas about the past and that form the substance of collective identity. For Connerton, "social memory" produces "master narratives," supported by material presence and embedding tradition in society. Critical features of master narratives are their continuing "unconscious" effectiveness as ways of thinking and their persistence as unconscious collective memory, whose images commonly legitimate present social relations. It is here that the collective memory of Nayeche's journey merits scrutiny, for the effects of ancestral past experiences, as recalled by storytellers, on the reshaping of memory. The active, fluid remembering of Nayeche's journey guarantees cultural survival through renovating tradition. When storytellers tell the story of Nayeche's journey on the waterless plateau they create knowledge about a place and time. Their narratives produce traditions with material presence in the Jie world.

In the twenty-first century, the way the Jie and the Turkana storytellers trace the memory of Nayeche and gray bull Engiro corroborates Halbwach's and Connerton's articulation about memory and place. The narratives of the memory of Nayeche's journey from plateau to the plain hold an important place both for the Jie and the Turkana. For both groups the memory of this journey has been a source of cooperation, conflict resolution, and political alliance. The journey of Nayeche, as narrated by storytellers, recounts how Nayeche walked and touched places in the Jie world and the Turkana world. Both Jie and Turkana, to elaborate their sacred past, locate the memory of their ancestors on the same terrain where Nayeche traveled, following the footprints of gray bull Engiro, where she drank water and ate wild fruits.

The Jie people often conceptualize their political and social relations according to memories that play an enormously important role in their "self-representation" (Abu-Lughod 1986 [also see Barber 1991; Caton 1990; Hofmeyr 1993; Krupat 1985; Tonkin 1988]). An examination of how and why the Jie past is remembered in certain moments and contexts reveals the strategies and ideologies that enable the actors to survive in a dry environment and to share scarce resources. Therefore, my focus on the Jie historical tradition as remembered memory images is coupled with a secondary but important aspect of this work: poetic discourses of vulnerability created by the arid environment. My argument is that we cannot understand the central role of historical tradition in the lives of the Jie people without understanding its profound relationship to the project of survival in an arid environment.

The ubiquity of Nayeche and the gray bull Engiro's story stems from multiple forms through which the journey of Nayeche and the gray bull Engiro is remembered. This remembering constitutes what Tonkin (1992) calls "production of historical knowledge," revealing highly entangled emotionally evocative collective experiences, and deeply embedded social practices (also see Bloch 1977, 1986; Cohen 2001). Like Tonkin's work, this book explores the production of historical knowledge, but it goes beyond that and examines the significance of remembering that reveals strategies and ideologies of the actors in the present. The memory of Nayeche and the gray bull Engiro underpins the workings of historical discourse.

The complex relationships among oral tradition, memory, and history have been convincingly argued by a number of scholars, for example, Bauman (1986) on the interrelationship between narratives and past social events; Basso (1995) on the Kalapalo oral history, memory, and narrative; Herzfeld (1982) on the Greek memory and politics; Bohannon (1953) on the fluidity of Tiv oral tradition; and Tonkin (1992) on the "narration of pastness." While all of these scholars' exploration of memory and history are relevant to my work in various ways, Tonkin's arguments on the narration of pastness in performance context provides me unique advantages.

Tonkin's formulation of the narration of pastness is drawn from Africanist historians' use of oral tradition in reconstructing Africa's past. Her formulation, however, goes beyond this in a way useful for anthropologists, historians, and folklorists exploring the use of past memory images embodied in historical tradition as a poetic device in the recalling of the past. The past and its representation, which Tonkin calls pastness, constitute a crucial poetic device in the construction of self in social interactions. Social life is, from this perspective, a set of transactions whereby social actors use the past as a "resource to deploy, to support a case or assert a social claim" and to create their identities, formulating their sense of who they are (Tonkin 1992, 1). For her, society is an arena of communication in which representation of pastness is accomplished. Tonkin defines pastness as a process of identification, which involves the "interconnections between memory, cognition and history" which help to shape individual identities.

Tonkin's finely honed argument on pastness is inseparable from the logic of Pierre Bourdieu's (1977) practice theory. Critical to her understanding is the process of remembering – distinct but not unlike Bloch's (1977) notion of tradition as historical knowledge – that is fueled by the effects of power and knowledge. From this perspective, remembering the past in the present can conceal multiple interpretations, and it is imbued with a shared rhetoric of the past that encapsulates and defines the forms of ideology and knowledge (Bloch 1977, 279). For Tonkin (1992), as for Bloch, the act of remembering is a force through which the past and the present unite social forms and human relations reconstructing the past in the present (see also Flores 2002).

The strength of Tonkin's notion of pastness lies in its remarkable emotional subtlety and semiotic richness, which connects the characteristics of the storytellers' memory and the act of recalling the past with those of their audiences. There is an interconnection in the representation of pastness in which the storytellers and listeners intersect at a point in time and space as well as at the time recounted (Tonkin 1992, 3). It is in this way that the past, emotion, and the act of remembering is contextually intertwined, through the dialogical engagement between the past of the storytellers and the members of their audiences in the present.

This way of looking at the past involves the act of recalling as a performance, which is congruent to my understanding of the storytellers' anecdotal references to past events in various present social settings among both the Jie and the Turkana people. From this point of view, I take the performances of oral tradition to be a transformational process through which the images of tradition are removed from the past context of their own making and represented in distinct political and social domains of the present (Anttonen 2005). As such, the effect of recalling in present is the redefinition of social identities as new images in light of the past, which allows the acquisition of a state that makes the remembered past "natural" (Bourdieu 1977, 104). For this process of dialogic representation of social identities in light of the past, people select not just any oral tradition but important ones such as that of Nayeche and the gray bull Engiro.

Tonkin's exploration of the past in dialogical engagement resonates with Tedlock and Mannheim's (1995) dialogical emergence of cultures. Drawing on Jakobson's challenge of the Saussurian focus on the individual actors as the source of *parole* or speech, Tedlock and Mannheim argue that language, as a shared system, is dialogical. Here they maintain that like language cultures are dialogically produced and reproduced and revised among the competent members of the cultures. Similarly, discourse articulated by oral tradition is both patterned and continually transformed, as the storytellers and the members of their audiences combine diverse ideological elements from diverse sources. Tedlock and Mannheim's telling formulation insists on the "emergent property of performance, conceived as a fully engaged social event and constructed jointly through the actions of all participants" (1995, 16). From this perspective, both the storytellers and the members of their audiences are positioned actors "embodying vectors of power and authority that are repositioned during the performance" (1995, 13).

Traditions may, as Corinne Kratz (1993) points out, seem timeless and immutable, yet they are continuously constructed according to the ideological changes in the society. In a related work, Bohannon (1953) has demonstrated these changes in a powerful way in his study of Tiv oral tradition. Bohannon has observed how the components of oral traditions changed along with changes in the present social relations in the Tiv community. Cunnison (1951) and Barber (1991) also observed similar processes in the Luapula and in the Okuku people respectively (also see Hofmeyr 1993). It is perhaps for this reason that the Jie storytellers' dialogical engagement with their past are always in full "communion" (Bloch 1977) with the present environmental and political circumstances.

The complex dialogic strands of tradition and interpretation have been brought together in two engaging studies, namely Schieffelin's (1976 [2005]) work among the Kaluli people in Papua New Guinea and Karen Barber's (1991) studies of the Okuku people of the Yoruba society and their creative use of oral tradition in identity politics.

For Schieffelin, the poetic discourse of the Kaluli people enables the teller and the listeners to express their experiences in culturally specific ways that may enable them to feel those experiences. Culturally specific configurations of experiences, as delineated by Schieffelin, are mutually infusing features through which the teller and the listeners think about themselves. His cogent analysis of the Kaluli people's performances delineates ways in which the performer and the audience can manipulate certain cultural themes, which he calls "key scenarios," using the memories of the ancestors, to create and maintain present political relationship and reciprocity among the people. For Schieffelin, these memories are embodied in the Kaluli landscape and in the Kaluli people's culturally important rituals.

Like those of the Kaluli people, the memory images of Nayeche and the gray bull Engiro oral tradition are symbolically embodied in the Jie landscape, in the phases of the harvest rituals, and in the marriage rituals (chapters 4, 6, and 7). In light of this, the story of Nayeche and the gray bull Engiro carries and recreates key "cultural scenarios" (Schieffelin 1976 [2005], 3), which I identify as cultural themes that inform the Jie and the Turkana peoples' understanding of their ancestral past. During the performances of oral traditions, for instance, the cultural themes surrounding the journey of Nayeche and the gray bull Engiro from the plateau to the plains, establish the frame for the Jie people to conceptualize their kinship ties with the Turkana people as they exchange and share their scarce resources (Mirzeler 2004). When we examine the story of Nayeche and the gray bull Engiro in specific performance contexts, we see how the diverse images of Nayeche's journey emerge more as an object of memory, with its multiple meanings, rather than as a fact of history (chapters 5 and 6). As a narrative resource, the story of Nayeche and the gray bull Engiro construes social actors and assures clear kinship ties between the Jie and the Turkana peoples.

In Karin Barber's *I Could Speak until Tomorrow* (1991), the author contributes to the study of oral tradition as performance art. Barber's study of the Okuku people's historical tradition known as *oriki* explores how *oriki* is created through various commentaries and utterances that enter in *oriki* genres during their performances. Barber describes how these commentaries and utterances become entangled with public discourse on various genealogies and kin groups who, by virtue of their dominant political position, embody society's ideology and sense of identity. The diverse cultural memories found in *oriki*, according to Barber, are not historical tales in the way we understand history in the Western world, but they are deeply grounded fragments of memory images through which communities express their heartfelt convictions about themselves to themselves.

The performances of *oriki* "open windows" to the past and enable the members of the audience to peek through these windows as they imagine present social relations in light of past events. The performances of *oriki* are, according to Barber, ways of "experiencing the past by bringing it back to life" (1991, 15) in the present. For Barber, *oriki* performances are deeply embedded social practices that inform the present actions in the society. "*Oriki* are," she says, "essentially historical in the sense that they are one of the ways in which the relations of the present with the past is constructed" (Barber 1991, 25). Barber's view of society has the Okuku community coming to terms with itself in light of the past.

This way of looking at historical traditions is congruent with my understanding of the Jie historical tradition and its performances. The memory images of the Jie historical tradition stem, in part, from story-tellers' poetic representations and valorization of political ideology in multiple contexts and performance situations. These performances constitute the dialogical creation of the past, those highly entangled fragments of remembered memory images that capture whatever may be "worth remembering" (Barber 1991).

An oral tradition such as that of Nayeche and the gray bull Engiro is created during performances only in the sense that the telling of the story is built upon both the previous and the present body of knowledge. The past in the story is not created in chronological order, but it is rather manufactured, or assembled, from existing memory images and body of knowledge, including myths and symbols. The story of Nayeche and the gray bull Engiro bears the sanctity of tradition, and it embodies an "efficacy" (Kratz 1994) exuding from the past experiences of the people.

The story of Nayeche and the gray bull Engiro, with its symbolic inflections, serves as a key example of a master discourse of the Jie and the Turkana oral tradition. Its reproduction through various forms, such as landscape, harvest rituals, marriage rituals, and popular biographies, articulates its depth and complexity and ambiguities with the continuing emergence of the Jie and the Turkana cultures and identities. It is the competent storytellers and the members of the audiences who unpack important cultural themes and representational aspects of signs embedded in the story of Nayeche and the gray bull Engiro.

In an ever rising spiral or a constantly growing palimpsest, the memory images of the Nayeche and the gray bull Engiro historical tradition arise out of myriad performance contexts and social climates that shape the symbolism of the remembered memory images of the past and its meaning. The symbols of the Nayeche and the gray bull Engiro tradition are beautiful and multivocal, and the meaning of their semiotics in a performance context informs people's knowledge of their past. As Bauman (1986, 4) argues, in a theoretical way, the structure and interactions in each performance influence the meaning of the oral tradition as each performance is dialogically played out within the context of the situated action. The performance context enables the storytellers and the audience members to reconstruct meaning of past events in the present.

During performances of the Jie historical tradition, the processes of identification and of remembering past are intertwined with a fresh cluster of social connotations and verbal icons of events and "abstracted sign images," evolving together dialogically with contemporary contexts that lead to what Fernandez calls (1986, 36) the differentiation of "Self" from "Other." Therefore, recalling past memories becomes a symbolic process that reenacts and modifies the images of historical traditions, constructing new personal and social identities and defining the boundaries between the communities and the people. At each performance, the Jie historical tradition takes on new shape and new meaning depending on their "abstracted sign images" (Fernandez 1986, 31), focusing on key symbols richly layered with powerful associations. Fernandez's abstracted signs are not distinct types of symbols, but rather they are endowed with different emphases and combinations of signs. They are critical to his understanding of the categories of Self and Other, which are subject to elaboration in performances. It is from this perspective that the images of the Jie historical tradition catalog kinship ties between those at the present time who are in adverse relationships and those who are friends. Sharing the memories of ancestors enhances social and political strategies and differentiates friends from enemies. With this background, I would like to rethink the story of Nayeche and the gray bull Engiro and its interrelationship among memory, tradition, and history.

If oral tradition constitutes a process by which past memories of events are dialogically reorganized between the storytellers and their audiences, what is the effect of these dialogical relations in the production of the past? It is this kind of question that enables me to reformulate Nayeche and the gray bull Engiro story as the master discourse of pastness, which maintains its links with the past events such as historical contingencies of pastoralism, agriculture, and myriad contemporary global forces emerging from the modern practices at the local level (chapter 1).

I have collected over two hundred historical traditions from the Jie and the Turkana people as well from among the surrounding communities, plus seventy-five versions of the Nayeche and the gray bull Engiro oral tradition from different localities both in Najie and in the Turkana land. The storytellers related the oral tradition of Nayeche and the gray bull Engiro to me, taking Nayeche to be their venerable ancestor who left Najie during a prolonged famine in search of water and food and settling on the upper Tarash River region. My conversations with the storytellers, regarding the interplay of oral tradition, history, and memory, confirm the symbolic importance of the story of Nayeche and the gray bull Engiro in the production of historical knowledge, in the context of political organization and interethnic relationships. The original event associated with the Nayeche and the gray bull Engiro story is not recoverable. Even though the story of Nayeche and the gray bull Engiro is very common, the symbolisms of Nayeche's journey are complex, articulating, on the one hand, the discourses of their differences and, on the other, their common origin, interdependence, and unity. As such, they serve not only as a way of reflecting the world, but also of shaping the identities and social relations. They are, as Geertz (1973) powerfully states, "models of" and "models for" social relations and cultural orders.

When I arrived in Najie during the rainy season in May 1996, after having spent a year in Turkana land, it was the beginning of the planting season. I spent thirteen months in Najie trying to complete my envisioned project about the story of Nayeche and the gray bull Engiro. Soon after I arrived in Najie, I met Lodoch, a sixty-five-year-old Jie storyteller, in a fly-ridden shop and sat with him behind the shop's mud-plastered cracked wall listening to stories of Nayeche as well as of Napeikisina, the villain trickster of the Jie oral tradition. I recorded both stories. After that day, Lodoch became indispensable to my project and I became his apprentice in the Jie oral tradition.[3] While hundreds of storytellers and their performances became the core of my studies of the Jie and the Turkana oral traditions, the centerpiece of my study was Lodoch, a traditional artist, regarded by his peers as a splendid storyteller, an eloquent speaker, and an animated performer. It was my privilege to study the Jie oral tradition under Lodoch. What really separated Lodoch from other storytellers was not only his vast awareness of his society and culture, but also his ability to contextualize and articulate his knowledge to an audience. Lodoch's artistic ability to invoke relevant images of tradition and situate them in relevant contexts in his performances was recognized by the members of his society. For this, he was highly respected. I am indebted to him for guiding me and teaching me the richness of the Jie oral tradition and encouraging me to explore it freely. His genius as a storyteller was based on his deep and thorough knowledge of his tradition, and he shared that knowledge with me generously and intimately. He insisted that I learn the tradition of his society not only from him, but also from other storytellers.

Together we walked on the dusty roads from village to village, participating in oral tradition performances.

Soon after meeting with Lodoch, I moved, at his suggestion, to Jimos
village, a few miles east of Kotido town. My decision to live in Jimos
village proved productive, for the people in the village were very rich
in oral tradition. They claimed to be the direct descendants of Orwakol,
the founder of Jie society, the father of Nayeche, the owner of the gray
bull Engiro, and the head of the Lokorwakol territorial division. They
also claimed that Nayeche had come from Jimos village.

The Jie tribal organization is, as one might expect, patrilineal. The pre-
ferred marriage arrangement is exogamous. Throughout Jimos village,
politico-religious elites are found who are reputed to be descendants of
Orwakol. Though descent is important to their high status, piety, ritual
knowledge, and competence in oral tradition are also important, since
the people in the seven clans look to these elite to solve their problems
and settle their disputes according to their tradition. Jimos village and
Daidai, the sacred Jie shrine, across the village on the banks of the
Longiro River, where Orwakol is said to have captured the gray bull
Engiro, are considered important ritual grounds and sanctuaries (see
map 4). Important communal congregations gather here. In precolonial
times, the Jie firemakers, the politico-religious leaders also known as
ekeworon, acted in Jimos village as the ritual functionaries of the Jie tribe
and were often in competition with the ritual specialists of other clans.
Toward the end of the colonial state, however, the political power of the
Jie firemakers had been eroded, and in the early-and-mid-1990s the position of the firemaker was reinstated by the people. Nakapor became
the firemaker and he exercised spiritual authority until his death in 2004.

The other important social group in Najie is the Ngikuliak hunter-
gatherers, who usually live in the bush. The origins of the Ngikuliak are
less certain, although there are numerous stories regarding them. They
are considered to be of low status, as they do not own cattle and they
eat wild animal meat. Most of the Ngikuliak and related groups live
in Rengen, in the Lokalodiny territorial section, and some of them are
settled in Kacheri, a new Jie community north of Najie.

The members of the Poet clan, who live in a village known as Poet
about a mile southeast of the Jimos village (see map 4), act as masters of
ceremonies during the harvest rituals. The Poet clan builds the master
granary of the Jie firemakers, entertaining large gatherings with their
sorghum beer, cooking and cleaning in ceremonial gatherings, and so
forth. In return for their services, the Jimos clan provides them protection.

There are certain prophets, ritual specialists, and healers known as *ngimurok*, who are important in the production and dissemination of oral tradition. They do not act as composers of the narratives but as skilled politico-religious leaders and healers who recall the memories of influential ancestral leaders and make predictions about the future of the tribe during important gatherings.

I sometimes roamed alone or with Lodoch carrying my tape recorder in the silence of the deserted landscape, from village to village, where I hoped to meet storytellers or to attend ceremonies at which stories might be composed. There were few vehicles, except for those of the Church of Uganda and the Catholic Diocese in Kotido town. I traveled on the dusty roads, along the dry riverbeds, carrying only my small backpack containing a notebook, a tape recorder, batteries, and a camera. I sometimes followed the shepherds' paths that crisscrossed the empty plains and isolated hills; I visited kraals in the distant grazing lands of Labwor Hills, home of the Labwor people in the west; I wandered the border of Karamoja Plateau and the Tarash River region in the Turkana plains in the east to meet potential storytellers and visit sacred shrines and various places where, according to the traditions, heroes of the past had traveled.

Upon reaching my destination, I would be greeted hospitably and offered sorghum beer and sorghum bread and if available sometimes a piece of meat. After polite exchanges, I would begin interviewing people, gathering biographical information, and tape-recording stories from people willing to tell them. If the storytelling sessions continued into late afternoon or if an important ceremony or gathering was going to be held, I would spend the night in the same kraal or village.

Most of the time I did not have to travel to meet storytellers, for they often came to Jimos village to consult with Nakapor, the firemaker, or with other elders, and in the process they also visited me. Most people in Jimos village knew me, and they would invite me to sit with them under the trees in the cool shade where they loudly chewed tobacco, spat, and chatted. If a person reputed to be a good storyteller appeared, my friends would introduce me to him or her. Sometimes the storytellers knew me by reputation as the collector of stories and hence they came to meet me on their own.

To learn the oral tradition and become well acquainted with devices of oral composition, I made efforts to mimic individual storytellers. When I tried to narrate the stories, they took my efforts seriously, even though they laughed at my pronunciation of the words and mimicking of the Jie storytellers' body language. I also joined in performances, even though it was embarrassing on many occasions; but I continued performing with children and women whom I knew and with whom I felt comfortable. Most evenings I visited the homes of friends and sat in front of the hearth fire with children and listened to the stories, and sometimes, haltingly, I repeated the story lines, which often caused much laughter among the children, amused by my pronunciation. Because of my relentless desire to better understand the Jie oral tradition, my feelings of embarrassment and my mistakes did not deter me from trying to learn. In fact, I learned more from making mistakes and evoking laughter.

In Najie and in the Turkana land, there were no professional storytellers. Rather, everyone was a potential storyteller. I worked with both men and women, young and old. I tape recorded, took pictures, and videotaped the performances, recording as well the landscape and documenting the broader cultural contexts, with the consent of the storytellers and the audiences, using the guidelines of the American Anthropological Society,[4] the American Folklore Society, and of general oral history practice. In this sense, my ethnography was a collaborative study with the storytellers.

The storytellers I interviewed were mainly non-literate but very articulate people. Some were diviners (prophets, healers, and traditional doctors), and some were literate people who were chiefs or primary school teachers who knew most of the people in the area. Most of the storytellers I interviewed were my friends or friends of my friends, which contributed to the liveliness of the performances.

The historical tradition I studied in Najie, in the Turkana land, and beyond is not produced haphazardly. The skillful storytellers artfully put together complicated sets of distinct yet interlocking practices – popular biographical memory images, metaphors, events, myths, and collectively remembered dreams of prophets – as well as a host of other speech acts. The sheer knowledge of culture, history, memory, local gossip, and politics required of a master storyteller in this tradition is astounding. Oral tradition is an important cultural reality for the people in this vast dry zone, and Najie is no exception.

Najie is a world in which *eemut* – oral tradition, or more specifically historical tradition – is central, not only in the sphere of the social and political lives of the people, but also in the most private sphere of everyday life. In the narration of historical traditions, artistic expressions and sociality are intertwined and indistinguishable. The model of historical tradition is often unconsciously used as a refuge, a means for individuals to tolerate current realities and to console themselves.

The plots of the Jie and the Turkana oral traditions, both in the historical traditions and in folktales, largely involve conflicts over food, water, and other resources. This drama provides the imaginative materials from which the storytellers develop the cultural themes of their stories. The fundamental human need for sharing food and water in an unpredictable environment is a common topic in the performances of the Jie and the Turkana stories. The desire to steal food and water and the destructive nature of refusal to share and cooperate become polar opposites of sharing in this moral world, both in historical tradition and in folktales.

In both the Jie and the Turkana cultures, the performance of oral tradition emphasizes social responsibility in behavior, and it also implies an aesthetic expression of moral judgment. The ethical standards of behavior appeal to tradition, with the acceptance of ancestral practice as a standard of reference. For both the Jie, and the Turkana people of the upper Tarash River region, appeal to tradition is a key to performance, a way of signaling assumptions, expectation, and social responsibility. The plots of historical tradition present the practices of the ancestral world as venerable and ideal. In the Jie land, a model of oral tradition informs important acts of life. In fact, the Jie people live their lives as in the stories they tell; this can be understood only if the oral tradition is examined within a theoretical framework that illuminates the centrality of oral tradition in the Jie social lives. That is to say, the Jie oral tradition must be understood, as I have outlined, as pastness, the poetic discourse of lives and social relationships.

Studies of oral tradition as discourse have long shown the biographical significance of oral traditions (for example, Abu-Lughod 1986; Hofmeyr 1993; Krupat 1998; Meeker 1979; Scheub 1988; Tonkin 1992, 1988). In listening to popular biographical tales, I realized how models of oral tradition are used in revealing important life events and milestones, and how narration of personal lives is traditionalized. In Najie, during everyday struggles, conflicts, and famines people are forced to wander in search of food, as in the historical tradition. In conflict situations, people usually imitate the model of historical tradition. In biographical tales, people seek out role models from the historical tradition whose behavior they can emulate to best deal with family conflicts or to survive during ecological crises. In many ways, biographical tales resemble historical tradition narratives.

In this book, I systematically examine the images of oral tradition against the backdrop of popularly known biographies. Such examination enables keen observers to see how the basic plot of oral tradition is analogously worked into real lives and events. Some of these events are actual stories of conflict that occurred within the memory of the living people during my ethnographic fieldwork. Historical tradition provides models for marriages, rituals, and basic human and kinship relations. In this respect, biographical narratives are real-life versions of oral tradition.

Michael Meeker (1979, 52) reminds us that biographical tales illuminate ways traditional plots are used in constructing personal identity. This fact speaks eloquently to how Lodoch artfully distills his autobiographical tales from his tradition and fuses the moments of crisis in his life with the crises of his society as depicted in historical tradition. In Lodoch's autobiography, we see how his sense of himself has to do with the stories that keep his past vital and vibrant, and we see his desire to pass on his knowledge of the past to the younger generation, so that the "old ways" (Krupat 1998) can continue to flourish. In his autobiography, Lodoch often talks about himself in the model of the gray bull Engiro. The centerpiece of his autobiography is the death of his older brother Achilla, the owner of the family herd who had inherited the *amachar* (cattle brand) from his father. The scene of Achilla's death is framed by the drama of Engiro's death in Lodoch's oral tradition.

In Lodoch's autobiography, the arrival of his first wife Napiyo to his home and her ritual return, during their marriage ceremony, to her parental home as a part of *awatoun*,[5] are synonymous with the metaphoric return of Nayeche during the harvest rituals, which itself coincides with the annual return of the Jie cattle from the plains of the Turkana land around the upper Tarash River region. Both the harvest ritual and the marriage ceremony are important cultural institutions in Jie society and in the life history of Lodoch, and as such they are "significant centers" (Scheub 1988, 7) of the storytelling tradition. Lodoch uses traditional plots to talk about his own life history, in part because his self-identity is defined in relation to his oral tradition.[6] The full autobiography of Lodoch appeared in my dissertation (Mirzeler 1999) and I draw from it my analysis of the autobiographical significance of oral tradition in this book (chapter 7).

It was natural for me to be fascinated with the oral tradition of another society, as I grew up in a culture where oral tradition played a significant role. During my fieldwork, I relived, in some ways, my childhood experiences. I shared with Lodoch about my apprenticeship to the Kurdish storytellers and I narrated some of the Kurdish stories to him. In this respect, Lodoch and I shared stories and experiences with each other. Lodoch was my confidant as I was his. During my ethnography, my role as an anthropology student and as an "objective scholar" shifted to that of a storyteller from a Kurdish village, and I became an apprentice to the African storytellers. I am happy to share these experiences and let my ethnographic narrative speak for itself about the rich and complex use of oral tradition in diverse social and political contexts.

I view this book as ethnography of the Jie and the Turkana historical tradition of the upper Tarash River region, though the main emphasis is on the Jie people in Najie. This book contributes to the anthropology of oral narratives as exemplified by the works of Lila Abu-Lughod (1986), Karin Barber (1991, 2007), Steven Caton (1990), and Michael Meeker (1979). As such, this work connects to folklore in several ways. For this book, I draw from my recordings of the storytellers during their performances and those made from dictation of oral historical traditions, folktales, biographies, and autobiographies, in English translation. I collected all the oral narratives in the field as an end for themselves. These recorded texts gathered in various settings, with their contexts, storytellers, and audiences, represent the very heart of the Jie and the Turkana folklore and expressive traditions. Although anthropology and folklore have their unique methodologies, they have tremendous common ground. As Dorson points out, the division between folklore and anthropology is a tricky ground. "Where does the one begin and the other leave off, is a question continually asked of the folklorists, whose field is often considered of anthropology" (Dorson 1972, 30 [also see Barber 1991, Hofmeyr 1993, Narayan 1989]). In my fieldwork as an anthropologist, I employed both ethnographic and folkloric methodology of collecting and recording oral texts as an end themselves. And hence, the book contributes to the fields of anthropology and folklore.

In this book, I engage in a wide range of theoretical debates on the studies of oral tradition, folklore, performance, and autobiography. The form of the book is deeply dialogic and, with my narrative approach, I explicitly position myself as an apprentice to the Jie and the Turkana storytellers. I was stationed in the Jimos village for thirteen months. In addition, I traveled for another eleven months throughout the vast dry zone from Labwor Hills among the western neighbors of the Jie people in Karamoja Plateau, including the headwaters of the Tarash River, to the shores of Lake Turkana, and to the Chalbi Desert in northern Kenya.

Various theories in anthropology postulate that ethnographic knowledge is to be positioned and to be based on "partial truth." It is in this sense that I recover and convey at least partial "truths" about the Jie and the Turkana oral traditions. I use the phrase partial truth as developed by Strathern in *Partial Connections* (1991), in light of fieldwork, ethnographic writing and self, and other issues on one of several senses. However, the sense that I focus on here is the sense that she identifies with the question of ethnographic representation of information. For Strathern (1991, 74, 76), contradictions arise in all ethnographic representation when we consider the compatibility of information across cultures and societies, because information is differently valued in each culture and society. She maintains that there is no standard baseline for analogy in the way information is used in representing cultures and, hence, accurate ethnographic representations are not possible (54).[7] It is in this respect that this ethnography presents partial truths about the Jie and the Turkana oral traditions. In many ways, this book is my intellectual journey of realizing "partial connections" between disparate cultural and social configurations relating to the story of Nayeche and the gray bull Engiro.

Living in Najie was sometimes difficult due to skirmishes and ambushes between the local people and the Lord's Resistance Army, which have plagued northern Uganda since the early 1980s. In addition, I had occasional distressing encounters with national security police, who naturally wondered what I, a Kurdish man with an American passport and speaking the local language, was doing roaming in the villages and in distant grazing lands where illicit gun trade took place, in this politically turbulent region (chapter 1). National security police officers often hinted that Karamoja was not the best place in which to conduct fieldwork at that time. I also was alone, having left my wife and my two young children in the United States of America. Naturally I missed my family and occasionally I even lost my desire for the project, wondering whether I was doing the right thing.

After about two years in the Turkana land and in Najie, I had collected more than enough materials to see the basic outlines of the oral tradition as a discourse, and I realized that any understanding of the oral tradition required multiple perspectives. During my field research and subsequent visits, I spent a good amount of time transcribing and translating the stories and biographies I collected. I worked with friends, especially with Lodoch, in translating and reflecting on the corpus of materials I had gathered. In addition, I hired a few other good friends, such as Joseph Lodungokol and Paul Longoli, and a few other acquaintances, who were sensitive to the nuances of the oral traditions, to help me with translation. The result of part of this research culminated with my 1999 doctoral thesis, "Veiled Histories and the Childhood Memories of a Jie Storyteller."

After my doctoral dissertation I continued to build on my research on Jie and Turkana oral tradition up to the present. In addition, in 2001 and 2002, I have conducted oral-history interviews with the senior anthropologists and colonial officers of the Karamoja Plateau and Turkana land. In 2003, 2010, and 2011, I returned to Najie and met with Lodoch and visited my friends. During each visit I realized that Najie had changed; it was much different from when I had lived there in 1996 and 1997. During my 2011 visit, I realized that Najie had grown tremendously and some modern buildings with tin roofs had begun to appear on the horizon in the distant grazing lands. Modernization and globalization had almost engulfed the whole of Najie. Some of my friends had died. The children with whom I had listened to the stories in the evenings, in front of the hearth fire, had become adults, and Lodoch had become a very old man.

One morning before the sun arose, after I had spent two months in Najie and around the upper Tarash River region in the Turkana land, Lodoch took me to Kotido to catch the bus to Kampala. We walked silently together on the dusty road where we had met seventeen years before. Thick mist hovered in the fields; the sound of cocks crowing and donkeys braying came from distant villages as beams of sunlight appeared on the horizon behind us. My eyes brimmed with tears when I saw the old bus parked in the corner of the lodge where I had once stayed, the first time I had come to Najie. I thought that perhaps this would be the last time I would see Lodoch and Najie.

When I was in the field, I realized that there are separate yet interdependent processes in the appropriation of oral tradition materials: taperecording stories that are performed to audiences in specific contexts and then transcribing the recorded text and translating the text for English-speaking audiences. Needless to say, in each process, the transcribers and translators transform the stories.

Another major difficulty involved the nonverbal aspects of the stories, which do not get recorded – the mimicking, the body language, and the untranslatable yet punctuating utterances that constitute the emotive aspects of the performances. These aspects of the storytelling form an essential element of the aesthetic performance contributing to giving meaning to the story, but they are not recordable or translatable. I did try videotaping, but found this to be very intrusive. Of all the processes of recording the oral materials, videotaping was perhaps the most distracting one, as the storytellers became conscious not only of their voices and words, but also of their appearance. Sometimes, the storytellers would become frozen and unable to narrate, including those most articulate storytellers. Hence, I limited my videotaping to public gatherings and occasionally to private storytelling sessions, knowing that neither the storytellers nor the members of the audiences were comfortable. As a result, I discarded videotaping altogether.

Most performances in which I participated were composed of dialogic exchanges between the storyteller and the members of the audience. During such performances, sometimes it was difficult to discern who was a narrator and who the audience. Sometimes stories were not told in their entirety; rather, certain key episodes were mentioned and repeated by the members of the audience, or the audience criticized the performer and disagreed with the narratives, as during dispute mediations (chapter 5). Every performer set up an interpretive frame within which to communicate the message. Ironically, those interpretive frames that figure prominently in the context are nonverbal and hence they cannot be found in the recorded text. All historical traditions have variants and sometimes there are significant discrepancies between the variants of a story. I have included divergent variants as well as generally known variants in my analysis.

My interpretation and understanding of the meaning of the stories in this book are influenced by the political and social climate of the narrative moment and performance. As I have indicated earlier, most of the oral tradition is created in poetic performances that include aesthetic expressions and body movement along with spoken words and gestures. Performance is an aesthetic experience. To capture the total aesthetic experience was beyond my ability and hence it was virtually impossible for me to present the oral tradition and its aesthetics as it unfolded before me during the performance while still keeping the story understandable. As a result, I have chosen the literal translation of the story, word by word, and checked the accuracy of the translation against the orally recorded text. I translated each oral material line by line, after transcribing the story. (See in part 4, the story of the gray bull Engiro, as an example.)

In the field, I took different approaches to interviewing the storytellers, depending on the subject topic of the interview as well as my relationships with the person whom I interviewed. At each interview, I provided small gifts such as tobacco, sugar, flour, and locally made beer, all of which are highly valued and consumed in the region. Before each interview, I informed the storytellers as well as the members of the audiences that I would be tape recording the performances, and I requested their permission to do so which was always granted. After the tape recording of the interviews, I played the tapes, while the people listened to their voices with great amusement. Such occasions often evoked laughter from the people and encouraged others to be recorded as they narrated their stories. It is true that the storytellers and the audiences became conscious of their words when I recorded them, however they gradually relaxed and performed their stories without paying too much attention to the recording.

Most interviews took one hour and they seldom went beyond two hours. The interviews were based on dialogic engagement and conversation, conducted in the Jie and in the Turkana languages. However, there were times when I could not understand the nuances of the conversations. To compensate for this, I played the tape-recorded stories in the presence of my friends who knew English well and they would clarify to me those aspects of the conversations that were unclear. Sometimes when there were additional problems in getting the meaning of the narrative passages, I would go back to the storytellers and play the tape back to them, and I would ask them to clarify the unclear sections. The storytellers were both patient and gracious in explaining things to me.

When I privately interviewed storytellers or recorded their stories, inevitably there was some sense of staging, setting a scene, for the storytelling. However, during the public gatherings, when the stories were narrated and anecdotes exchanged during dispute mediations in their cultural settings (chapter 6), I would record the stories discreetly with the knowledge of a few authority figures who were in charge of the gatherings. Hence the public performances were more authentic and natural as the storytellers hardly paid any attention to me with my tape recorder sitting in the corner. These were all very different contexts and storytelling productions.

Sometimes, when a storyteller felt uncomfortable with being tape recorded, I would ask that particular storyteller, after the performance event, to dictate the same story to me and I would write it down line by line. Dictating stories usually took place in private without the presence of the audiences, of course. Dictating stories was a very slow process, and there were times when the storytellers omitted various parts of the stories, to summarize aspects of the overall narratives. Although dictating stories usually created a relaxed atmosphere, giving me an opportunity to ask the storytellers to clarify their stories, dictation and transcription took away the aura of the performance context. Likewise, when the storytellers performed the stories, as I tape recorded them, they became conscious of their words and of the flow of their narratives. Also sometimes the members of the audiences would make unnecessary and loud comments, so that their voices would be recorded. This was disruptive to the performances. As I've already mentioned, videotaping was even more disruptive, and I stopped it altogether.

To prepare for my future analysis of the stories, I asked both the storytellers and the members of the audiences about the meaning of the stories. Sometimes, both the storytellers and the audiences provided me with similar interpretations; at other times, however, interpretations by audience members and the storytellers were vastly different. Of course, during these moments I also had my own interpretation based on my academic knowledge of the oral tradition as performing arts, as well as based on my participation of the storytelling performances in the Kurdish villages during my childhood. It is in this spirit that I try to find "partial connections" between disparate interpretations and points of views as I analyze oral traditions and biographical and autobiographical materials in this book.

The difficulties of transcribing and translating oral materials often reduce the moorings of the language, and they eliminate the culturally understood artistic expressions and emotions (for example, Abu-Lughod 1986; Barber 1991; Caton 1990; Cashman 2008; Hofmeyr 1993; Mills 1990). The inevitable problem of transcribing and editing oral texts, although real, should not render ethnographies of oral tradition as fatally flawed. Through grappling with these issues, anthropologists and folklorists have found improved results through creative writing and representations, and it is these techniques that I have employed.

In this book I use "the Jie" and "the Turkana," to refer to the Jie and to the Turkana people in general. However my intention is not to totalize people, and I trust that the reader will understand that "the Jie" or "the Turkana" does not mean all the Jie and all the Turkana people. I also use Najie and Turkana land loosely, realizing that neither Najie nor Turkana land are bounded territories. In addition, when I refer to the Turkana people, I refer to the Turkana people living around the upper Tarash River region. Turkana land is an enormous territory where diverse communities live. I have traveled, researched, and collected stories in various parts of the Turkana land and Chalbi Desert, however for the purpose of this book, I confine my analysis to the upper Tarash River region. Inclusion of all the Nayeche and the gray bull Engiro stories that I collected from various parts of the Turkana land in my analysis would take the course of this book in a different direction because of the sheer size, magnitude, and the diversity of the region.

This book is divided into four parts. Part 1 has two chapters (1 and 2), part 2 has three (3, 4, and 5), part 3 has two (6 and 7) and the conclusion, and part 4 contains translations of stories. Part 1, chapter 1, sketches the precolonial and colonial histories of the Jie, their ecology, social and economic adaptations, and their contemporary predicament in the context of postcolonial state violence. It also discusses the relationships between the Jie and the neighboring peoples, and the significance of storytelling in shaping the modern perceptions. Chapter 2 explores the book's ethnography by weaving descriptive cultural scenes about the animated world of the Jie, as the rhythm of everyday life unfolds, with a continuing dialogue concerning storytelling, oral tradition, performance, rituals, and my interactions with the storytellers. This chapter is in part a narrative of my entry into the community, and it is about my experiences of living there, traveling in the kraals, and about my participation in the storytelling performances and the stories of the storytellers.

Part 2, chapter 3, explores the patterns and images of Jie historical traditions from a regional perspective and illuminates their interconnections with biographical narratives and folktales. This examination of historical traditions and biographies reveals the parallels between images of individual biographies and fictional tales and those of historical traditions. This illustrates the possibility – probability, even – of their influence on each other. Chapter 4 explores the complex relationship among oral tradition, memory, landscape, and the Jie worldview. The Jie land possesses a variety of ecological features: barren land with bushy patches, sacred groves, dry riverbeds, granite hills adorned with desert foliage, manmade landmarks such as pathways, and the plateau and the plains. These environmental features house the memories, keeping them alive, as they are the landscape where traditional heroes roamed; and where the original clans were founded, at the place Orwakol, the ancestral hero, captured the gray bull Engiro; and where Nayeche gathered the teeming wild fruits. Discussions in this chapter bring structure to the historical traditions and tales, and give a better sense of the geographical images in the stories. Chapter 5 examines rhetorical representation of oral tradition in dispute mediation and conflict resolution, showing how recalling the past shapes the identities and social relations of the people. Here I elaborate on Caton's development of rhetorical persuasion to illustrate how the images of oral tradition shape social identities and promote unity between an ideal ancestral past and the present (Caton 1990). Here I also suggest that the motifs and themes of Nayeche and the gray bull Engiro, and various other oral traditions, are tokens of a generalized ideal Jie identity, which are frequently recalled during dispute mediations and various tribal gatherings. The storytellers embellish their narration of past events with images of popular biographies, folktales, and myths, and by doing so they assert their authority to speak to particular audiences. An understanding of the art of rhetorical persuasion in dispute mediation is critical to appreciate the implications of the poetic power of remembered memories and "meaning making" (Flores 2002).

Part 3, chapter 6, argues that the story of Nayeche and the gray bull Engiro is the centerpiece of the Jie historical tradition and is connected with important rites of passage and rituals, such as marriage and the harvest ritual. The Jie harvest ritual distinctively features the role of women in the political thought of the interethnic relationship between the Jie and the Turkana, which is clearly linked to the Nayeche and the gray bull Engiro oral tradition. The examination of the linkage enables one to explore the participation of women in their identity politics. Indeed, the linkage between the Nayeche and the gray bull Engiro oral tradition, the harvest rituals, and the marriage ceremonies creates a powerful space for women in the Jie–Turkana interethnic discourse. Two different versions of this chapter, each exploring different yet complementary themes and aspects of the same tale, have previously been published in the journals *Ethnohistory* (Mirzeler 2004) and *History in Africa* (Mirzeler 2009). Chapter 7 provides an analysis of oral traditions in light of Lodoch's autobiographical tales, revealing historical traditions as not only about events, but also as possible sets of relations, and that these events can appear in the biographies. These biographical images are not visible in the events themselves, but are added to the remembered events by skillful storytellers such as Lodoch. In this respect, the story of the gray bull Engiro is not a story about a real life bull. The bull stands for something else. The gray bull is a symbol of tradition that holds the society together. Parts of chapter 7 are drawn from my dissertation (1999) as well as from my predoctoral and post-doctoral research from 1995 to present.

The conclusion reintegrates crucial points about oral tradition, performance, and the general orientation of Nayeche and the gray bull Engiro as a master narrative. Understanding the story of Nayeche and the gray bull Engiro as a master narrative requires, I suggest, exploring it in the processes of remembering and meaning making in performance contexts. Here, I also gently nudge storytellers' representation of Nayeche and the gray bull Engiro and other oral traditions, disagreeing with Africanist historians' interpretation of oral tradition as history. I take stories like Nayeche and the gray bull Engiro as providing models for people's deeply felt convictions that shape and inform wide ranges of social experiences, laden with meanings that have not been noticed and explored previously.

Part 4 provides translations of oral traditions (sixteen historical traditions, twelve folktales, and three biographical narratives). The first historical tradition is presented using line-by-line translation, accompanied with the line-by-line transcription of the original text, to give an idea about the translation of the entire oral materials in this book. Some of the oral traditions analyzed in the main text are drawn from the selection presented in part 4. Those interested in a better sense of images and symbolism of Nayeche and the gray bull Engiro and other oral traditions can turn to part 4.

PART ONE

PART ONE

1 Jie Past and Present: Ecology, Economy, Guns, and State

This chapter discusses the relationships between the Jie and the neighboring people as well as the significance of the storytelling in shaping modern perceptions. It also sketches the precolonial and colonial histories of the Jie, their social and economic adaptations, and their contemporary predicament in the context of postcolonial state violence.

Like others who are a part of the Karimojong Cluster,[1] the Jie people interact regularly with their neighbors – the Turkana pastoralists in the eastern plains of Turkana; the agriculturalist Acholi and Labwor people in the west; the agropastoralist Dodoth, Jiye, and Toposa in the north; and the Matheniko, Bokora, and the Pian on the Karamoja Plateau in the south. In addition, the Jie people have always interacted with their hunter-gatherer neighbors such as the Ngikuliak and the Tepeth.

The Jie live in a network of interethnic relations affecting their economy, culture, history, and identity. Relationships between the Jie and their Karimojong Cluster neighbors are complex and in constant flux. For example, interactions between the Jie and the Dodoth, Bokora, Matheniko, and Pian are generally hostile. The relationship between the Jie and the Toposa and the Turkana are friendly, characterized by sharing resources and forming alliances against their common enemies. However, the relationship between the Turkana and the Toposa are characterized by hostility and enmity, yet all these three communities claim a common ancestral lineage dating to the early settlement around Daidai in the late eighteenth century. The Toposa depend on the Jie for important ritual resources such as sacred clay found in the course of Longiro River, which the Toposa use in their initiation ceremonies as well as in healing sickness. When the Toposa separated from the Jie at the beginning of the nineteenth century, they brought along with them a black stone from Daidai, which then became an important part of their rituals.

The relationship between the Jie and the Labwor is generally friendly and there is extensive trade between the two communities, while the relationship between the Jie and the Acholi is marked by peace interrupted by occasional conflict. The relationship between the Turkana and the neighboring Southern Nilotic Pokot, who live adjacent to Turkana in eastern Karamoja in Uganda and in northern Kenya, is generally hostile, marred by violence and constant cattle raiding. Nevertheless, intermarriages among these communities continue, and their alliances and enmities are in constant flux.

The Jie people are by reputation a dominant group in the area, long regarded by their neighbors as fierce fighters (Gulliver 1955; Lamphear 1976; Marshall-Thomas 1965; Neville Dyson-Hudson 1966). In the late 1940s and in the early 1950s, P.H. Gulliver, the first anthropologist to study the Jie people, calculated the total Jie population to be 18,000. In 1969, Lamphear, an historian, reported the Jie population to be 33,000. In 1996, when I did my fieldwork in Najie, the Jie population had increased to 53,000. Today, the Jie population exceeds 60,000. Most Jie people live in Najie, in the central Karamoja Plateau, whose altitude is more than 3,500 feet, encompassing about 1,300 square miles and dropping steeply at the Uganda escarpment. On the west, Najie is surrounded by Labwor hills, and in the east near the escarpment, by the Koteen Hill and by the Nangalol Apolon, a seasonal river winds through the area. On the south, the broad shoulders of Mount Toror border Najie (see maps 1 and 5).

As an ecological zone, Najie has thin, wild vegetation and a dry climate. The Jie people cultivate many different crops, each of which is acclimated to the dry environment. Sorghum, the most important crop in the Jie diet and economy, is grown along the banks of the seasonal rivers. Several varieties of sorghum grow well in Najie. A number of different kinds of medicinal plants, tobacco, and maize are interspersed among the edges of the sprawling sorghum fields, and numerous varieties of wild fruits and clumps of thorny thickets important to the economy of the Jie people also endure the harsh climate.

There are two major territorial divisions in Najie. The larger one in the south is Lokorwakol (literally, the place of Orwakol), and the smaller one in the north is Lokalodiny (literally, the place of Lodiny), dividing the whole of Najie into southern and northern sections named after the ancestral founding fathers Orwakol and Lodiny. The Lokorwakol territorial

division, which is the focus of this book, is subdivided into seven territorial subsections: Losilang, Kotyang, Kanawat, Kotido, Komukunyu,
Panyangara, and Nakapelimoru, which derive their names from the
seven mythical wives of Orwakol (see map 3). The Lokalodiny territorial division is divided into four territorial subsections: Lokatap,
Kadwoman, Kapelok, and Chaichaon. Both the Lokorwakol and
Lokalodiny have their own politico-religious functionaries, such as a
firemaker, and both perform various ritual performances such as the
harvest rituals. The subdivisions of both territorial sections are strewn
primarily around the banks of their respective rivers. In Lokorwakol,
the four main rivers are the Longiro, Lokibuwa, Lokwakiel, and Mesua
(see map 3). The Jie subdivisions are further differentiated into villages,
and each village is composed of a number of homesteads that claim
descent from the same agnatic or adopted ancestors. Most Jie people
presently live in family homesteads (*ere*, singular; *ngirere*, plural) in
Najie. Homesteads are not isolated but are clustered under the over-
sight of the eldest male of the household.

As the Karamoja Plateau begins to tilt downward from the Koteen
Hill region in the east, a myriad of small seasonal streams and runoffs
converge and form the headwaters of the Tarash River, which flows to
the plains of Turkana land. In the center of this descending slope, on the
northern banks of the Tarash River, there is a hill called Moru a Nayeche
that derives its name from Nayeche. This hill forms the political border
between the Jie and Turkana people. Across from the Moru a Nayeche,
beyond the southern banks of the Tarash River, Moru Apolon (the great
hill) rises, overlooking the escarpment and the descending Rift Valley
(see map 5). As one stands on the lofty shoulders of Moru Apolon and
looks toward the east with the Najie at one's back, the Turkana land appears as a vast, sandy plain where the monotony of the dry scenery is
interrupted only by thinly vegetated volcanic hills and whirling dust
clouds rising in high columns on the horizon. Desert shrubs cover the
steep eroded gullies and ravines that constitute two-thirds of the country. Thorny trees, wild fruits, and some sharp-pointed plants are the
only vegetation in the plains around the Tarash River. With its wild
fruits, faded green thickets, clumps of tufts, and thorny brushes, the
headwaters of the Tarash River is a beautiful place. During the hot season, the Turkana cattle browse in its thickets while, in the bush, wild
animals sleep during the day and roam in the darkness of night. The
sound of insects mingles with the sound of wild animals that drone in
the deep gullies of the dry riverbed.

Around the headwaters of Tarash River there are a few semipermanent Turkana villages: Oyakwara, Lopedur, and Loitan. These villages
are clustered near one another and the people of the villages have close
ties with the Jie people. Their relationships have been tightly woven
through intermarriages. The dome-shaped houses in the villages are
made of thorn bushes and various other local shrubs, and the large
round cattle enclosures are also made of thorny bushes. The people in
these villages, just as most of the rest of the Turkana people, are pastoralist nomads.[2]

According to John Lamphear (1976, 34–41), when the Jie settled in the
early nineteenth century along the banks of the Longiro River, when and
where their current ethnic identity emerged, they developed complex
social structures and organized themselves into territorial groupings
and kinship clusters of agnatic descent structured around cattle pastoralism and sorghum agriculture. However, cattle pastoralism occupied
a central position as both a source of subsistence and a means of political
power used in the transfer of bridewealth and religious sacrifices. In addition, the Jie along with their Karimojong Cluster neighbors developed
a new system of politico-religious institutions determined by complex
generation-set (asapanet; singular; ngasapaneta, plural) and age-set organizations (anyamet, singular; nganyameta, plural).[3] The Jie generation-set
system is based on genealogical generations, involving the initiation of
sons into the generation-set following one's own father. The generation-
set system is cyclical in that two of the alternating generation-set and the
names Ngitome (those of the elephants) and Ngikoria (those of the gi-
raffes) recur in alternating fashion.

Generation-sets are divided into age-sets. Each generation-set contains around three age-set sections consisting of men initiated over a
few years. Becoming a member in an age-set enables a man to become
a member of a generation-set. For Lamphear, the gerontocratic aspects
of the generation-set system emphasized the ritual authority of the elders, which verged on political power. The surviving eldest members
of the most senior age-sets commanded respect and obedience because
of their symbolic association with Akuj (God). The eldest men of the
senior age-set had supernatural power to conduct effective prayers in
making decisions about their community.

Among the Jie, each major division has its own generation-set and age-
set system, cutting across clans and uniting men of different lineages into
a cohort of equals enjoined to observe norms of friendship. According

to Muller (1989, 98), the transmission of power from one generation-set to the next is dependent on factors such as peace and an adequate food supply. The changing demographic balance between the two alternating generation-sets regulates the succession between the two alternating groups. For the Lokorwakol territorial division, the opening and closing of the generation-set is commemorated by a formal inauguration ceremony held at Nayan, a ritual grove in Kotido area. According to Lamphear (1976, 39), the opening of a new generation-set began when the surviving members of the grandfathers reached an age when they could no longer produce sons who could be initiated in the final age-set of the father's generation. When the eldest son of the previous generation-set leader reached proper age for initiation there would be pressure by the uninitiated mature or elderly men to close the generation-set and open the new one. The generation-set system of the Jie and their Karimojong neighbors defined and still defines the organization of social relations.

In the generation-set system, the elders' politico-religious power was articulated in the *akiriket* (*ngakireta*, plural), the sacred assembly, which functioned both as religious and political ceremony in which sacrifices were offered to Akuj (God). During these ceremonies *ngimurok* (*emuron*, singular; prophets and healers) and the *ngikarachuna*, the junior men (*ekarachunait*, singular), assisted the senior elders of the generation-set in their performances of important politico-religious functionaries. According to Gulliver (1953, 157), the disobedience to elders evoked curses by the elders, which the young men feared. The elders often demonstrated their power and authority with the threat of *ameto* (traditional mechanism of punishment) in which they would force the offender to slaughter oxen for the elders and order the next younger age-set to beat the offender.

The elders' economic power was vividly expressed in *akiwodoking* ceremony in which they gave permission and blessing to young men to drive the cattle in the distant kraals on the condition that they must return when the elders called them to do so. The elders had the power to stop fights by simply drawing a line between the fighting groups and ordering them to settle down. Lamphear (1976), in the leading work on the early history of the Jie, maintained that in the late nineteenth and early twentieth centuries, the elders controlled the military activities. The young men sought the blessing of the elders before they went to war. If the elders favored the war, they smeared the young warriors with sacred clay and blessed them. When the firemakers died, the elders then had also the power to choose new firemakers. The power of elders thus extended into economic, political, and judicial practices.

For Lamphear (1976, 202), patterns of warfare changed in the course of the nineteenth century. Whips, not spears, were the earlier weapons. At around midcentury, the Jie began to form military organizations. Armies were arranged by age-sets and led by the battle leaders (*ekapolon ka ajore*), and men began to fight using spears. Although the war-leaders were regarded as commanders, the senior elders led actual planning of large-scale raids and other military activities, while they relegated the ritual preparations to the firemaker. With the emergence of Loriang as a war-leader in the late nineteenth century this changed. Loriang concentrated power and authority in his own hands, leaving less for the elders and establishing himself as the major military leader.

Origins of the Jie

Reliable data on the Jie's history before 1900 has come to students and scholars in the form of John Lamphear's historical reconstruction, *The Traditional History of the Jie of Uganda,* and various other writings that sketch aspects of the Jie history, such as the works of J. Barber (1968), M. Cisternino (1979), P.H. Gulliver (1952a 1955), N. Nagashima (1968), B. Novelli (1988, 1994, 1999), B.A. Ogot (1994), A. Pazzaglia (1982), J. Tosh (1978), G.S. Were and D.A. Wilson (1968), and J.B. Webster et al. (1973). Lamphear's work is, however, the most comprehensive history of the Jie people, touching the early Nilotic migrations, detailing historical and semimythical or wholly mythical events ascribed to the eighteenth and nineteenth centuries, such as the succession of the heroes and the ancestors to the office of the firemaker, and, finally, analyzing the proliferation of local warfare and the emergence of Loriang as a Jie warrior leader in the early twentieth century.

Lamphear correlated the stories of the early Najie settlement that are embedded in Jie oral tradition with the complex problem of identifying Nilotic origin and migration, with particular reference to events that took place around the Koteen Hill area on the Karamoja Plateau. As the Nilotic-speaking communities rapidly expanded, pushed, and absorbed the preexisting communities, they settled around Koteen Hill. The people of these early Nilotic migrations had three economic specializations: agropastoralism, agriculture, and hunting and gathering (Herring 1974; Lamphear 1986; Pazzaglia 1982; Wilson 1970).

It is in the Koteen Hill area, according to Lamphear (1976, 1986, 1988), where the original fragmentations and splintering of the ancestral families took place. This is when the Ngimonia clan separated from the Jie and migrated down to the plains, during the initiation of Ngipalajam generation-set, and settled around the upper Tarash River region, sometime in the 1720s. Later, these settlers became Turkana and adopted a more pastoralist economy fueled by the resources of Zebu cattle power and of the eastward expansion to the shores of Lake Turkana. In about 1740, another ancestral clan from the Koteen Hill area migrated to the north and settled around Daidai on the northern banks of the Longiro River, forming the embryonic Jie community. From about the 1740s on, the ancestral Jie families on the central Karamoja Plateau and the Turkana people around the headwaters of the Tarash River shared a common universe and ideology, including common origin stories, rituals, traditional forms of authority, political systems involving firemaking institutions, and generation-set and age-set organizations. They also shared the oral traditions of the lost gray bull Engiro, the father of all the cattle, and Nayeche, the daughter of the Jie and the mother of the Turkana.

Two semimythical ancestral leaders, Orwakol and Lodiny, founded Jie polity on a cattle-based pastoralism and sorghum agriculture around the Longiro and Dopeth rivers and divided the area into two territorial sections: Lokorwakol and Lokodiny (see map 3). While Orwakol led the people living around Daidai on the banks of the Longiro River, Lodiny led the people who settled around Lokatap Rock on the banks of the Dopeth River. The earliest Jie political system, based on the agropastoralism founded by Orwakol and Lodiny, derives its politico-religious power from the firemaking rituals associated with sorghum agriculture. These rituals involved the ceremonial making of new fire by the firemaker, after the extinguishing of prior fires. Originally, these rituals were first performed during times of crisis and, consequently, the firemakers were accorded tremendous respect (Lamphear 1976, 120–2). Although the early firemakers officiated at various rituals, their roles in the harvest rituals were supreme and remained so until the death in 2004 of Nakapor (Mirzeler 2009). The harvest ritual performances in particular were designed to legitimate the spiritual power of the firemakers.

The office of firemakers was most likely influenced by the Acholi concept of *rwot* (*rwodi*, plural), which refers to the hereditary king or chief. Similar to an Acholi *rwot*, Orwakol, the first firemaker, was responsible for creating many of the pastoralist and agricultural rituals including the *asapan* (male initiation ritual) and *angola* (a type of ritual performed to expel famines and diseases), as well as the harvest rituals. Orwakol had exceptional mythic attributes, and some people considered him the first human as well as the one who discovered the sacred clay (*emunyen*) that is used in rituals along the banks of Longiro River and who captured the gray bull Engiro, the progenitor of the Jie and Turkana cattle (Lamphear 1976, 124–9).

Like Orwakol, Lodiny is a semimythical ancestral figure still revered today. As firemakers, both Orwakol and Lodiny had judicial and ritual power and they were charged with the opening and closing of the agricultural cycle. Harvest rituals played, according to Lamphear, a major role in legitimizing the firemaker's cosmological power, particularly for those in the Lokorwakol territory. The office of firemaking and the performances of harvest rituals continued until the death of Lotum in 1960, after which the office became dormant and no one was elected to the position until Nakapor became firemaker in the mid-1990s (Mirzeler 1999, 2004, 2007a, 2007b).

In the late eighteenth century, the Jie community moved beyond Daidai and Najie as a new territorial entity began to form. The Lokalodiny and Lokorwakol territorial divisions had different experiences in terms of encountering and assimilating the original populations (Lamphear 1976, 136). For example, during the second part of the eighteenth century, the Jie people developed close relationships with the Labwor people who were affected by the Laparanat famine. (The Jie people name the various ecological disasters such as famines in their history. Laparanat was one of the severest famines, which took place in late 1800s.) Many of the Labwor people were skilled smelters and smiths who forged iron from the iron deposits of their lands, an activity that would play a large role in shaping Jie economy. The Jie, who controlled the iron-rich Mount Toror during the mid-1800s, engaged in iron trade with the Labwor smelters, becoming intermediaries in supplying iron tools to their neighbors, the Turkana pastoralists to the east below the escarpment. In various parts of the Labwor hills, R.S. Herring (1974, 245–80; also see Wayland 1931, 196–200) found artifacts suggesting an ancient iron trade between the Jie and the Labwor communities, which contributed to the considerable expansion of agriculture and pastoralism. Indeed, certain elements in the oral tradition attest to basic patterns of pastoralist expansion and early agricultural concentration from at least the middle of the second millennium AD. For example, J.G. Wilson (1970, 134) distinguishes various categories of agricultural implements, presumably belonging to the Oropom people (among the original settlers in the region), suggesting the presence of earlier pastoralist and agricultural developments. Similarly, Lamphear finds ancient traces of agricultural tools near the Koteen Hill area, remnants of various ancient water canals and an aggregation system near Panyangara in Najie, further indicating the existence of ancient agriculturalist communities in the broader region (Lamphear 1976, 60–2, 78–9, 137).

Lamphear (1976, 170) postulates that Orwakol, who was from the Toroi clan, ruled the Lokorwakol territorial division until the 1740s. After Orwakol's death, his son Loyale became the firemaker, but he lacked his father's charisma. When Loyale died during the Laparanat famine, his son, Lowatamoe, became the firemaker. When Lowatamoe died, the firemaking position passed on to the Jimos clan in Losilang. The succession of firemakers of the Jimos clan brought changes to the office, and the firemaking rituals went through several transformations. First, they changed the ritual fire-sticks from the *ekale* tree to the *essegessege* bush that grows in large numbers in Moru a Eker, a sacred grove a few hundred yards southwest of Jimos village, across from the Longiro River (see map 4). In addition, new rules and dietary and ritual prohibitions and observances were created. The firemakers had to follow strict dietetic rules, as they were prohibited from eating the meat from cattle that died of natural causes or food that had been grown outside of Najie. Planting and harvesting became more ritualized. When planting time came, the people of Lokorwakol had to gather at the Lomukura sacred grove to ask for the blessing of the firemaker to begin sowing. "If he decided the time was right, he would bless them by smearing them with clay. Having given his blessing to the people, the fire-maker would bless the seeds, which implied his permission for planting to begin" (Lamphear 1976, 172).

According to Lamphear (1976, 179), with the rise of the Jimos firemakers, the power of firemakers increased and began to "eclipse" the power of the senior elders and the judicial system. For instance, the firemakers took active roles in military matters, such as smearing warriors with sacred clay and blessing them. However, preparation for war continued to be in the hands of the elders and the hereditary war-leaders. The firemakers and the elders cooperated in the performances of important rituals, and the elders began to take important matters to the firemakers.

This continued until Loriang emerged as a war-leader and command-er in chief of the Jie army in the late nineteenth century. Lamphear main-tains that Loriang's military achievement began to overshadow the spiritual power of the firemakers, and his leadership and authority impinged on the congregation of the elders. Soon he assumed responsi-bility and made decisions for the entire community, usurping a respon-sibility of the elders. As Lamphear (1976, 246) points out, "While they [elders] continued to provide valuable foci for the ritual unity and the political homogeneity of their respective major divisions, their practical role became ancillary to that of Loriang, whose leadership transcended the major divisions to embrace the Jie community as a whole."

Loriang's emergence as the supreme war-leader in the Jie society co-incided with the coming of elephant hunters and ivory traders to Karamoja from different parts of the world during the first decade of the twentieth century. During this momentous period, the hunters and trad-ers of the world met in Karamoja and competed with one another for resources, creating a new economic and social fabric for the Jie and their neighbors in Karamoja Plateau and Turkana land. In the course of these developments, Loriang forged his economic and political relationships with the merchants and traders from Ethiopia and from various parts of East Africa, which elevated him to international power (Ocan 1994, 113).

During this period, elephant hunting and ivory trading became prof-itable to the Jie and various other communities in the Karamoja Plateau and Turkana land below the escarpment. As Loriang developed close relationships with international communities of ivory and gun traders, he sought to assert control in the region by means of warfare and raid-ing. Warrior-minded young men from Acholi, Labwor, and Turkana trekked to Panyangara seeking out Loriang, offering their loyalty and assistance in elephant hunting, gun trading, and raiding. Ivory trade, warfare, and raiding assured an intricate economic and social network for Loriang, enabling him to strengthen his relationships with traders and to become the single most influential warrior. Loriang reimagined and redefined the Jie's relationship with their neighbors during this crit-ical period, which coincided with the emergence of colonial control.

Elaborating on Lamphear's historical reconstruction, Ocan (1994) maintains that Loriang, as a war-leader, exerted his power among the elders and firemakers and brought the elders' council under his control. The social position of a warrior as a war-leader was one of privilege: "The warriors were organized into an army and the war-lord became their supreme lord. The army without the control of the elders ceased to be a community-centered army, but instead became an instrument of private accumulation and central coercion. Because of more efficient organization, it was able to accumulate surplus by raiding far and over-running several other communities" (Ocan 1994, 139).

Loriang was – and still is – considered the most fierce and creative warrior of his time. His raiding expeditions were regarded as an ulti-mate model of warfare and political achievements. He was celebrated in Labwor and Najie, and his friendships with Swahili-speaking traders were the sources of a new means for the Jie to replenish their livestock. During the years of ivory trading, the cattle population swelled dispro-portionately, and people's herds became much larger than they had been before the rinderpest (a common cattle disease in East Africa) wiped them out in the 1890s.

Lodoch, the Jie storyteller, told me about Loriang's interesting con-nections with Ethiopian, Swahili, and various Muslim traders who roamed the region. Here I consider one of these memories as an occa-sion to reflect how the Jie remember Loriang and his relationship with ivory traders of his time:

> In his disposition, he [Loriang] was cheerful; in his person as a warrior his talents were far above others; he spoke perfect Swahili, which he had learned from the Muslim traders coming from Mombasa. The ivory hunters and traders who lived in Tshudi Tshudi [Kaabong] were Somali, Ethiopians, Arabs, and other Muslims and often visited Loriang in his ere (homestead) ... they sometimes held dances and feasts on moonlit nights that lasted un-til morning. The warriors would fire their guns in the sky, which could be heard all the way in Nakapelimoru. People cultivated for Loriang and herded his cattle. They would hunt elephants at Loriang's request. At that time there were many elephants that yielded the heaviest and largest tusks that brought more and more cattle and guns.

The memory of Loriang dancing with Muslim traders is a telling one, for it locates these traders in the same frame as the Jie, in the kind of everyday interaction that went on between these traders and the elite members of the community, such as Loriang. Academic scholarship on northern Ugandan history and anthropology has often neglected the interactions and trade relationships of Ethiopian, Swahili, and various Muslim communities. Like their European counterparts W.D.M. Bell (1925), A.H. Neumann (1898 [1994]), and H. Darley (1935), the Ethiopians and Somalis and Swahili ivory traders also ventured into Karamoja and searched for commercially exploitable resources and engaged in ivory trade. In this respect, they were no different from the European traders or hunters, yet the colonial officers and various European travelers characterized the Muslims as slave traders and illegal elephant poachers, in consonance with standard elements of "colonial tropes" (Pratt 1992). What we read, then, in colonial documents and various travelers' accounts are not simply reports about their observations of the lawlessness created by "illicit" Ethiopian, Swahili, and various Muslim traders and "fugitives," but rather the ordering of their observations informed by the political imagination of their times (Mirzeler 2006b). As Ocan (1994, 113) points out, it was the merchants and traders of these non-Western empires who linked Northern Uganda to the international political economy. Emin Pasha, who spent a long time in Istanbul, had intriguing diplomatic and political relationships with high Ottoman officials before he became the governor of Equatorial East Africa and traveled to parts of Karamoja (Schweitzer 1898). All the political and diplomatic interconnections between the Ottoman Empire and Karamoja are yet to be explored.

During the first decade of the 1900s, Karamoja was outside of the British colonial administration, and a general "lawlessness" presided over the entire region. The European hunters, who competed with the Muslim traders, reported the presence of guns and widespread disorder in Karamoja, as they sought intervention. Yet the colonial government persistently refused an official intervention until the possibility of the Ethiopian Empire's claim for Karamoja and the Turkana land became a real threat. It is this geopolitically critical context and its perceived threat that finally prompted the colonial government to intervene in this far-flung colonial territory, after they received a complaint from Karimojong reporting the Jie aggression in the region in 1910 (Barber 1968, 124). It was this complaint that set the stage for H.M. Tufnell's famous patrol, which led him to an encounter with Loriang near Mount Toror in 1911, at which time Tufnell told Loriang that the days of raiding were over, ordering him to return the women and children he had taken from the Bokora during his most recent raids in the region. When Tufnell's soldiers searched Loriang's homestead, they found some rounds of ammunitions in his possession, but no guns. Before leaving the Jie land, Tufnell selected Loriang and Lodoko (another respected Jie leader) as chiefs for the Lokorwakol territorial division and Lopetum from the Rengen for the Lokolondiny territorial division.[4]

The Karamoja Plateau and Turkana land area is vast, and a number of decentralized communities have occupied it. Tufnell felt he would be able to bring down the resistance and pacify the whole area with the help of the chiefs. With the establishment of chiefs, Tufnell sought to reframe and design the control of the Jie and the entire Karamoja region under the military administration. Despite the difficulties of guns, traders, hunters, and fierce competition for ivory prolonging the violent colonial intervention in the region, Tufnell was successful in his patrols and, as a result, he was offered the district commissioner position in the region. He then tried to prevent raiding and to disarm the people in Karamoja and beyond.

On the heels of Tufnell, several administrators and colonial police officers descended upon Karamoja, including C.A. Turpin, who sought to develop the region as part of the twentieth-century world. While Tufnell created the administrative system, Turpin built upon it and developed it, and with his extraordinary energy he built roads and connected various centers in the region. Both Turpin and Tufnell left their mark and became significant actors in Karamoja's history.

While such colonial interventions were taking place in the Karamoja Plateau, the British Imperial forces made a number of military raids in the Turkana land in an attempt pacify the "belligerent" Turkana. Despite their modest number, the Turkana resisted the British conquest and defended their livestock, water holes, and grazing land, until the infamous Turkana Patrol of 1918, which is still remembered by the Turkana as "Apataret" (scattering). The patrol had a devastating impact on the Turkana and threatened their survival as a community, causing them to lose thousands of livestock. Without their livestock, thousands of Turkana died of hunger, and they never fully recovered from the Turkana Patrol of 1918, economically, socially, or psychologically. In the words of Robert Collins, the patrol was the watershed in the disintegration of the traditional society of Turkana (2006, 117; also see Lokuruka and Lokuruka 2006).

Under military administration, Karamoja was greatly changed between 1911 and 1921. The days of ivory were almost over except for in the Turkana land. The Lango and Acholi were under civil administration and began to develop rapidly. Yet, raiding and general lawlessness continued in Karamoja and Turkana land because of the inadequacy of the military administration. Between 1911 and 1914, military posts were established in Tshudi Tshudi, Morongole, and Loyoro. Moroto had become a small town, which later became the administrative headquarters.

As the colonial administration set out to establish control in the region, new colonial chiefs were assigned by the British and were charged with collecting taxes, keeping records, and maintaining peace and order. This situation led to tense conflicts and resentment between the people and the chiefs and was most vividly and publicly expressed when elders in Karamoja murdered Achia, who had been placed at Nabilatuk in 1923 as a chief by the British colonial state. The murder of Achia shook the British colonial fantasy, with disturbing implications for the colonial administrators, who realized that the elders and the traditional structure in Karamoja wielded significant power, regardless of the presence of the colonial government (Barber 1962).

In 1923, Governor Sir Geoffrey Archer held a critical meeting during which it was decided that the elders should be allowed to control the internal affairs of the clans, although the system of chiefs and courts would remain under the control of the colonial state. After this decision, Karamoja was left to its own devices and no significant developments took place except with regard to cattle-buying schemes and the appointment, in 1948, of the first district veterinary officer to replace the veterinary scouts (Barber 1968, 208).

Although the government made some efforts in the 1950s to establish new projects, introducing plow farming, education, and marketing facilities, by 1960 Karamoja was still starkly different from the rest of Uganda. However, the 1960s brought new changes in the district, as Indian and Somali entrepreneurs opened shops selling manufactured goods. Both Catholic and Protestant missionaries, who had been in the district since the 1920s, began to influence the situation with evangelical, educational, and medical initiatives. In 1961, a governmental committee was formed and led by Basil Bataringaya (who later became a victim of Idi Amin's regime) dedicated to finding new ways to improve the region and to reestablishing the presence of the government security forces to incorporate the district into a nation-state (Young 1994, 282–92; also see Mirzeler and Young 2000, 415). In fulfillment of the incorporation project, a second battalion of the Ugandan Army, headquartered in Moroto, housed substantial arms and ammunition, but the battalion was composed of ill-trained recruits, leading to conflict with the Karimojong.

The development of Karamoja as envisioned by Basil Bataringaya essentially influenced state initiatives (Mirzeler and Young 2000). Shortly after independence, state-sponsored projects were launched with the goals of modernizing, developing, and incorporating Karamoja into the broader Ugandan nation-state. Modernizing bureaucrats desired to incorporate "backward" Karimojong into the modern nation-state, with the expectation that "undeveloped" communities in the region would follow in the footsteps of the rest of the modern and developed nation. The modernizing projects of the Ugandan state have been vastly different from the paternalistic vision of the colonial authorities and their desire to civilize the backward tribes. The postcolonial state's nation-building project demanded immediate cooperation in the name of "social progress" (Young 2012).

When Obote I assumed power, his regime initiated various developments to incorporate Karamoja into the rest of the nation, but the Karimojong resisted the state efforts and continued in their traditional ways. During the Obote II period, the Karimojong continued to rebuff the government's efforts to incorporate them into the nation-state, and adamantly remained marginal (Mirzeler and Young 2000).

In 1971, when Idi Amin seized power, his administration took radical measures to impose modernization on the Karimojong through violence, eliciting rebellious responses from the people. In early 1979, when Amin's regime fell, soldiers fled Uganda and abandoned the well-stocked armory in Moroto. The sudden flow of dangerous firearms into the hands of the civilian population in Karamoja opened a new era in pastoral politics in northeast Uganda, transforming the local modes of conflict. This transformation has had far-reaching effects, both on relationships between the Ugandan state and its local representatives, and within Karamoja's societies.

One of the most profound transformations in the lives of the Jie and their Karimojong neighbors emerged from their new economic and political relations and their integration into the national government since the 1979 incident. The widespread availability of the AK-47, and other automatic weapons, and the Jie people's involvement in national politics effected an extensive undermining of the traditional tribal system; but the ancestral memories detailed in their historical traditions and embodied in various places at the center of their ancestral landscape continue to be ideologically compelling and to have a powerful hold on the Jie people. The new political authority and power created by the Jie's involvement in Uganda's national politics through participation in the election of local representatives has radically altered the traditional power and authority structure (Gray 2000; Mirzeler and Young 2000), but at the same time it has allowed the realization of the traditional ideals of Jie's unity and solidarity with other Karimojong communities. This would have been almost impossible through tradition-oriented politics alone. The new politics have pressured the Jie to establish alliances through lineages with other tribal communities, thus orienting them toward achieving unified agnatic alliances on the model of the original extended family that exists only in the traditional stories.

In the 1980s and 1990s, the Uganda People's Defense Forces (UPDF), commanded by General Yoweri Museveni (president of the country since 1986), suppressed a long-standing rebellion in north-central Uganda by the Lord's Resistance Army (LRA) under Joseph Kony. When the LRA began receiving large arm deliveries from Khartoum, the UPDF introduced a new strategy to fight against the growing power of the LRA, and invited the owners of AK-47s to register their weapons in return for a 10,000 shilling monthly retainer (about $10.00 US at that time). The armed herders in neighboring Karamoja thus became a critical force for containing the encroachment of the LRA, by blocking their potential operations in Karamoja. However, when the LRA left the political scene in northern Uganda and retreated to the Congo in early 2000, the UPDF – no longer needing Karimojong warriors as buffers between themselves and the LRA – decided to disarm the warriors to affect a new pattern of security and order in the region. The disarmament project, however, characterized by an ominous record of human rights abuses, went well beyond its stated aims, causing major demographic, socioeconomic, and political changes, ultimately challenging the region's environment and overall security (Mkutu 2010; Sundal 2010; Gray 2010; Mburu 2001; Mirzeler 2012).

Voices of Jie Storytellers

In a work similar to the present one, Scheub (1996) argues persuasively for analysis of the voices of storytellers as they shape the contours of resistance against the intrusion of external forces. For Scheub, when storytellers talk about their societies, they manipulate the images and metaphors of both past and present. For example, in resisting external intrusions like apartheid, the Xhosa storytellers of South Africa often blended the conflict felt by traditional heroes, torn between loyalty to tradition and acceptance of change, with a vision of a new community. For Scheub (1996, xxii), "[t]here is a double hero in the southern African tradition: the hero who embodies change at the expense of tradition, and the hero who stands for tradition with no chance of change." Jie oral traditions representing the double image of hero – in historical traditions, folktales, and biographical tales – actually reflect upon contemporary issues. Like the world of the Xhosa, the world of the Jie is periodically renewed through the artistic commentaries of storytellers who, as they blend the old and the new, invoke truths embodied in the images of tradition. Generally committed to tradition, Jie storytellers struggle between loyalty to the cultural past and the inevitable change that modernization is imposing on their society. They are aware that within their tradition, the heroes with a double nature can help the society move into new forms, yet the impetus for change, with the example of the heroes, seems to arise within Jie traditions, not outside. When external forces, such as the disarmament of the first decade of 2000, intrude into society, the heroes' role in the stories is to resist, to re-energize tradition. Forces of change from outside that are too powerful to resist undermine the heroes' role as protector of Jie society.

In talking about contemporary predicaments within the Ugandan state, the storytellers, evoking the symbolism of ancient Jie polity, compare their own heroic firemakers to the Ugandan rulers endowed with extraordinary power and authority. The Jie firemaker had long been characterized as a father figure cum politico-religious leader both in a political and a cosmological sense (Mirzeler 2004). On behalf of the people, the firemaker ritually solicited supernatural powers to ensure the production of sorghum crops and reproduction of the cattle, as would a protective father figure. In sharp contrast, the president of the Ugandan state has been, according to a Jie storyteller whom I will call Akiru, "like a hyena, the consumer of the human and cattle. He is no different than the colonial masters were." Symbolic equivalence of a state ruler as an anti-father and anti-heroic bearing the characteristics of colonial power is, indeed, recorded in various scholarly interpretations of the postcolonial African state leadership. As Young (2012) points out, the African postcolonial state is "a hybrid creature," combining "residues of colonial state" and "neopatrimonial practices" (70). Yet the rulership (the moral matrix) of the African postcolonial state uneasily evokes the father "who had parental obligations to nurture and discipline," expressing his power as a "consumer-in-chief," simultaneously feeding the state bureaucrats and patrons. Tripp's (2010) study further illuminates this hybrid with the example of the Ugandan state, delineating its moral matrix as a father figure with "semidemocratic" and "semiauthoritarian" character. For Tripp, the forms of neopatrimonial practices permeate the political realm of the Ugandan nation-state, which, although privileging democratic practices, has limited the scope of democracy with authoritarianism. The Ugandan state, according to Tripp, has drawn upon its legitimacy and obligations to intervene militarily to disarm, to civilize, and to develop its peripheries, but, in reality, it has enabled its patrons and bureaucrats to engage in a predatory extraction of public resources.

It is illuminating to examine the disarmament of the first decade of 2000 in Karamoja in light of Young's and Tripp's interpretations of relationships between the state and civil society. While the Ugandan military disarmament of the Jie and the Karimojong people displayed a modernizing impulse supposedly prioritizing "development" and "progress," the predatory extraction of resources by state patrons and bureaucrats severely compromised normative state precepts, forcing "nude savages" and "cattle rustlers" to leave their land, guns, livestock, and various other resources behind and migrate into urban areas where their survival became precarious.

In the midst of these conflicts, the storytellers are appropriating new forms and new interpretations and creating new authoritative relationships that link the past with present. In stories about contemporary postcolonial conflict, traditional images appear rhetorically to denote newly relevant historical meanings. Jie storytellers are becoming increasingly conscious of global connections and environmental changes, and they use local strategies in responding to broader issues such as tensions between elders and the young men and unease about the hybridized state's neopatrimonialism, with large-scale economic restructuring and the political power of modernizing agents in the region. Intertwined with modernization goals, the interest of the Ugandan state continues to marginalize the Jie and their Karimojong neighbors and to pressure them to accept the state's agenda. These conditions have instilled a sense of urgency in the storytellers to reconceptualize Jie traditions so they will speak to contemporary situations. The state's persistent efforts to disarm Karamoja sharpen the conflict, further encouraging storytellers in their efforts to guide change to work to keep their traditions strong and adaptable. The Jie storytellers, as they broach themes of resistance and accommodation in public discussions, continually grapple with their society's contemporary predicament as they negotiate social values, cultural selfhood, and the loss of tradition. The storytellers have developed a variety of strategies to deal with the loss of tradition. They explicitly and self-consciously reimagine their past while they try to influence their present reality.

For the storytellers, the story of the Jie is the story of their land where they cultivated and grazed their cattle, and shared the plenitude of cattle and grains with their neighbors. For hundreds of years, they cultivated their fields with their hoes and protected their cattle with their spears made from the soil of Mount Toror. Then in the last one hundred years came the hunters and ivory traders, who slaughtered the elephants in their land, and the colonial governors who introduced ploughs, intensive agriculture, and cattle marketing. With these, their traditions began to change. The Jie storytellers often lament the passing of tradition, the passing of a time when society waged warfare with spears, and when people lived lives in which they experienced the metaphorical insights of their tradition. In their lamentations, they rhetorically and politically appropriate the images of tradition and create historical meaning in their efforts to form a relationship with the global forces and hybridized state that limit their traditional powerstructure. The storytellers often invoke the memories of past warfare waged with spears made from the soil of Mount Toror as they draw upon rich clusters of forms and themes embodied in Mount Toror. Their stories reveal how metaphors of hoes and spears made from the sacred ore of Mount Toror supplied the tools for agriculture and warfare, life and death. War waged with the spears made from the ore of Mount Toror had spiritual sanctions, which once regulated customary forms of warfare and violence. As the hoes made from the ore of Mount Toror ruptured the earth which gave life to sorghum grain, the spears made from the same ore pierced the bodies of the warriors and released their spirits. Traditionally, at the beginning of each harvest, the people ceremonially buried the hoe, which initiated the cultivation of the soil. In the same way, they also buried the spear, which initiated war. Both hoes and spears remained firm beneath the earth until they rusted and become mingled with the soil and disappeared. This is said to fill the granaries of the women and to multiply the cattle of the men (Mirzeler 1999, 2007a, 2007b; Mirzeler and Young 2000, 423). The spear made from the ore of Mount Toror is a part of the Jie landscape, containing a force that is destructive but at the same time creative.

The spear and hoe made from the iron ore here is a narrative device articulating the metaphoric and fantasy elements of tradition emphasizing the ideals of justice, social responsibility, and moral action in warfare and death. This came to my attention during one of the peace ceremonies I attended in which a Turkana elder who negotiated the peace ceremony stood up and told the group of elders from Matheniko and Jie *"kapana atanyama ngalup a Toror"* (let us eat the soil of Mount Toror), after which they literally placed soil in their mouths. The soil during this ceremony symbolized the iron ore of Mount Toror.

The eating or tasting of soil is not an uncommon metaphoric response in Jie and Turkana tradition (Mirzeler 2007a and 2007b). The soil is said to contain the souls and spirits of the dead. According to Jie and the Turkana traditions, when people die, their spirits go to the hills, bushes, and riverbeds. I was told again and again when I inquired, that when a person dies the spirit flies out of the mouth along with the life of the person and becomes a part of the landscape. That is why some Jie storytellers make a distinction between spears and the bullets of AK-47s. According to some Jie storytellers, when the spears rupture the body of the victim, they release the spirit, and the spirit of the dead person travels to bush and seeks redemption from the ancestors. The fear of retribution forces warriors to take responsibility toward their victims, but death caused by the unblessed bullets of an AK-47 causes the spirit of the dead to become confused and wander in the landscape aimlessly (also see Mirzeler and Young 2000).

When the tradition becomes associated and synonymous with human life force and spirit, change induced by modernity and global connections, such as the AK-47, is felt as a loss and a threat to the sense of cultural continuity, a rupture in time and history. Thus the interpretation of past memory images, embodied in Mount Toror and other landscapes, demonstrates how the images of tradition are "transformed" and "lifted up" in the process of traditionalization (Anttonen 2005, 35).

The storytellers modify the content of the tradition to redefine the memory of Mount Toror and the spear made from its ore in light of the changes of modern life. The fantasy element contained in the ore of Mount Toror likens the ore to an endangered species, the loss of which is parallel to the loss of diversity in the Jie landscape, and is a discursive response to the presence of the modern AK-47. The loss of the spear made from the ore of Mount Toror is closely related to alienation, which denotes the loss of the political and spiritual influence of the remembered memory images of tradition embodied in the landscape of Mount Toror. The loss of the spear is thus the loss of the ancestral memory embodied in the landscape that sways traditional authority and demands social responsibility for death and violence, which was a great integrative paradigm of the Jie people. In many ways, the sense of the loss of the spear is an irreversible loss of cultural memory and a loss of tradition. The contemporary blessings of the AK-47 by elders is a local strategy to re-appropriate the traditional power of Mount Toror and to incorporate it into the changes created by the broader global connections of modernity, because the memories of past warfare around Mount Toror stress justice, protection, and self-defense against encroaching neighbors. Thus, the sentiments expressed in memory of this place demonstrate the customary forms and the spiritual significance of warfare, based on defense rather than offense.

More important in the present context is the way in which the images of AK-47 bullets made from the ore of unknown lands, as opposed to spears made from the ore of Mount Toror, had become dissipated. Of course, the Jie and their neighbors have not forged their spears from the ore of Mount Toror for perhaps a hundred years now, but the metaphoric significance of the iron ore of Mount Toror has remained powerful.

The tasting of the soil of Mount Toror is a nostalgic reflection on past warfare conducted with spears made from the ore of Mount Toror: all these suggest that places of memories are still in use, with the implication that, although modernity may transform the landscape, the same tradition continues without interruption. And it is not as if the past is forgotten: the Jie and Turkana peoples still pay tribute, by their visits, to the places of memory that they continue to admire. The places of memories are recalled during ceremonies to highlight the changing political and social circumstances in Najie.[5]

The Storytellers in Exile

The Jie's transition in the contemporary context during which they, like their neighbors in northeast Uganda, are moving into the boundaries of society where transformations are taking place. The storytellers and their audiences are actively and effectively incorporating contemporary experiences with the forces of guns and disarmament projects into their traditions. From this point of view, the Jie society is contending with the disruptions caused by both internal and external forces: the power and authority of the elders are challenged by the heavily armed young men and postcolonial nation-state's military power. The traditional power of the elders has become ineffective in struggling against these forces, and the result is disruptions leading to dispersals and migrations to Kampala. This divergence between past and present is graphically drawn in the narratives of the Jie storytellers, in which they contrast present-day destroyed villages and landscape with a better past. The voices of storytellers reveal the revitalization of traditions initiated by the threat of external forces.

The Jie traditions with rich lineages provide clear structural underpinnings encompassing the breadth of a story of continuity and growth and of loss. In the narratives of storytellers the larger context is represented as loss and attack to their tradition. The disorientation of loss felt can be clearly detected in the narrative of Jie storytellers living in exile in Kampala. The storytellers in exile lament the passing of tradition as well as mourning over the loss and the destruction of the landscape. They conceptualize changes and modernization as a loss of tradition. They long for what has already been lost or has become distant. The sense of loss for the storytellers in exile is the story of an alienated self. Longing with nostalgia and homesickness, the storytellers in exile long for metaphorical home and the time prior to change. The storytellers' tale about forced migration and their aloneness become what Scheub calls "necessary prelude to newness" (1996, xxvi).

The storytellers reminisce about the landscape and the village of the past, but also about the authority once held by the elders over young men and the young men's fear and respect for the elders. The current violence in the region is linked to the declining power of elders that followed on the modernizing developments of the last thirty years. For many storytellers, the current situation in Jie life is far from the golden age image of a younger generation respecting their elders and fearing their retribution. The storytellers reminisce about the past, about when the senior generation-set stepped down, and their promotion of the eager junior generation-set of male elders to become senior elders. However, it has been some time since this pattern was disrupted in broader Karamoja. Since the late 1950s, there has been stagnation in the succession of power from senior generation-set to junior generation-set due to unsettling security concerns, food shortages, and the heavy presence of army.

According to Stites (2013), the existence of multiple generations of uninitiated adult men has created discordance in the traditional patterns of relations governing the generation-set system, which was marked by deference on the part of the youth and influence on the part of the elders. The tension from the multiple uninitiated generations creates an environment in which young men seek new forms of status, authority, and respect to achieve status within a system that no longer afford recognition of young men. Because of this, heavily armed young men with AK-47s in northern Uganda become motivated by individual peer group goals. Without the possibility of amassing personal wealth or of establishing reputation, young men are increasingly questioning the validity of the actions of elders and are disrespecting their traditional position as peace negotiators and diplomats.

The presence of large numbers of young men armed with AK-47s and the subsequent forced disarmament dominated the storytellers' narratives in 1990s and in the first decade of 2000s. The storytellers' narratives display two important effects of the AK-47s on society: the marginalization of elders' status and the disempowerment of women. The storytellers do not address the presence of guns and violence in a direct or concrete way, but they allude to a contemporary crisis. For example, the rabbit, traditionally an ambivalent character, becomes the symbol of the greedy young men with the AK-47s.

For the storytellers, the AK-47 empowers young men and increases their mobility across state boundaries, enabling them to interact with the representatives of the nation-state, while at the same time it denies similar opportunities to women. Whether or not the course of modern development is destructive and violent may be debated, but it nevertheless has negatively impinged upon women's traditional rights, resulting in violent disruptions, first by the expropriation of women's traditional rights to land, then by the disarmament of the men who had used guns to protect cattle. Under these circumstances, both women and men have become less and less effective in resisting external influences.

The divergence between tradition and modernization has been obvious since Museveni's regime launched a violent disarmament campaign against the northeastern Ugandan people (Stites 2013; Gray 2010; Eaton 2010), an act often contrasted, by storytellers, with the stories of the great mythic heroes and representatives of the people of the past. While guns and disarmament are not obvious themes in oral traditions, they nevertheless loom large in, on the one hand, the imagination and, on the other, in the real world. When the tales are performed as commentaries on the present, the messages become obvious and evident, without direct reference to the violent disarmament that continues into 2013. The images and themes have the effect of sharpening consciousness. Many storytellers are supportive of a gun-free society even though firearms are used to protect cattle. Yet because of the way the government arms one ethnic group while disarming another, gun ownership is given urgency, driven by powerful emotions with roots in the ancient motifs of the people.

Storytellers often evoked images of disarmament that cluster around memories of their villages as they were in the past. Here, anecdotal references to the memories of their grazing lands and the lives that unfolded within it index their relationship to their lost guns and their grazing lands, the places where their ancestors settled and lived. References to the images and memories of guns and the ancestral grazing lands and their loss enable the storytellers to recreate a framework in which the "memory of the loss" (Gray 2000) reshapes their sense of self, their identities.

Relying on such images, the Jie storytellers reveal how the victims of disarmament lost their family herds, homes, and villages, and how some of them crossed rivers and hills to migrate to Kampala to escape hunger and death. As a narrative resource, the story of their migrations to Kampala constructs social actors and assures clear friendship ties among the victims who experienced this trauma of disarmament, and these stories help them keep the memory of violence and dispossession alive.

Those Jie and those Karimojong who fled live as refugees in slums, abandoned structures, and bus stations in Kampala. Important changes in the lives of the Karimojong refugees came about not only because of the disarmament, but also of urban conditions. For many Karimojong, the abandoned structures and bus stations in which they are compelled to live are emblematic of their destroyed homes. This association evinces strong emotions of deep mourning for their lost homes, so the storytellers talked of living in Kampala while referencing and critiquing the world's indifference to their lives. And so, in recreating the lost gray bull image, the Jie storyteller captures, reflects, and reevaluates the political reality of living as refugees in one's own country. When we analyze the stories of these storytellers, we can see how the personal narratives give voice to an alternative discourse and become an integral expression of the dispossessed and dislocated, serving in the imagination as an eventual return to a lost way of life and new beginnings, the creation of new landscapes, engendering new memories of a past that differs from their current lives living in the crowded cities and revealing the beginning of new possibilities and horizons.

With the loss of guns and grazing lands, the Jie and their Karimojong neighbors encountered new boundaries and horizons within the global economy and the context of contemporary political forces. The changes in their lives, in their stories and rituals, can potentially help them to become part of the global world. Although the Jie and the Karimojong people recognize the worthiness of their guns, they maintain an ambivalent attitude toward them. They reject the destructive nature of guns, yet they embrace the security they provide. This duality, long familiar in Jie oral traditions, allows the storytellers to express both positive and negative feelings about firearms, much as they articulate contradictory feelings in the dual images of their heroes.

Memories of violent disarmament among the Jie have become powerful and effective tools in healing the wounds of the past and in creating a new consciousness; yet some Jie kraal leaders have actively engaged in exploiting memories of trauma for their own political and economic purposes. They invoke the memories of state violence to bring symbolic meaning and purpose to warring groups, gaining legitimacy through the memories to raid villages as a means to demonstrate their resistance against the state.

Seeking legitimacy, some of the kraal leaders have claimed their raids have the approval of the national authorities. It is in this context that unscrupulous warlords secured their political authority by means of invoking memories of trauma. The frustrated and threatened young men engaged in agitation against the state; however, these protests and resistance were often countered with state violence. In addition to the increasing militancy of youth in the region, gun traffickers from Somali, Sudan, Ethiopia, and Kenya have taken on a wide range of political roles conventionally reserved for state institutions, such as providing internal security. Some warlords and their allies disrupted authority, ignoring the international frontier boundaries as they clandestinely compete to control the cattle and gun markets (Mburu 2001; Mkutu 2003, 2010).

Since the disarmament began, the government has disrupted the patterns of the traditional pastoralist movement in the outlying grazing lands by creating "protected kraals" (Mkutu 2010, 97) outside of which pastoralists cannot graze their cattle. To accomplish this goal, the government employed certain young men, supplying them with arms and ammunitions, to provide security for the cattle in the protected kraals. Through these new state guards, according to a well-educated Jie scholar, whom I will call Lowatomoe, the state is able to provide guns to its constituent supporters to enhance its patronage system and informal political networks outside of state institutions. Meanwhile, these constituent supporters pursue their private interests while pretending to serve the interests of the public. Lowatomoe was clear about how some of these new kraal guards are like the trickster rabbit of the Jie oral tradition. While they jettison all pretenses of providing security, they are essentially dangerous rivals or allies of unruly warriors and warlords across state boundaries, undermining the collective interests of the people. At this extreme, these so-called guardians of the kraals are in reality unruly warriors, warlords, racketeers, and as such, they and their associates are more international criminals than "traditional" war-leaders, especially if one thinks of the latter as supposed to be serving collective interests.

For many Jie elders, the new guardians of cattle are like the ambiguous trickster characters of the folktales, like the rabbit with a sacred gray color, who dupes people and mimics the selfless heroes of the past, yet steals from people.[6] The critical difference between the unruly warlord, racketeer, the new guardians of the protected kraals, and the "traditional" war-leader may seem to lie in the fact that the war-leader works for the community. However, it is difficult for observers to grasp the distinctions among the contemporary warlord, the war-leader, and the racketeer as they all embody divergent impulses, each pursuing collective and private interests, depending on what processes and/or actors one is analyzing. To say a war-leader with powerful linkage to tradition and elders serves the collective interest is not completely accurate, since war-leaders are motivated both by public and private interests and are known to manipulate the traditional systems.[7] On the other hand, a warlord may provide protection and services to villages because of his networking interests. Thus, the vision of a contemporary war-leader as "traditional" and benevolent or as serving a collective belies the material desire for power that motivates him. Thus, it is difficult to categorize who is a warlord and who is a war-leader, as different observers characterize them in a variety of ways that are not entirely compatible (Mkutu 2010, 93).

Contemporary warlords or war-leaders, who I was told are mainly political urbanites and international entrepreneurs, are the primary agents orchestrating violent raids as well as state elections (Dr Lokuruka, personal communication, 2011). They pay for raids conducted by local pastoralist warriors. Their political and interregional connections help to organize the transition of stolen cattle across state boundaries. This urban-centered activity is increasing on a large scale in Najie, Karamoja, and Turkana land, adding additional layers of insecurity to the threat of intertribal raids.

The Burning of Jimos Village

Complex layers of political and economic maneuvering create insecurity and force local people to risk their lives and resist the state and its disarmament project. One particularly symbolic resistance occurred in Kotido, which culminated in the destruction and the burning of Jimos village by the Ugandan army in 2007. Jimos was the village of Nakapor, the late Jie firemaker. The event occurred when the army went looking for a young man, whom I will call Lojulukan. Lojulukan was, according to some storytellers, an unruly warlord and racketeer yet, according to others, another war-leader. Lojulukan colluded with the guardians of the protected kraals in the Kacheri area and successfully raided nearly two hundred head of cattle and took them to the Turkana land. A few days after the incident, the news spread that Lojulukan was hiding in Jimos village. When the UPDF soldiers went looking for him there, a young man from the Toroi village who happened to be in Jimos village at that time, trying to negotiate for his marriage, fired at the soldiers thinking that they were there to confiscate his gun. At that moment, the soldiers, firing their guns indiscriminately, surrounded the village. In the process, the village caught fire. The fire spread from Jimos village to another village, causing several people to lose their lives in the flames, while both villages burned to the ground, with the exception of the sacred granary of the firemaker in Jimos village.

The explanation given by the storytellers about the resistance of the granary to the fire offers pivotal instructions on how to remember and interpret the destruction of Jimos village. The refusal of the fire to burn the ancient granary is understood in terms of the creation of a new Jie ethnic consciousness in the twenty-first century – one without guns, the very absence of which is an ironic contradiction to the Jie's fighters (Ngijie) identity. The new village, which exists on the rubble of the old village with its surviving ancient sacred granary (left intact after the fire), was built by people relying on memories. The new palisades and passageways serve to delineate the boundaries of the village as it was before and as it is now.

The storytellers' narrative strategies connect the new village in the present with the old one, linking its untouched, undestroyed granary to living, surviving eyewitnesses. For some storytellers, the granary that refused to burn will continue to nourish the Jie communities of the future through the spirit of their ancestors. Listening to narratives of this memory told in various ways, gave me a good insight into how storytellers transmit knowledge of the traumas experienced by the Jie. The destruction of Jimos village and the continuing horror of disarmament are perceived as what Heike Behrend (1999) calls "epistemological fragmentation," a total loss and utter helplessness. The disarmament dispossesses the Jie and the rest of the Karimojong of their means of survival, creating a chronic and debilitating memory of violence different from their historical experience. When the Jie storytellers talk about the destruction of Jimos village, their narratives used both ancient and contemporary images to create an unbroken Jie identity. The storytellers talked about the way the old village existed before its destruction and about the community of memory and experience that came after. Some storytellers drew the outline of the village on the parched earth with a stick to show their audience the outlines of the old village before its destruction, making tangible their memories.[8]

The new Jimos village constitutes not a mere village built on the old one, but a community of memory whose existence and continuity are made real by the people's memory of its destruction. Jimos village does not consist only of a land with families residing on it, but also of the memories of Orwakol, Nayeche, and the gray bull Engiro that make the village flourish. They always have been and always will be there to protect not only Jimos village but also the entire Najie area, providing them the very source of their sacrifices, including the memory of the selfless bravery of the ancestors of those living there now.

The narrative strategies of the Jie storytellers are congruent with ways that oral artists in general function in society as the voices addressing social mores and experiences (Amadiume and An-Na'im 2000; Bivins 2007; Hofmeyr 1993; Scheub 1996; Schneider 2008). Jie storytellers create a moral topography through the use of the images and metaphors of their oral traditions in talking about the destruction of their village and the ongoing disarmament. Their tales are filled with grim allusions to violent episodes that detail their experiences of the last ten years, rooted in the anguish and trauma caused by the ongoing disarmament, and encapsulating their deepest fears and hopes, dreams and nightmares. Through these images, the Jie storytellers evoke memories of the traumas associated with the trickster characters in their oral tradition whose victims seek redress and implement strategies for social regeneration. The storytellers bring the experience of the contemporary incomprehensible and grotesque predicament into perfect conjunction with the world of their oral tradition's exaggerated trickster, Napeikisina, and the cunning rabbit.

It is in the storytellers' artful conflation of these memories with the trickster theme that the disarmament process becomes a transcendent metaphor against which to construct the ruthlessness of the soldiers and the horrors of their violent acts. For example, in the subversive versions of the rabbit stories, the storytellers enable the rabbit to join the people in digging ditches to bury their guns before the government soldiers come to search the villages, thus enabling the trickster to become a part of the society. There is a message in the rabbit helping to bury the guns. While in real life, some warriors buried their guns before the army searched their villages, the knowledge about the buried guns must also be buried, since this knowledge is dangerous, and must be erased from memory – society must find different means to survive.[9]

Another example of a storytellers' solution to the violent conflict caused by disarmament emerges in another subversive version of a story about conflict between the farmer and the rabbit.[10] By situating the Jie people's current predicament of the disarmament drama in the context of the conflict between the rabbit and the farmer, the story suggests that the current government's life will not be long enough to merit deep concern, like the rabbit in this story, which ate the farmer's crops.

The meaning of the distinction between the farmer and the rabbit, in the context of disarmament, is not found in the details of the folktale structure, but in the allegorical existence of the morally upright, indestructible Jie institutions, embodied in Jimos village, versus those of the corrupt government. To read the images literally relegates the message of the story to a mere morality tale. Instead, we need to read it as the storytellers' artful presentation of the successive history of the Jie people, who, in the face of immoral destruction, fight back through their memory and tradition rather than through weapons of destruction, which were used not only by the Ugandan army during the disarmament process, but also by previous colonial and postcolonial state entities.

In the context of performance, the storytellers weave the images of folktales, historical tradition, and private memories to recreate Jimos village as it is remembered before its destruction, as it existed in the past, and as it is imagined into the future. The weaving of the real world with the fictional world of the animals and the long-gone ancestral worlds is what the storytellers communicate to their audiences. This weaving of memory, fantasy, and history is a powerful political tool, which the storytellers artfully utilize to address the not yet complete violent destruction and cultural annihilation of the Jie people, such as that brought about by the disarmament.

The Return of the Exile

After the destruction of Jimos village, many of the storytellers with whom I worked in the late 1990s escaped from Najie and went to Kampala. The voices of the displaced Jie storytellers on the streets of Kampala captures yet another moral mandate embodied in the history of the Jie. Many Jie people whom I met in Kampala during my return visits in 2010 and 2011 suffered from an acute identity crisis. They called themselves Karimojong, not Jie. I saw in Kampala a sixty-year-old Jie storyteller, whom I will call Nacham. I originally worked with Nacham in 1996 and 1997 when he was in his mid-forties. Nacham escaped the horrors of the destruction of his village in Kotido and walked to Kampala on foot with his family. When Nacham and his family were forced to flee, they were confronted with survival in an alien place, not as an individual Jie family, but as bands of homeless Karimojong wanderers in a cosmopolitan city that did not welcome them. There is budding research about the displaced Karimojong living in Kampala and other cities (for example, Sundal 2010; Stites et al. 2007). The displaced Karimojong people on the streets of Kampala have created a new diasporic community. What unifies these people ranges from the memories of their villages, the dusty roads they traveled, and the sound of cowbells coming from the distance, to a common language, folklore, and traditions.

Memories of village life and of the violent disarmament, told by displaced survivors, are valuable historical materials documenting dilemmas of communities experiencing tragedies (Jackson 2006; Scheub 1996; Slyomovics 1998). Storytellers in exile retain the memories of displacement. Nacham and other storytellers use folkloric genres to document the recent history of Najie. These narratives capture aspects of village life before the disarmament and various aspects of the treatment of the Jie and Karimojong by Ugandan soldiers during the disarmament.

Nacham now identifies himself strongly as Karimojong rather than Jie or Ugandan. His narrative describes his flight with his family from their village, their brutal life in Mbali, the death of his son, and his wanderings in Kampala, where he now lives. Nacham's narrative is like a memoir, recounting his brief return visit to Najie in 2010, finding the new village built on the rubble – one that looked starkly different. Kotido

had become an expansive shantytown, largely a multiethnic community, and the homestead where he grew up, which had been burnt, had
been replaced by a single room made of corrugated iron belonging to
a different family. The soldiers occupied the entire district and many
people there now spoke different languages. In his narrative, Nacham
discloses how he wandered and begged on the streets, and how he
struggled with alcoholism, hunger, and survival. He describes Kampala
as a place of alienation, though it became his new home. Nacham identifies himself with the Karimojong street beggars with whom he struggled
and survived through the brutally humiliating world of a big city, and
where he suffered with many Jie and Karimojong people. As a self-iden-
tified "Karimojong" living in Kampala, Nacham confronts his otherness
and the government's indifference to him and many other Karimojong.
Of all the memories, one event from Nacham's life is pivotal: the destruction of his village. It was this village that gave the Jie the central
metaphor of their history. Its destruction became the symbol not only of
the oppression of the Jie people, but also of the entire Karimojong's
oppression from which Nacham escaped.

2 Ethnography of Storytelling

Traveling north from Soroti, leaving behind the run-down Indian buildings and broken concrete boulevards, one enters the Moroto Road, the
old dirt road, which leads all the way to Karamoja in northeastern
Uganda. This was the road that H.M. Tufnell built with forced labor,
connecting Karamoja with the rest of the world – the world that swallowed its elephants. Continuing on this road, one passes rows of identical round thatched houses with open courtyards crowded with trees,
under which sit men and children. Women carrying huge loads of firewood on their heads shout across the courtyard to the children. Before
entering Karamoja, one must cross several tiny bridges, each of which
can accommodate only one lane of traffic. There, all must wait their turn
alongside other vans and passenger cars packed with people, goats,
and chickens.

Once across the bridge, leaving the tall reeds and humid marshes
behind, one enters the beginning of a dry sandy plateau dotted with
shrubs and tall fruitless trees and isolated hills. Traveling northward,
the vegetation thins out and gives way to clumps of desert shrubs, and
lone acacia trees here and there, surrounded by scrubby dwarf trees.
The crisscrossing of the dry riverbeds is a sure sign that one has entered Karamoja.

When I first traveled this road to go to Najie, the land of the Jie people, it was May 1996 soon after the presidential elections in which
Yoweri Museveni had become president. This dry flat land was the place
I had read about and had become fascinated with, while in the cold
library rooms at the University of Wisconsin–Madison. The wooden
palisade villages with round thatched houses on both sides of the dusty
road resembled very much the picture I had seen of them in P.H.

Figure 2.1: The dusty road to Jimos village. Author photo (Losilang)

Gulliver's book *The Family Herd*. The cattle were returning home and the women were walking on both sides of the road with their hoes on their shoulders.

During my first arrival in Najie, in 1996, I stayed for about a month in a mud-plastered hotel near the edge of the town, and I went to the surrounding villages during the day to meet with storytellers and collected, among others, the story of Nayeche and the gray bull Engiro. One memorable afternoon, I set out to go to Jimos village, in Losilang, about five miles northeast of Kotido, to meet Nakapor, the Jie firemaker. On the way, I stopped to buy gifts of tobacco and sugar at a shop where I used to sit behind the counter and chat with the owner. It was in this shop that hot afternoon that I met Lodoch, and, from that day, I became his apprentice and began learning Jie oral traditions from him. We walked together many miles on dusty roads and visited places where mythical heroes such as Nayeche and many others had been born or had passed through during their journeys. I participated in many storytelling sessions with Lodoch under the trees, in the bush, and in remote villages. My research on oral tradition and my interest in Nayeche's journey provided a frame for our interchange. As I became familiar with Lodoch and his family, I felt less interested in collecting stories and more in meeting people I did not yet know.

My relationship with Lodoch, his family, and his neighbors opened up horizons in my research project that I had never anticipated. I became interested in social life in Najie, the complexities of interpersonal relationships in the Jie society, and the way its people understood their world. Lodoch was generous as well as articulate about himself and his culture. His wife and children welcomed me to their home when I visited them. Nakapor, his two wives, and daughters and sons, as well as the families belonging to the firemaking clan all spoke and maintained a relationship with me.

During my first research expedition, at Lodoch's suggestion, I made arrangements with Nakapor, the firemaker of the Jie, and moved to a mud hut at the edge of Jimos village, near Nakapor's home. My new place was also only minutes away from Lodoch's home. Although both Nakapor and Lodoch insisted that I live with one of them, I declined their generous offers. I did not want to burden them and intrude in their lives any more than I already had. The mud-plastered traditional round homestead in which I had settled was located on a poorly cultivated lot of high ground. Except for a few dusty acacia trees, nestled outside the fences, and isolated tall tamarind trees, nearly all the trees had been cut down and used for fuel or for thick palisades surrounding the homesteads. Rainfall was scarce when I was in Najie, and consequently the earth was parched and covered with thick dust that burned one's ankles like hot ashes. In the wet season, the Longiro River overflowed its banks, flooding sorghum fields. At night the moon and stars shone intensely.

This decision to stay in Jimos village to be with people whom I already knew, who had accepted me, instead of moving from village to village collecting stories, was not minor. I sometimes despaired, thinking that I was not collecting enough information or compiling enough historical traditions about Nayeche and the relations between the Turkana and Jie peoples. But by staying there I gained a depth of knowledge of both village life and individual lives on which my later analysis would draw. Learning about people and listening to village gossip, in addition to my close relationship with Lodoch and various other friends, convinced me about the importance of becoming a part of the community and developing interpersonal relationships with people as

Figure 2.2: Lodoch, the Jie storyteller. Author photo (Jimos village)

opposed to collecting a very large corpus of stories. My return visits in 2003, 2010, and 2011 further cemented our relationship. Despite these scattered visits, I felt as if I had never left the village, as if I had aged along with the people whom I had come to know.

Jimos village is on a high ground in Losilang territorial division along the southern banks of the Longiro River. Standing high, about thirty miles east, near the border of Najie, Koteen Hill looms on the horizon. Several miles beyond Koteen Hill, the Karamoja Plateau drops sharply to Kenya on the Rift Valley floor, the desert plains – the home of the Turkana people. Standing in the bare stretches of Jimos village, the chains of villages are visible along both banks of the Longiro River, a seasonal river, which swells in muddy torrents during the rainy seasons and flows with flash floods from north to south.

To the southwest, one can see Nakapelimoru, the largest village in East Africa, with its myriad round huts surrounded by round, thick wooden palisade fences. Nakapelimoru stretches over the broad plains situated near the low-lying Magos hills. East of Nakapelimoru is an

Figure 2.3: Jimos village. Author photo

expanse of brush-covered rolling land, which stretches for miles to the edge of the escarpment. No one lives in this rolling land except for shepherds who graze their cattle in its sparse brushes, perennial shrubs, and wild fruits, watering their cattle in Nangalol Apolon, a seasonal river that winds through this area.

In Najie, from May to the late August, small ponds of brown muddy water accumulate here and there amid the sparse brushes and perennial tufts, but in December, January, and February, during the height of the dry season, the faded greenery and water ponds disappear, leaving behind only turtles in the quickly disappearing dampness of the cracked earth. During the dry season, Jimos village, like its neighbors, becomes barren and waterless as the dry-season wells, far from each other, dry out, except a few in the dry bed of the Longiro River. In May, June, and July, dark clouds hover and occasional torrential rains drench the cracked earth. Then seasonal rivers flow in muddy torrents. Soon after the rains, bushes and spiny trees flower and the land becomes muddy.

Even though not large, each of the homesteads of Jimos village is a home to thirty to forty people. Inner walls divide each homestead into subsections and clusters of courtyards that contain thatched-roof round houses and a cluster of granaries. The houses are plastered with brown mud, and the roofs of the houses are thatched with bundles of grass attached tightly to wooden frames in a cone shape. In the middle of each courtyard is the *arii* (cattle enclosure), crowded with livestock in the evenings.

Early in the morning hours, people open the gates of the cattle enclosures to let out their herds. When the cattle, with beautifully shaped horns, move on the dusty paths, steam from their breath mingles with the thick clouds of the dust in the air. But the sounds of the herders and the cling-clang of the cowbells slowly diminishes as the cattle move toward the Longiro River in the distance.

Later in the day, before midmorning, the women walk with hoes over their shoulders, singing songs as they set out to weed their gardens. There were about thirty to forty hard working women in Jimos village with many acres of land under their care. Various types of sorghum were visible: red, white, yellow, and purple sorghum bushes standing several feet high. Along with sorghum, the women grew a variety of crops, including bulrush millet, finger millet, pumpkin, gourds, and many other squashes.

In the evening, women often returned home as the last streaks of the sinking sun could be seen over the high palisade fences. At this time, the cattle returned home as well, bustling and moving in procession. Some women were bent down carrying heavy loads of firewood. Some sang as they carried calabashes full of water, pumpkins, sorghum, and millet for the evening meal. While the men attended the cattle in enclosures, some women milked their cows, and others churned the milk, while yet others tended the young children building fires to cook the evening meals. After the cattle gates were closed, people gathered around the cooking fires and talked about the day that had just passed. After the evening meal, young children often gathered around to listen to the stories, singing songs around the flickering fires. The children huddled around the fire, warming their hands over the dying embers, as the storytellers transported them into the fabulous realms of fantasy and imagination, realms where animals spoke like humans. In the growing darkness the voices and the body movements of the storytellers shaped the experiences of the children in that fabulous realm.

In Jimos village, all the homesteads, with their crowded houses, granaries, goats, sheep, and cattle, belonged to a few men: Nakapor, his brothers Naletom and Lomulen, and his paternal first cousins Rianaro and Urien, the heads of the Jimos clan who claim descent from Orwakol, the first firemaker of the Lokorwakol territorial division. Although the official firemaker was Nakapor, the most influential man in Jimos village was clearly Rianaro, a man well versed in his tradition.

Rianaro was a wise man in his late fifties. Every morning, he walked for miles to check on his cows in various grazing lands along the banks of the Longiro River and beyond. He was also well known for his exceptional skills in speaking for his community. He was allied with most of the villages in Najie through the marriages of his sisters, daughters, and sons. His sister was married to Lokeo from Nayese village, located northwest of Jimos village. Lokeo was a well- known *emuron* (traditional doctor) who had prophetic dreams. He also told fortunes by throwing sandals in the air. Rianaro's eldest daughter Logwee was married to an influential kraal leader from the Lokomebu village, in the Kotido area. While his youngest daughter Nadon was being courted by a rich kraal leader, his son Lotipe had already accumulated over fifty cattle to initiate his marriage arrangements with a girl in the Wotakau village, in Nakapelimoru. Rianaro's full brother Urien had two wives, both named Lomuriya. Both women came from influential families in the area and got along well with each other.

Perhaps the richest man in Jimos village, Rianaro owned many cows. His wives and daughters cultivated larger gardens than did the other women. Rianaro was well respected by his family members, who obeyed him. When present, he spent most of his time sitting under the shade of a tamarind tree at the edge of his lot. When all the women went to weed their gardens, he watched his homestead and cared for his grandchildren. Old men, including Lodoch, often visited him during the day, and they told stories and shared current local gossip. During one of these visits, I met Lokapilan, a stocky middle-aged man of medium height who wore a flat ivory disc lip plug. Lokapilan often came in with Lodoch and spent the whole morning talking with Rianaro and other older men who were there.

Lokapilan's home was in the Toroi village, across from Jimos village to the south, near the Roman Catholic mission. Like Rianaro, Lokapilan was also known for his fierceness. Despite his advanced age, his strength was obvious. He could walk miles to the grazing lands to check on his cattle. He was a politically influential person in Najie. He was an excellent storyteller, with a hearty laugh, and he was regularly invited to political meetings, during which he would skillfully narrate the stories

Figure 2.4: Nakapor, my neighbor and the Jie firemaker, in front of the master granary. Author photo (Jimos village)

of tribal legends to convey his opinions. People generally liked his stories and narrative voice and they valued his opinions.

Although Nakapor was a firemaker, people in Jimos village occasionally questioned his position. After the death in the 1960s of Lotum, Nakapor's father, the Jie people did not select a new firemaker to succeed him. But in the early 1990s, the people realized that traditional rituals had not been practiced and that, since then, they had had many problems coping with frequent diseases, droughts, and raiders, who generally used AK-47s and various other automatic weapons. When the people decided to start their traditional ceremonies, the elders gathered together to talk about choosing a firemaker and three people were recommended for the position. The first choice was Naletom, the older stepbrother of Nakapor. The second choice was Lomulen, the youngest brother of Nakapor. The third was Nakapor. People chose Naletom, but he refused because of dietary restrictions saying, "If I become a firemaker, I would be restricted from eating the meat of dead animals. Neither would I be allowed to eat food or drink beer from other places." At that point people thought that Lomulen was too young to become a firemaker so they offered the position to Nakapor. He accepted (Mirzeler 2007b).

The Poet clan, who traditionally made the master granary of the firemaker, built a new granary for Nakapor and put it in the courtyard of his eldest wife, Nadul. That year, each of the seven clans of the Orwakol people collected a calabash full of sorghum and gave it to Nadul, after which Nakapor poured each into the master granary. This was done a few years before my arrival to Najie.

During the installation of Nakapor as the firemaker, the Jie people slaughtered a spotless black goat and smeared Nakapor with *emunyen* (sacred clay) from the Longiro River, and they gave him the power to smear people with the clay and to make fire from the wet branches of the *essegessege* tree. Despite this, because of Nakapor's left-handedness and his habit of eating the meat of dead animals, some people had reservation about his position as the firemaker. Hence some elders had decided to postpone the sacrificing of a bull in Moru a Awor, a sacred hill surrounded by sacred grove, to seal the installation of Nakapor to the firemaker position.

As a firemaker, Nakapor possessed much knowledge about his tradition and he was articulate in talking about his community in traditional contexts. His only weakness was his inability or unwillingness to follow the dietary restrictions set for the firemaker. When I first visited him, I was with Lodoch. On that first day, Nakapor talked about his father's encounter with the British colonial officers, various agricultural developments in Najie, and the introduction of automatic guns.

"Our land has a lot to do with our traditions and our past," said Nakapor. "After the death of my father, nobody distributed sorghum seeds to the people, except the white people, when they introduced their brand of sorghum and polluted our granaries. One day the white people came and told my father to move from Jimos village, and to settle somewhere else. But my father refused and said, 'This village and this land are the places of the firemaker since the time of Orwakol, our first firemaker. It is prohibited for a firemaker to leave his home and settle elsewhere. We keep our traditional granary here. This is the land where we grow our sorghum handed down from our forefathers. This is the granary where we store our grains. This is our river from where we get our water.' After this, the white people stopped asking for the land. So, my father refused to surrender the land to the white people who wanted this land because it is a highland and fertile on the banks of a river."

"When my father refused to give the land," continued Nakapor, "the white people left but they returned shortly afterward and took our young men, forcing them to build roads, and sent our young children to the government school in Dodos land. People resisted this, and they refused to send their children to school, and that is why they buried the pen and the book."

"The white people later introduced automatic guns, which enabled the young men to wipe out villages and families whenever they went raiding. That is why there is so much raiding in the kraals and why there are so many deaths. The hills, the rivers, and the wells in Jie land have become restless." Nakapor continued, "Today, with their guns, many of the young men are stealing what belongs to everyone. Rather than sharing resources and being responsible to one another, large numbers of young men routinely and violently have been attacking innocent people and denying water and grazing resources to the weaker members of the society. There are ancestral memories and ancestral traditions in this place," he said, "And nothing can touch those memories and traditions, neither the government, nor young men with guns. Those memories and traditions are part of our stories. They can deny us water and pasture, but they cannot take our ancestral memories and traditions."

"In the Jie tradition," said Nakapor, "there is the idea of sharing hunger, thirst, and friendship. One of the things about our culture, which the whites have never understood, is the idea of sharing hunger and thirst. *Akoro* is the Jie word for hunger and thirst. In Jie culture, one of the ways in which we greet people is by saying 'kanyamit ayong akoro' (I am hungry). This way of greeting is a kind of talking about our shared experiences of hunger. This land is like the one breast of Napeikisina, powerful, full of milk, but it cannot feed the twins at the same time. The twins have to take turn to suckle the milk of their mother. When there is no milk in the breast of Napeikisina, both will be hungry. So the sisters and brothers have to share their hunger, and comfort one another. Or fight with one another."

Nakapor continued, building on the folkloric motif of his society. "Sharing your hunger is an act of friendship and recognition. In everyone's life in Najie, there is a moment in which one experiences hunger and thirst. Greeting someone with the word *akoro*, is a way of acknowl-edging that you are a part of this world. You understand others with your hunger and thirst because you can relate to them. When you talk about your hunger and thirst you are not pretentious. You remember the story of the rabbit which I told you."

"I remember the story," I replied.

"One of the first stories we, the Jie people, hear as children is the story of the greedy rabbit who deceives humans and animals as he steals their water and food, which he has not worked for. When the thieving rabbit gets caught while in the well, and the animals ask, 'Rabbit, why are you at the bottom of the well?' the rabbit responds, 'Because I am thirsty.'"

"You know," said Nakapor, "when the rabbit pretended that he didn't drink the water, he didn't fool those other animals. Of course, they knew the rabbit had lied. The rabbit had robbed the people of what was most precious to them and what they had worked for the hardest. The rabbit had said he had not drunk water, yet he got caught at the bottom of the well while drinking the water, and he still denied it and pretended to be upright."

"When you are not hungry or thirsty while others are, you have robbed the people, because you have failed to share. The rabbit had robbed peo-ple and had lied to the people and had pretended that he was not an animal and that he does not drink water. Yet he was an animal and he was thirsty and hungry, just like the rest. Where you are hungry and thirsty, you are with us and we understand you. When you tell some-one that you are hungry and thirsty, it is a matter of seeking friendship. The rabbit was not seeking friendship. He was interested in stealing the water, which he did not work for. We all experience the feeling of being thirsty and hungry during famines, and we all remember what is im-portant in this harsh world. And do you know why we, the Jie people, like to tell rabbit stories?" asked Nakapor rhetorically, and he answered, "Because that's where the wisdom is. My mother used to say, 'If you are going to grow up and become an adult, the first thing you have to do is to listen to our stories and trust your own encounters with rabbits and hyenas before you go to the kraals.' And I used to believe in my moth-er's stories. Listening to her telling stories at night in front of the hearth fire took us far away from this world, yet it brought us back to it only for us to see that the fantastic world of the animals in the stories is where we actually live. The rabbit, the hyena, Napeikisina, and the rest, are a part of this world."

"There are a lot of rabbits today. Some young men with automatic guns go out and raid the cattle. Like the cunning rabbit, they steal the food from you. They eat the food they did not work for. With their guns, some young men have become like the rabbit and the hyena. With guns they feel secure and powerful, but in reality there is hunger, vulnerability, and the political uncertainties that one can find everywhere."

Nakapor's household was typical of those of most of the Jie. His vast homestead was a beautiful place to stay. It hummed with the sounds of men and women at work, churning milk, grinding sorghum, shuffling woods, and burning fire. The naked little children ran about the courtyards and played near the cattle enclosures. As a husband, Nakapor was somewhat terse and had a hot temper. His eldest wife, Nadul, lived in Jimos village and kept the master granary, belonging to the firemaker, in her courtyard. She was very nice to Nakapor, waiting on him and offering beer and food to the people who visited her husband. Nakapor's second wife was from Kacheri and she was related to Nacham, a well-known elder who had founded the Kacheri community north of Najie. This marriage provided Nakapor with appropriate political connections.

In the summer of 2003, when I returned to Jimos village, Nadul had died a few years before. But the people had blamed her death on Nakapor's inability to follow the traditions of the ancestral firemakers. Because of all of this, an important sacrifice was postponed until the following year in deference to Nadul's death. Unfortunately, before the performance of the key sacrifice, Nakapor died in 2004, from a sudden and unidentified sickness.

During my stay in Jimos village, I occasionally visited the Jie kraals in the Labwor hills and on the Karamoja Plateau. Because of the scarcity of water and the pasture, the Jie kraals traveled to the Labwor Hills in the west during the wet season and to the east during the dry season as far as the headwaters of the Tarash River in the Turkana plains. When the kraals moved, people built makeshift grass huts or sometimes simply marked the ground and built temporary fences from thorn bushes. In the grazing lands, the young men were very protective of their cattle. They slept beside the herd, never leaving the animals for a moment and never trusting anyone else to guard them. When the young men returned from the kraals with well-fed cattle that had multiplied, they felt proud of earning the trust of the elders in the villages.

Figure 2.5: The Alerek Hill in Labwor. Author photo (Abim, Labwor County)

During the month of May, when the first rains came, the women in the Jie villages began to till their gardens and prepared them for sorghum, millet, and various types of pumpkins and gourds. The young men began to drive the cattle toward the Labwor hills where they would settle the herd in the grazing lands around Abim, a small agricultural town well known for its traditional iron smelters.

Abim town was located in an outpouring of the green at the edge of the harsh semidesert plateau. It was nothing like Najie, or, rather, it seemed to have no connection with it. With its high hills covered with reeds, elephant grass, savannah, and tall, lush trees, I found it was dazzling, filling me with curiosity and wonder. But the wonder soon vanished, gradually giving way to mysterious respect, as I heard about the old Labwor traditions and stories attached to every hill, well, and old tree, and, above all else, the wondrous Alerek Hill, the home of the sacred python.

The distance between the Jie and the Labwor communities is a day's journey on foot. The shepherds and traders passed several freshwater wells and seasonal springs and traversed trails that bear red earth. According to the Jie people, omens of good and rainy seasons were always determined by the blessings of the ancestors of both the Jie and the Labwor people. It is for this reason that during prolonged droughts and famines the Jie people would often join the rain making rituals of the Labwor people. When the rains were delayed and dry seasons were prolonged, the Karuwot clan of the Labwor people would intervene. The rainmaking specialist of the Karuwot clan would request intervention at the cave of the sacred python in Alerek Hill.

I have visited the Labwor hills with Lodoch many times and there have met many storytellers. To get there, we would take a long road, one that people almost never used. We would set out on our journey at dawn and reach there at dusk. During one of these memorable journeys, we went to visit Owilli, one of Lodoch's friends. We traveled on foot, taking our usual long road to avoid any possible attack by wandering gunmen or Kony's Army. On the journey we walked in silence, but occasionally Lodoch related memories of his days in the Labwor hills and the death of Achilla, his older brother in the hospital in Abim. His eyes brimmed with tears and his lips trembled in nostalgia. But he smiled when he talked about his memory of Napiyo, his wife, and the child she bore him in Abim in their home on the slopes of the Labwor hills.

When we reached Abim, Owilli and his friends were happy and excited to see us; Owilli's home was in the Kiru village, situated in a valley at the foot of a hill rising in the west. Because the hill was high, its shadow fell over the village on the valley floor. Owilli's daughter lit a lantern and hung it on a tree in the courtyard, where we sat and drank tea.

That summer night in the Labwor hills was beautiful. The dusk came late, bringing in its shadow a cool breeze that swept down intermittently from the cliff tops, a cooling air that contented us all. The half-moon rising over the reed-covered slopes of the hill cast a bright silvery light. It was so bright that I could see the rippling reeds on the slopes of the hill. Truly a serene night! Lodoch and Owilli reminisced for hours. That night Owilli told us the tale of Logo, a venerable ancestral figure of the Karuwot clan, in the Labwor oral tradition, which appears in their popular stories. Owilli had a beautiful voice, and the words flowed from his lips, like the wind blowing from the slopes of the high hill across from us, telling a story in perfect Jie language.

The story was about a long-ago quarrel between the dry and the wet seasons and how the dry season prolonged his stay for several years, until the crops withered and the rivers and the ponds dried. The land became so dry that people and animals died of thirst and hunger, and the bleached bones of the cattle and of the humans were strewn on the parched earth. During that time Logo went to Alerek Hill to plead with the sacred python, hoping to soften his heart and secure intervention. At last, the sacred python was moved to pity and Logo penetrated the sky with the python's tail and the rain poured like rivers. It rained so heavily that it soaked the entire earth in the Labwor hills. When the people in Najie saw the dark clouds hovering on the Alerek Hill, they drove their few emaciated cattle and settled around it, offering their sacrifices to the python in a cave in the hill. When the Jie people did this, Logo was very pleased, and told them that since they had observed their customs, they had become brothers with the Labwor people. "From now on," he said, "when the rainy season comes you may drive your cattle to the Labwor land for grazing." When Owilli finished his story, he said, "That is why, the Jie people still settle their kraals on the slopes of the hill during the wet season. And that is also why, when the dry season is prolonged, the head of the Karuwot clan offers gifts to the sacred python in the Alerek Hill, requesting intervention."

In Najie as well as in the Turkana land, around the upper Tarash River region and beyond, oral tradition is performed on various occasions. In the Turkana land, where most semipermanent homesteads (*awi*) are widely separated, storytelling sessions are usually held at one of the homesteads or in a dry river bed at night, during a time of leisure from herding and gathering wild fruits or woods. Men and women from different families assemble on moonlit nights around flickering fire, and they sing and dance or tell stories. Because of the space between the homesteads, people hear the sounds of songs from a distance and they begin trickling in. Some people arrive late for these performances, while others arrive early and leave early. Some spend the whole night participating in singing, dancing, and narrating tales. Sometimes the storytelling session is interrupted by important news or gossip.

In the grazing land, the herders of the nearby kraals drop in for a short while to sit and talk, chew tobacco, drink beer, and listen to the men singing and telling stories. During such times, young men come and go. There are traders who occasionally pass by with merchandise from Somalia, Sudan, Ethiopia, or nearby towns, and stop on their way through. Not infrequently the travelers will spend the night. Many of

Figure 2.6: The dry course of upper Tarash River. Author photo (Turkana land, northern Kenya)

these men are also gifted storytellers and they tell stories as well as listen to others tell their stories. What is true of the gatherings of the Turkana people on the dry riverbeds during moonlit nights is true of the gatherings of the Jie people in the kraals in the grazing land or in the villages.

In the kraal centers such as the Nangalol Apolon, Moru Apolon, Koteen Hill, Apule River, and the banks along the headwaters of the Tarash River, the moonlit nights usually bring people from different kraals to the *etem* (men's gathering place) of a respected person, where they dance and sing all night. Some of the business of buying guns or exchanging cows and establishing new friendships are done there during the night's gatherings. Some visitors might spend the night in the dancing ground and leave the next day.

This is a good time for the storytellers to show their oratorical skills and tell stories, both folktales and historical traditions, or sing songs or share gossip. Even though the storytellers are not professionals, their audiences offer them beer, tobacco, or milk while they tell stories. If the members of the audiences are favorably disposed to the storyteller and the telling of the story is right, the storyteller would savor his narration and lengthen his tales, gossip, or songs. However, if the members of the audiences are not receptive, the storyteller would usually shorten his narratives or songs. The length of the stories usually depends on the audience. For this reason any one person may tell the same tales in various ways. If the storyteller is with the Turkana people and tells the story of Nayeche, for example, he or she would end the story in such a way that it would be pleasing to the Turkana people. The Jie and the Turkana oral traditions are not fixed but fluid, and the storytellers are conscious of the expectations of their audiences.

In the villages, as in the kraals, the evenings are the best times for the performances of oral traditions (both folktales and historical traditions), when women are not in the fields and the older men are not sitting under the trees gossiping with their neighbors. Then all are relaxed and sit back and listen to the performers. During one of the performances, I recorded a story from Ngimerichadai, a Turkana storyteller in Lateya, a semipermanently settled Turkana village in the plains of Turkana about twenty miles from the Uganda Escarpment, in a semi-desert area where the Tarash River bends and twists its way. Ngimerichadai was about forty years old, and exceptionally gifted in telling both folktales and historical traditions. With her creative body movement and her deep voice, she vividly portrayed the characters of her stories.[1] When I visited Ngimerichadai one night, she was sitting in her courtyard overlooking the dry course of the Tarash River, enjoying a calabash of beer. She was a beautiful, tall woman. When she saw me, she called to her daughter to bring some beer for me. It was a brilliant moon-washed night when the damp earth of the dry river course after the day's heat gave up a fragrance of soil. That night, while young people went to the dancing place in small groups, the old men and women and children gathered around Ngimerichadai and formed a crescent in the dry riverbed. The moonlight shined on the children's beautiful faces as they leaned toward Ngimerichadai listening to the stories and sometimes joining her in singing as they repeated the words after her. That night, Ngimerichadai performed several stories and I recorded them all. Here I share one of those stories, about a honey badger and a baboon who became friends and invited each other for dinner:

Long ago, a certain baboon and a honey badger became friends. One day the baboon invited the honey badger to her home for dinner and

Figure 2.7: Storytelling session near Jimos village. Author photo (Losilang)

offered her some *ngapongo* (a type of sour wild fruit). The honey badger tried to eat the fruit but, when she found out that they tasted bitter, she pretended to be choking and said to the honey badger that *ngapongo* chokes her, and that she could, therefore, not eat these fruits. But, being impressed by the hospitality of the baboon, she wanted to be polite to her and, hence, the honey badger immediately invited the baboon to join her for dinner. The baboon, greatly pleased by this counter offer, immediately thanked the honey badger and accepted her kind invitation. The baboon put her child in a *nyanapet* (a goatskin bag for carrying babies on the back), carried on her back, and walked along with honey badger. The honey badger and the baboon with her child on her back walked and walked until they reached the home of the honey badger.

Upon arriving in her home, the honey badger told the baboon to sit and wait for her a bit. The honey badger climbed a tree and skillfully blew air into a beehive so that the bees came out. The honey badger then gathered some honey and came down from the tree and offered some honey to the baboon. The baboon ate some honey and loved it. She said, "Ooi, this is sweet. This is sweet." The baboon ate hurriedly and gave some to her child as well. While the baboon was eating the honey in such a manner, the honey badger was disturbed by her gluttony and said, "Eee, it is enough! You ate all my honey. How about my children? We have to leave some for my children. You have eaten enough!" Disgusted by the uncouthness of the baboon, the honey badger politely told her that it was time for her to go home, and she showed her the way out, escorting her some distance on the path. As they were walking, the baboon continued to think about the delicious and sweet taste of the honey, and thought upon how she could come back and finish eating the rest of the honey. Suddenly an idea came to mind and she said to the honey badger, "I left my *nyanapet* in your home. Can I please go and get it. I will be very quick." The honey badger responded politely, "Oh, yes. Please by all means you go ahead and get your *nyanapet*. If you like, you can leave your child here with me and I will wait with her until you return." The baboon then said, "It is very gracious of you to offer to look after my child while I go to get my *nyanapet*, but I have given you enough trouble already. I will take my child with me. It is no trouble at all." The baboon then went very quickly to the home of honey badger and immediately put her child on the ground and got a big stick and climbed the tree and poked the beehive. The bees came out and swarmed on the baboon. The baboon tried to escape the swarming bees but she was not successful. She got stung very badly all over and was in great pain. The baboon desperately tried to run away from the swarm of bees, but the bees followed her. The baboon desperately ran into the dry course of the river and hurriedly dug a hole and buried herself and her baby in the sand, but the tail of the baby remained outside.

The honey badger, who was waiting for the baboon, became concerned about her and went back to see what was the matter. When she reached her home, she saw the disheveled beehives strewn on the ground and realized that all the honey was gone. She smiled and immediately realized why the baboon pretended to have forgotten her *nyanapet* at home and why she was so eager to go back and get it. As the honey badger looked around for the baboon, she noticed some footprints and followed the footprints until she reached the river. In the riverbed, the honey badger called baboon, but there was no response. The honey badger looked and looked and then she saw the tail of baboon's baby sticking out from the sand. The honey badger came and pinched the tail of baboon's baby and the baby cried. The baboon whispered to her to be quiet, but the honey badger pinched the tail of the baby again. The baboon said, "You shut up. If you continue screaming the bees will find us here." The honey badger pinched the baby again, and the baby cried again and said, "Mother someone is pinching me." The baboon pressed her baby steadfastly against her bosom and closed her mouth with her hands. The honey badger continued to pinch and pull the child. As the honey badger pulled the child from the baboon, which was buried under sand, the baboon held onto the child. In the end, the honey badger pulled the child and dusted off the sand and told the baboon sarcastically, "Eeeh, I thought you forgot your *nyanapet* and you went to get it. Where is your *nyanapet*? What happened to you? Why are you so swollen?" The baboon kept quiet.

Storytellers

In the Jie land and to a large extent in the Turkana land around the Tarash River, while women narrated folktales (generally recognized as fictional), men narrated historical traditions. However, in both Najie and in the Turkana land, I met some women who were excellent performers of historical tradition and some men who were marvelous performers of folktales. The lines between the performances of folktales and of historical traditions are fluid. Although men generally performed historical traditions, I met women who were great performers of historical traditions with excellent knowledge of tribal politics, history, and legends. Most Jie and the Turkana women performers I met, however, insisted that they were not gifted in performances of historical tradition, yet they did participate in these performances.

The styles and artistic expressions of the performers varied from person to person and from place to place. Of all of the storytellers that I met, Lodoch was the most skillful. He was a splendid performer of the Jie oral tradition. His ability to create fabulous scenes fusing contemporary and ancient images, accompanied by his poetic voice and body movements, gave his performances extraordinary depth and breadth. Through his gestures and artful style, he created some of the most fascinating stories, evoking excitement and participation from the members of the audiences. Lodoch was fluent in both folktales and the historical traditions. Once he began his story, his sentences flowed like a river and he never struggled for words. He knew his audience and his tradition so well that he skillfully unfolded the plots of his narratives, stressing particular episodes or topics that connected with the contemporary discourses of his society. While his imitation of the cunning rabbit and the villain Napeikisina (see part 4) often brought laughter to his performances, his portrayal of Nayeche's forlorn journey moved the audience emotionally and connected them with their past. With his body movements and the subtle adjustments of the tone of his voice, he powerfully dramatized the movement of Nayeche and the gray bull Engiro from the plateau to the plains. In the stories of Lodoch, the negative and the positive attributes coexisted in the image of the ancient Jie heroes of historical traditions. These heroes sometimes acted positively, pulling the society toward unity by sharing resources with the members of the society. At other times they were represented as selfish and destructive.

Lodoch had learned the art of telling stories from his parents and from other children when he was a child. When he was a young boy, the boys told stories to each other whenever they went to herding goats and calves. Some of these boys were just as good at telling stories as some of the older men in the villages. When Lodoch was growing up, there was a boy called Locham who was a gifted storyteller, and he told stories better than most of the older men. Lodoch remembers well when Locham told the story of Napeikisina and some other very funny stories that they all "laughed and laughed."

Lodoch's father was also a good storyteller and he told him and his siblings the stories of Nayeche and the gray bull Engiro, as well as the stories of Orwakol and Lodiny. Lodoch remembers how he would sit with his father under the trees, and listen to him tell those stories to the old men. Lodoch admired his father very much and he learned the art of storytelling mainly from him. Lodoch also learned the art of storytelling from his mother who was a good storyteller, and who told him and his siblings the stories of Napeikisina and that of the rabbit.

In the evenings when his father went to sit in his *etem* (men's gathering place), Lodoch would sit next to him and listen as he told them more stories. One day, Lodoch asked his father about the different versions of the stories which he had heard from other people, wanting to know why there were so many different versions of the same stories. His father told him, "Of course there are many different versions of the same stories. Everybody has different stories about the same thing. If everybody had the same version of the same story, there would be no need to tell stories to each other."

When his father told him the story of the gray bull Engiro and how the bull drank the water at the well in the Longiro River, Lodoch wanted to have a bull, "just like that," when he grew up, a gray bull with a beautiful hump. When he was a young boy Lodoch became fascinated with the story of Nayeche, and her struggle over the cattle in Koteen

Hill. Whenever the Turkana women came to get sorghum from Lodoch's family during the harvest rituals, Lodoch would ask them, "Is it true that you are the grandchildren of Nayeche? Do you also come from the Tarash River?"

Lodoch had a particular attachment to the story of Nayeche. He always connected the story of Nayeche to one of his earliest childhood memories about Atoot, a Turkana woman from the Lateya village, along the banks of upper Tarash River in the Turkana land. Atoot used to come during the harvest and help Lodoch's mother to harvest and thrash the sorghum. Lodoch remembers well how whenever the Turkana women came during the harvest time, the firemaker went around banging on the granaries of the homesteads, telling the women in the village to be "generous to the daughters of Nayeche when they come to ask for sorghum."

Lodoch also remembers that whenever Atoot came, she brought sacks (*ngichueei*) full of dried wild fruits from the Tarash River region and sacred clay from the Moru Apolon for his mother. Atoot stayed with them every year throughout the harvest and helped his mother grind sorghum, collect firewood, and fetch water from the wells. At the end of the harvest, his mother gave her sacks full of sorghum, which Atoot loaded on her donkey and transported back to Turkana land.

What perhaps brought me closer to Lodoch than to anyone else in the village was his fascination with the Nayeche and the gray bull Engiro stories as well as the kind of memories that he shared with me. Every time Lodoch told the story of Nayeche and the gray bull Engiro, it was different. It differed depending on whether he told the story at night or during the daytime. If he told the story to his children at night, it sounded different than if he told the story in the kraals to the young men or to the old men in the village under the trees. At each telling, the story of Nayeche and the gray bull Engiro were knitted differently with all the survival fantasy images: Nayeche traveling in search of water and food on the plateau in the plains, in the bush, in the dry riverbeds, or around the hills.

One memorable evening, Lodoch told us the story of Nayeche in front of the hearth fire as we gathered around him. That moonlit evening, he cleared his throat in his usual way before he began his story:

Kolong ayai apese ngina anyaritae Nayeche. Abeokoi kerai bo Nakapelimoru kenyonia Nayeche kerai bo iwache. Kire cho ebeokoi amekini akoro, torotok esaki ngigeron. Anging amamakutor ngakipi ka nginya, apotu ngitunga tomiyasi ngaren ngibaren iwarito nagakipit ka ngingya. Alosit Nangalol Apolon ngun apotu ikes kiboyoto aneni temasi, "Adaun nginya eyotosi nabo ngaren iwadio." Toloto apei paka tar moru ngolo enyaritae Koteen kiboyoto kaneni. Ani kiboyoto aneni apotu togeut nabo atemar, "Okoe, ikokinio ai, be adaun bo nginya daang adaun nabo tar akimuj aono a kwap ikokinoi ai." Apotu ngiche tunga temassi ebe, "Atobongosi lore Najie," nai apotu ngiche temasi, "Emam ayaa nabo ngaren iwadio kidiama ngirongan." Apotu ikes tota-matamata temasi, "Bas, nguna ajwakak, alosit robo tomiyarai mono." Apotu ngiche tunga tomiyasi anyeriamut ngakipi dang, apotu cho to-bongut. Apotu ngiche tunga temasi, "Amwanu a kolong atowotokisi lore," cho apotu towotokis lore.

Long ago, there was a girl named Nayeche. They say Nayeche left from either Nakapelimoru or from some other places. She was chased by hunger and she went in search of wild fruits. There was a drought and people went in search of pasture and water. When they reached Nangalol Apolon (the Great River), they stayed there and said among themselves, "The grass is finished here, let us go a little bit ahead." They went up to a hill named Koteen and stayed there. After they stayed there, they again said, "Oh, what can we do, all the grass is finished, and even the food is finished and the place is dry. What can we do?" Some people said, "Let us go back home to Najie," but other people said, "No, Najie is dry, even dryer than here. Najie is a cursed land. For many years now, there has not been a drop of rain in Najie. The Longiro River has refused to flow. The people in Najie are dying from disease, hunger, and thirst. Why should we go back to a place which has been cursed?"

As the people in Koteen were saying these things, the old men came from Najie. They asked for some cattle to take home because people there did not have anything to eat. The people refused to give them any cattle. The old men began to beat the young men with their sticks, but the young people were much stronger, and they chased the old men away. The old men then cursed the people of the kraals and said, "If that is the case, you can take these cattle and go. Your cattle will multiply, but they will all die and you will never be able to settle anywhere. You will just move from one bush to another."

After the old men cursed them and left, the people of the kraal thought and said, "Let us stay here and send somebody again to search for water and pasture." Some people went to search for water, but they came back without finding anything. These people continued their journeys and many of their cattle died along the way from hunger and thirst. People roamed around Koteen Hill, Nangalol Apolon, and around the Lomogol River with the hope of finding some water and green grass, but all the wells were dry and there was no green grass. Cattle died as these people moved and the vultures ate the carcasses until they became white bones.

One morning when the kraals had come back to Koteen Hill, Nayeche got up early in the morning and went in search of wild fruit far away to the east of Koteen Hill at the foot of the smaller hills. She searched and searched for wild fruits and came back. The next morning she did the same and went even a bit further ahead and found the footprints of the bull [the gray bull Engiro]. The people said that the bull had become lost and had disappeared a long time ago. Nayeche followed the footprints of the bull and followed the footprints and said, "Oh, it is true, it is true; the bull must know where there is water. I am thirsty."

Nayeche followed and followed the footprints of the bull and reached a place where the bull had found a well in a dry valley between the rocks. She found that the water there had just been finished because the baboons had drunk it. She continued her journey following the footprints of the bull and she reached a place where the bull had smelled the water in a faraway place. She followed and followed the footprints of the bull and said, "This bull must know where the water is."

She continued to follow the bull's footprints. She followed and followed until she reached the smaller hills above the escarpment. She climbed down the escarpment and there found a small well and abundant wild fruits. She said, "This place is good. I should settle here for now and gather some wild fruits." She gathered and gathered very many wild fruits and spread them under the sun to dry.

Nayeche stayed in this place until the water was finished. Then she continued to follow the footprints of the bull and said, "Ohh, the bull must have passed here, and here. He must have gone this way all the way down the escarpment." Nayeche followed and followed the footprints of the bull until she saw the bull in the distance moving in the direction of the Tarash River. The bull went and went, and it entered the dry riverbed.

There, in the bed of the Tarash River, the bull moved slowly under the heat of the sun and Nayeche followed it and followed it. The bull reached a well in the dry riverbed, and drank water from it and went into a bush on the northern side of the river. Nayeche came and drank the water from the well too. She then went to the bush looking for the bull. In the bush, she saw the bull climbing on a hill. Nayeche also climbed the hill. There, in the hill she found a cave and entered in it. She said, "Oh, it is very good. I will settle here, in this cave. If it rains, this rock will cover me from the rain."

Nayeche stayed on that hill and made that cave her home. There was water nearby, as well as abundant wild fruits. She gathered the wild fruits and spread them on the hill to dry. There were no baboons or other wild animals but only a few foxes, which ate the leftover fruits. Nayeche stayed there with the gray bull Engiro. At night, she made fire and slept next to the bull to keep herself warm.

One day, the people in Koteen Hill went in search of water and pasture, and they found the footprints of Nayeche and said, "Ah, these are the footprints of Nayeche and the lost gray bull Engiro." As these people followed the footprints, they said, "Oh, so Nayeche went this way to the east down the escarpment. The footprints of the lost gray bull are also here."

These people followed the footprints of the bull and of Nayeche all the way to the Tarash River. They followed and followed the footprints until they reached the cave where Nayeche stayed. People said, "Ehh, this place is good. There are pastures and water here."

They saw Nayeche sitting on a rock near the cave. They said, "Ehh, this is Nayeche."

They asked Nayeche, "What are you doing here?"

Nayeche replied, "This is my home. I gather wild fruits here and I eat them."

People asked her again, "What are all these things?"

Nayeche replied, "These are my wild fruits, *ngidomein, ngaponga, engoma*, and all the other kinds of wild fruits whose names I don't know. Would you like to eat some of them? I know you are hungry. Eat them."

These people ate the wild fruits, which Nayeche offered them. They all ate and drank the water. When they were all satisfied, they said, "Oh, this place is good. What should we do? Should we also all go back to Koteen Hill and bring our cattle here?"

One of them said, "You people, let's migrate here. This place is good, with water and green grass and plenty of wild fruits, which we can eat. Let us migrate here."

Other people said, "It is true, if we migrate here, the cattle will produce enough milk since there is enough water and grass here. The gray bull is also here. He will mount our cows, and our cattle will multiply and become many."

These people went back to Koteen Hill and called for an *etem* (gathering). When the people in Koteen Hill gathered together, they said, "We have found a place with plenty of water and pasture. That place is full of wild fruits and there are no wild animals. We saw Nayeche and the gray bull Engiro there too. We should go to that place instead of going back to Najie. If we go back to Najie, we will die of hunger just like those people out there. Let us go to that hill, to the hill of Nayeche near the Tarash River. The Tarash River is big and there is plenty of water under the ground there. We can dig wells and water our cattle. Our cattle will become fat again. We can spend the whole dry season there and when the rainy season comes we can go back to Najie."

The people in Koteen Hill said, "In that case, let us migrate there tomorrow morning."

In the morning before the sun rose, the people saddled their donkeys and drove their cattle toward the east. They truly migrated. These people went down the escarpment and followed the Tarash River until they reached the hill in the bush near the river. They settled around the hill, and went to Nayeche and said, "Nayeche you have become our mother. We have migrated and settled around your hill. We have separated ourselves from the Najie, and we shall not go back there. This place from now on is our home."

Nayeche replied, "I only care for my life. I was chased by hunger and I followed the footprints of the gray bull Engiro. I followed the gray bull Engiro because I was thirsty and hungry. I live here with the bull and this hill is our home. If you have also migrated here, you have also separated from Najie like me and the gray bull Engiro."

The people settled down around that hill and they went to visit Nayeche on the hill. Whenever they went to see Nayeche, they brought her some milk. Nayeche mixed the milk with wild fruits and drank it. Sometimes they slaughtered a cow and took meat to Nayeche.

These people stayed there for a long time and Nayeche grew old. These people said, "Since we have separated from Najie and settled here, Nayeche has become our mother and our leader. Let us go back to Nayeche and ask her for advice and see what we should do in the future. Should we go back to Najie, or stay here? You see we have become many now. Our cattle have also multiplied and become many."

These people truly went to Nayeche and asked her for advice, "Mother, what should we do? Should we go back to Najie or stay here?"

Nayeche replied, "I don't know what is happening at home. Nobody knows what is happening there. We don't know if they are there in

Daidai or if they migrated to somewhere else."

The people said, "Mother, we would like to stay here. This place has become our home."

The people continued to stay in Moru a Nayeche, and Nayeche became very old and unable to walk. One day Nayeche sent a message and asked young men to come and see her. The young men from the kraals came and sat near Nayeche on the hill.

Nayeche said, "You have become many. There are many kraals around the hill and some of them even go further down along the Tarash River. Take me around and let me visit the kraals in faraway places before I die."

The people put Nayeche on the back of a donkey and went to visit the kraals. When they reached a certain kraal, they found people drinking water. Nayeche asked, "Who are these people who are drinking water?"

The young men replied, "We don't know who these people are."

Nayeche asked these people, "Who are you and where have you come from?"

The people said, "We are just people and we have been living here since you came and settled here."

Nayeche said, "Okay, if you don't have a name let me give you one. When I first saw you, you were drinking water; therefore, I will name you Ngikamatak (those who drink)."

Nayeche and the young men went to different places to visit the kraals. They went to a kraal in the bush, and Nayeche asked, "Whose kraal is this?"

The young men said, "This is the kraal of so-and-so people." Nayeche said, "Okay, I will name this kraal Ngimonia (people of the bush)."

They went to a different kraal and Nayeche asked, "Whose kraal is this?"

The people replied, "It is the kraal of so-and-so."

Nayeche said, "Take me to that kraal and let me see who these people are."

When the young men took Nayeche there, Nayeche saw cattle and goats of black and white color. She said, "I will name this kraal Ngingoroko (animals with white and black patches)." Even now, these people are called Ngingoroko.

The young men continued to take Nayeche around. They came to a flat land without a tree along the Tarash River. Nayeche asked again, "Whose kraal is that settled here?"

The young men said, "It is the kraal of so-and-so."

Nayeche said, "Do you know the name of this kraal?"

The young men said, "We don't know the name of the kraal."

Nayeche said, "This whole plain here is white, the bush is white, the cattle are white, the goats are white. I will name this kraal Ngikwaatela."

The people who live in this place are called Ngikwaatela even now.

Nayeche got on the donkey and continued to move with the young men until she reached another kraal where people were polishing the surface of long spear sticks. Nayeche asked again, "Whose kraal is this?"

The young men said, "It is the kraal of so-and-so."

Nayeche asked people, "Does your kraal have a name?"

The people replied, "Our kraal has no name."

Nayeche said, "Okay, since you have the long spear, I name your kraal Ngioyokwara (those with long spear)." Even today, people call these people Ngioyokwara.

After moving along the Tarash River, the young men returned with Nayeche back to that hill where Nayeche stayed. The young men asked, "Mother, you have been staying in this hill for a long time now. What is the name of your hill?"

Nayeche replied, "I will name this hill Moru a Nayeche."

Shortly after her journey along the Tarash River, Nayeche died, but the people continued to stay there, and they called themselves Turkana. So this is how those people below the escarpment became Turkana.

There were many gifted storytellers in Jimos village. Rianaro was one of those storytellers who often captivated the members of the audience during his remarkable performances. Like Lodoch, Rianaro performed both folktales and historical traditions. He unfolded the plots of his stories and developed his characters fully and imaginatively. Rianaro was an engaging person and this helped him during the critical exchanges with the members of the audience. What characterized the stories of Rianaro was the overwhelming presence of the good and the evil, the importance of compassion and cooperation, and the sharing of scarce resources in a dry environment – one of the basic Jie cultural principles.

Similar to Lodoch, Rianaro too emphasized the double nature of the ancestral heroes. Sometimes Rianaro critiqued the images of miserly Lokolong, who refused to share his bull Ngolengiro, the only surviving bull in the entire Najie, without receiving its first offspring. At other times, he made Lokolong an example to follow for his virtues in sharing the offspring of his bull. Rianaro often emphasized the importance

of being generous and of sharing and respecting, not only in the historical traditions, but also in the folktales.

Rianaro was critical of the thieves who stole food and water, like the
rabbit. He often emphasized the respect for others' food and water
resources. His habit as an elder and a moral authority came out most
vividly in communal disputes over resources. I have also seen Rianaro
perform during dispute mediations on several occasions, stressing and
developing the themes of sharing as the ultimate human virtue when
living in ecologically difficult places such as in Najie and in the Turkana
land. Every aspect of a modern Jie political dispute reflected so much of
Jie and of Turkana ancestral politics as portrayed in the historical traditions. It always seemed appropriate for Rianaro to link the contemporary disputes to the conflict resolution of the original Jie families.
Rianaro indeed had intimate knowledge of tradition, for he ended up
time and again with an emphasis on moral generalization illustrated by
the events of Jie/Turkana ancestral families.

Logwee, the daughter of Rianaro, a young woman in her early thirties, differed from her father. She was quite verbal in her narratives, and
she often used loud voices when describing the deceitful hyena and
the rabbit. Her narrative style was vivid, vigorous, dramatic, full of fantastic scenes pregnant with chaos and order. Often unexpected moral-
izing themes unfolded in her stories. She was more interested in the
art of performance, and hence she often embellished the plot of her stories with songs, particularly when performing the Napeikisina stories.
Her individual narrative style was replete with typical phrases and motifs familiar to her audience. Logwee was particularly good in describing the wit and stupidity of Napeikisina and her wretched death on the
back of the hyena, which defecated from fear of capture. Logwee
amused her audience with her descriptive word choices. She brought
laughter to performances when she imitated the mother who exchanged
her ugly baby with the evil Napeikisina in the form of a beautiful infant,
emphasizing the evil nature of a mother who becomes victim to
Nakpeisina's evil plot (see part 4).

Logwee also excelled at recounting historical traditions. In performing the historical traditions, she tended to expand the plots and embroi-
der them with memory images, songs, and chants. For example, she
particularly enjoyed her favorite episodes in the story of Nairanabwo
in which Nairanabwo rescued the Jie society from the famine. She often
concluded the story of Nairanabwo with illuminating comments, which
gave unity to the story line.

Figure 2.8: Logwee, repairing her palisade fence. Author photo (Jimos village)

One intensely dark night Logwee, a few children, and I sat on a mat on the floor after supper of boiled sorghum and fresh milk. The fire in the hearth gave a yellowish dim light. The world was silent except the occasional braying of donkeys, which was part of the night. Rianaro had eaten and he was now reclining against the wall. Logwee, the children, and I were taking turns telling stories. It was Logwee's turn to tell a story. After clearing her throat she began telling the story of Nairanabwo, an Acholi/Jie prophetess of long ago; here it is as I recorded it:

In the year of Nairanabwo, the people in Najie, from Rengen to Nakapelimoru and from Panyangara to Mount Moroto, suffered under the hot sun, which blistered and burned all the vegetation. The very earth cracked wide open and swallowed everything. Some women went to the bush with their children to gather wild fruits, but there was nothing there – not even a dry seed. All the wells were dry and no life was left in Najie. Turtles became so skinny that, when they walked, they rattled in their shells. It was during this time that Apabelo, a well-known Jie prophet, had a dream in which Akuj told him about

Nairanabwo saying to him to bring Nairanabwo to Najie. So, the people traveled far to bring Nairanabwo from Katap, the Acholi land to Najie. When people reached Katap, they saw Nairanabwo sitting under the *epong* tree (a leafless cactus-like tree with milky juice) near a well known as Loongor.

When the people brought Nairanabwo to Najie they went straight to Emamlope village, to the home of Apabelo, the great prophet who had dreamed about Nairanabwo. Later that evening Nairanabwo told women to go to their gardens and sprinkle wild cucumber seeds for the birds to eat. The women went to their gardens in the morning and did as Nairanabwo had instructed. The birds came in large numbers and ate the seeds. Nairanabwo then told the people to harvest *esaale* (a woody plant with bushy leaves) and to boil its leaves, to drink it in their gardens, and then to sprinkle the remaining water on the sorghum plants. People did as Nairanabwo instructed. She told the women to sacrifice a black male goat and to smear themselves with its *ngikujit* (the undigested food of its intestines), and to drink the sorghum beer. The women did as they were told: they sacrificed a black goat and drank some beer. After that they danced all night.

After the women followed the instruction of Nairanabwo, it rained and rained and the sorghum plants grew thick, yielding rich seeds. When the sorghum ripened, Nairanabwo sent messages to the villages telling women not to chase the birds from their fields. But some women said "Ehh, what does she mean not to chase the birds when the birds eat our sorghum?" But other women said, "Let us listen to our mother Nairanabwo, and let's not chase the birds away from our fields."

When the harvest time came, all the women who listened to Nairanabwo had plenty of sorghum. Those who did not listen to her words did not have any. Their sorghum plants were choked by wild weeds and dried up. The women whose fields failed went to the women who had good harvests and asked for food, and when they did not receive enough, they fought with the women who refused to give them food. As a result, women began to fight. When Nairanabwo saw that women were fighting over food, she became very upset and left Najie and returned Katap. The following year, the sun burned hot again, scorching the fields. The women went to their fields and sacrificed a black ram and smeared themselves with *ngikujit* and prayed to Akuj, uttering the name of Nairanabwo. That year their gardens again yielded plenty of crops. That is why even today, the women follow the words of Nairanabwo when they cultivate their fields and offer sacrifices in her name.

"Was Nairanabwo an Acholi," asked one of the children at the end of the story. "Yes," replied Logwee, "she was an Acholi. It was the Acholi woman who saved us from death. That is why we sing praising Nairanabwo when we till our gardens." Logwee then began to sing the song, and all the children and I joined her:

Akimuju na ekimuji esuwa na
Talalau kingenyar
Akuj, keena, Nairanabwo keena, ngokosikiro nguna ekilipit iyong

(This food, which we are eating now
Let it be more and more
God, hear us, Nairanabwo hear us, what we are asking you for)

PART TWO

3 Patterns and Images of Historical Tradition

During my travels in the vast dry zone in Karamoja Plateau, on the shores of Lake Turkana, and around Chalbi Desert, I engaged in extensive conversations regarding the inhabitants' historical traditions. I learned that the Nayeche story is very common among the hunter-gatherer, pastoralist, and fishing communities in the region. The story depicts in various ways episodic memories of ancestral journeys and struggles over food and water. Such narratives are called *eemut* among both the Turkana and the Jie people. The *eemut* has endured, perhaps for centuries, to the present day. It is a prose narrative typically characterized by origin stories touching on famine, thirst, hunger, survival struggles, and migration. The plot of the historical tradition unfolds against a familiar desolate landscape, near a dry riverbed or a well. It gives specific features of the landscape, such as the names of the animals, vegetation, specific water resources, and the bush. Often, it also contains utterances and speeches of the characters, discussions of their emotions, and descriptions of the basic social relations, kinship obligations, and political concerns of the time. These elements are set against a backdrop of hunger and thirst, common in the daily life of Jie and Turkana societies.

These aspects of the historical tradition are not unique to Jie society. As the works of various scholars in the region (Kassam 2006; Lamphear 1976; Karp 1978; Sobania 1980; Schlee 1989) clearly indicate, hunger and thirst motifs are found in the historical traditions of various communities of hunter-gatherers, pastoralists, agriculturists, and fishermen throughout the dry zone that stretches from the Karamoja Plateau in northern Uganda to the Chalbi Desert in northern Kenya. Their shared vulnerability to starvation explains the similarity of these traditions among the peoples of this vast area. These communities engage in frequent warfare and conflict over water and grazing resources, but they also have a remarkable concern for sharing the meager resources needed in basic survival and for fostering or creating political alliances.

Here, scarce resources and unpredictable arid conditions force people across the plateau and the plains to construct networks of interethnic relationships. Sobania (1980, 1988) points out that throughout the arid zone in northern Uganda and Kenya, pastoralist, farming, and hunter-gatherer communities find solace in their historical traditions, which encode for them the images of ecological disasters, famines, and feasts. This encoding records, according to Sobania, the repeated patterns of events that have forced people to disperse and migrate in search of food and to help one another during times of crisis. The motifs of the historical traditions vividly portray a discursive history of ecological crisis, which forces people to establish political alliances.

In the plot of historical traditions, various environmental and political factors set the stage for the "culture hero"[1] to appear at a critical moment. From this moment unfolds the narrative plot. The culture hero, whose quest is aided by external circumstances, is associated with mythical themes. As such, these themes shed some light on ancestral heroes' adventures and strife as well as revealing certain patterns of ancestral motivation that have shaped the experiences of the people living in the region. There is a close relationship between the ancestral motivation and the moral responsibility of sharing the scarce resources of the region. The invocation of a few images and motifs of ancestral experiences of survival in crisis provides a glimpse of the social and political forces of the past. This can reveal more about the contemporary forces at work.

In an earlier study, I analyzed the ritual and biographical characters of historical tradition (Mirzeler 1999). Here, I will expand the scope of my research by including additional historical traditions, folktales, popular biographies, and newly acquired culturally relevant data that will help me flesh out historical traditions in light of Harold Scheub's theoretical framework.

For the last several decades, Harold Scheub has been delineating the recurring ancient memory images in the *ntsomi* oral tradition of the Xhosa people, which he refers to with the phrase "thematic image" (1969, 148). Conceptually, the notion of thematic image refers to the dramatic performance, the storyteller's effort to produce a work of art before an audience through the combined use of body, voice, and oral tradition. The thematic image is, according to Scheub (2002, 3–4), the finished production distilled from the entire tradition, reflecting the poetically conceived ideal world of the community.

Scheub's description of the thematic image, following a sequence of conflict resolution elements in *ntsomi* tradition, has led him to a useful approach to oral tradition. His analysis consists of an abstraction that includes all vital elements crucial to folklore studies: performer-audience relationships and the poetic, biographical, historical, verbal, and nonverbal dimensions of oral tradition as a performing art. The significance of memories is conveyed in performance as the storytellers bring together complex networks of collectively remembered images to create the individual *ntsomi* performance, and it is this that determines the meaning of the thematic image.

For Scheub, during performances the ancestral world becomes a part of the everyday and fits into the context of the contemporary world, as both the storytellers and the members of the audiences dialogically mold the "allegorical" images (1998, 26) of past events with the present circumstance. The allegorical images of these parallel yet separate worlds are unified through the unfolding of the conflict resolution in the context of the performance. For Scheub, the allegorical images are the building blocks of the tradition and provide the fundamental materials for the development of the plot, revealed poetically and artfully.

Within the thematic images of Jie historical tradition, ancestors work out their relationships with themselves and others. The storytellers who work with historical tradition have witnessed countless performances of it. Hence, they skillfully bring together the strands of tradition and confront the present moment allegorically and literally in feasible and acceptable terms. The storytellers never state the theme or the specific moral message, but rather juxtapose the networks of meaning into useful conjunction, addressing the moral good within humans as well as their potential for evil.

Like the Xhosa storytellers, Jie storytellers and the members of their audiences work together to control the potentially destructive forces of human society, to mold and channel them into a work of art. The performance of historical tradition, therefore, is an attempt to explore the potential evil vices and disharmony that threaten to fragment society, leading to crises of identity, dissolution of the family, and disruption of interethnic relations during famines and droughts.

Jie historical traditions are an organic extension of customs and traditions established by the ancestors, reflecting a perfect and balanced human society. The storytellers give order and frame contemporary society by means of the remembered images of the ancestors. The storytellers' artistic creation of the ancestral world envisions a future that has its roots in the past. The force of the historical tradition depends not only on a story's images and plot, but also on an individual's experiences with that familiar tale – dimly recalled memories that resonate and echo through the emotionally felt real-life experiences of the members of the audience.

The repertoire of most historical traditions in the vast dry region recalls interminable conflicts within families and between clans. Very few characters are involved in their plots; generally, the heroic characters are ill-treated by powerful family members, then leave their homes and wander forlornly in the desolate landscape until they find a new place in the bush or near the dry riverbeds, usually in a new ecological zone. The motifs of all these traditions are united in the wandering of the rejected hero during ecological disasters and prolonged dry seasons and famines, when all the rivers dry up and the land becomes parched by the scorching sun. Usually, when survival becomes precarious, the hero departs from his or her home and wanders in the desolate landscape until finding a new place with water and food. This aspect of heroic adventure is well illustrated in the wondrous adventures of Nayeche and the gray bull Engiro.

The thematic images of rejection, separation, and the subsequent journey of the hero are all elaborations of significant beginnings and the birth of a new society. Thus, out of rejection and a conflict situation, the hero emerges with new possibilities.[2] When the hero wanders in this desert landscape, he or she enters into a life-threatening situation, which potentially could swallow him or her up. However, nature welcomes the hero. This untouched virgin nature – the bush, the hill, or the unknown river, or the island – becomes like a womb nourishing the hungry and thirsty hero. It is in this womblike oasis that the hero evolves and becomes independent, which is possible only if the hero separates from his or her origin. Famine, hunger, and conflict over resources are the necessary conditions for the hero to separate from origins. The wandering of the hero is, in many ways, the genesis of the *elope* (self) (Campbell 1972). The miraculous survival of the hero is the most tremendous experience of the heroic journey. This journey of the hero usually includes a certain experience of anticipation and hope for new, yet unknown possibilities.[3] The Jie historical traditions, in their tales of journeys of the ancestral heroes, exemplify this experience of hope.

A moving example of this anticipation and hope is well illustrated in the journey of Nayeche.[4] She follows the footprints of the gray bull Engiro with anxious anticipation to find water. "Oh," she said, "... the bull must know where there is water. I am thirsty ... This bull must know where water is."[5] Eventually, the gray bull leads her to a well in the headwaters of the Tarash River. After she drinks water from the well, she goes into the bush where she finds a mysteriously seductive place, opulent and beautiful, reminiscent of Daidai, the original cradle land. In this new cradle land, she is protected from the dangers of famine, and she is nursed and healed from the pangs of rejection.

The wandering of Nayeche and the gray bull Engiro on the plateau in anticipation of new possibilities has a "biographical significance" (Bakhtin 1981, 89 [also see Scheub 1988; Basgoz 2008]). The biographical elements of Nayeche's life are preserved in various historical traditions, even though these traditions may not adhere closely to her entire life story. Her biography remains as discourse embedded in the common plot of the historical tradition. Similar to Nayeche's, certain biographical memory images of various other ancestral heroes are also preserved in various historical traditions, serving as archetypal models for human relations. The thematic images of the Orwakol and Lodiny historical traditions describe certain episodes from the lives of the legendary ancestral heroes – their relationships with their family members, and the fears, desires, dreams, and tensions that underlie the patterns of the social and political lives of people.[6]

These symbolize at once the ideal kinship relationship within the family and between the politico-religious leader of the community and people in the new cradle lands. They illustrate traditional conflicts and tensions within the family, against whom aggression can be projected or with whom resources can be shared. All of the good and bad elements of kinship and social and political relations are depicted in such historical traditions. The critical implications of the good and bad kinship relations have been preserved since Orwakol's arrival to Daidai, his finding of the gray bull Engiro, Nayeche's departure to the Tarash River, the sacrifice of Engiro, and the meaning of the universal communion that was performed in Daidai, distilled from the biographical memory images of the ancestors. The following passage from a historical tradition performed by Lodoch, for example, reveals the disturbing implications of the memorable communion on Engiro's flesh:

All the men now dragged Engiro toward the rock of Daidai and they speared him one by one until Engiro fell on the rock lifeless. Orwakol, his seven sons, and the young men of Turkana and Toposa all set in the *akiriket* under the tree and ate the charred meat of Engiro all by themselves, as the Ngikuliaks, the children, the women, and the old infirm men indignantly watched them eating. The aroma of Engiro's meat engulfed the whole of Najie; even Lodiny and his people smelled it all the way at the Lokatap Rock.

As the young men consumed the meat, there started conflict over the flesh of Engiro. The Topasa men wanted to eat the right thigh of Engiro, but Orwakol refused and instead gave it to his people. The Turkana and the Topasa than said, "Ehh, if it is like that let us leave." The Toposa then left and went in the direction of north and the Turkana then went toward the east.[7]

The communion depicted in the passage quoted from the historical tradition both unites and divides the original family. The protecting older brother Orwakol refuses to share the meat of the sacrificial animal with his brother. We know this because the aroma of Engiro's burning meat reaches Lodiny all the way to Lokatap Rock; that symbolic communion initiates new life and new birth for the Orwakol people. While it unites the seven territorial divisions of Orwakol clans through the body of Engiro, it fractures it by defining as other Lodiny, the Toposa, and the Ngikuliak hunter-gatherers, the original inhabitants of Najie.

This is the meaning of the memory of the universal communion in Daidai, remembered and interpreted endlessly by storytellers. This is the sense of the ancestral relationships embodying the good and evil character of the ancient past. Thus, we see that two mythological themes come together: the unity between the Orwakol and Lodiny clans brought together by gray bull Engiro and its offspring; and the denial of the sacrificial meat of gray bull Engiro, which fragments the unity of the ancestral family. For the first time, the Jie learn that brothers are separated and the land is split in two halves and named after the two ancestral founding fathers respectively: Lokarwokol and Lokalodiny. The tension, created by the communion in Daidai, has alarming implications for the contemporary Jie. Through this, we can better understand the patterns and variants of the conflict between members of these communities living in the same environment.

When Lodiny experienced rejection from Orwakol, he felt threatened and separated from Orwakol and traveled in the wilderness in search of food and a new place to stay. In a variant of Nayeche stories, we see the expression of a similar theme. When Nayeche was rejected and denied food, she too wandered aimlessly on the plateau in solitude. As in historical traditions, we also see similar wandering of characters in the folktales. In these, when humans and animals meet on equal ground, we see the unfolding of famines and thirst, the objective calamities that threaten life as well as social and political order.

In the variants of Napeikisina stories, for instance, Napeikisina is prosecuted and rejected by her sisters, chased away from society by the tainted world of her family. Although Napeikisina runs away from her society, she wants to be a part of the very society that rejects her. She aimlessly wanders in the wilderness outside her village in search of human contact and friendship. She, who was originally innocent and who followed the established customs, becomes corrupted after she falls victim to her sisters' trickery. After this event the innocent Napeikisina transforms into a villainous figure, who moves about aimlessly as she tries to reconnect with people and reenter society. She begins to act like her villainous sisters, tricking people and causing them to abandon their homes, kraals, villages, and children. She always tries to share something with people, but unable to do so, ends up dying on the back of a hyena.[8]

There are certain thematic parallels between Napeikisina's story and various historical traditions, and this parallel is not limited to Napeikisina's story.[9] As we will see later in this chapter, the thematic images of folktales and historical traditions are almost inseparable from biographical narratives.

Similar to the characters of folktales and historical traditions, we see family conflict situations between the characters of the biographical narratives and their kin that offer no way out, ultimately causing them to leave their families and wander in the bush to start a new life.[10] However, the ancestral figures of historical tradition or biographical narratives are not the only characters to do this. We also observe similar processes at work in the fantastic world of the folktales. I examine the biographical and folktale significance of historical tradition later in this chapter.

In historical tradition, we observe survival strategies, where the desire for independence and individuation from the bonds of family and tradition often act as the enabling impetus to go beyond society and to survive alone in the world. We see this happening during prolonged droughts and famines when the full range of ancestral memories are let loose. The story of Lodiny's persistent search for water and grass during that long dry summer allows us to see more deeply into the desire for independence. After his search for water and grass, Lodiny, Orwakol's younger brother, finally migrates to Lokatap Rock near Orwakol. After ten years living with Orwakol near Daidai, Lodiny decides to separate from his brother and become independent. Here is what young Lodiny said to his people in anticipation of his independence: "My kraal is also large. I also have many children. I will divide my *ngagulei* [clans] as Orwakol divided his." When the anticipated moment comes, Lodiny separates from Orwakol and gives his command to his people to make their fire facing north, thus declaring his independence from Orwakol.[11]

In some historical traditions the rejected person is rendered helpless and vulnerable and mistreated by the powerful members of the family and thrown out into the dangerous world, yet despite his or her help-lessness, he or she overcomes the obstacles and survives against all odds. The urge and compulsion to survive transforms the rejected an-cestral member of the society into a hero. Ancestral power is revealed often by the miraculous actions of the rejected and seemingly power-less member of the society. From this point of view we see the redeem-ing power associated with the rejected person, who eventually helps the society go through the difficult moments. As the reader will recall, Nayeche,[12] in some variants, is a rejected child who survives the famine conditions and later becomes a savior of her people and the founder of a tribe. Lodiny, who was intimidated, mistreated, and denied food by Orwakol, his maternal uncle in certain variants, leaves his home and finds a new clan in Lokatap Rock.[13] The very grandeur of the rejected ancestors' power is bound up with the fantasy of survival, manifested in certain basic historical traditions, but not confined to the Jie people. We find similar survival fantasies in the historical traditions of the Turkana, Elmolo, the Rendille, and the Samburu people, all living in disparate parts of the dry zone (Mirzeler 1999; Schlee 1989; Sobania 1980).

The memories of survival fantasies embodied in historical tradition bridge the people with their past, anchoring them with their ancestral roots and assuring them the promise of survival in the unpredictable dry environment where these people experience political turmoil. Thus, we see the thematic image of ancestors' search for food and water and their turmoil leading to the formation of a new society. They are as-sured the redemptive power of nature. Like some of the ancestors who left their society and disappeared, they too can reappear in a new cradle land and begin a new life surrounded by the virgin bush, wild fruits, water, and opulent pasture.

Bush, river, and hill are the recurrent images in historical traditions as well as in biographical narratives as we will explore below. The forced departure of the heroine and her subsequent journey leads her to cross new boundaries, which are allegorical and have their parallels in the real world. This kind of equivalence exists in historical traditions and is recognizable as well in popular biographical narratives.

Oral material, whether it is historical tradition, folktale, or biography, evolves over time, and its plot and content change depending on the space, social milieu, and language of numerous storytellers (Barber 2007; Basgoz 2008; Scheub 2002). However, in this analysis I identify the salient characteristics that most historical traditions share. Some of the popularly known biographical narratives referring to more recent times share the basic thematic images of historical tradition, so perhaps they must also be granted historical tradition status.

In the realism of their plots, some of these popularly known biographies have characteristics in common with the historical tradition genre. For example, the biography of Nacham,[14] who lived within the context of modern Najie, should be included in the historical tradition genre, not biography. The biography of Nacham is so typical of the structural model of historical tradition that one might assume it is a part of the biography of Nayeche, insofar as the plot of the biography includes many of the elements of Nayeche's story. Wandering in the dry landscape, following the footprints of the animals, finding a place in the bush teeming with wild animals, drinking water from the well – these all parallel the story of Nayeche. I have included some of these biographical narratives, including Nacham's, because they were created by storytellers and performed orally on certain occasions. Similarly, the story of Nakapor's installation to firemaking status also seems to have a structural connection to some of the historical tradition genres, such as the story of Orwakol and his seven wives regarding the original distribution of sorghum and fire. Lodoch composed both of them. In another story relating to Nakapor's biography, composed by Rianaro, the plot of the biography is so similar to the biographical memory images of Orwakol, that the storyteller even invokes the ancient memory of a ritual event in Nyanga, one of the ancient Jie cradle lands.[15]

The typical form of the historical tradition structural model is found in the stories whose main characters are ancestral mythical heroes who lived in the distant past. Of those characters, Orwakol, Lodiny, Nayeche, Kadanya, and Lobeyekuri lived perhaps in the eighteenth century or earlier (Mirzeler 1999). Loriang[16] and Nairanabwo[17] lived in the

twentieth century within the memory of living people. The stories of
Nairanabwo recount the recent historical memory of the survival of a
famine situation, and they are shaped into the historical tradition model. The biographical elements in these stories parallel those found in the
historical tradition of Kadanya, documenting the ancestral memory of
the Jie. The story of Nairanabwo begins with an episode of a prophetic
dream cycle. This is followed by the heroine's travel during a long dry
season and her performance of a sacrifice to prevent calamities. This
stays true to the classic model memory image of Nakadanya in Jie, and
the memory of Lokorijam[18] in Turkana historical traditions, respectively.
Unlike the story of Nakadanya and Lokorijam, the story of Nairanabwo
is long and it contains certain personal biographical details about her
daughter and her marital status. This is perhaps because she lived during recent times within the memory of some living people.

Unlike folktales, which are considered fictional, historical traditions
refer to specific geographic settings and real life situations unfolding
within an historical or pseudohistorical time.[19] The thematic images of
historical traditions are formed when the storytellers select the memory
images embodied in ancient traditions and combine them with circumstances of the present, shaping them before an audience to create a
work of art without a record. At the poetic center of the thematic image
are the members of the ancestral family with all their cosmological and
politico-religious trappings.

In the historical traditions referring to the beginning of societies,
parents or grandparents of the heroes are not mentioned, as if these
ancestral heroes were the first humans. The names of siblings rarely appear, except in Orwakol and Lodiny historical traditions, which sometimes depict the two as brothers and sometimes as a maternal uncle
and nephew, respectively. In one historical tradition, Orwakol's wives'
names are mentioned in relation to the founding of the seven territorial
divisions and clans during a key ritual event.[20] The storytellers do not
mention the hero's children, except in one of the Nayeche stories, in
which some storytellers claim Nayeche was Orwakol's daughter. In another historical tradition, the storytellers make reference to Orwakol's
sons, but they do not mention their names or give any details about
them. Generally, references to kinship relations are minimal and without
detail. Heroes usually experience famines and so travel in search of food
and water, making it easy for the storytellers, who themselves have experienced such crises, to identify with the stories of the heroes, sharing
their destinies and feelings. Lodoch, when he depicted Orwakol's abuse

of his authority toward his brother Lodiny, says, "I identify with Lodiny, so much. His relationship with Orwakol reminds me of my brother, who sold everything I had and disappeared" (Interview, Kampala, 2011).

In other Orwakol stories no mention of family is made. The plot of the narrative does not fall into the established pattern, but takes the form of ordinary patterns of life in the kraals and mentions no extraordinary famines resulting in dispersal, no search for water and pasture. In the stories, conflict sometimes occurs between Orwakol in the kraals and the elders in village, causing Orwakol to move the kraals away from the settled villages.[21]

The storytellers usually present the heroes within real life situations, experiencing political turmoil that forces them to make decisions within a social and historical context. Names of popularly known geographical locations, grazing lands, bushes, hills, wells, and rivers with their attendant resources are mentioned. Historically, the majority of these places are considered centers of creation (Eliade 1960) that embody memories of famine, war, and survival.

In the historical tradition, reference to time is not as important as reference to geographical space. Some historical traditions omit references to time altogether. Sometimes historical references are inconsistent. At other times, the storytellers refer to important rituals and age groups to indicate the time of the story, but the performance of the same story by the same storytellers or others may mention different rituals or age groups, or sometimes omit them. Sometimes reference to time is rather general such as "long, long ago" or "during the great famine and hunger of long ago," as in many classic folkloric formulae. On the other hand, in some stories we find certain popularly remembered ritual moments or famines imprinted in the collective memory of the people, such as the Ngipalajam generation being associated with Nayeche's journey, referring to approximately 250 years ago.[22] At other times, however, the journey of Nayeche is associated with Lokolong's bull,[23] the only bull surviving the great famine of long ago, which Lamphear correlates with Loriang's time (Lamphear 1976, 224; Lamphear and Webster 1971, 24). According to some storytellers, however, the story of Lokolong's bull is a much more recent event, which took place within the memory of the living people who actually lived through the great famine.[24] Close scrutiny of the majority of historical traditions in our collection demonstrates rather vague and contradictory references to time. However, sometimes the storytellers include the dates to convince the audience that the heroes of the story are real and lived in a certain time and place.

In addition to contradictory and inconsistent chronology and geneal-
ogy details, the details of the historical events may differ from performance to performance. In the story of Nairanabwo, for example, the
person who dreamed and prophesied about Nairanabwo's ritual power
was a woman,[25] but in another one is male.[26] In some stories, Nayeche
appears as an old woman, in others as a young girl. In addition, in some
Turkana variants of the Nayeche stories, no mention of gray bull Engiro
are made. According to some storytellers, two bulls followed the footprints of Nayeche rather than the other way around.[27] Similarly, in some
stories, Orwakol appears as Lodiny's older brother; in others, he is the
maternal uncle.[28]

The representation of the ancestral heroes by storytellers also varies
from performance to performance. The images of the ancient Jie heroes
are often contradictory – these heroes sometimes acted positively, pulling
society toward unity by sharing resources with the members of society.
At other times, however, they are represented as selfish and destructive.
In historical tradition, the negative and positive attributes coexist.

Once Rianaro recounted to me a story during an interview about the
Jie oral tradition and about the personalities of Orwakol and Lodiny.
The story takes place in Daidai. Here's how Rianaro artfully forged that
fantasy memory into a story to illustrate both the good and bad sides of
his protagonist. This can shed light on the dual nature of the ancestral
heroes:

When Orwakol and Lodiny first came to Daidai, they both went hunting
in a place called Ngityang, some distance north of the Longiro River. That
place was called Ngityang because there were a lot of wild animals there
at that time. They hunted all that day but they could not find a single wild
animal. They had almost given up on hunting and were about to return to
their homes when Lodiny killed an antelope. Orwakol became jealous
of him. They carried the carcass of the animal to Daidai where Orwakol
wanted to make a fire to cook the meat. But he was so jealous and resentful
of Lodiny that he offended Akuj, and when he tried to make a fire, the fire
refused to burn. Orwakol became angry and frustrated and blamed Lodiny
for his inability to make the fire. Lodiny then said to Orwakol, "We are
brothers and you should not blame me for not being able to make fire. Let
me try and see if I can make fire." When Lodiny tried, the fire started and
flames rose. Seeing Lodiny making the fire annoyed Orwakol and he became indignant and took the meat of the wild animal and the fire from
Lodiny and told him to go away. Lodiny left Daidai and went to Lokatap

Rock and hunted another antelope and made a new fire and cooked the meat and ate it. (Rianaro, 14 July 1996)

What we see in this story is the image of the ancestral brothers in which the negative image of Orwakol as an older brother unfolds. No matter how morally upright, virtuous, and mature Orwakol might seem, he can be immature and immoral. And as an immature human being, he lives in a world with so much possibility that he can shape and create his relationships in this world and live in it. As a venerated ancestor, Orwakol has the double image of hero and frail human associated with him.

On one level, what Rianaro was actually trying to do with the story was to raise a question about the jealous spirit of a benevolent ancestor. The story, though seemingly simple, is a very sophisticated, imaginative narrative full of metaphors, meanings, and drama by which people can guide their lives. The message here is that deep within the heart of each individual, there may be a greedy, immoral, immature self. Thus we see an evil capacity within a seemingly benevolent ancestor. "We are all capable of being immature and evil, not only in ancient times, but also in this contemporary world," Rianaro points out, and continues. "We know the flip side of Orwakol's hero image; we know from him appropriate, exemplary ways of behaving, ways of creating friendships, and of growing with others. We also know how greed and jealousy can result in destruction and conflict even between brothers."

What Rianaro told me is especially true in a dry and unpredictable environment, such as Najie, with its political uncertainties and where everyone is vulnerable, including those who own and control the resources. One can lose it all at any moment. One can possess many livestock and be well and secure today, but lose all and be hungry and insecure tomorrow. The future with cattle wealth, which is vulnerable, is unpredictable and that is why Jie storytellers say, "No one knows what tomorrow will bring to us." Orwakol had the ability to make fire, but he lost it unexpectedly. Orwakol lost it because he offended Akuj with his jealousy and greed.

The negative image of Orwakol is not confined to the variant, which Rianaro recounted, but also appears in other variants I collected from other storytellers. Various storytellers' accounts of Orwakol's relationship with Lodiny reveal intricate kinship relations between uncles and nephews. Some relate the problem of misused authority, some recount political adventure involving cattle raiding, and some recall sharing resources.

In an interesting variant of an Orwakol/Lodiny historical tradition, which Lokopelan recounted, Orwakol is depicted as an unreasonable and oppressive maternal uncle who ruthlessly appropriates his
nephew's hard won cattle.[29] While Lokopelan portrayed Lodiny's accumulation of cattle through raiding as an innocent youthful activity, he
described Orwakol's attempt to possess Lodiny's cattle as vicious behavior bringing disharmony to society. In this incident, Orwakol goes
beyond the bad uncle figure to become the egregiously aggressive cattle
grabber who unreasonably demands an unpaid-for bride-price for his
sister from his innocent young nephew. Similar to the story of Rianaro,
what Lokopelan does with this depiction is to use the depravity of
Lodiny to illuminate the depravity of nephews by their cattle-grabber
maternal uncles. Orwakol demands the unpaid bride-price from Lodiny's
mother so that he may ask for his traditional right to receive the bride-
price of his sister. But Lodiny refuses to consent. He leaves Daidai and
settles at Lokatap Rock. Thus, Jie society becomes divided as a result of
Orwakol's greedy desire to amass resources.

The contradictory images of ancestral heroes illuminate that historical traditions are not only about the past, and the past is not just about
what happened; they are also about how people remember the good
and bad of the past. Talking about good and bad images of historical
traditions and learning from them are an essential part of becoming human. The Jie historical traditions express the good and the bad, through
their depiction of the ancestral heroes, and yet both good and evil are
potential healing force attributes. These attributes coexist in the double
image of Orwakol, the ancient Jie hero. The future depends on the past,
a past, which the Jie people are actively involved in receiving and shaping. The past is connected to the material world around them in their
contemporary relations, as in the memory images embodied in Daidai
on the banks of the Longiro River.

In addition to double attributes of the heroes, we also see certain
patterns of tension between individualism and obedience to custom in
various historical traditions. In a version of the Orwakol and Lodiny
stories, for example, when Orwakol demands cattle, Lodiny obeys the
custom and gives him more cattle. In another version of the same story,
when they separate, each making new fire facing different directions,
they continue to share the meat of their sacrifices. In other words, separation does not stop them from sharing food, which is proper conduct,
behavior that is an integral part of the society. By affirming the positive
action of sharing food, which is imposed by *etal* (tradition), they fulfill

an inner part of their human nature. As humans, they did not become victims of the whims of their evil potential. *Etal* (tradition) brought out the positive potential in the ancestral heroes. Hence the members of the contemporary society are informed that they too can diminish their evil nature, making it possible for people to maintain harmony and good relationships with one another. It is for this reason, Lodoch once told me, that people share food even though they may not share fire. Even though there is both good and evil potential in the ancestral world, tradition emphasizes an ordered harmonious human society in which sharing food and cooperation for survival are the central images of the tradition.

In identifying with the contradictory thematic images of oral traditions like these, the contemporary people themselves must make their choices on which advice of their contradictory ancestors they should follow. Although Orwakol may be oppressive to Lodiny in certain variants of the story, he rescues him and his people during a prolonged famine situation by sharing his resources in Daidai. The desire of Orwakol to share his resources is a reflection of the longing of humans to share, but it is also symbolic of the human capacity for good. Orwakol in this performance becomes a representation of people's humanity by means of artistically expressed generosity. This is how people survive in this unpredictable dry environment, and hence how people cooperate for survival during famines. It is in the combination of the ancestral heroes' many appearances and actions that the full concept of being human in the contemporary world emerges. It is in these complex networks of memory images, which wind their way throughout the entire tradition, that the thematic image of historical tradition is woven.

In another performance, the developing and growing evil is represented allegorically when Orwakol refuses to give cattle to people in the villages. As the conflict grows between the people in the village and the kraals over cattle, the venerable elders in the village allegorically come together as an evil force and become involved in raiding, stealing, and killing. Thus, the venerable ancestral elders take part in killing.

In yet another performance, the ancestral family experiences conflict when they refuse to share the meat of the gray bull Engiro with the Toposa people, causing the Toposa to separate and become a different people.[30] "It is for this reason," Lodoch told me, "when the Toposa people come to collect *emunyen* (sacred clay) from the Longiro River for their rituals, we [the Jie people] show our generosity and offer food to our Toposa visitors, thus we redeem the past injustice committed against the Toposa people by our venerable ancestors."

The contemporary Jie people's desire to share their resources generously with the Toposa people becomes the image of the redemptive
power of a larger good. The ancestral families are thus not always seen
as ideal. They are seen to be like the contemporary people themselves,
full of conflict. Both good and evil are expressed in historical traditions
in literal and allegorical ways. If the denial of resources disperses the
society and causes conflicts between them, the sharing of resources
brings people together and saves people from death.

It is impossible to type ancestral characters as fabulous, heroic, or
even evil. A venerable ancestor might be an ideal figure in certain performances of historical tradition but may become evil in other performances. Nayeche might be an ideal daughter, but in certain performances
she is depicted as being a rebellious daughter who refuses to give cattle to the elders in Koteen Hill.[31] We can thus argue that, at one level,
performances of historical tradition deal with past historical events,
but at another level with human nature.

It is thus necessary to define the remembered image in historical tradition on the basis of performance event. The meaning of the historical
tradition can only be revealed when we analyze the content of individual performances against a broader context (Bauman 1986). Therefore,
the key to understanding the remembered image in historical tradition
can be found in the performance, which embodies the network of allegorical and literal representations of tradition. Sometimes Orwakol as
an older brother or a maternal uncle figure is depicted as the unreasonable affine, yet in others he is a reasonable and benevolent father, brother,
or uncle. The contradictory thematic images of such historical traditions are not surprising; they are features of the Jie world the way trickery and discord are to the folktales, as we will see later in this chapter.

These contradictory double images of heroes are themselves allegorical and have universal value. They become projected onto the Jie
experience of living in a dry and unpredictable environment, and can
accurately describe real experiences through the thematic images of historical tradition. As with other oral tradition genres (folktale and biography), the thematic images of historical traditions tell something about
universal themes of vulnerability and interdependence created by living
in unpredictable dry environments where survival necessitates political
alliances, cooperation, and the sharing of scarce resources.

The thematic images of historical tradition with their double images
speak a symbolic language of myth, articulating the need for survival
in dry environments. Like the allegories, symbols of historical tradition

are represented by the Jie world itself. Through the allegorical image of Orwakol, the Jie world tells about the presence of contradictory images of fathers or older brothers and maternal uncles.

Similar to the Orwakol and Lodiny stories, the fate of Nayeche, as depicted in the variants of the Nayeche stories, is distilled from the stuff of everyday life experiences as well as the stuff of the mythical past. What appears to be mythical in the narrative is distilled from biographies and traditional rituals. The thematic image of Nayeche's forlorn pursuit of the gray bull Engiro tells something about *awotoun*, a phase of a marriage ritual involving the return visit of the bride, along with her husband, to her natal home bringing with her the cattle that serve as the final payment of her bride-price.

In its connection with the marriage ceremony, the motif of Nayeche's journey appears as a manifestation of a rite of passage, a cultural process whose existence can be observed in individual biography. Nayeche is not only connected with the marriage ceremony but also with the harvest ritual. Her connection with harvest ritual, however, involves traditional forms of repeated and cyclical forms of event categories hearkening back to historical moments whose structural elements can be observed in Jie politico-religious thought. The story of Nayeche at this level is a part of the new society, in which the primal granary of the firemaker is conceived as the womb of the mother. The metaphor of the granary is a primary phenomenon in Jie history and politico-religious thought, expressing the mythic creation story. The combined image of the gray bull Engiro and the granary is symbolic of Jie agro-pastoral identity. Lodoch asserts over and over again that everything comes from the granary of Orwakol, and the same allegory is applicable to the womb image of Daidai and the masculine creative power of the Longiro River. Like the womb image of Daidai, the muddy floods of the Longiro River are an organic part of the image, giving the original family a sacred aura. While the Longiro River gave life to the entire Jie community, Daidai rock is the womb image, which bore and nurtured the ancestral family. Because Engiro was sacrificed here, it is fitting that the choice to share or refuse to share the meat of Engiro distinguished the people and defined their ethnic identity. Thus the river metaphorically fertilized the rock, which gave birth to two distinct clans: the Orwakol and the Lodiny clans. The place where the gray bull was sacrificed is a significant site for the Jie. It was from that very place, according to some storytellers, that Orwakol distributed *amachar*, the cattle brand, to his sons. Just as Daidai is the womb image for the Jie, Moru a Nayeche is the womb image for the Turkana. Moru a Nayeche is the beginning of things, the cradle land and mythic source of their identities.

The storytellers emphasize the interdependence and complementary aspects between these ancient images. These divine images and their attendant memories are associated with the survivors of ecological and political disasters. That is why the basic thematic images of ancestral family echo the Jie social relations with the Turkana, representing both Nayeche and the gray bull Engiro as the victims of ecological and political tragedies who found respite in the bush and survived.

The discourse of Nayeche's journey on the waterless plateau is infused with various other historical memories as well as popular biographies of contemporary people. The numerous representations of her journey by storytellers in various contexts align the empirical experiences of people with the experiences of Nayeche. The motif of Nayeche's journey is universal and describes how people experience their historical reality of living in an unpredictable environment with political uncertainties. In their performances and anecdotal exchanges, the storytellers and the members of the audience poetically recreate the diverse images of Nayeche and various other historical traditions as allegory, giving vital meaning to the present.

The gray bull Engiro and Nayeche travel together in the desolate landscape as concomitant forces; Engiro, as the divine bull, serves as Nayeche's companion. They are both victims of famine. The essential affinity between Engiro and Nayeche as the victims of famine is best shown in their survival strategies. They depend on each other. Their interdependence is symbolic of the interdependence between the Jie and Turkana as well as between two ecological zones – the somewhat lush plateau and the dry desert plain. Likewise, the interdependence between men and women represents agriculture and pastoralism, respectively. The historical traditions of the Jie and Turkana living around the upper Tarash River region articulate these archaic elements of survival strategies – the recognition of complementary experiences and interdependencies. Their oral historical traditions, in particular of the gray bull Engiro and Nayeche, in the eyes of the Jie and the Turkana people whom I interviewed, have a discursive meaning informing both their interdependence and their vulnerability living in an unpredictable environment where they can both become victims of famines and political uncertainties.

That is why the popular traditions of these communities describe ancestral heroes invoking a moral standard of sharing food and resources to survive, a point well illustrated by Sobania's (1980) studies in the region. The norms of sharing for survival often take the concept of kinship obligation as a political strategy. The articulation of political strategies through Nayeche is at the core of the Jie and Turkana interethnic dependency. The storytellers illustrate how this is so. Presented by the poetic departure of Nayeche and the gray bull Engiro from the plateau to the plains, both the Jie and the Turkana turn to the possibilities this poetic journey creates for both communities. It is notable that the storytellers emphasize the lesson from this journey in the conclusion of the tale when Nayeche refuses to return home. She describes Jie life on the plateau as full of hunger and famine, and she then creates the Turkana society, from the Jie, on the headwaters of the Tarash River. The Tarash River, which is fed by the floods of the plateau, cuts through the desert landscape in Turkana land, is associated with the birth of Turkana from the embryonic Jie society.

The varying interpretations of Nayeche lend understanding to the plot of the tale. After the gray bull Engiro gets lost and wanders on the dry plateau, Nayeche disappears and follows the footprints of the bull. Luckily they both reach the Tarash River. They both seek refuge and rest on a hill in a thicket beside the river. Barely surviving hunger and thirst, there they find protection and respite from famine. Next we see some Jie men arriving and settling with their families on the headwaters of the river and creating a new society. This recalls the division of the original Jie society into two pairs: the Lokorwakol and the Lokalodiny clans, named after Orwakol and Lodiny respectively, in Jie land on the plateau; and a pair of societies, the Jie and the Turkana, in the plains, which is where the story of Nayeche ends. The Turkana tribe successfully evolves and becomes nomadic pastoralists who depend on their kin on the plateau. Although the place where the newly created Turkana society settles does not enable them to grow sufficient grain and vegetables, they can still get by in the desert because they can always get the grain from their maternal kin, the Jie. Kinship can transcend the problems of desperate circumstances. Because of this, the Turkana people feel secure despite their unavoidable experience of frequent famines in the desert.

Even though the Turkana feel the fragility of life in the desert, they know there is a place on the plateau where they can turn. This is perhaps why, in Nayeche performances, people reach different conclusions as they ponder their interethnic experience. Sometimes the interpretation of the story does not raise a mythical kinship obligation for deeds and words. Instead it suggests the meaning of norms for moral responsibility and political strategy, and how what really matters is the response to political uncertainties and hunger during famine.

Thematic images of Nayeche's survival strategies can be found in the historical traditions of people throughout the dry zone in northern Kenya and Uganda. Sobania (1980) illustrates this point in his richly documented thesis. My apprenticeship experience with storytellers in this vast dry region concurs with Sobania's findings. My work on the presence of common basic themes and parallels in the oral historical traditions of the peoples living in different communities takes Sobania's work further. An understanding of the role of the thematic image in oral historical tradition promises insight as to why the people of this region share similar traditions. Throughout this vast area, the plots of popular historical traditions and their thematic images describe the articulation of survival strategies and political alliances.

Although these societies individually have different divinities and concepts of world order, their traditions have remarkable parallels in their plots and thematic images. These plots try to answer questions about moral order, celebrate the appreciation of hope for survival, address conflict resolutions within the family, and emphasize the importance of sharing scarce resources and establishing political relationships.

In the traditions of each of these societies there are thematic images of wandering ancestral heroes in search of water and food until they find a new cradle land, giving birth to a new society. For example, the wandering of the hero for survival is perfected in the adventures of Sepenya, the heroine of the Elmolo tradition, and its variants.[32] In the Sepenya tradition we find highly developed types of journey motifs, which are remarkably similar to those of Nayeche and are composed of the same thematic elements. Both Nayeche and Sepenya are exceptional in their endurance and survival virtues. They are also exceptional in their devotion to life and continuity. A sudden drought and prolonged famine strikes the land, threatening the continuity of life and society, forcing Sepenya to wander in search of food and water. The story ends happily when Sepenya arrives on the island and starts a new society, which eventually is united with the original society, as in the case of Nayeche. Sometimes the Elmolo storytellers frame Sepenya as a victim in mythological categories, in her journey to South Island with her pregnant goat in a camel trough caught in a violent storm. The plot unfolds in a definite geographical space and time on an island separated from the Elmolo on the mainland by dangerous deep water. These parallel the dangerous waterless plateau that separates Najie from the headwaters of the Tarash River in the plains.

The story of Sepenya's journey, which is well remembered by the contemporary Elmolo people, is poetic and all encompassing. The thematic image of the story contains information about Elmolo philosophy, the human passion for survival, maternal love, and identity politics. Adventure and conflict motifs, such as the original conflict situation, pregnancy, giving birth both literally and allegorically, vulnerability and rejection, and flight from society are worked out in Elmolo traditions. Certain other motifs, such as the transformation of tribal identity from pastoralists to a fishing people and vice versa, are well developed in their hippo myth and its ritual performance, paralleling Nayeche's connection with the harvest ritual. The recognition motif is also pervasive in Elmolo traditions: the recognition of cows that are transformed into hippos and the recognition of the tragedy experienced by victims upon return to the mainland are parallel to the Jie men's recognition of Nayeche in the bush. Finding gourds containing babies that are floating in the swamp represent the promise that life will continue (Mirzeler 2006a).

The historical significance of the Elmolo traditions may be variously assessed, but one cannot deny the syncretism of these traditions. In their structure, their tragedy stories fuse together almost all the genres of their oral traditions. In a variant of a Sepenya story, Sepenya arrives in Sarima as a pregnant woman and parts the lake to cross to the island. The end of the plot is Sepenya's marriage to her son Merisiya.[33] The poles of the plot movement are crucial events in Sepenya's life and have biographical significance as they do in the Nayeche stories (Mirzeler 2006a).

The moments of heroic journeys take place during specific times, at moments when everyday life is interrupted by droughts, famines, and ecological tragedies. These moments provide the necessary condition for the intrusion of the supernatural forces to shape history, as the individual hero, such as Sepenya, tries to survive. The Elmolo people, like the Jie and Turkana, understand the experience of famines and political turmoil through mythic heroes, such as, Sepenya and Nayeche.

Everything that Sepenya experiences during her journey, she does through the discourse of the Elmolo people in its specific forms, as Nayeche does through the Jie and Turkana discourses. No matter how many contradictions and insoluble conflicts Sepenya experiences, her journey is affected by the semantic and expressive impulses of the Elmolo people's fantasy of survival and social and political ideologies associated with being the victim of a lake tragedy. The discourse of Sepenya's journey personalizes her as a victim of a lake tragedy, like Nayeche be-ing a victim of famine. The island where she arrives becomes a new cradle land where she gives birth to the fisherman Elmolo tribe. The story of Sepenya's tragic journey and her miraculous survival may or may not be a true historical event, but it encodes Elmolo people's poetic logic (Mirzeler 2006a). The story is discursive, political, and biograph-ical, and speaks through the voices of the Elmolo, orchestrating their unique themes.

It is impossible to think of the journey of Sepenya to South Island in search of food as being independent of the political strategies between the Elmolo and the pastoralists who, with them, lead interdependent lives. The pastoralist Turkana, Samburu, and Rendille living around the lake depend on the Elmolo people during times of crisis. It is per-haps because of this that Sepenya is sometimes depicted as Samburu, but at other times as a Gabra or Rendille pastoralist. This fluid identity enables these communities to manipulate the ethnic boundaries, and create kinship ties with the Elmolo people to secure political and eco-nomic alliances, but also to gain access to fish during ecological crises. This point is well documented by Sobania (1980), Schlee (1989) and Mirzeler (2006a).

As in the Nayeche story, the basic themes of the Sepenya origin stories are connected with staple food, which helps her to survive in a famine situation. During prolonged famines, while Nayeche eats wild fruits, Sepenya eats fish, drinks goat milk, and gathers honey. Similarly, Lmasula, the ancestral hero of the Samburu clans living around Mount Kulal, eats honey. As various studies have shown (Galaty 1986; Ohnuki-Tierney 1993; Karp 1980; Kratz 1994; Mirzeler 2004, 2009; Sobania 1980, 1988), staple food is commonly used as an identity marker among the hunter-gatherers, pastoralists, agriculturalists, and fisherman commu-nities of East Africa. These communities often share their staple foods to survive during ecological crises and political turmoil. As they share food, they also share their survival stories about themselves and ne-gotiate marriages. There is a constant pressure among the pastoralist nomads throughout the arid zone to invest in political and economic alliances (Schlee 1989; Sobania 1980), which enable people to share food. Since there is never any clear boundary between these ethnic communi-ties, the threat of ecological turmoil is very much a problem for all of them, a threat present since ancient times. In this respect, similar to the Nayeche story, the performance of Sepenya historical tradition can be seen in part as a political strategy and moral response to the problem of famine, raiding, and the uncertainties of living in a dry environment.

In the dry zone, important social interactions are revealed, modeled by traditional heroes. The Jie and various other communities almost live their lives as the stories that are told. Listening to the biographical tales of people enabled me to glimpse at the forms of Nayeche and Sepenya stories, where the central concern is survival. An examination of the forms of popular biographical narratives illustrates how individuals might unconsciously use historical traditions in them, and shows how their structures are analogously worked into real life events and personages. I recorded over twenty biographical narratives among the Jie, Turkana, Elmolo, Gabra, Rendille, and Changille from northern Kenya.[34] I list some of these oral sources in part 4, and their transcriptions are in my possession. I will consider here some of these stories. They are mostly actual stories of conflict and survival, which occurred within the memory of living people. In these biographical narratives, we find traditional heroes or heroines reenacted in the depiction of real life circumstances. In these stories, we find real life versions of familial conflicts, found in historical traditions. The biographical narratives express certain elements or phases of life that are depicted in historical traditions, but always within the discourse of contemporary lives. Similar to historical traditions, the biographical narratives raise the question of how traditional models might be used in constructing personal identity in a hostile family situation in which individuals are trying to survive. Again, in the case of the biographical narratives, the question is posed not at the level of myth, but at the level of real life situations.

In the biographical narratives of certain people of recent times, we can see more visibly a working basis of archetypal themes. The stories surrounding some of the real biographical characters, even though recent and contemporary, are simultaneously ancient, as they express the characteristics of the ancient historical traditions and mythological themes. Thus, we see the projection of historical traditions into real life situations where real people experience ecological disasters and political turmoil and wander in search of water and food. At the heart of both recent biographical narratives and ancient historical traditions are philosophical premises and political ideations that are saturated in mythic images. The portrayals of Nacham[35] and Koryang's[36] respective journeys, Apesa-Arengan's[37] conflict with his brother, Nakol's[38] conflict with his father, with their correspondences to the experiences of Lepiiso[39] among the Elmolo, and Edapal[40] among the Turkana are replete with mythic images. These images, in turn, are compatible with the mythic images of Orwakol, Lodiny, Nayeche, or Sepenya's world orders as expressed in various traditions. The story of Nayeche is never about her biography, as is often concluded by observers. Rather her story and its variants are more than a biography, even though it tells a phase of her life, that is, her departure from her home, her journey, her settlement around the Tarash River, and her death.

What is remarkable about the story of Nayeche is that it tells about famine, hunger and thirst, and family conflict and dispersal in a discursive way. These lives unfold in the unpredictable dry environment in the full perfection of the discourse, which involves biographical thinking (Bakhtin 1980). Thus, although the story includes biography, it is more than biography. Although it tells us something about the biography of a particular person, it enables the Jie people to comprehend their historical reality. The figure of Nayeche as a daughter is like that of a marriageable daughter. The wild-fruit-gathering daughter at the height of famine, hunger, and thirst is a frequently occurring phenomenon, and the visible expression of many popular biographies. Whether Nayeche depicts archaically the classically experienced situations or not, the journey of Nayeche and her search for water and wild fruit has symbolic value that is rich with meaning. The nature of Nayeche's journey is conceived from biographies of contemporary people. The popular biography of Koryang, for example, who lived within the memory of living people, is depicted as a wild-fruit-gathering daughter at the height of a great famine, and is seen to embody this thematic image of Nayeche's biography.

Koryang was a poor girl who was mistreated by her family members. The portrayal of Koryang in the biographical narrative is one of a reasonable young woman who attempts to gather wild fruit to help herself and her family to survive in a famine situation. Her ungrateful parents accuse her of sleeping with warriors and chase her away. Koryang wanders in the Lopetei bush and finally settles under a wild fig tree in Kacheri. This biographical narrative resembles a variant of a Nayeche story in which Nayeche's parents and her brothers chase her away during a famine while she is trying to survive. The journey of Koryang to Maaru Hill in search of wild fruit is not a mere biographical memory, but rather is laden with emotion, articulating universally felt experiences of the people in the region. Koryang's search for food speaks to the general experiences of people and, as such, it is part of the popular biographies of all time. The plot, which Koryang's story embodies, is discursive and immediately understandable within certain hidden cultural and historical connections; it also has its implicit connection with the story of Nayeche.

In the thematic images of the narrative, it is apparent that Koryang's behavior is approved of, but that of her unreasonable parents is condemned. The persistent appearance of famine and the need for survival create irresolvable conflict within the family. This marks the separation of Koryang, who is mistreated by her family. The story of Koryang repeats the journey of Nayeche in real life action, abandoning her family and starting her own life in Kacheri, in a faraway place. When she goes to Kacheri, she gets married and becomes a successful farmer and refuses to return. This actualizes Nayeche's paradigmatic journey at a personal level. Koryang as a famine victim disappears and she survives. Her reemergence in the bush as a successful farmer imitates the actions of Nayeche and situates her identity with this heroine as closely as possible.

Let us examine the biographical narrative of Nacham, another renowned real life personage, who was regarded as a hero and became famous for having established Kacheri as a farming community. Similarly to Koryang's story, Nacham's heroic journey begins at the height of famine and prolonged drought. The mythic image surrounding the journey of Nacham parallels the journey of Nayeche. In fact, anyone listening to the story of Nacham being recounted by storytellers would be hard pressed not to notice the presence of characteristically Nayeche-related elements. The portrayal of Nacham's journey by various storytellers is replete with mythic images, which are compatible with the historical tradition of Nayeche's world order. Like Nayeche, he creates a new society. While Nayeche emphasizes the pastoralist identity of the society, Nacham's success in Kacheri emphasizes its agriculturalist identity, highlighting its importance for survival.

In some way Nacham is identical on the one hand to Nayeche, the emblem of the famine victim who was rescued by the mythic bull Engiro and survived; on the other hand, he is similar to Orwakol, an archetype, equipped with a mythical biography. Like Orwakol, Nacham makes new fire and distributes sorghum to his people in Kacheri. What we see in the biography of Nacham is a mythicization of an actual person. Nacham, the protagonist of popular Jie biographies, becomes famous for his courage. His historical existence is unquestionable, and people believe his historical journey to Kacheri was around 1950. People also know that he died in 1999. Nacham's personality entered the popular biographies during his lifetime.

In 1996, I had an opportunity to record Nacham's autobiography depicting his admirable success in creating a new society and transforming the site of his arrival into a shrine. When he was a young man, a British colonial officer gave him a gun. It was this gun that he flung over his shoulder and then wandered in the bush in search of food until he reached the Lomuton River in Kacheri. There, he drank water from a well and tasted the soil. Finding the soil fertile, Nacham decided to settle there and grow sorghum. After seeing Nacham's success, a British missionary assisted him and helped him establish an experimental farm there. When people saw Nacham's sorghum fields, they migrated to Kacheri. Kacheri grew in size and the people who migrated there became Ngikacherian.

Even with its real chronology, dates, events, and real people, the story of Nacham is full of mythic allusions. The story of Nacham is a story of a courageous young man who created a modern farming community. This has a significant meaning that can only be revealed via its connection to myth.

Nacham brought about decisive changes to Jie society during the last twenty to thirty years. Through his connection with missionaries, he linked the Jie economy to the outside world. Because of the influence of the European market, experimental farming applications in areas of mechanization, fertilizers, and selective agricultural breeding, Jie farming has achieved unprecedented levels of success. Nacham had repeated the success of the historical character Nayeche celebrated in Jie historical traditions. During his lifetime, the story of Nacham's historic accomplishments were shaped by the refining action of mythicization. The emergence of Kacheri as a distinct farming community became a part of the popular biographical memories, kindling the poetic imagination of the storytellers. It is remarkable that the collective memory did not preserve the personal and historical elements of Nacham's biography. Yet when I interviewed him, he gave me a detailed account of his journey to Kacheri with relevant dates and chronologies.

When we compare the storytellers' accounts of Nacham with the story of Nayeche, we can see the transformation of a live person into an ancestor and the fusion of individual into archetypal category. The lack of details and specific dates in people's memories of Nacham, in a certain sense, signifies his identification with the impersonal archetype of an ancestor in numerous historical traditions. The story of Nacham takes us to the core of the heroic image where we find the equilibrium of two frequently occurring states: prolonged famine and the certainty of survival, which characterizes lives in this vast dry zone. When the storytellers speak of Nacham, they speak of a folkloric hero, a fearless hunter, and the great farmer who rescued people from hunger and death. Nacham thus embodies something of the venerable past and recent hero, evoking an immemorial image.

Another interesting biographical narrative that reveals the elements of oral historical tradition is the story of Nakol and his father, from the Orwakol clan, living in Rengen. The story transpires during a long dry summer when Nakol decides not to give any more of his cattle to his father. Nakol's father is portrayed as an unreasonable man, abusing his traditional authority. Nakol, on the other hand, is portrayed as a reasonable son, a successful raider, who accumulates many head of cattle. However, his father uses these cattle as bride-price to marry many wives. The relationship between Nakol and his father becomes sour and conflict flares up between the two in the kraals. This conflict situation sets the tone of the biographical narrative, and draws upon the motif of abuse of authority by older brothers and fathers. These are some of the persistent themes in Jie historical traditions, which often culminate in irresolvable conflicts. In many ways, the conflict between Nakol and his father is a repetition of conflicts introduced by the ancestral families. The narrative of this conflict is intricately distilled from the historical tradition recounting Orwakol's abuse of his authority and Lodiny's eventual separation.

What the story of Nakol and his father does is to illustrate fathers' temptations to abuse traditional authority and their sons' rebellion. Rebellion against abusive authority figures is a common reaction to this traditional dilemma. Young men are often inspired by the persistent desire to free themselves from their traditional obligations to submit to the authority of elders. As the storyteller composes this biographical narrative, he uncovers the personal problem inherent in the traditional authority of fathers over their sons. Is Nakol's father unreasonable in appropriating the cattle that his son has amassed through risky cattle raiding? Does he have the right to use his son's cattle to marry many wives? In contrast, is Nakol justified in rebelling against his cattle-monger father?

The thematic image of the narrative reflects the disruption and degeneration of a father-son relationship over cattle. The covetous father provokes his son, and the son rashly confronts his father, in violation of the Jie convention of respect for paternal authority. His father responds to him by reminding him how he cared for him as a child, feeding him with the milk and blood of his own cattle, an image that demands irresistible obligation and submission. Clearly, the words of

Nakol's father have the traditional power to unsettle the enraged son, but Nakol is determined to take his cattle and separate from his family. The theme of separation threatens the Jie familial conventions and tradition itself. This is poignantly exemplified in Orwakol's and Lodiny's kinship relations.

Nakol's final decision to separate and settle in Kacheri fragments the family, which leads his father to deny him of the right to use his *amachar* (cattle brand), a powerful symbol that unites the family herd, affording sanction against any possible transgression that might disrupt that unity. Hence, Nakol's action in the face of his father's provocation does run counter to tradition. The resentment and the outbreak of separation are attributed to Nakol's refusal to submit to parental authority because he recognizes his father's abuse of traditional authority. This recognition causes him to confront the father rather than ignore him. Eventually Nakol's actions lead to the very thing a son must avoid: the fragmentation of the family and the family herd.

The details of Nakol's conflict with his father are recalled in great detail, and remain intact, as if a haunting memory. But Nakol's life outside of this particular conflict, it seems, does not matter. Whatever memories there were of his life outside this conflict have vanished; only the memory of his conflict with his father during a prolonged famine is, it seems, of a true occurrence. There may have been other details that preceded that particular conflict during that hot summer, important in their own ways, but they had not seemed so to Lodoch, who recounted the story of the conflict. Nakol's conflict with his father was a special event for Lodoch, like a long awaited event in which the conflict between Orwakol and Lodiny were made apparent. There might have been other difficulties during that summer; and many people may have died and vanished in the bush, but they were not remembered. The incident of Nakol and his father, however, flourished in the popular memories of the people. It was not important what preceded the conflict or what happened afterwards because the conflict between Nakol and his father took over the memory and made that event the most remembered happening of the dry summer of a long ago. It alone moved Lodoch to appreciate his relationship with his father.

In another popular biographical narrative, we see the problems of traditional authority and morality, the importance of sharing resources as well as various survival strategies during famine. This particular biography involves a conflict between Aonyot[41] and his older brother. The story begins with Aonyot's mistreatment by his older brother, which clearly had a disturbing implication for Logwee, the Jie storyteller who recounted the story to me. The story, in many ways, is about the testing of traditional kinship relations during a prolonged famine situation and the importance of helping one another to survive. The story addresses a number of socially accepted moral standards of behaviors, with various implications during a time of famine when survival becomes a pressing issue. Various features of this morality tale also illuminate how kinship obligations may be unsettled by famine situations, and how morally proper behavior is necessary for survival and success in such times. The story shows how one can be assured of survival through sharing food and cooperating with others. Refusal to share and cooperate can only result in conflict and suffering. In addition, the story also illustrates how Aonyot's personal morality led to success against all odds.

Aonyot suffered from hunger, yet his older brother, with many cattle, refused to help him. In the end, Aonyot is rewarded with success and wealth, causing jealousy in his evil older brother who dies at the end. The storyteller portrays Aonyot as a reasonable younger brother who struggles to survive. His stealing food is defined as a reasonable behavior under the circumstances. Aonyot is an ideal young man: he steals cattle without killing anyone, marries the woman who helps him survive, and compensates for the ram he stole by offering a cow in its place. Hence Aonyot's success is associated with Jie proper human behavior.

The theme of Aonyot's biographical narrative appears at the beginning when his older brother tells him, "You should not come to disturb my children and you should not come to eat food." Aonyot's brother is clearly an unreasonable person and he is short on the Jie standard of morality by not accepting social responsibility toward his younger brother. In addition, Aonyot's older brother acts unwisely in not recognizing the political and economic uncertainties of living in an unpredictable environment where it is possible to be rich and lose everything or become poor and then gain riches. The plot of the narrative is framed to show how sharing scarce resources and cooperation are the only basis for survival.

At the beginning of the tale, Aonyot's situation is desperate. With the help of a woman, he is forced to steal a ram for his sustenance. His brother's wife secretly gives him some vegetables to eat. The behaviors of these two women are portrayed as ideal representatives of Jie behavior. If they are caught stealing from their own families to assist a man, it could lead anyone to believe that they are engaging in some deceit and treachery. The course of the events however will eventually show that what they are doing is right.

The storyteller carefully builds the plot of the tale to demonstrate that although the hungry man who steals to survive seems to be dishonest, he is in fact honest. Stealing cattle without harming or killing anyone is a virtue. Aonyot takes the stolen cattle to his friend in Nakapelimoru, and his friend assists him, as a friend should. After another successful cattle raid, Aonyot drives the cattle again to his friend's home and tells him, "I will marry the girl who helped me." This is most admirable behavior. Such a proposal is the proper recognition of help for what one receives among the Jie. By marrying this girl he can build an ideal family.

The next episode describes the marriage arrangements between Aonyot and the father of the girl. Here we see how the ideal behavior of the generous girl is contrasted with her opportunist father. While the father believes Aonyot to be a thief, he immediately rules him out as a possible suitor, but he changes his tune upon hearing about Aonyot's cattle wealth. Then he anxiously promises his daughter in exchange for cattle. He becomes even happier when he receives a cow for his stolen ram. At the end of the story, the theme of the plot fully develops. The moral of the tale surfaces explicitly when Aonyot becomes the richest man in Najie, marries nine women, and has many children while his brother dies of jealousy, regretting his improper behavior.

The preceding analysis allows us to see parallels between historical tradition and biographical narrative. But which came first, the historical traditions or the biographical narratives? Is the story of Nayeche the result of biographical thinking or vice versa?

This question becomes even more urgent when we reflect on the parallels between historical traditions and folktales, which enable us to go more deeply into the historical tradition genre. In these parallels, we discover the elements of the fictional points: we find ourselves outside the realms of historical tradition and biography, where ancestral memories reside and flourish, yet simultaneously inside. It is in these parallels that we see the possible fusion of biographical memories, the ancient mythic worlds of historical tradition, and the fictional world of folktales. Reflections on these seemingly separate yet parallel worlds show how the thematic images of good and evil in historical traditions are so intertwined, not only with biographic memory images but also with the fictional world of animals found in folktales. Reflections on these parallel worlds lead us into the combined fantasy and reality embodiments of historical tradition.

In the fantasy world of animals and humans, we observe that Jie folk-tales never express any biographical elements or phases of life, but rather always the nature and essence of life. Whether portrayed in classically idealized form or otherwise, the actions of animals or humans in folk-tales have, above all, a symbolic value: in them, we find ideal moral values and lessons to be learned in life. Their very nature removes folk-tales from biographical or historical relationships. Yet, thematic images of the folktale characters are surrounded by, and evoke, an aura of his-torical tradition and biographical narrative. This is so, not for any ac-countable historical and biographical reasons, but rather because of their discernible and clearly recurring themes of conflict resolution over food and scarce resources, which are common to the plots of both his-torical traditions and biographical narratives. The key to folktales is the transformation of images into social models, which reveal the theme. As Scheub (1998, 130) suggests, the storytellers manipulate the images of oral tradition and create new models to comment on the real world. Models constructed from the fantastic world of the folktales flow into the cultural discourse from which the members of society are judged.

My analysis of the thematic images of folktales shows how human experiences are analogously worked into the fictional experiences of folktale characters. I recorded thirty-five folktales of the Jie, Turkana, and Elmolo peoples. For this analysis, I considered twelve of these. All of them are popularly known stories, and they express certain ele-ments of the social life of the people, but always within the discourse of the world of animals. Similar to historical traditions and biographical narratives, they are used as models in constructing personal identity in an unpredictable dry environment or a hostile social situation where fictional or real characters are trying to survive. The models in the case of the folktales are represented at the level of parody and fiction, but always in the context of life situations.

In the folktales, we can see the basis of ordinary social situations. The stories surrounding some of the folktale characters, even though fic-tional, are simultaneously real, contemporary, and ancient as they ex-press the characteristics of the ancient historical traditions and fictional themes. In the context of the folktale storytelling, the worlds of humans and animals come together to create a fabulous reality (Scheub 1969). When these parallel yet separate worlds merge, unexpected conflict oc-curs and fantasy and reality mesh, creating disharmony in the process.

Similar to historical traditions, the plots of Jie and Turkana folktales depend largely on the drama of conflict resolution, which provides the imaginative raw materials from which the storytellers develop the themes of their stories. This conflict resolution is dialogically worked out in the narrative plot and formulated by the storytellers and the members of the audience anew at each performance. Skillful storytellers bring the complex network of images together as they develop the themes in each performance.

Characters of folktales, like the characters in historical traditions or biographical narratives, are often threatened by hunger and thirst, and they are forced to cooperate and share resources for survival. The storytellers use the animal characters to create proper models for human behavior and moral standards for harmonious society. That is perhaps why the moral standards of the animals are tested when the everyday patterns of life are threatened by prolonged drought, famines, hunger, and thirst.

It is not surprising to see the themes of folktales, historical traditions, and biographical narratives arising from similar conditions. The themes and plots of folktales resemble the types of images in historical traditions and biographical narratives so much so that we must consider them as related. The fantasy of the folktales emerges from the shared discourse of the animal world where the stereotypical attributes of animals define certain human states and affairs. In all of these states, the hold on the moral standard of sociality becomes loosened in folktales, and all the unacceptable treachery, cunning, and deception streams out allegorically through the narrative plot into human consciousness during performances allowing conclusions to be drawn regarding the contemporary world. It is therefore possible that the themes and images of historical traditions, too, make their appearances in much the same way as the manifestations of the fictional world into the real life situations of the contemporary world. The storytellers create these fantastic realms of folktales with their attendant paradigms to judge human society. The folktale images often move the members of the audience into emotion-laden realms during the course of performance to exploit the traditional meanings. The plot of folktale becomes a trope during performances, as Scheub (1998) writes, in which the storyteller and the audience members work together to rearrange traditional images for new connotations and meanings.

These new connotations and meanings intrude into the flow of the contemporary world as they do into the mythical world of the ancestors during the performances of historical traditions; for instance, the wandering of Napeikisina[42] is a thematic image parallel if not exactly the same to the wandering of Nayeche. The wandering of Napeikisina speaks about the theme of rejection, but in the world of the folktale it challenges the fantasy of survival and success as depicted in the case of Nayeche. It challenges the assumption that the rejected one will survive and will eventually reenter society. While in the historical traditions Nayeche becomes a hero, in the folktale Napeikisina becomes the evil trickster.

Unlike historical tradition, the plot of the folktale does not proceed from a fantasy of survival to eventual success; it tells a different version of the story of the rejected person. It comments on the wretched experiences of the forlorn wandering of the rejected person until her eventual death and, in so doing, it challenges the redemptive theme of the rejected person becoming a hero of survival stories. Napeikisina, for example, turns the story of heroic success upside down and tells us about the experiences of becoming a trickster and how a trickster behaves toward the society that denies her access to it.

Napeikisina, the one-breasted villain trickster, often appears on the Jie and Turkana cultural scene to disrupt harmony. The storytellers and audience members work out the images that characterize Napeikisina in her appearances, and embellish the story with diverse meanings. Napeikisina, like the despicable hyena and the cunning rabbit, represents the negative trickster character of the Jie and Turkana oral traditions, and her negative activities disrupt society rather profoundly. Thus, the various themes found in the performances that feature Napeikisina deploy the various representations of the evil trickster found in the artistic traditions of the Jie and the Turkana people.

The one-breasted Napeikisina is a cannibal who loves to eat human flesh. As a cannibal, she is not a part of Jie society. She has one long breast, which occasionally hinders her movement, but despite this she can move faster than most people. Napeikisina, who was once an innocent child, lost her innocence, and thus her humanity, when she was deceived and rejected and made fun of by her friends with whom she went to gather *ngalebulebwo* (a kind of wild fruit). With her one breast she is less than perfect, living at the margins of society because of her desire for human flesh. She always tries to become a part of society, but her desire for human flesh constantly frustrates her, and keeps her from achieving her aspirations, hindering her from meeting even basic human standards.[43]

Napeikisina and her actions inform multiple themes as she transforms herself from a gourd, to a fish, to a feather, to a human. The transformative power of Napeikisina lies in her ghastly confrontation of innocent people whom she tricks. She often confronts her victims in remote desolate places where there is no help. There, she frightens and victimizes people. In most performances Napeikisina pays dearly for her inhumane treatment of people: when she falls asleep or becomes distracted, her victims successfully escape and she herself becomes a victim and drowns in a river, or gets abandoned in a desolate place, or drops dead on the back of a hyena who is defecating from fright.

In most performances Napeikisina appears in guises familiar to people, and her evil tricks unfold in contexts known alike to the storytellers and the audience: on the dusty road, in abandoned kraals, in homesteads, in villages, on the banks of rivers. In these familiar settings, people encounter the evil trickster creature, Napeikisina, masquerading and disguising herself in various forms.

Performances of Napeikisina stories usually open up with ordinary scenes; children are weeding gardens or young girls are gathering fruit. While the children are weeding, Napeikisina's blind child watches the children. Similar to historical traditions, here we have an example of the subtle contradictions found in these stories. On the surface Napeikisina is the trusted aunt, as an aunt should be, but in truth she is a cannibal and she should not be trusted. Napeikisina's child is blind, but she is able to watch the children weed the garden. It is crucial to understand the contradictory nature of Napeikisina to note how unrecognizable evil can emerge unexpectedly in a context familiar to the storyteller and audience. In one of the variants of the Napeikisina stories, she transforms herself into an abandoned beautiful child in a ditch and tricks a woman into getting rid of her own child. This speaks not only to the evil nature of Napeikisina, but also to the inhumanity of the mother who lives in the society. Here we have interesting contrasting fates: in the historical tradition, the ancestral uncle or older brother figure mistreats the younger kin; in the folktale the mother throws her own child. At another time, Napeikisina transforms herself into a child, but this time steadfastly attaches herself to the head covering of a man who tries to help her.

Sometimes the storytellers bring together the hyena, another evil and despicable creature that threatens human society, with Napeikisina. In these stories, they both end up destroying each other from fear; the evil hyena becomes frightened when Napeikisina attaches herself to it, and as it begins to run it defecates from fear and finally drops dead with Napeikisina on its back.

In depicting the animal and human characters in the folktales, the storytellers focus on the nature of the villain and evil rather than on the animals themselves (Scheub 1969). Since it is the character of evil with which the performer and the members of the audience are concerned, the hyena and the fox become an extension of Napeikisina when they deny eating the child. A child ignores the advice of his father, and takes his cattle to a faraway place and is devoured by the hyena. The wickedness of the hyena and the fox is allegorically transmitted to the child when the father of the child gathers the bones of the hyena from the fire and the bones of the child and puts them together in the gourd to bring the child back to life. By churning the bones of the child with the bones of the hyena, the father mixes the child with the wickedness of the hyena.[44]

The mixing of the bones characterizes a struggle between good and evil. The folktale plot moves the positive father figure character into relationship with the negative child character. As the child disobeys the father and moves into a distant alien place, the plot of the story unfolds, the pattern is disrupted, and the good and the evil become unified. The attendant traditional emotions of "sympathy" and "revulsion" (Scheub 1969) toward the father and child become interwoven and interact. The good father and the bad son images feed into emotions having to do with the timeless struggle between affines that are embroiled together in the story. The narrative plot that deploys these contradictory emotions sustains the mixed emotions expressed between Orwakol and Lodiny in historical traditions, and these emotions become strengthened in such a way that they become the felt experience in the folktale.

The folktale of the child who did not listen to his father, and became eaten by the despicable hyena, uses the theme of conflict between kin and the attendant emotions of sympathy and revulsion, which are the major means of arranging the materials of historical tradition. In Jie folktales, the hyena is always evil and grotesque: it eats rotten human flesh, so that the very introduction of such an animal image into the performance ensures that the members of the audience will know the broad significance implied in ignoring the advice of a father.

The performer thus blurs the boundary between human and animal, between good and evil, and between revulsion and sympathy, showing how humans can become like the hyena. In this story, the performer emphasizes sympathy for the father and revulsion for the child who ignores the father's advice. Although the child possesses the evil capacity of the hyena, the father is equally bad to exact revenge on his son and transform him into a hyena. The father's metaphoric fusion of the child with the hyena indicates the father's evil punishment of his son, which parallels Orwakol's unreasonable treatment of Lodiny in some historical traditions, and that of Nakol's father's abuse of his traditional authority while dealing with his son, or Aonyot's older brother in dealing with Aonyot.

The members of the audiences are familiar with these contradictory images, and concentrate on the thematically significant tensions expressing contradictory relationships. It is in the arrangement of these familiar images that the storytellers bring fictional experiences into metaphorical relationship with the real world, through their proximity in meaning and implication, as expressed in historical traditions and biographical narratives. In the folktales, the realistic processes of historical traditions extend into emotion-laden fantasy images of the folktales, as the storytellers systematically reorganize the familiar images to construct meanings. Take, for example, the fundamental need for sharing food and resources for survival as expressed in historical traditions, and how such common topics are elaborated in the performances of Jie folktales. If refusal to share resources causes conflict in real life situation as depicted in historical traditions and biographical narratives, the cunning employment of trickery to steal food and water create similar results in the world of the animals in folktales. The desire to steal and the destructive nature of stealing becomes the counterpart of the greed and the refusal to share in historical traditions and biographical narratives, and, thus, a part of being evil. The rabbit's cunning ways in stealing food and water for which it does not work is also symbolic of the human inclination toward evil, which includes the venerable ancestors when they become greedy, amassing cattle, refusing to share resources, and mistreating their close kin.

In the folktale, the cunning rabbit becomes a representation of a person's inhumanity toward society, when it is caught while stealing food from a garden or water from a well for which it did not work. Equally bad is the action of the turtle, which is lured to cooperate with the cunning rabbit in stealing the water, water for which it refused to work, from the well that other animals cooperated to build.[45] Interestingly, we find that good and evil are not mutually exclusive categories in these stories. For example, the turtle's final capturing of the cunning rabbit in the act of stealing is not motivated by his desire to protect the common resources of society from the thief, but rather his desire to exact revenge on the thief who betrayed him after the turtle had cooperated with the rabbit in stealing the water. Hence, the turtle himself is a part of evil, yet was trusted by the society. They are both cunning and evil as they both try to get something for nothing. And they are both as intertwined in their evil actions as are Napeikisina and the evil hyena.[46] While the rabbit is caught, the turtle is not.

Thus, in the manifestation of Napeikisina's many evil characters and in the actions of animals in various stories, the Jie conception of evil becomes apparent. It is in this complex manifestation that the basic recurrent themes of the Jie and Turkana folktales can be located.

The evil nature of humanity is expressed through the manifestation of Napeikisina's symbolism, but good is also reflected both figuratively and literally. Sometimes good and evil are intertwined and seen as inseparable. For instance, the blind child of Napeikisina informs the children about the cannibalistic schemes of her mother and saves. them from being slaughtered and eaten.[47] Good is almost always portrayed in performances, which depict cooperation in positive actions. Figuratively, sometimes good arises from evil, which means evil itself is capable of positive results and action. So we see that in spite of rabbit's uncooperative behavior, other animals worked together and dug a well.

In the same way, all the animals cooperate with the father of the child who was eaten to find the culprits, the fox and the hyena, that ate the child.[48] And sometimes, even nature responds to the plea of innocents who are being persecuted by evil. For instance, the river responds to the plea of the children and saves them by opening for them an escape path from the evil Napeikisina.[49] The blind vulture, with the despicable habit of eating rotten flesh, mirroring that of the evil hyena, helps the wives of the elephant to catch the culprit fox, who cunningly killed their husband.[50] In the same way the children saved themselves from being eaten by the evil Napeikisina through their own wit and cunning. So we see that, similarly to good, evil action also requires cooperation. All the animals and birds cooperated with the bat and carried out a successful raid against the wish of Akuj (God).[51] In the folktale, it is the bat that goes off to raid cattle; however, in reality it is people who raid cattle, and thus the performer blurs the distinction between human and animal, rendering such distinctions irrelevant. And the tree cooperates with Akuj's wish and frees the cattle from the evil actions of the raiders. So we see the themes of the real life images superimposed in folktale fantasy images. The interaction of the historical tradition, biographical narratives, and folktale images together convey the universally felt emotions having to do with good and bad images.

Even though evil seems to be a necessary part of the society, people are always able to fight against it and defeat it. When Nayeche is rejected, the gray bull Engiro assists her to survive in the wilderness and leads her to the sources of food and water. When Aonyot's older brother mistreats him, the wife of the evil brother helps him survive. The images of good and evil found in Jie and Turkana performances epitomize the basic concept of human relations centered around conflict resolution. The cunning rabbit eats the crops of the hard working farmer, but in the end is defeated, becomes food, and is eaten.[52] The ungrateful baboon steals food from the honey badger, which generously shares her food with it, and then becomes victim to the attack of swarming bees.[53]

The evil Napeikisina reflects both good and evil, and the deceitful baboon both gluttony and generosity. The fabulous world and the real human world, fantasy and imagination are all embodied in tradition and dialogically worked out between the storytellers and the members of the audience during performances. The storytellers unfold the good and evil embodied in their tradition. Conflicts and their resolutions form the basic plot of the stories and are conveyed in performances that reflect the human desire for cooperation, sharing, and the respecting of others' resources; it is this which ensures order and harmony in society. In fact, most Jie performances, through the artful manipulation of images, articulate the basic human desire to achieve harmony and order in society. Conflict usually reveals the presence of disruptive forces, such as the deceptive rabbit, the hyena, the fox, the gluttonous baboon, and evil Napeikisina. The resolution of conflict brings harmony and restores order and equilibrium.

The performer weaves fantastic and realistic images to reveal the themes of morality in conflict resolution. The images of the Jie and Turkana stories reflect the necessity for an ideal society free from evil and disorder. To establish social equilibrium, stories thematically emphasize adherence to tradition. The performers portray resolutions of conflict between animals in the realm of traditional order, which society struggles to achieve and uphold. While the tricks of Napeikisina and the hyena are disturbing, they are not important, and the chaos and disorder they bring about are passing. They have no power to cause permanent disruption. The cunning tricks of Napeikisina, the rabbit, the fox, and the hyena may play significant roles in disrupting harmony and threatening survival in a difficult environment, but the power of the evil is seen as transitory. Even when the evil Napeikisina, the grotesque hyena, the cunning rabbit, the gluttonous baboon, and the fox continuously disrupt the society, the traditions handed down from generation to generation bring about harmony in Scheub's sense of these terms (1969, 169). The evil forces are always neutralized or defeated by their own evil. From this perspective, evil forces roiling contemporary Jie society will eventually be defeated and harmony re-established. Modernizing forces will be tamed and a readjusted society will be harmonious.

4 The Jie Landscape, Memory, and Historical Tradition

To fully understand the Jie historical tradition, it is necessary to appreciate the beauty, the poetry, and the symbolism of their landscape, and the metaphors, rhythms, and patterns of the lives unfolding within that landscape. Landscape and the memories it contains are a major feature of Jie historical tradition. Jie storytellers cultivate memory images that are embedded or captured in their landscape. What really fascinates the storytellers is that Najie is not just a geographical space, but a world full of memories. Najie's landscape speaks to the Jie storytellers, in that they absorb its beauty into their inner world and they receive the wisdom of the ancient ancestors from these places. Landscape is an important resource for the storytellers, not only in describing the mythical ancestral world, but also in talking about the contemporary changes people experience. That ancient image of the shores of the ancestral world stands apart from the contemporary imperfect world and in some ways becomes artistically and poetically articulated during performances of historical tradition.

Throughout history, Jie storytellers have been inspired by the layers of past and present epochs they have seen scattered and inscribed in the landscape of Najie. Landscape as a major feature of Jie historical tradition references the past during performances, and the ubiquity of Jie landscape is reflected in the multiple and cumulative representations of past events in poetic performances. The diverse representations of memories of place in Najie by storytellers during their performances have etched compelling stories of famines and feasts into the reservoir of historical tradition. In these performances, the Jie storytellers shape the contours of Jie geography and places of remembered memory for their critical interpretative purposes. This chapter will examine the poetic engagement between story, memory, and landscape as well as investigate how memory engages with landscape in the performances of historical traditions.

How do we examine the engagement of memory and landscape during performance or the engagement of historical tradition with memory and landscape? Various works have attempted to provide answers to the kind of question I pose in this chapter. Some recent studies on the tangible features and physical remnants of cultural memory on the landscape have focused on how political elites fix the remnants of the past for selective interpretation. These arguments generally invoke Hobsbawm and Ranger's formulation of "invention of tradition" (Hobsbawm and Ranger 1983), suggesting the presence of an invented knowable past. According to Herzfeld (1991, 24 [also see Spear 2003]), the problem with this approach is that we cannot reliably know which history is invented and which is not. Herzfeld interprets Greek memory embodied in the urban landscape as not simply a unilateral phenomenon immune to contestation. When, for example, various state authorities negotiate their sense of place, they seek to incorporate the power of the past emanating in the physical spaces into their own structures of authority and political process, as they redefine the forms of tradition and history (Herzfeld 1991, 14). For Herzfeld, negotiations are often animated in the writings of novelists and poets referring to cultural memories of place.

In a similar work, Richard Flores (2002) argues that the past inscribed in the landscape cannot be recalled without reference to heroes of the past. The actions of heroes that transpired in the physicality of place evoke different meanings when they are recalled. The memories about the actions of heroes surrounding the physical remnants of the past influence the actions of the social and political actors of the present. Flores's argument can be extended to the way Jie storytellers recall the actions of their heroes who once lived in the land and left their traces on the physicality of the landscape.

For Guiomar (1989, 193), memory of place refers to those aspects of memory that exist in the details of narrative entanglement with geographical place. When Guiomar considers how France is remembered through the grand narrative of Vidal de la Blache, a French historian and geographer, he explores how la Blache's narratives of remembering are entangled with France's landscape and its national discourse. Similar to Guiomar, Pierre Nora (1989) examines how the place of memory is constructed from the complex interplay of memory, place, and history, "when memory crystallizes and secretes itself ... at a particular historical moment" (1989, 8). The most fundamental purpose of memory of place, says Nora, "is to stop time, to block the work of forgetting" (1989, 7). It is this kind of understanding of memory and place that fascinates Nora. The interplay between memory and place has, Nora insists, its center in the mythic experience of people. Whenever memory and history intersect in a place, there is a move "to the undifferentiated time of heroes, origin and myth" (1989, 8). For Nora (1989, 11), memory and place are the keys to a "laboratory of past mentalities." I agree.

In this chapter I draw principally from the work of Flores, Guiomar, Herzfeld, Nora, and various others (Cunnison 1950; Halbwachs 1950; Lefebvre 1974 [1984]; Slyomovics 1998), to examine how Najie and its history are entangled with Najie's geography as well as how these entanglements are sorted out by storytellers' representation of them. The Jie oral storytelling genre of historical tradition is not of a fictional tale but rather it is a collection of narratives of "remembered memory" deeply grounded in folkloric motifs (Mirzeler 2004). The thematic images of historical tradition are the images of real events of famines, dispersals, and feasts that combine to express people's sense of their past embodied in the landscape. A thoughtful consideration of the interplay of memory, landscape, and history is not a matter of sorting fact from fiction, but rather is one of exploring how cultural memory and history are entangled in particular places. Because memory inscribes places with meaning (Flores 2002; Herzfeld 1991; Nora 1989; Slyomovics 1998), it is necessarily involved with social and political relations, which, in their turn, enhance historical discourse with certain evidence and interpretations. As discourse, the interplay between memory and landscape is available through the performance of historical tradition, and, therefore, it is a part of the *eemut* genre, a blend of historical tradition and cultural memory. The Jie landscape is a part of historical discourse, entangled with memory and, consequently, it participates in the production of historical tradition.

Ancient Najie's landscape arouses memories through its massive historical tradition. Certain spaces in Najie's geography are preserved and marked out by its present inhabitants. In their performances, the storytellers often draw on the sensation of these places and their former inhabitants. Such places are part of the historical tradition. Frequently, memories about these places are assigned evidentiary value, not only because they document and seal collective and individual rights, but also because they embody memories about past conflicts over resources that have given rise to those rights. These rights are negotiated anew at each performance. In these performances, skillful storytellers transport the members of the audience away from the disturbing present day and into the realm of the ancestral world, which is embodied in landscape. Because landscape imbues the act of remembering, it is also involved in the formation of identities, as Flores (2002), Herzfeld (1991), Slyomovics (1998) and Basso (1995) attest. The Jie storytellers refer to memories embodied in the landscape, entangled with both good and bad times in history, and the geography of Najie is instructive for the way storytellers construct their historical images. The storytellers' poetic references to the landscape invoke the established themes of Jie culture as they guide people's imagination through the interplay between past and present, the fabulous world of the ancestors and the tainted contemporary world.

With its hills and winding seasonal rivers, Najie is not merely a geographical space where the social lives of the Jie unfold, but it is the place where collective memory is located. Jie historical traditions and places are rooted epistemologically in what happened in the past in certain places. Symbolic imaginary realms convey the order of the ancestral world and place emanates memories saturated with nostalgia. For Herzfeld (1991, 66), nostalgia "is a key strategy in the claims people make to cultural legitimacy." The memories of the original ancestors embodied in the landscape are nostalgically remembered during performances as they claim legitimacy to resources. The original ancestral memories embodied in the landscape, depicted in historical tradition refers to the event of ancestral dispersal and migration around the foundational cradle lands or original settlements strewn in the landscape, places like Dongiro, Longiro River, Tarash River – the places of the myths and ceremonies, the point from which the cattle move to the kraals in the grazing land in the east and west.

Daidai, as a place of origin, for example, possesses the fundamental remembered images and themes of Jie historical traditions that imply the thick discourse of life itself, a discourse that enables the storytellers to glimpse nostalgically an ideal world order. The gray bull was found· there. It was there that gray bull fathered all the Jie cattle. It was also there that it was sacrificed and its flesh was eaten before Orwakol offered the *amachar* (cattle brand) to his sons, beneath Moru a Eker, the phallic rock (see figure 4.3), near Ebur (see figure 4.4), the pit where Losilang pounded the sorghum grain before putting them in her granary. Across

Figure 4.1: Daidai Rock, the birthplace of Jie people. Author photo (Kotiyang)

Figure 4.2: Nakapor standing behind the master granary during the performance of the harvest ritual. Author photo (Jimos village)

Figure 4.3: Moru a Eker, the phallic rock. Author photo (Jimos village)

Figure 4.4: The Ebur, where the Jie women in Jimos village pound sorghum grain, radiates a female fertility image. Author photo

Figure 4.5: The Longiro River. Author photo (Losilang)

Figure 4.6: Lokatap Rock. Author photo (Lokalodiny Territorial Division)

from Daidai, located in Jimos village, Moru a Eker and Ebur form a combined mother and father emblem around which annual sacrifices are offered. Moru a Eker, a phallic image, symbolizes the father image, the sun, the Akuj; and Ebur is the symbol of female and moon, the Ekipe, both connected and juxtaposed in Jimos village, the village of the firemaker.

The memory of the original ancestral Jie family and the divine images are embodied in Daidai, which exudes the aura of something mythic, spiritual, and historical. Daidai and its representation in various historical traditions are the basis of the complementarity of Akuj and Ekipe (male and female representation of Jie deities), the sun and the moon, sorghum and cattle, Orwakol and his seven wives and the womblike Daidai and the fertilizing masculinity of Longiro River – all of which give birth to the thick discourse of Jie historical tradition. Daidai is the primary ground, where the memory of origin is embodied and understood and from which the various themes of historical tradition emerge and speak the sentiments of vulnerability created from living in a dry environment, and the importance of interdependence and complementarity among the members of the original family. From Daidai the remembered memory images of the Jie ancestral family well up and flow into historical traditions, shaping and clarifying Jie discourse. From these remembered memory images, the Jie storytellers draw the sources of their imagination when they talk about Orwakol and Lodiny, Losilang and her granary, Engiro and its offspring, and Nayeche and her pursuit of the gray bull Engiro's footprints from Karamoja Plateau to the Tarash River in the plains of Turkana land.

Across from Daidai lies Jimos village, the natal home of Nayeche, on the southern banks of the Longiro River. Jimos village embodies the physical images of the Jie's past. In the center of Jimos village is the homestead of the firemaker, where the master granary containing the grain of the women of the seven territorial divisions rests on the wooden tripod (see figure 2.4 and figure 4.2), next to the *arii* (cattle enclosure) of Nakapor, the firemaker. On the way to this granary, lies the dry Ebur (a hollow rock) (see figure 4.4), brimming with symbols of female fertility. In the Ebur the Jie women who live in the Jimos village pound their grain as they refresh their historical memory of Losilang, who was the first woman to pound her grain in the Ebur, before putting it in her granary.

A few hundred yards west of Jimos village is the Moru a Eker (the hill of power), the phallic rock symbolizing male fertility (see figure 4.3). In the center of these two images lies the home of Nakapor, encircled with protective palisade walls, on the model of the regenerative uterus. The master granary, nestled against the palisade walls of the cattle enclosure, inside the home, contains the sorghum grains that have been nourished by the flood of the Longiro River.

The master granary is built on the model of a womb, its mouth the center of the symbolic circle of the Jie universe around which the sun is said to revolve. The plaster covering the walls of the master granary is eradicated by the wear and tear and is transparent, the same way the universe is depicted in the Jie cosmology, allowing the rays of the sun to keep the seeds of the Jie clans warm in the symbolic womb. According to the Jie storytellers, the shrines, the trees, the cattle, and the sorghum fields of all the Jie clans grow from this point. This granary is the nurturer of the Jie society. The energy of the sun penetrating its walls symbolizes the communication of the divine energy to the womb of the world. This granary is said to be the hub of the Jie universe.

During the harvesting time, the *apwela*, an indigenous small bird, which symbolizes death and sickness, is said to hover over the master granary at night, emitting lights from its anus, threatening the survival of the Jie society. This granary is in many respects the navel of the Jie world, the umbilical point, and the symbol of continuing creation. According to many Jie storytellers, the Jimos village, with its master granary, is the home of Nayeche, the daughter of Orwakol. This is the reason why, they say, the Turkana women come to Najie during the harvest time to ask for sorghum from the Jie women. When storytellers evoke the images of these places in their narratives, they immediately indicate not only what collective memory is inscribed in that space, but also the politico-religious implications of the economic resources therein, thus conflating the memory and resources at the cosmological level. Resources within the physical space seem to have no meaningful existence without the memory of events embedded within the space. In a sense, the Jie storytellers mediate the relationship between the memories and the resources of the physical spaces, referring to the memories of past famines and struggle over food in an infinite number of geographical points in Karamoja Plateau and beyond.

At the heart of the Jie historical tradition is the memory of the original Jie family who settled around Daidai and later spread out along the banks of Longiro River, the symbol of the ancient geography of Najie. The Longiro River has a prominent position in the Jie historical tradition not only because the original Jie family settled on its banks, but also because it was the muddy water of the Longiro River that attracted the gray bull Engiro, the father of all Jie cattle. The collective identity of the Jie was born and shaped by the memory of Engiro's capture by Orwakol, the first firemaker of the Jie on the banks of the Longiro River. The storytellers maintain that when the Longiro flowed through the rocky ground, it cast a gray mud color, the same as the gray bull.

At the time of writing, the Jie villages on the banks of the Longiro River were compact, juxtaposed rather than linked. Each village was established near a shrine, which provided a passage between the village and the river. Each shrine portrayed the characteristic structure of Daidai, the center and birthplace of the Jie, along the banks of Longiro River. According to Jie storytellers, during the ancestral time, each territorial division was occupied and inhabited for the purpose of growing the seeds of Orwakol, which he gave to each of his wives as a gift. That is why the contemporary *akimwaar*, the Jie harvest ritual, glorifies Orwakol and his family as the archetypal model for all creation. The ideology of *akimwaar* and its ritual structure was established by Orwakol in Daidai and Moru a Eker as the system of the annual movement of cattle from west to east. As the politico-religious leader of the Jie, Orwakol played a considerable role since he was regarded as the first firemaker. As such he was responsible for the regularity and rhythm of nature, wellness, and continuity of the entire society. This is why we can see the themes of fecundity and fertility in the symbolisms of these sacred spaces where the original sacrifices were offered. The Jie marriage ritual has its model in *akimwaar*, the harvest ritual, and in its mythic plot (Mirzeler 2004). The myth depicts the marital union between Orwakol and Losilang, his eldest wife, the night before the distribution of the sorghum seeds to his wives and the cattle brands to his sons on the banks of the Longiro River. The marital union reflected in *akimwaar* is a rite integrated with ecological rhythms, which validates the integration of the seven territorial divisions of the Jie on the plateau and the Turkana people on the plains.

The Jie people love and protect all their rivers, but they are enchanted by the Longiro River above all others. Unlike the Nangalol Apolon, and Apule Rivers, the Longiro River has, near Daidai, a granite bed with copious wells filled with water even during the long dry seasons. According to storytellers, when Orwakol came to Najie in search of water, he heard the humming sound of the Longiro River flowing from miles away. The muddy water of the Longiro River was pure and luxuriant –

a gift to the Jie from Akuj (God). That is the reason that while the Jie storytellers commemorate all the rivers in Karamoja Plateau and beyond, none is treated with greater emotion than is the Longiro.

The emotional symbolism of Longiro River as a place of memory and collective identity resonates with the symbolism elsewhere of place and memory and collective identity, ethnicity, and nationalism. Flores (2002, 17) describes how Alamo, as a place, mediates emotionally charged memory symbols key to Mexican identity and unity. In his analytical discussion of the place of memory in defining the contemporary Greek identity, Herzfeld (1991, 130–1) repeatedly emphasizes how in Rethemnos the memories embodied in certain places emotionally and symbolically link the present Greeks as a community and as a nation to their past. In a similar work, Whitehead (2003, 62–3) points out how as certain ecological locations secrete emotionally felt experiences of the ancestors they play a role in defining the identity of the Patamuna people of the Guyana highlands.

The Jie storytellers emphasize the presence of ancient agro-pastoral villages along the edges of the Longiro River close to the water wells in the river's dry path. Ancestral families lived on the banks of the Longiro River, and they made use of every well on its dry route. In the course of the Longiro River Engiro impregnated the Jie cattle. On the banks of the Longiro River Orwakol made the first fire and offered sorghum grain and blood sacrifices. The memories of these mythical instances, which are alive in Jie oral tradition and cultural practices, presuppose the continual regeneration of the Jie society.

The Jie historical traditions beautifully illustrate how Jie ancestral family rooted itself on the soil of the Longiro River via sorghum agriculture and incorporated itself in a portion of the dry plateau that storytellers so admirably describe. The storytellers detail portraits of local life, describing how people settled in certain places and recalling the type of land they settled, portraits that reflect the nature of the soil and the physical geography. The performance of Jie historical traditions show how the original polygamous family gave birth to seven territorial divisions in Daidai and spread throughout the Jie geography. The historical tradition provides a "logical model" (Levi-Strauss's term, 1953, 443) capable of linking the land and its inhabitants, explaining how the Jie began in Daidai in one place, with one polygamous family, and then spread out along the banks of the Longiro River. It also tells us that the descendants are encouraged to emulate their ancestors.

That is why Jie storytellers reconcile Jie polity and kinship during their ritual performances. That is also why we find the poetic reconciliation of Jie polity and kinship in the plot of Jie historical traditions. That is also why Jie storytellers say if all Jie are descendant from one polygamous family, and all the cattle and grain also come from the same family, then all the people are related and they share in common the grain and cattle. In this way the storytellers metaphorically and economically unite the Jie along kinship lines around Longiro River.

Since the unified descent of the Jie and their material wealth come from a particular geographical space within the plateau, there is a logical reason for the prevalence of sharing both cattle and grain in this ecologically unpredictable environment. The historical traditions stress the kinship overtone, weaving the relationship between villages in Jie geography through the concept of descent. While agricultural production throughout Najie is linked through the seeds of Orwakol, the supreme ancestral figure, Engiro, and the distribution of Engiro's offspring among his sons, serves to link the agnatic lineage of Orwakol's clan.

The continuing connection with the original family on the Jie geography is symbolically represented by the ritual bond, through the exchange of sorghum during the *akimwaar* (the harvest ritual) (Mirzeler 2004). As descendants of one original family, the seven territorial divisions' mutual involvement in the performance of *akimwaar* enables them to confirm their kinship ties, reminding them of their mutual political and economic obligations. The annual performance of *akimwaar* renews the ritual bonds and kinships, reinforcing the obligatory economic and political reciprocity between the seven territorial divisions of the Jie.

The Jie historical tradition offers extensive accounts of the formation of two separate Jie polities in the central Karamoja Plateau. While the Lokorwakol division became powerful because of the rich sources of the Longiro River, the Lokalodiny division became powerful from the sources of the Dopeth River. Both rivers over time crystallized the geographical bonds and connected the two principal parts of Najie in the heart of the Karamoja Plateau.

When the Jie ancestral families arrived in Najie, they transformed certain natural spaces, such as Daidai, Lokatap Rock, Koteen Hill, Moru a Nayeche, and Tarash River, into shrines to commemorate the events of capturing the gray bull Engiro, the journey of Nayeche, and the establishment of their seven territorial divisions. The Jie storytellers locate the memories of their ancestors in these places with their own rhythms, ideologies, and representations of everyday lives. The poetics of Engiro's journey from Longiro River to Tarash River possesses a cyclical rhythm that is fused with the Jie harvest ritual, during which Nayeche, the Jie ancestral heroine who gave birth to the pastoralist Turkana on the headwaters of the Tarash River, returns metaphorically to the dry plateau. The fusing of Engiro's journey with the rhythm of harvest reveals images that testify to the ancient struggles that occurred among the members of the original family over the capturing of the gray bull Engiro along the twisted banks of the Longiro River. The way the Jie and Turkana storytellers around the upper Tarash River region entangle the memories of gray bull Engiro and Nayeche with Longiro River and Tarash River are congruent with the various notions of place and memory as articulated by Flores, Herzfeld, Nora, and Guiomor.

The dry-season wells, beneath the Longiro riverbed near Daidai, preserve the water unspoiled below, even when the riverbed becomes dried and cracked. During the rainy season, the course of the Longiro River is expanded directly from the flooding of the marshes of the northeast and the many tributaries flowing throughout Najie. The flood of the Longiro River meanders like a giant river this way and that way, watering the sorghum fields of the women around Daidai and beyond. When the river floods the sorghum fields around Daidai, thickly woven sorghum stalks and blossoms become hidden in the muddy water. The earth around Daidai is rich soil and it remains moist for a good part of the year, and because of this, rushes, wild fruits, and unsown and uncultivated wild sorghum bushes grow.

Daidai, the original settlement of the Jie ancestral family on the banks of Longiro River, emanates memories redolent with symbolic imaginary realms, conveying an order of the ancestral world paralleling Nora's conceptualization of the relationship between memory and place. When Orwakol arrived on the banks of the Longiro River, he developed various *ngitalio* (traditions) and performed sacrifices and rituals in Daidai, the sacred granite rock, rendering memory of events tangible. On this granite structure of Daidai Orwakol kindled the first fire and distributed it to his wives. Napeyo, an impressive Jie storyteller, recounts that event in the following way:

> The people said that the story of Orwakol goes back to ages past when he came to Daidai with his seven wives and made a new fire. When Orwakol

made the fire, he started new *ngitalio* (traditions) and established new taboos. They (members of Orwakol's family) put the master granary in the *ekal* (yard) of Losilang, the eldest wife of Orwakol, and Orwakol gave her the first fire. After this the fire was given to Kotyang, the second eldest wife, followed by the third wife, Kotido, followed by Kanawat, and so on, until all the seven wives had received the new fire.[1]

I was once told that there is no place in Najie as beautiful as Daidai. Thorny bushes frame a narrow path that emerges from the large granite mass of Daidai and then sweeps down to the dry riverbed of the Longiro River. The gray colored granite mass of Daidai (see figure 4.1) is surrounded by wild bushes that create a closed, compact environment, almost like a protected womb, connected to the Longiro River by a single path adorned with desert foliage and thorny bushes. The central granite mass is organic, so organic that it resembles the slightly swollen belly of a woman who has just given birth. This gives additional authority to Daidai's symbolic association as the center of creation. The fertility images in Daidai and their representation in various historical traditions are metaphorically arranged to create a sequence of emotion – Engiro walking on the path to the river course then bending down to drink. This ostensibly mythic image reveals itself by the tensions created in the storytellers' representation of the memory of Engiro drinking water near Lodoket, the path that connects the granite mass of Daidai with the Longiro River.

According to Lochoro, another Jie storyteller, the place where the gray bull drank water before his capture is the most important image of Daidai's landscape, not only because of its association with Lodoket, the single path, the metaphor of the umbilical cord, but also because of its association with the bed of Kaarbokol, the sacred clay, which is found there. The storytellers depict Engiro's capture by Orwakol and Engiro's fathering of the Jie cattle around the space where the sacred clay is found. By virtue of their suggestive forms of sacredness and fertility, the path and the place where the sacred clay is found have become one of the most important spaces of creation for the Jie people. I was once told that it is this clay that women smear around the umbilical cords of their newborn infants. The central granite mass in Daidai, with its single path connecting to the river, looks so possessed of life that Jie storytellers link their creation to the center of that granite mass. When the Jie ancestors first arrived there, it is said they sat on that granite mass and received from it the warmth of the rising sun while they experienced the beginning of a new day, a new society.

It was from Daidai that Nayeche left during the prolonged dry season, following the footprints of the gray bull Engiro, and went down to the plains and gave birth to the Turkana pastoralist community. Daidai was the birthplace of the original Jie family, the place where the original gifts were exchanged between humans and Akuj (God), and between Orwakol and his sons and his wives. In Daidai Orwakol offered sorghum grains to his wives for them to sow in their respective lands along the banks of Longiro River. Also in Daidai, Orwakol was known to have plunged the *anyuli*,[2] the sacred iron bar, made from the ore of Mount Toror, into the earth, consecrating the annual movement of the cattle from the villages to the kraals and offering his *amachar* (cattle brand) to his sons, thus symbolizing the basic trust Jie fathers have of their sons. In another version of the same story, it was in Daidai where Orwakol sacrificed the gray bull Engiro with the spear made from the sacred ore of Mount Toror, and offered its flesh to his sons, symbolizing the offering by Jie fathers of their cattle, their "inalienable possession" (Mauss's 1967 term), to their sons as a gift. Although the sons receive the cattle, the gift is inalienable from the father's point of view insofar as the cattle remain in his family.

According to some Jie storytellers, when Lodiny came to Daidai, the land around the banks of the Longiro River had already been inhabited and cultivated by the wives of Orwakol. Orwakol took possession of the wild, uncultivated land from the Ngikuliak hunter-gatherers and transformed it into agricultural land. Akuj led Orwakol to Daidai on the banks of the river that watered the land of his wives, and gave him the gray bull Engiro, which sired his cattle. Also in Daidai, Orwakol sacrificed Engiro with the spear forged from the ore (*elelo*) of Mount Toror and soaked the ground of Najie with its blood.[3] In Jie discourse, Daidai, with its sacred granite mass and its association with Engiro's blood, attests to the zone of creation. According to Jie storytellers, it was in Daidai that Orwakol and Lodiny experienced their conflict over resources, which caused Lodiny to separate and settle at Lokatap Rock, after which he gave birth to the Rengen people.

The Jie villagers in the seven territorial divisions periodically perform ceremonies together in Daidai to chase away sickness, renew their social and political unions, and deal with the problems brought about by the long dry season characteristic of the area. Kaarbokol, the sacred clay found in the Longiro River near Daidai, is used in most ritual performances to integrate the seven territorial divisions. People smear themselves with Kaarbokol to escape disease and to chase away evil spirits as they repeat the archetypal sacrifices in Daidai, originally performed by Orwakol and Lodiny, the ancestral heroes. Daidai has a supreme symbolic function in Jie society.

The Longiro River and Daidai are not the only places of memory of union and creation. Lokatap Rock (see figure 4.6), the earth's navel, is another locus of creation for the Jie people, specifically the place where the Rengen division of the Jie people originated. In the Jie collective memories of origin, Lokatap Rock is represented as a sanctuary to the people of Lodiny and it symbolically imitates Daidai's creation. Similar to Daidai, Lokatap Rock is also situated on a secluded high ground associated with past memories of not only pastoralism and agriculture, but also of the presence of the Ngikuliak hunter-gatherers. Lokatap Rock is thought to be the original settlement of the Ngikuliak and Rengen people, with a large number of hyraxes considered to be sacred (also see Lamphear 1972, 505).

Unlike Daidai, the Lokatap Rock more readily recalls Lodiny's presence than it does Orwakol and the Orwakol clans. Perhaps it is a combination of storytellers' mythic representations that marks this early landscape as a separate and different place, a place for the people of Lodiny alone. The storytellers' artistic imagination exerts a strong influence on the early memories of Lodiny and his clans embodied in Lokatap Rock, the ancestral cradle landscape of the Lodiny clans, the Rengen people. The images of Lodiny's personality are woven into Lokatap Rock, and his association with peacefulness is amplified by the presence of a sacred python, which people believe embodies Lodiny's spirit. The gray colored granite structure of Lokatap Rock rises out of flat plain and is emblematically represented by the peaceful python, the hyraxes, and the sparse shade of the trees around the edges of the granite mass. This artfully establishes the mood and setting within the landscape that gives life to the spirit of Lodiny.

The storytellers who recount the first night that Lodiny spent beneath Lokatap Rock translate the images of the ancient memories embodied in the landscape and transform the rich granite of the place into a place of creation, very similar to the Daidai. The granite structure and its close proximity to the Dopeth River seem to have provided Lodiny a view through which he envisioned a sacred space, a space of creation on the model of Daidai. The Dopeth River embodies some of the same qualities that are complexly merged in Daidai's connection with the Longiro River. Surrounded with palisade villages of the Rengen people, Lokatap Rock, like Daidai, is a center of creation.

The particular gray color of the granite stone structure of Lokatap conveys its sanctified position, which is parallel to that of Daidai. The themes of creation suggested for Lokatap Rock have no direct connection with the gray bull Engiro whose presence sanctifies such places with images of creation. Only skillful storytellers, like Lodoch, attentive to tradition, envision the animated connection of Engiro with Lokatap Rock. Lodoch's evocative portrayal of this connection is well worth quoting:

> All the men now dragged Engiro towards the rock of Daidai and they speared him one by one until Engiro fell on the rock lifeless. Orwokol, his seven sons, and the young men of Turkana, and Toposa all sat in the *akiriket* under the tree and ate the charred meat of Engiro all by themselves, as the Ngikuliaks, the children, the women, and the old infirm men indignantly watched them eating. The aroma of Engiro's meat engulfed the whole of Najie even Lodiny and his people smelled it all the way at the Lokatap Rock.[4]

Lokatap Rock's landscape, as storytellers describe it, expands upon the motif of ancestral conflict which corresponds to what transpired near Koteen Hill, another granite landscape where Lodiny's kraals had been established before coming to Daidai.

Koteen Hill is one of the most powerful and profound landscapes ever to fascinate the storytellers. It is a most mysterious landscape, lending mythological themes to the historical traditions. The hill abruptly emerges in an unbroken flat landscape, exhibiting a sanctified image, a massive round granite structure surrounded by a semidesert wild landscape. It is a rocky outcrop topped by an inaccessible shrine that highlights the consecrated nature of the entire hill. At the foot of the hill are myriad wild fruit thickets mimicking the topographies of Daidai, Lokatap Rock, and Moru a Nayeche, with traces of ancient kraal structures, campfires, rolling grazing lands, and rivers.[5]

The storytellers' evocative portrayal of Koteen Hill's resources provides discursive images worth remembering. The patches of pastures, wild fruit bushes, and seasonal rivers, such as Lomogol River in the north, as well as Nangalol Apolon, the great river, on the west. The immense resources, along the great rivers, with bulrushes arching downward on their sharp slopes, illustrating the great life-supporting capacity.

The hill's seamless and nearly perfectly round image suggests something larger at work within nature's grandeur. The hill, so sharply defined and shaped that visitors ponder the hand of a giant artist sculpting the hill from the mass of rock; embodied in it is a sheer physical tension. It seemingly propels itself upward against gravity, as if against the oncoming threats of famines and thirst that so often devastate the waterless plateau. The hill stands out, and yet it is a part of the dry plateau, but a part of that is animated and powerful. It is suggestive of elemental memories of ancestral struggles, giving its gray tinge a sacred quality, the same color as Daidai's granite structure and the color of the gray bull Engiro. With its gray color and immense structure, the hill appears ancient and sanctified. On its rising shoulders, appearing barren, there are immutably fixed ancestral images, exuding memories of the ancient and recent struggles over resources.

Koteen Hill is indeed an object of memory par excellence in Nora's sense of the term. The storytellers link this hill to the earliest ancestral migrations from Dongiro to the Karamoja Plateau before they became pastoralists and learned to cultivate seed. According to Lamphear (1976, 73–99) and Pazzaglia (1982, 26), Koteen Hill is one of the earliest cradle lands of the Jie people corresponding to the times of the ancestors when people perhaps had not yet domesticated animals. This is how Lodoch describes Koteen Hill:

> The people who had a few cattle settled in Nakadanya near Magos, and the people who had no cattle settled in Koteen. Those who had settled in Koteen had no cattle and they hunted wild animals. They built their homesteads there. They went around naked, except the women, who wore the skins of animals that they had killed. Those who went to Nakadanya in the Magos area had cattle and they stayed there.[6]

About thirty miles east of Koteen Hill, below the plateau, looms the image of Moru a Nayeche, the hill of Nayeche on the headwaters of Tarash River. Descending from the plateau, going down to the headwaters of the Tarash River, one can observe a wild thicket on the left bank of the river that extends miles inland. Upon entering the bush, the tip of Moru a Nayeche comes into view, tucked away a few hundred feet from the banks of the Tarash River. To the left of the hill, between the hill and the river, is the grave of Nayeche, marked by piles of small stones strewn by travelers, and surrounded by desert scrub (see figure 6.1). Yet the hill next to the grave radiates fertility, teeming with wild fruit bushes, life and creation. A narrow path adorned by desert thickets connects the hill to the seasonal Tarash River, the veritable sap of life that carries in its currents the themes of survival and creation. Patches of opulent pasture secluded behind the bushes and water holes serve to create the image of a mythical cradle land.

Moru a Nayeche is a significant landscape in the Jie and Turkana oral traditions of origin and it is the center of creation for the Turkana people. Through this mythical landscape, the Turkana and the Jie are connected with a shared past and resources. Moru a Nayeche, as a part of the origin story, offers the Jie and the Turkana storytellers a tangible means of expressing important traditional ideas about their shared memories and histories.

Located between the plateau and the plains, Moru a Nayeche represents the principles of balance and order between the Jie and the Turkana communities. Moru a Nayeche keeps their kinship ties from dissolving into confusion and turmoil. The river/hill dichotomy is a metaphor of kinship between these people, who engage in complementary economies, pastoralism, agriculture, and hunting/gathering, all of which become central themes for storytellers. The landscape functions as a narrative that contains the memory of the famine that inspired Nayeche to follow the footprints of the gray bull Engiro to the plain to create a new cradle land. Storytellers reveal the meaning of the landscape in their stories when they talk about Nayeche's desperate pursuit of the gray bull in search of water on the dry plateau, and her descent to the plains where she finds the headwaters of the Tarash River. In the story of Nayeche performed by Lodoch, there is a famous passage:

> When she [Nayeche] reached the Tarash River, she found the footprints of a bull there and said, "These are the footprints of the bull which they said disappeared in the kraals. The bull must know where the water is." Nayeche followed the footprints of the bull until she reached a place where the bull had found water.
>
> Nayeche said, "This is the water it [the bull] drank, and it is finished." Again Nayeche followed the bull. She followed it to the place where the bull had drunk, and she drank the *ngiorok* (the last bit of water, the remnants of water mixed with mud). She walked and walked again until she

found where the bull had just grazed. "Okoe, it just walked here, here, around here," Nayeche said. "It was just around here," said Nayeche.

She followed and followed the footprints of the bull and gathered wild fruits as she went. She walked in the river until she reached a rock. That rock later became her home.[7]

The features of Moru a Nayeche continually interact within the context of everyday discourse and enable the storytellers to create their stories about the former inhabitants of Najie and beyond. The storytellers describe Moru a Nayeche as an oasis located at the foot of the sharply dropping plateau and the headwaters of the Tarash River, which meanders through the dry and barren desert landscape. The Turkana people are proud of Moru a Nayeche's features, its isolation from other hills, its special place on the banks of the life-giving river, and its embodiment of the memories of the ancient settlements, which convey a mythical theme around the venerable ancestors. The images of Moru a Nayeche's landscape thus play a crucial role in the oral tradition of both the Jie and Turkana communities.

Landscape is an important resource for the storytellers, not only in describing the mythical ancestral world, but also in talking about the contemporary changes people experience. These contemporary changes affect the complex relationship between landscape, memory, and tradition in profound ways in Jie society. During my return visit in 2011, clusters of square cement houses were more noticeable amidst the traditional mud-plastered, cone-shaped, and thatched round houses. But people referred to both types of houses as *akai*, and they are not seen differently. A new modern economic situation had been created via the Jie people's involvement in commercial agriculture, privatization of land, cattle sale, and illicit gun trade, and has changed the political economy in profound ways. The old traditional economy, based on subsistence agriculture in scattered small family plots and dependent upon the erratic rainfall, has been steadily altered since the 1950s by the introduction of new crops and more efficient cultivation techniques and technologies, including a new irrigation system (Gulliver 1955, 1971; Mirzeler 1999, 2004). The historical traditions having to do with memory and ancestral landscape merge in contemporary ritual performances, revealing society's struggle to achieve a vision of a healthy and vibrant community.

Contemporary performances of historical traditions and rituals are fused with tradition and modernity. The sacred ancestral landscape now providing a new structural foundation for the disruptions caused by AK-47s and the heavily armed young men who threaten tradition. The storytellers' reflections are particularly helpful in understanding the changing relationships between landscape, memory, and history in this age of globalization. When relating the history of changes in Najie, the storytellers all included the changing relationship between the Jie landscape and their memories, and put that landscape into a contemporary context.

This changing relationship between memory, place, and history was powerfully shown to me when I sat down with Logwee, the Jie storyteller, one afternoon under an acacia tree in front of her mud-plastered homestead and recorded our conversation about oral tradition and landscape. Logwee had a fascination with what she called the *ngiemuto* (folktales and historical tradition). She saw the contemporary world as a continuation of the long gone world of the ancestors, through which the storytellers intertwine the past experiences of the ancestors with the experiences of the humans living today. That ancient image is the horizon of the ancestral world which separates the contemporary imperfect world and, in some ways, becomes artistically and poetically expressive during performances of *ngiemuto*. This is in line with Guiomar's (1989), Flores's (2002), Herzfeld's (1991), Nora's (1989), and Slyomovics's (1997) interpretations of the complex relationship between memory, history, and landscape.

Logwee told me how she was blessed by being born in Jimos village near the banks of the Longiro River, which is marked out by a scattered granite landscape. "The grayish color of granite is the same color of the gray bull Engiro," she told me. She shared with me her memories of playing childhood games on and around these granite patches near the Longiro River around Daidai, when she went to weed their family gardens there. She also shared memories with me of the flowing muddy water of the Longiro River during the rainy seasons, which gradually grows into a giant river yearly, corresponding in her imagination to the ancient memory of Orwakol's capture of Engiro while drinking the muddy flood water of the river.

"When I was a child I used to wake in the morning and went with my mother and sisters to weed our gardens on the banks of the Longiro River, near Daidai" said Logwee:

In those days, we used to walk into a world which was once occupied by our ancestors, who themselves went to their gardens with their hoes on their shoulders, and who drove their cattle to get to places of water and grass. When I was a young girl, I used to go occasionally with my mother to distant kraals in the east around Nangalol Apolon to visit my father and uncles. The ancestral world always revealed itself to me there. During the long dry season, when the kraals were in Koteen Hill, my father used to come and visit us. And when he came, he always brought with him fascinating stories about Koteen Hill, and the Lomogol River that flowed there.

During our conversation, Logwee told me how a lot of developments in Kotido, particularly tin-roofed square houses around the Longiro River, have destroyed the scenery with their unattractiveness. "Those people who think they are educated and want to live in those square cement houses have become so different, so different that it is difficult to understand them." "Yes" I said to Logwee, "returning to this place, I don't think Najie is the same as it was seven years ago. Back then, there were no square houses with tin roofs in the distant villages to be seen on the horizon."

What Logwee was telling me about landscape and the tin-roofed cement houses was not only about the Jie landscape where the Jie cattle still go for grazing and return to the villages in the evenings. She was also referring to the rhythm of these places, where they have changed along with the landscape. The memory images inscribed in those places that sustain the plot of stories with a sense of rhythm and ancient beauty have changed. When the Jie storytellers think of historical traditions, they think about the past and about the landscape with a sense of its rhythm and ancient patterns. The storytellers know about the rhythm and patterns of their history, and they know their landscape and its memories that give meaning to a long gone world, which they struggle to connect. This world for them is always better, greater, and is always more distant than they can ever reach. And "that is the beauty of the landscape," Logwee told me. The storytellers have a vital role in creating the rhythm and patterns of past memories and histories embodied in the landscape (Cashman 2008).

"In the past when a girl got married, her mother gave her a piece of land for her to cultivate, and that land became the *ngalup nguna anakini toto* [the land of the mother]," Logwee continued:

When I was a young girl, I remember people never sold land or whatever they grew on it. Whenever people were hungry, they went to each other's villages and got some sorghum. I remember when people started selling sorghum and other food crops. I also remember how the *wazungu* [referring to white people] introduced the serena sorghum, that distasteful sorghum that polluted our granaries. We used to grow our traditional sorghum, which tasted much differently than the serena sorghum we grow today. I was a young girl at that time. When my mother and sisters cultivated our family plots, our friends came and helped us. Even our enemies came and helped us. This gave us an opportunity to make peace with them and become friends again.

"You remember the story of Napeikisina, which I told you?" "Yes," I said. "Do you know why those girls go to the garden of Napeikisina and help her even though they knew that Napeikisina was a cannibal? I'll tell you why," she said. "You see, in Jie culture when a woman asks other women to help her clear or weed her garden, women would go and help her even if she is as evil as Napeikisina. It is our custom to help and support each other in all sorts of ways. Today, you cannot get anyone helping you in your garden unless you give some money. This is how bad things are today."

"Land was not private property. It was a communal asset." Logwee continued:

> Traditionally, when people migrated to new places, the women of the house went and looked for a piece of empty land, and when they found it, they negotiated with the women who inhabited that place. If you had good character and you had no problems with other people, with the women of the land where you wanted to settle, they gave you a piece of land to cultivate. When you were given a piece of land, you offered sacrifices in the *akiriket* (shrine) of that land and learned the *ngitalio* (tradition) of the people who lived there, and the piece of land given to you became your land (*ngakoni lup*). When you sacrificed a goat in your land and offered the meat to the people, the people remembered that and they talked about how so and so offered sacrifices in this and that place, and how so and so shared the meat from the goat and offered beer made from the sorghum of her garden in this and that place. This is how things were before the government owned the land. Today the government owns the land, and if you want to cultivate the land, you purchase the land. If you want to purchase the land, you have to go to the government office in Kotido and survey the land and buy it. People don't have to know what your character is, and you don't have to learn the *ngitalio* of the place you settle and offer sacrifices in the *akiriket* of that new land you purchase.

In Logwee's narrative the memory of the sacrifices and offerings of food by the new settlers in the land was set within the strands of the past interwoven with the memory of the ancestors and with the threads of the present, legitimating access to resources. This is changing.

5 Historical Tradition and Poetic Persuasion of Pastness

In this chapter I focus on the role of the rhetoric of "pastness" in dispute mediation and conflict resolution, and show how the representation of pastness, as portrayed in historical tradition, shapes the identities and social relations of those signified by them. I illustrate how the images of Nayeche and the gray bull Engiro shape social identities and assure unity between an ideal ancestral past and the present. Storytellers embellish their narration of past events with images of popular biographies, folktales, and myths, and by doing so assert their authority to speak to particular audiences. An understanding of the art of persuasion in dispute mediation is critical to appreciate the implications of the poetic power of remembered memories and meaning making.

Poetic exchanges of anecdotes about the past are a veritable passion for the Jie in circumstances of dispute mediation, during which individuals strive to portray themselves as conforming to the ideals of their ancestors. Various images evoked during dispute mediations cluster around competing connotations and give meaning to potent "public symbols" that enable people to understand and relate to the past and reconstruct their personal and social identities. Here anecdotal references to the images of oral tradition and cultural memories index kinship ties, reminding people that they are descendants of the same ancestral family and that their cattle too are the descendants of the gray bull Engiro and, as such, they should respect their kinship relations – share food, water, and pasture; and acknowledge their interdependence in the face of the unpredictable environment in which they live.

Sharing memories of the past and talking about their ancestors persuasively legitimizes contemporary political alliances and enhances the possibility of sharing the scarce resources, maintaining peace, and differentiating enemies. It does so by giving people the substance of an ideal past world in which the ancestors behaved in certain ways under similar circumstances; it demands identification with their ancestors and calls for them to behave as did their ancestors in the past in similar situations.

In the performance of rhetorical persuasion, we see not only how people secure access to resources, but also how "personal identities are composed" around "political investment" of resources, as Meeker suggests in the case of the Bedouin nomads of the Arabian desert (Meeker 1979). The articulation of political strategies by means of poetic "rhetorical devices" (Fernandez 1986, 41) is at the heart of Jie society as well as that of the Turkana and various other communities in this region. I suggest that the rhetoric of persuasion defines poetic and artistic expression to a significant degree in the *eemut* verbal art form. As I have shown elsewhere (Mirzeler 2004), the images in *eemut* oral tradition are based on cultural memories, and they are simultaneously poetic and politic, reinforced by anecdotal references to past events during dispute mediations.

The rhetoric of persuasion in anthropological, and folklore studies has an intrinsic generic significance. Various conceptualizations of oral tradition have shown the inseparability of the art of oral tradition and the rhetoric of persuasion (Abu-Lughod 1986; Bauman 1986; Caton 1990; Meeker 1979). At the heart of these studies is the argument that the poetics of oral tradition is constitutive of rhetorical and artistic expressions. The *eemut* tradition in this sense is not only the story of the past, but also the poetics of persuasion, which provides the Jie with the map of survival strategies on their dry plateau. Sharing and making persuasive anecdotal references to the images of *eemut* during dispute mediation reminds people of the problem of cattle as a "vulnerable wealth" (Meeker's term, 1979) and of their interdependence necessitated by the vicissitudes of their dry environment. For this reason people refer to the various adventurous initiatives of their ancestral heroes to arrive at and legitimate the survival strategies and political alliances in their *eemut* tradition. Through references to the *eemut*, people redefine their political and economic boundaries while expressing their "vulnerability" and "interdependence" poetically (Mirzeler 1999).

The discourse of pastness articulating vulnerability and interdependence is composed of varying categories, survival strategies, and social and political relations that enhance the public self-image. Rhetorical references to pastness during dispute mediation therefore provide an opportunity for "self-presentation" and a space to build a "respectable

self-image" (Caton 1990) in the eyes of others. What is useful in persuasive rhetorical references is the "recognition of the role of mediation in
association and the recognition that a metaphoric predication is a hypothesis about the world" (Fernandez 1986, 55).

To analyze the image of *eemut* performance as a form of persuasive
rhetoric requires conceptualizations, which I will draw first from similar yet distinctive studies of the persuasive rhetorical power of oral tradition explored by Michael Meeker (1979) among the Rwala Bedouin
nomads of northern Arabia. I then will draw from Lila Abu-Lughod's
(1986) work with the Bedouin tribal society of northern Egypt, and from
Steven Caton's work among the Khawlani tribal people of Yemen. In
addition, I will draw from Elizabeth Tonkin's conceptualization of history and memory to demonstrate how dispute mediation can be understood as the locus of dialectic and persuasive recalling of pastness,
where individuals verbalize "social memory" and imagine the past in
light of the present and vice versa (1990, 108).

Narrative persuasion has a primacy over sociopolitical organization
in explaining the political violence and poetry in Michael Meeker's analysis. Rwala Bedouin nomads living in a dry and unpredictable environment are forced to maintain the integrity of their vulnerable domestic
wealth for their survival. To overcome conflict and to ensure survival in
an uncertain environment and unpredictable situations, the actors have
to form independent herding groups across the desert and establish
political alliances to fend against the patterned social and political insta-
bilities that threaten their herding groups. However, sometimes the political community and authority are not effective in resolving conflict
and protecting human lives. To overcome this, the Rwala Bedouins developed a distinct form of political institution, which Meeker refers to as
"the ceremonial narratives," that involves retelling stories of actual wars
and raids, most having occurred within living memory (1979, 52). The
act of composing a ceremonial narrative is also the construction of a personal identity. Writing about "how a personal identity might be composed in a world where one must struggle to survive," the storytellers
harness sometimes disturbing memories laden with emotions familiar
to the members of the audience (Meeker 1979, 52).

Ceremonial narratives, observes Meeker, are persuasive and assume
for nomadic pastoralism a way of life, which demands routine political
strategies (1979, 7). The construction of personal identity has an interesting correlate in the ceremonial narrative. The content of the ceremonial narrative is patterned and expresses certain themes, such as "the

relationship of men and personal instruments of aggression," which, according to Meeker, is a "central feature of North Arabian Bedouin political experience" (1979, 151). The storytellers, in developing interpretations of the ceremonial narratives, attempt to explore strategic possibilities of actively dealing with contemporary political experience and conflict situations. They appeal to memories of past events, and urge their audiences to consider what kinds of behavior might be the basis for standard human interaction living in hostile environments and political uncertainties in which human life must be protected and supported.

Ceremonial narratives are expressed via certain artistic and poetic conventions that invoke the moral authority of "political investment" to protect and support human life against "environmental uncertainties," political crises, and human aggression. The very process of telling the ceremonial narratives provides a window on historical processes and "some indication of the way in which popular motivations took shape within a pattern of circumstances"; this reveals "something about the general character of a people's historical experience" (Meeker 1979, 151).

The forms of artistic expression observed by Meeker in the ceremonial narratives among the Bedouin are intrinsic to the performances of Jie historical tradition. The Jie, like the Bedouin, live in a dry environment, cope with similar political uncertainties, and deal with the problem of protecting the integrity of vulnerable domestic wealth and resources. Here, Meeker's analysis of the Bedouin ceremonial narratives sheds light on the storytellers' anecdotal references to historical tradition and their invocation of ancestral moral authority. Similar to ceremonial narratives, historical traditions are forms of persuasive expression; they are a response to the Jie political and historical experience expressed in certain fixed forms dealing with fixed themes. Moreover, they provide not only a glimpse at the political and historical experiences of the ancestors, but also at certain patterns of political motivations and events important to the Jie people.

Abu-Lughod's work on the poetry of the Bedouin of the western desert of Egypt builds on aspects of Meeker's argument to focus on the way in which poetry relates to the concept of self. In Abu-Lughod's analysis of ideologies, we see how honor and the code of modesty require that Bedouin women not to speak about their love for men or express their sexuality. Public expression of love for men and sexuality is synonymous to admission of dependence and vulnerability which

conflicts with the Bedouin ideals of dignity, autonomy, and independence. According to Abu-Lughod, Bedouin women use poetry as a way
to express their love for certain men without losing their honor and dignity. The persuasive set formats and conventional structures suggest a
universality in poetry that gives a certain aura of protection to women
to express these sentiments otherwise deemed unacceptable. The use of
poetry depersonalizes these expressions and gives women a measure of
independence and autonomy and contributes to the honor so prized by
the Bedouin (Abu-Lughod 1986, 245 [also see Caton 1990, 111]). The
persuasive discourse of poetry not only provides protection to women,
but also gives them an added advantage of persuading the lover to respond to their appeal.

Abu-Lughod goes beyond Meeker's formulations of the poetics of
persuasion and situates persuasive appeal within the sociopolitical order in the discourse of poetry and in everyday language and practice,
tying poetics and politics to the construction of identity. It is from this
point of view that I will analyze the persuasive use of *eemut* in dispute
mediation. Such analysis is pertinent to understanding the Jie people's
construction of personal identity during performances, as certain forms
and conventional structures contained in historical tradition are critical
markers of identification among the Jie people.

Building on notions of poetic persuasion, Caton too works out the
relationship of poetry to self in the Khawlani male society of Yemen.
Distinct, but not unlike Abu-Lughod's notion about the relationship between a society's official ideology and individual experience that fuels
the construction of an honorable and reasonable person in speech acts,
is "an act of constructing the self" (1990, 113). For Caton, the poetic
composition of a self is a public performance through which the poet
makes an argument to "instill in the listener an attitude of respect toward his person" to create himself as a respectable person (1990, 113).

For Caton, the most important means of persuasion is the argument
couched in a certain style of articulating the matters at hand. For him,
persuasion is effective when the performer evokes emotional responses
from his or her audience through the effective use of symbols and metaphors. Therefore, knowing what to say is not sufficient, but rather how
one says it and how one uses poetic forms, metaphors, and symbols is
the key to persuasive engagement. Similar to Abu-Lughod, he defines
persuasive engagement as a process in which the actors allow themselves to be transformed by identifying with the ideal self-image. The
process of identification with the ideal self-image serves not only as a
way of reflecting the world but also as a way of shaping it (Caton 1990,

159). The persuasive character of the speaker is constructed during performances as the speaker attempts to evoke the emotions of his audience so as to "impel" them to act in a certain way. This is, according to
Caton, "the traditional concept of oratory," a kind of "syllogism" based
on a cultural understanding of reality and poetic forms. For Caton, poetic performance and the ability of the speaker to bolster his messages
poetically, subliminally using symbols, metaphors, and images, is the
key to persuasive performances.

Meeker's, Abu-Lughod's, and Caton's basic analytical concepts are
crucial to my analysis of anecdotal references to *eemut* images in dispute mediations in Jie society. The expression of poetics found in the
eemut tradition is persuasive and consonant, at the conceptual level,
with the findings of these researchers. From the point of the poetic anecdotal references to the image of *eemut* uttered in dispute mediations,
there is an attempt to persuade people to link their experiences to ancestral ideals, asserting the universality of their experiences and persuasively demanding social conformity with the norms of reciprocity,
and the ideology and moral codes set by their ancestors.

Conformity with cultural ideals and moral values is important for Jie
people in perpetuating the standards set by their venerable ancestors
that guarantee survival in the dry environment. The images of historical tradition expressing the ancestral deeds are circumscribed by tradition and authoritatively structured by the discourse of everyday life.
Performance of historical traditions evokes memory images that deliv-
er the messages of cultural ideals. Historical tradition is expressed in
certain forms and conventional structures, and stylized genres, rendering the message of tradition as persuasive and universal.

Particular oral traditions are associated with universally occurring
social conflicts, and ecological and political crises of everyday lives. In
their anecdotal references, the storytellers draw upon these common
themes during dispute mediations and express the universal experiences of the people and their neighbors, such as hunger, famine, and
conflict over water or cattle, all of which have caused the dispersals of
people and are still closely linked with everyday situations. When the
storytellers invoke the images of mythical ancestors and their experiences of famines, for example, they often draw an analogy between the
ancestral world and the contemporary world, which elicits sympathetic
responses from the members of the audiences.

The Jie and the Turkana people admire the heroes and heroines of
their historical traditions, and they believe that their traditions reflect
the truth of the past. The rhetorical link to tradition evokes "traditional

sympathy" (Bauman 1986) and provides a way of expressing sentiments of vulnerability and norms of reciprocity. The rhetorical persuasion in dispute mediation is thus both poetic and persuasive and enables people to express their experiences in a culturally valued way to win the traditional sympathy of the people. Indeed, such poetic discourse often moves people and induces the desired course of action.

As I have shown earlier, the Jie people's past involves emotionally felt cultural experiences, such as memories of famines, hunger, and vulnerability arising from living in an unpredictable and dry environment. The storytellers foreground the aesthetic of their rhetorical composition with the emotionally felt cultural experiences of people during dispute mediations. Anecdotal references to the memory images of past events of famines and dispersals give a clear means of persuasion to identify with the ideals of the ancestors. As expressed in dispute mediation, pastness is grounded in the conception of being vulnerable and living in an unpredictable environment and, accordingly, stresses and poeticizes the glorious deeds of ancestors living under similar circumstances. It is for this reason that I draw from Tonkin's highly provocative notion of pastness. Following Tonkin, I argue that identification with the past logically occurs in a situation of dispute mediation in which storytellers, who are actively participating in the dispute mediation, strategically and poetically persuade the conflicting parties to identify with a commonly shared ideal past and thereby achieve agreement.

In Jie thought, the values of interdependence, cooperation, and sharing food and water, as reflected in their oral traditions, are associated with decent human behavior. This association reinforces the reality of both the unpredictable environment and their economic system, in which older males, who control resources, depend on the younger men and women for sustenance. This vulnerability and their interdependencies, which are crucial to the Jie experience, are those between parent and child, between people in villages and those living in kraals, and between different ethnic communities occupying distinct ecological zones and practicing varied economic activities.

The vulnerability created by their dry environment is an important aspect of Jie dispute mediations and is perhaps the most distinctive feature of not only the Jie but most peoples of the arid region, from the Karamoja Plateau in Uganda to the Chalbi desert and beyond in northern Kenya. This unavoidable vulnerability is perhaps the basis for why people of this vast area share similar traditions. Pastoralists, agriculturalists, hunter-gatherers, and fishermen of this vast region engage in

frequent warfare and conflict over resources, but they also have a remarkable concern for political alliances and the sharing of meager
resources (Dyson-Hudson 1966; Gulliver 1955; Karp 1978; Schlee 1989;
Mirzeler 1999; Sobania 1980).

Here scarce resources and unpredictable arid conditions force people
to form political alliances across the plateau and the plains and construct networks of interethnic relationships. Throughout the arid zone
in northern Uganda and Kenya, communities share food and water and
cooperate for their survival. Indeed as the corpus of historical tradition gathered in this vast region demonstrates, the repeated patterns
of events, which have forced people to disperse and migrate in search
of food, and to help one another during times of crisis, have forced
people to establish political alliances. In this vast region, the obligation
to share resources is a distinctive feature of the norms of personal and
collective integrity, and is tested in times of ecological disaster. People
find the "promise of survival" (Meeker's term, 1979) in examples and
definitions of sharing and cooperating. During famines, when survival
is threatened, people engage in obligatory reciprocity similar to that depicted in historical traditions. Sharing the cultural norm of reciprocity
with their neighbors, the Jie people ensure their survival.

The Jie territory is a well-defined geographical unity, bounded by networks of seasonal rivers and surrounded by the foothills of the agriculturalist Labwor people in the west and the desert plains of the Turkana
pastoralist people below the plateau to the east. The principal enemies
of the Jie are the Dodos pastoralists in the northeast and Matheniko pastoralists in the south.

During the dry season, the Jie cattle are vulnerable to attack from the
Dodos, while they are in the grazing land in the east and faraway from
the villages, near the Koteen Hill and the Lomagol River. The threat of
cattle raids by Dodos and Matheniko people at this time often causes
the Jie to move their cattle back to the safety of Nangalol Apolon, a great
river that winds some twenty miles east of Nakapelimoru, where they
can graze in safety. During this time however, the scarce grazing and
water resources, and the presence of Matheniko and Dodos and other
pastoralist groups from farther south, forces the Turkana to settle their
kraals alongside the Jie, their traditional allies. Thus, the Jie and the
Turkana around Nangalol Apolon stand together with their backs to
the Nakapelimoru, facing the open grazing land, which stretches toward the plains of Turkana below the escarpment near the upper Tarash
River. The main reason for this movement is defensive and strategic on

the part of the Turkana: in grouping their kraals closely together with the Jie in Nangalol Apolon, near the vicinity of Nakapelimoru, the largest Jie village, they increase the distance from their mutual enemies, the Dodos and the Matheniko, who would be around Koteen Hill and the Lomagol River. The transitory settlement of Jie and Turkana together around Nangalol Apolon gives them the added advantage of not only being able to defend their cattle against possible raids, but also enables them to organize effective raiding, usually during the moonlit nights.

Sometimes, however, resources around the banks of Nangalol Apolon become scarce and unable to sustain all the kraals, and hence fights erupt between the Jie and the Turkana over water and grazing. When this happens individual heads of the kraals responsible for the maintenance of the herds meet to informally discuss these matters in their respective *etem* (men's gathering places) to resolve the conflict situation. If they are unable to resolve these conflicts informally, the next step is to take the matter up at *akiriket* (public gatherings), in which individuals are allowed to speak and express opinions.

Meetings in *akiriket* are cultural public performances, "bounded events that transform everyday spaces into places of heightened social significance," as Flores postulates in his study of the ritual practice and cultural performances of the Los Pastores among South Texas "mexicanos" (1995, 148). Debates and discussions in *akiriket*, sometimes attended by a relatively large number of people, are accompanied by certain ritual performances. These meetings are usually scheduled and take place in sacred places, such as under the shade of a tree, at dry riverbeds, or near a well, that are sanctified and spatially marked. Before the formal discussions begin, people usually chat and gossip about the local issues. When the time is ripe, one person makes a speech, announcing the beginning of the public speeches, and sets "the interpretive frame within which the messages being communicated are to be understood" (Bauman 1977, 9). Immediately after the announcement, silence usually falls momentarily, until the second speaker begins his speech using conventional phrases and expressions. Thus, the public discussion proceeds as people "take turns" in giving speeches from wherever they are sitting. Some speakers get up and move back and forth, pointing in different directions, using a stick or a spear and uttering persuasive conventional rhetorical phrases, "validating" (Briggs's term, 1988, 124) the performances. Such speech acts continue until consensus is achieved and formal decisions are made.

At the height of the performance, the storyteller paces back and forth in front of the audience, seated in a semicircle arranged respective to age and social status, and tries to elicit responses from the audiences. The place of onlookers, usually older women, young men, and children, is at the edge of the *akiriket*. The debates in the *akiriket* involve almost everybody in the community. People take part in the performance at the event in a number of ways, including killing the sacrificial animal and cooking and eating it. Some young men may collect firewood and do the roasting for the older men and distribute the meat according to rules that reify social status within the society.

The social position of the people is also represented by the physical distribution/placement of the participants. For example, people form groups according to age and gender who eat together; women, if present, will sit with other women or serve sorghum beer in calabashes, while the younger men may cook the sacrificial meal. The choicest pieces of meat are usually reserved for the elder male participants, with some meat and beer also given to junior elders and to uninitiated men. Men who possess the skills necessary scrutinize and read intestines laid out on the ritual ground to provide guidance for the community's future. At the public feast, the eating of the sacrificial meat defines and affirms the ideal authority structure of the society as a prelude to public decision making.

While no one person chairs the discussions, some people gathered in the *akiriket* do articulate short speeches and command the attention of the audiences. Debates during these scheduled occasions not only enable the public to reach a decision which affects the whole community, but also provide an opportunity for community members to reaffirm their ideals, norms, and ideologies and to reconnect themselves with their ancestral world, for these debates are often linked to some past events that might be considered integral to the present.

In November of 1996, just before the harvest rituals began, the heat grew oppressive, and the Turkana kraal residents who were settled in the Koteen Hill area came to the banks of Nangalol Apolon in search of water.[1] Upon settling on the banks of Nangalol Apolon, they prolonged their stay around the river at this time of the year. This meant that more than double the number of animals were drinking at the wells and overcrowding them, spawning arguments and conflict. Nobody knew what the state of the water supply would be if the Turkana continued drinking large quantities, watering their animals as if water were a plentiful commodity.

Despite the Jie's good nature and their usual welcoming attitude toward the Turkana, they were exhausted by their preparations for the harvest season and became peevish and did not hide their annoyance at the Turkana cattle at their wells, using up their meager water resources. The continuing tension resulted in a major fight between Turkana and Jie warriors which culminated in bloodshed. Several Jie men from Nakapelimoru began fighting with the Turkana men in the kraals using AK-47s and, in the process, a Jie herder and several of his livestock were killed and several Jie and Turkana men were severely injured. When the news of the violent skirmish reached the villages in Najie, several elders immediately went to the kraals and tried to defuse the situation to prevent further bloodshed. The elders returned to the village with some Turkana women and children in an effort to help them stay in a safe place until the explosive conflict was resolved.

When the elders returned to the village with some Turkana women, the young Jie men, who were alarmed and ready to attack the Turkana kraals, calmed down and expressed their desire to socialize with the Turkana women instead, which calmed their annoyance. After a few days, when the male relatives of the Turkana women came to fetch their wives and children, the relatives of the Jie man who had been killed, along with the Jie who had been wounded, induced the Jie elders to keep the Turkana people in the villages and kraals on the banks of Nangalol Apolon until the peace talks could take place and negotiations were made. The Turkana people were willing to participate in a peace talk and negotiate for the death, losses, and injuries, but they insisted the peace talk to be held in Nangalol Apolon, and expressed that they wanted a great Turkana kraal leader, whom I will call Apamulele, to lead the peace talk between the feuding factions. Nangalol Apolon was a half a day's journey from Nakapelimoru. Since Apamulele was the key person negotiating the peace talk, people thought of waiting for him to come, but Apamulele did not come. Fear gripped the villages in Najie and men grew rash and nervous. The delay in the arrival of Apamulele meant that the Turkana people would linger longer and have to depend on meager Jie water resources.

The Turkana people continued, however, to insist that only Apamulele was capable of negotiating and establishing peace between the two communities, as he was the most respected elder and an indispensable kraal leader. This request was considered by some Jie to be strategic on the part of the Turkana people. This was giving them the opportunity to prolong their stay around Nangalol Apolon and Nakapelimoru, buying time in this prolonged dry season to survive. Confusion and an atmosphere of uneasiness and fretfulness engulfed all of Najie.

Despite the presence of various other Turkana elders who were capable of negotiating peace, the absence of Apamulele brought new fears. With each passing day, there was a tacit agreement among the men to postpone the harvest ceremony one more day. In the meantime, the Turkana people continued to come, bringing news from the kraals. The Turkana women helped the Jie women gather firewood, harvest the fields, brew beer, and make bread, as well as engaging in barter and trade. Thus, the preparation for *akiriket*, the primary arena of performance event, became an arena for the exchange of gifts and labor which encouraged "exchange of favors" (Flores 1995, 152) and linked relationships, bonding the people together.

Finally Apamulele appeared and the news of his arrival traveled quickly from house to house. The Turkana and Jie in Nakapelimoru were eager to participate in the peace talks. As night closed in and during the next day, young and old, men and women, I was told, roamed about where Apamulele was staying in Nakapelimoru. They all knew the stories about Apamulele's powerful oratorical skills and they grew impatient to see how he was going to lead the ceremony. They were overjoyed when the sister of Apamulele, whom I will call Atung, passed through the village gathering sorghum grains from various homes to make beer for the ceremony and take it to the peace talk.

Atung made the beer in Jimos village at the homestead of Nakapor, the firemaker, while Nadul, Nakapor's wife, helped her. At this point, I joined her. Nadul boiled the grains in several earthen pots as other women helped her, while Atung stood nearby guiding her. I had the privilege of helping Atung cook the grains and brew the ceremonial beer. Whenever I followed her instructions appropriately, she looked at me with pride and stood up shouting for me to put more wood on the fire. As I helped Atung bring more firewood, carry water, and perform other tasks, the women were amused and their amusement reached amazing heights. Their shouts grew louder, accompanied by waving from the elderly and young women congratulating me.

At that moment a group of young men fired their AK-47s. Rianaro went outside and scolded the young men for bringing their guns, telling them never to operate guns during the preparation for a peace talk. Rianaro was not afraid of the guns, but felt the guns should not be present, out of respect for the upcoming ceremony as an event of peace and sharing. With guns, he said, people kill. He said he did not respect men who would come to the ceremony with them. He then said to them, "If you are going to shoot a gun, shoot at your enemies, the Dodos and the Matheniko. But there is no enemy here. These are helpless Turkana women."

The next day the ritual participants gathered on the dry riverbed of Nangalol Apolon. Elders from all over Karamoja were invited to attend the ceremony, and most Jie neighbors were represented by their respective elders. Some of these men were very elderly and had to be carried on the backs of young men to the ritual grounds. This was quite a feat since Nangalol Apolon was almost a day's journey from Jimos village.

During the ceremony, a Jie elder, a very old man, got up and smeared himself with *ngikujit* (undigested food content from the intestines) and walked back and forth praising Akuj (God) for his generous gifts and blessings. It was a great day for many people. Dancers stamped their feet on the ground, and the smell of ghee (melted butter) blended with the aroma of roasting meat. The men made an extravagant show in front of the members of the audience. They made a large sacred semicircle on the sandy ground using leaves and green grass. People smeared themselves with the gray sacred clay drawn from the sacred rivers in the region. The Turkana warriors wore black and white ostrich feathers, leg-bells, and whisks and gathered under a huge tree near the dry riverbed and started to dance, imitating bellowing cattle and various wild animals and birds. A young man holding a spear drove a black and white spotted fat bull and encircled the ritual ground four times. Some young men poured water over the bull fetched from a well in the dry riverbed. Other young men sprinkled water on the ground and purified the *akiriket*, the ritual ground. The young man leading the fat bull raised his spear over his head and petitioned Akuj for help in the peace process saying: "Akuj, give us peace, protect us from the spears and guns of our enemies; hear our prayer as you heard the prayers of our ancestors."

Some young men then sprinkled the spear and the bull using the branches of *ngidomein* (from a type of wild fruit tree typically used in traditional ceremonies, and also known to be used by Nayeche who gathered *ngidomein* fruits during her journey on the plateau). The man then drove the bull in front of the *akiriket*, where the elders were sitting in semicircle on their stools and ready to spear the bull. The elders then put away their stools and sat on the ground to show their respect for the sacred performance about to take place and watched in anticipation of the young man spearing the bull. When the young man speared the bull through its heart, it instantly fell to the ground. The sacrificial victim (*ajulot*) was then cut into pieces and roasted in the center of the semicircle where the elders were sitting. The roasted meat was first offered to the senior elders at the *akiriket*, and then placed on the *ngidomein* leaves in front of the elders. More meat was cut, and then distributed to the people. Elderly men gathered around the carcass of the bull sacrifice and began to eat while younger men carved out the internal organs and milked the *ngikujit* (undigested food in the intestines) and smeared their bodies with it. Others made sorghum bread into balls, and with one hand, tossed them into their mouths while, with their other hand, they sipped their sorghum beer.

At this point, a very senior Turkana man wrapped in red cloth removed the cloth, almost theatrically and, remaining completely naked, smeared himself with *ngikujit* while holding the spear which was used to kill the bull. Next, holding the spear with its blood-stained blade raised above his head, he praised Akuj for his generosity. Next he praised the person who provided the sacrificial bull. Then he praised the ancestors and threw some roasted meat toward the east in the direction of Moru a Nayeche (the hill of Nayeche) and performed the prayer. The elders who were sitting in the semicircle put their stools away again and sat on the ground and repeated the words of the performer. The performer occasionally stopped and nodded with his head saying, "Eee," an "interrogative" utterance prompting the members of the audiences to respond.

Iyong! Iyong, Akuj. Kingarkinae
Aku,j nakinae akiyar, nakinae ngibaren, nakinae ngitunga; nakinae ngakipi; nakinae ekisil
Iyong Aku,j kiteyarae, nanae ngakipi
Akuj, akiring na kon tanyam
Akuj, emong lo kon lo tanyam

(You! You, Akuj. Help us
Akuj, give us life; give us animals; give us people; give us water; give us peace.
You Akuj, make us live, give us water
Akuj, this is your meat, eat it
Akuj, this ox is for you, eat it)

After the prayer, the performer stood silent, and pointed the blood-stained spear toward the Moru a Nayeche saying: "That is the place where Nayeche settled with Engiro and drank water from Tarash River. That is the place where Nayeche offered wild fruits to the Jie men; that is the place my ancestors ate with the Jie. That is the place where Engiro mounted our cattle and our cattle multiplied." After making these statements, the man sat near the carcass, rejoining the old men.

Sitting with a few distinguished kraal leaders from each of the various tribes that gathered that day, Apamulele was joyful and excited. He spoke only to the people immediately beside him until, at a carefully chosen moment, he stood up and said, half jokingly, as a way of creating a bond between himself and the visitors, *"Ebeyote ejok, mam nyechamitae ngibore ngini erai nyading ka ngitunga ngulu ebei Ngijie."* "Let us stay well in peace. We don't want hatred with the Jie." Everybody listened and laughed and looked his way. His slim face with a broad smile exuded strength and confidence. After he straightened the white cloth wrapped around his body, and when he was sure they were paying attention to him, he delivered a long speech about water, cattle, and women.

With his speech, Apamulele organized the discourse of the performance and created expectations regarding the outcome of the peace ceremony. By and large, Apamulele placed himself in the position of the "principal speaker," while the members of the audience supplied the "back-channel cues" (Briggs 1988, 86), saying, "Eee" (that is, "yes," "we understand," "we are listening"). Continuing with his theatrical performance, Apamulele raised his stick in the air and, with the rhythmical movement of his body, created anticipation in the members of the audience. Suddenly, with a loud voice, he shouted, *"Inak Nayeche ngaberu."* "Nayeche gave them women." The members of the audience responded with back-channel cues and repeated the words of Apamulele to indicate their agreement. With the last statement, Apamulele clearly established a pattern for the conflict resolution in the imaginations of the members of the audience. He continued. "From the time of Nakadanya, we bound ourselves together by way of our women. When a man gets married he binds himself to the clan. He becomes one with the clan." The men looked at each other and then at Apamulele and responded to him again with back-channel cues. Things were clear now, or they were becoming clearer, but no one said a word. Addressing the young Jie and Turkana men who were sitting behind the elders, Apamulele asked, "Do you want us to welcome the cattle of our brothers, Turkana and Jie, into each other's cattle enclosure?" The way the ritual participants laughed and looked at each other made it plain that they were in agreement with him, and that the feuding parties should offer their cattle and daughters in marriage to one another's men in cleansing the blood of the dead man and the wounded men. The participants of the peace talk chanted together the following formulaic phrase after Apamulele: "*Erai Ngijie ka Ngiturkana ngipei.*" "The Turkana and the Jie are one."

With this rhetorical phrase, the patterned emotion is worked into a trope of the past, into a layered relationship between the Jie and the Turkana, who were prefigured in the heroic adventure of Nayeche, transforming the spoken word of *eemut* into an enactment, an event, with Apamulele orchestrating. When the formulaic image of the Nayeche historical tradition and the realms of the contemporary world brought into contact, the members of the audience who were involved in the feud were persuaded to cut a deal with one another and resolve their conflict. Apamulele's skill in completing the story with a rhetorical flourish enhanced his persuasion, thus establishing the overall rhetorical power of his story.

"We are one," responded an old man from the audience, affirming the statement made by Apamulele. The congregation followed suit and nodded their heads saying, "Eee." "We will share our food and water with our brothers," laughingly affirmed another old man. The Turkana men shouted with laughter and looked at each other approvingly and said in unison, "We will share our food and water with our brothers, the Jie. We will give our daughters and take theirs." Apamulele stood and joined in with their speech. "The cattle of one is cattle of all!" he said, looking at the elderly men sitting in front of the carcass and smiling. "And the daughter of one is the daughter of all!" To affirm this view, Apamulele moved forward and, with stick raised, pointed to a well in the dry riverbed visible in the distance. Apamulele declared, "It was there that the foot prints of Nayeche got blended with the foot prints of Engiro. It was there that Nayeche smelled the water. We are the children of Nayeche and the gray bull Engiro. We will share our water and pasture with the Jie when they come to Tarash River. We will be generous to one another. If not today, we will be hungry tomorrow. We shall share water and pasture forever." Shouts and joyous laughter filled the air.

Apamulele then requested that the women gathering wild fruits in the grazing land and visiting in the kraals be treated with deference and that the men make sure they were safe. He reached out to a bush

nearby and plucked a wild fruit and put it in his mouth, poetically re-
enacting Nayeche gathering wild fruit. He continued his reenactment,
imitating the thirsty Engiro moving sluggishly in search of water. After
a while he enacted Nayeche again following the footprints of the gray
bull Engiro, thirsty and hungry. The Turkana women, standing behind
the crowd, showed enthused admiration for Apamulele's enactment of
Nayeche and the gray bull Engiro.

In the dry bed of Nangalol Apolon, senior men from all the tribes surrounded Apamulele as he broke the hind legs of the sacrificial bull, and
then broke the spear. People tried to get near, but they were told not to
get close. The children, who had been running around from one place
to another, shouting, stood silently as if dazed. A few moments later the
bones and spear were buried and people craned their necks to see. In
spite of continued warning to stay away, several women shouted. After
breaking the bones and the spear, an old Turkana man sang a song that
required repetition from the members of the audience. The joyful shouts
and singing filled the air in an atmosphere of overpowering happiness.
The shouts shook the bushes and echoed resoundingly. With the rising
and falling of melody, many old men energetically danced in the bush,
uttering the name of Akuj, the gray bull Engiro, Nayeche, and Orwakol
simultaneously.

After clearing his throat an old man told the crowd, "You have had
your food and you have drunk your beer, and Akuj has blessed the Jie
and the Turkana. There are several feast days a year, and today is one
of those."

Everybody listened to the old man silently. It was so silent that one
could even hear the breathing of the orator who now spoke without
words. His body language was such that there was no need for words.
He looked at the AK-47 carried by a young man and said, "Our ancestors fought with spears made from the soil of Mount Toror and not with
the guns of white men." His eyes roamed in the distance and he shook
his stick toward Mount Toror that loomed in the distance. Then, silence
prevailed as only the eyes of the old man spoke. They shone in an appeal for the presence of the ancestors. The words came out of his mouth,
"Mount Toror, the hill of my ancestors; Engiro, the bull of my ancestors;
Longiro, the river of my ancestors. Nayeche, our mother! Engiro, the
father of our cattle!"

The old man's appeal to the ancestors plunged the audience into
depths of sorrowful longing. The silence was broken and the audience
was momentarily transported to the time of the ancestors. The old man

reenacted the actions of Nayeche following the footprints of the gray bull, and Orwakol capturing the bull in the Longiro River, as he poetically narrated the story. The old man, drenched with droplets of sweat, which he wiped away with the palms of both hands, was joined by Apamulele who smeared him with the ashes of the sacrificial fire.

He told how Nayeche shared the wild fruits with the Jie and how the gray bull Engiro went to Tarash River and drank water from a well. Apamulele told the story of the ancestors in his own way, bringing together the varying themes from a range of historical traditions and various communities to enhance the mood of the audience.

It was the old man who set the mood and won all the admiration, but Apamulele was no less appreciated. In the dry bed of Nangalol Apolon, they both fascinated and captured the complete attention of the audience. The performance of Apamulele provided the fundamental framework for the comprehension of historical tradition as "social action" by engaging the audience to comprehend the relevance and significance of the actual verbal performance of the ancestral heroine to social life of today. What Apamulele did, essentially, was to tell the story of Nayeche's adventure on the waterless plateau and turn it into the experience of others (Bauman 1986, 2).

As they spoke and made reference to the themes of varying historical traditions, it was impossible to record and capture all the nuances of this theatrical narration of pastness. There was no single narrative, but rather an intertwining of subnarratives, as a number of poetic anecdotal references were made to certain episodes of the wandering of Nayeche on the waterless plateau. The structure and interaction within the performance patterned expectations and rearranged the structure of social relations between the Turkana and the Jie within the performance event and perhaps beyond (Bauman 1986, 4). The multivocal meaning of the historical tradition emerged in a dialectic played out within the context of the situated action, as Tedlock and Mannheim's formulations delineate (1995, 5). The memory of Nayeche's prayer and her appeal to people became a verbal icon of the performance event; as Apamulele recalled this memory image, he made the flux of Jie and Turkana experience comprehensible. Apamulele's poetic performance of pastness embellished the words of Nayeche in the interest of greater dynamic tension, and created acceptance between the Jie and the Turkana.

When the old man and Apamulele stopped performing, the members of the audience began to exchange jokes, ambiguous allusions, and other pleasantries, revealing their understanding that the Jie and the

Turkana offered their daughters in exchange for the blood of the dead man and the wounded men, and the cattle were killed; an offer which they accepted.

Apamulele must have been signaling his trust that the Jie and the Turkana were willing to settle the conflict if they each offered their daughters for marriage. Thus, he was proposing a workable solution in his suggestion that Jie and Turkana enter into marriage negotiations. Apamulele's emotion-laden poetic message deeply intertwined verbal icons with the contemporary society in an attempt to end the conflict and violence. With the rhythmical movement of his body and the music of his words he moved the performance into the realm of the ancestors.

Apamulele's nonverbal demonstration of Nayeche's pursuit of the gray bull Engiro in Nangalol Apolon reminded the people of their ancient kinship ties, peaceful relationship, common ancestors, and common border and territories, persuading them to share resources. Here the effect of poetic references to a peaceful relationship is not entirely unconscious. Indeed, Apamulele tries to achieve, and does indeed achieve, a poetic juxtaposition of the violent contemporary moments with the peaceful ancestral past. With his rhetorical anecdotal reference to the motifs and images of the historical tradition, Apamulele skillfully forged a connection between past and the present in an attempt to establish the necessary associations for people to avoid violence and maintain peace.

Apamulele's anecdotal reference to Nayeche's journey linked the dispute mediation to the Jie and the Turkana religious tradition, with practical political procedure connected to the ancestral moment. The reference to Nayeche's journey was explicitly aimed at persuading the members of the audience to end the violence and conflict and establish security and peace. In the memory of Nayeche, Akuj appears as the transcendental peacemaker to whom the ancestors prayed during political crisis. Nayeche's journey revealed how Akuj, as an ultimate authority, would support and protect human life. The presence of Akuj connected with Nayeche, the venerable ancestral heroine, the creator of the Turkana tribe, seems crucial for the feuding parties to be motivated to end the warfare and violence. The interesting aspect of this connection is not that it advances a moral claim, which is confirmed by the obvious predicament, but rather that it sanctifies the Turkana people's rights to water and grazing resources around Nangalol Apolon. The memory of Nayeche's journey thus also undercuts the implication of conflict over resources and it establishes the resolution in *akiriket* as a part of the struggle shared by both communities.

The initial prayer offered by the old man before Apamulele's speech also emphasizes the moral implications of religious idealization in the statement *"Tolilimer, tolilimer, tolilimeto, tolilimeto"* (Become cool, become cool, all of you, become cool), suggesting the avoidance of anger and violence. Heat symbolizes anger and destruction, while becoming cool signifies the calmness and peacefulness both for Akuj and human beings. The performances of Apamulele and the old man therefore left the audience with the understanding that the very act of offering one's women for peace and as a means of stopping of the violence is more a religious ideal than a political mandate. Apamulele idealizes Nayeche's peaceful journey on the waterless plateau; he then underpins the implication that it is the ancestors that created the Turkana from the original family. Precisely because of this, the Turkana, the descendants of Nayeche, have the hereditary rights to water wells and grazing lands. This sets the stage for a comparison of the notion of ancestral authority based upon the rule set by Akuj, and with the authority claims of the contemporary tainted world, which resulted in violence.

The poetic images of Nayeche fetching water from Nangalol Apolon, her prayer for the protection of the cattle and people, and the possibility of her people and cattle being eaten by the vultures and hyena, inspires the audience by the possibility of the real threat of violent conflict between the two communities. Thus, the poetics of survival is brought into useful conjunction with the reality of violence, urging people to focus on the moral authority of the ancestral heroes. As Apamulele recalls the memorable journey of Nayeche, he juxtaposes the troubled contemporary human relationship and the ideal conditions of the ancestral world. With his effortless interpretation he first conceives the contemporary conflict as a genuine human concern for peaceful survival in the face of violent conflict; he then conceives the past political strategy as a necessary model for current political experience. He discovers the political strategy in the entanglement of poetic memory images in the semiotics of the landscape and in historical tradition, as he nonverbally enacts the adventure of Nayeche and the verbal icon of the Jie oral tradition into popular interethnic political procedure. He thus persuades the members of the audience to favor investment in peaceful relationship rather than violence.

With his performance, Apamulele demonstrates the basic design of the ancestral experience that transpired on the dry bed of Nangalol

Apolon on the plateau and around upper Tarash River in the plains. His artistic reenactment of Nayeche's peaceful adventure on the waterless plateau is antithetical to violence, which is the root cause of the Jie and the Turkana experience of conflict, and which prompted the dispute mediation. Focusing on the dimension of Nayeche's peaceful adventure, Apamulele insists that whatever is the contemporary situation between the two communities, the very emergence of the Turkana society from the embryonic Jie was peaceful. He demonstrates this by providing a nonverbal account of how Nayeche peacefully gathered wild fruits in the bush. There was no violent threat of the natural order and the gray bull Engiro was on her side. The thirsty landscape did not prevent Nayeche from going to the Tarash River. Indeed, Engiro shared water with her. Nayeche fetched water for the Jie people from the Nangalol Apolon, from the very river whose water the Jie were refusing her descendants. However, it was the generosity of Nayeche that tempted the Jie men to go to Tarash River and take risks. The original Jie family settled in Moru a Nayeche peacefully and rescued themselves and their cattle from the threat of famine of the waterless plateau. Apamulele's invocation of Nayeche's adventure therefore reminded the people that every aspect of Turkana life was and is so much a part of the plateau and the patterns of circumstances that are found there that it seems appropriate to observe the norms of mutual reciprocity.

I participated in another peace talk, in Lokatap Rock in October 1997, at the height of the dry season. The gathering for the performance involved a dispute over a man, whom I would like to call Lochor, a Rengen man from Lokatap Rock who had consistently been watering his cattle at a well near a place called Lodoket by the Longiro River near Jimos. The other man, whom I shall name Locheng, from Nakapelimoru, disputed vehemently that Lochor, as a Rengen man from the Lodiny clan, had any rights to water his cattle at the Longiro River, which belonged to the Orwakol clan. The elders had consequently decided to hold a gathering to discuss the matter and resolve the potentially explosive conflict situation.

I went to the gathering with Abdulkarim, a Jie friend. It was in the afternoon when we reached the Lokatap Rock at the edge of the congested village. When we arrived, the performance had already begun. The members of the gathering were mostly older men but included some young men in their thirties and forties. The adolescents and children lingered and watched as the cultural scene unfolded. Ritual participants were nearly finished eating the roasted meat of an ox, sacrificed for the occasion, while they were discussing recent warfare, marriages, and other tribal gossip.

Abdulkarim and I sat at the foot of the great rock and listened to the men talking about things of the past while honey badgers roamed and ate grass. There was a very elderly Rengen man who sat at the foot of the rock near me engaged in friendly exchanges, sharing his memory of Tufnell, a colonial officer who traveled to Najie on several occasions during the early 1900s. He remembered as a child seeing Tufnell standing on the rock in his impeccably clean uniform where we were sitting and questioning people about guns. As I listened to the childhood memory of this elderly man, the members of the gathering finished the last bit of the meat and their beer.

At a deftly chosen moment, a very old man from the Orwakol clan, whom I will call Longoli, stood up on a high rock with a stick in his hand and, pointing it in the direction of the Longiro River, he initiated the talk by invoking the formulaic images and the sentiments of historical tradition, with the intention of persuading the members of the audience to be more sympathetic to Lochor's predicament in the midst of the long dry season:

> People do not know that people of Lodiny and Orwakol are one. This is how things were. There was no foreigner. All of them were Jie people, one nephew and one uncle. Today, because of the relationship of the great old men, we still consider Lodiny's people as our own nephews, we are people of Orwakol and they are people of Lodiny. After sprinkling water and smearing with *emunyen* (sacred clay), Lodiny and Orwakol became brothers again and began visiting each other. These people are not foreign to one another. They are all one. Orwakol is one. Lodiny is the nephew but they are all Orwakol. Whenever the Orwakol people performed sacrifices at Daidai, they invited five to ten Lodiny people to come and hear the words of the people about their land. The share of Lodiny and his people was always given to them, even if there was only one bull sacrificed. Today people no longer know that there should be some share for Lodiny's people; Lodiny's people do not know that there should be share for their uncle also. Yet they know. Even though those who know, they know very little. It was my father who told these.

To appreciate Longoli's closing statement, I must explain that Longoli's father was one of the most respectable elders of the past whose extraordinary deeds are still remembered to this day. When Longoli said that the source of his knowledge was his father, he signaled to the members of the audience that they should not risk contradicting his statements about past relations. However, some younger members of the Orwakol clan elders who were present at the meeting were unwilling to share the scarce water resources of the Longiro River with the Lodiny people at the height of the dry season and thus politely rejected Longoli's mediation. After repeated efforts to get the Orwakol clan to cooperate and accept a truce, another old man from the Orwakol clan, whom I will call Lopore, stood up, and holding on to his staff, he said with a trembling voice, "Ikoni ngakwap itiyao nege, tokerite ngikapolok, tokerite apa kon" (This is how things are done in this place; respect the great people, respect your father).

After this Lopore remained silent and stared at the members of the audience and walked slowly back to where he had emerged and sat down. This short statement followed by his silence could either mean that Lopore was not well informed of his tradition to take up the challenge and elaborate on his statement, or, more likely, that he refused to respond to the challenge, which is an insult to the contesting party. Soon after Lopore returned to his place, another elder, whom I will call Ekeno, stood up and responded in defense of the younger men of the Orwakol clan who rejected Longoli's appeal: "Dig a well at Dopeth River, get your black *emunyen* at Koromwai[2] and let your cattle drink water from there! This is what Lodiny instructed people to do when he came to this place. Lodiny also told people, 'When it is dry season take the cattle to drink water at the wells of the Dopeth River.' Those were the instructions of Lodiny of long ago which are followed in this land, and forever."

Ekeno, quoting Lodiny, the ancestral founding father of the Lodiny clan, provided a powerful punch line with a disturbing interpretation, offering a contrasting set of ideals and assumption regarding the rights of Lodiny clans. The tone of Ekeno's voice was one of frustration and anger with Lochor who, in his estimation, should have watered his cattle in the Dopeth River, the river which belongs to the Lodiny people, instead of watering the cattle at the wells of Longiro River, which clearly belong to the Orwakol clan; he hence steadfastly refused Longoli's mediation on behalf of Lochor. Ekeno's punch line reorganized the mood of the audience and created an unfavorable expectation regarding the predicament of Lochor.

As soon as Ekeno sat down, a tumult and uneasiness broke out among the members of the audience. The mediation lasted several hours, but in spite of Ekeno's punch line the members of the audience seemed to be more in agreement with Longoli, the original speaker. This time another man from the Lodiny clan, whom I will call Logwee, stood up in his bid to remove the people of Lodiny from their defensive position during mediation. By this time of the mediation process, large groups of people had arrived speaking in low-pitched voices trying to persuade the Orwakol clan to mediate. Here is the anecdotal reference which Logwee made as he paced back and forth in front of the crowd, uttering the following persuasive formulaic images of tradition with a trembling voice, with members of the audience responding to him with validating back-channel cues, saying, "Eee" (yes, we understand):

Lodiny ka Koorwakol erai ngipei daadang!
Emam ngini erai!
Emam ngini abuni alo Katap!
Emam ngini abuni alo Turkan!
Emam ngini abuni alo Dodoth!
Ngijie ikes daadang
Ngikaitotoi, Ngikaitotoi ikes!

(Lodiny and Orwakol are one!
There is no outsider!
No one comes from Katap (the Acholi land)!
No one comes from Turkana!
No one comes from Dodoth!
They are all Jie people
They are brothers, they are brothers!)

These popular formulaic phrases were explicit statements made by Logwee about the interethnic relationship and kinship ties between the Orwakol and the Lodiny clan. They appealed to their ancestral kinship ties, hoping to persuade the two sides to share resources as their ancestors did. This meaning is nicely articulated in the phrase *"Ngikaitotoi, Ngikaitotoi ikes!"* (They are brothers, they are brothers!). The parallelism in the sound and syntax persuasively suggests the traditional kinship ties presupposing and preparing the members of the audience to accept the equal rights of Lodiny people for the resources of Longiro River, as kinship dictates. Thus, Logwee defined the relationship between the two communities in terms of the broader regional ethnic politics, emphasizing the importance of the kind of close kinship the Lodiny and Orwakol have with each other in relation to the Turkana, Katap (Acholi

people), or Dodoth. Therefore, both Lodiny and Orwakol people should
appreciate one another, he suggested, and respect their ancient rights to
water wells.

Logwee's persuasion changed the course of the mediation and encouraged Longoli, who was silently watching the mediation process. Longoli
stood up and walked up and down, without a word, poetically evoking
anticipation from his audience. After a few moments of such silent movement, with a low voice he performed a version of a story of the Orwakol
and Lodiny historical tradition in which he emphatically tried to interpret the rights of the Lodiny people to the dry season wells of the
Longiro River. Here is the translation of the story which I recorded during the performance:

> Lodiny and Orwakol were hunters. People did not yet have cattle and they
> moved in the bush and stayed in the camps. Lodiny and Orwakol were the
> people who found the gray bull. They were hunting wild animals when
> they found that bull. They found Engiro in a place named Lodoket. The
> bull was drinking water from a well when they found it. That place is near
> Daidai, along the course of the Longiro, near the place where there is stag-
> nant water. When they found the bull it was drinking water. They did not
> do anything to it because Akuj prevented them from killing it. Akuj pre-
> vented them from killing the bull in that place where *emunyen* (sacred clay)
> is. That is where you can find *emunyen* now; which is why the Longiro River
> is called Longiro. They found the bull there. They did not know where
> the bull came from; they (Lodiny and Orwakol) had come long ago from
> Nyakwai[3] to kill wild animals there.

The interesting aspect of this performance is the way it reinterpreted
and validated the Lodiny clan's rights to the wells of the Longiro River
in a way relevant to the predicament of Lochor. The story first depersonalizes Lochor's situation and then it traditionalizes the current affairs by
drawing upon certain images and associations that support the idea that
the Rengen people (Lodiny people) have rights to not only the wells of
the Longiro River in general, but also the well in Lodoket where Lochor
was accused of stealing water. Through its depiction, this tale associates
the rights of the Rengen people to the dry season wells in Lodoket since
the story hints at the discovery of the *emunyen* (sacred clay), the sacred
bull, and the well in Lodoket, not only by Orwakol but also by Lodiny,
the ancestor of the Rengen people. What the story tells is true because
the continuing presence of the sacred clay in that place where Lodiny

and Orwakol found the bull testifies to the memory of Lodiny's and Orwakol's simultaneous encounter with the gray bull there. The concurrent encounter legitimizes both Lodiny's and Orwakol's equal access to the wells in Longiro because the ancestors of both saw the sacred bull when they were together.

It was also apparent from the narrative that, since both Lodiny and Orwakol found the ancestral bull Engiro in the Longiro River, and since all the cattle of the Jie are descended from gray bull Engiro, all cattle in Najie had the right to drink the water of the Longiro River, including the water of the wells in Lodoket. As soon as Longoli completed his story, he immediately and skillfully made reference to popular stock memory images in Jie oral tradition, thus expressing and intensifying the emotional force of the pastness in the following anecdotal references to historical tradition:

Kiparae cho tonoku, kinokokinae Daidai.
Kiparae cho tonoku, kinokokinae Lokatap.
Kinokokinae cho nyakin ani cho enokoni kiyela kirae lotunga daang daadang.

(In Daidai, they [Orwakol and Lodiny] rubbed the sticks, fire fell out, and they made fire.
In Lokatap, they [Orwakol and Lodiny] rubbed the sticks, fire fell out, and they made fire.
They made the fire and distributed it to the people, all the people, all the people.)

Hearing these stock memory images, the rest of the members of the audience replied together in one voice saying: "*Kinokokinae cho nyakin ani cho enokoni kiyela kirae lotunga daang daadang*" (They made the fire and distributed it to the people, all the people, all the people).

Although the first and second lines refer to the making of fire in two important ancestral shrines, Daidai and Lokatap Rock, respectively, and reveal the differences and separateness of the Orwakol and Lodiny clans, the last statement about making fire and distributing it to all the people makes it clear that even though their ancestors made fire in two different places, meaning they are different people, they nevertheless share the same fire since the source of the water, cattle, and fire are diffused and shared, and hence they are one people. The idea here is that even though the people of Lodiny and Orwakol are different people, their ancestors found the resources together and they have shared the same vital resources because everything was handed to them by their common ancestors.

At that point, an unexpected objecting response came from a member of the audience. It warned people, in a humorous way, about the ill effects of stealing water for which one did not work, by drawing on the images of a cunning rabbit which drank the water without laboring for it in the popular Jie oral tradition. The audience laughed. The humor presented the members of the audience with the more human side of the situation describing Lochor's action. But this was also discomforting, as everybody knew who Lochor was. After the initial laughter, people became solemn again and shook their heads commenting that it is true that one should share the water, but people should work together to get the water. No one should steal the water from a well that they did not help to dig.

After the performance of the peace ceremony was over, people talked among themselves and continued to laugh at the comment the man made with its association to a cunning rabbit. It was apparent that people enjoyed the peace talk and narrative performance. One reason why people appreciated the story was that the objection that was raised with the image of rabbit was both disturbing and amusing at the same time. An objection uttered in an amusing manner avoided a possible tense outcome. This point was made beautifully and effectively with improvisational talent and the ability to utilize both forms of oral tradition (folktales and historical traditions) valued by the storyteller and the members of the audience. Even though the performer and the members of the audience were drawing from stories familiar to everyone, the ability to evoke the right image at the right moment was admirable and effective in resolving the conflict.

It would be a mistake to assume that storytellers' skills are judged exclusively by their ability to handle the stock images of the historical tradition; on the contrary, he or she must show some level of originality in interactions with the members of the audience. The image of sharing fire is the stock memory image of pastness which, skillfully used by a storyteller, can intensify the force of the pastness. The comment regarding the ways of the cunning rabbit uttered by a member of the audience balanced the ways of imagining the past in the light of the present situation in an amusing way.

Of course, the persuasiveness of the arguments was embellished with appropriate body movement, intonation, and the rhythmic elements of the storyteller and the members of the audience and this highlighted

the competing points of view of pastness. Longoli's narration of historical tradition and his poetic expression was powerful and rendered with
a beautiful voice. The contrasting but familiar images of the cunning rabbit and the venerable ancestors were beautifully juxtaposed with their
different but connotative richness, and subliminal intertextual comparison was useful in resolving a potentially explosive conflict situation.
Such invocation of the images of traditions reminded the people of
their vulnerability in such a harsh environment, articulating the importance of sharing meager resources, but it also reminded them of the
value of being ethical in their actions and, in particular, the value of
not stealing.

People knew that Lochor was from Rengen and that he had been married to a woman in the Orwakol clan. The few cattle he had given his
wife who lived in Kotyang village on the banks of the Longiro River
had to be watered in the wells of either the Dopeth River or the Longiro
River. They also knew that it was the peak of the long dry season and the
wells of the Dopeth River were barely able to support even a few cattle.
The people in Rengen depended on the wells of the Longiro River.

But people also knew that the residents of Kotyang village resented
Lochor's uncooperative and socially questionable attitude. Also of relevance was Lochor's sad personal relationship history. He was not kind
to his wives and sons, and he had become abusive. One of his wives
escaped to her natal home in Losilang after the death of one of her sons.
People said that Lochor became abusive to her after the death of her
son. After a period of time, she was persuaded to return to her husband's home, but Lochor and his other wives and daughters mistreated
her again.

After the performance of the peace talk, people privately talked about
Lochor's abusive attitude toward his grown sons, in their mid-twenties
and thirties, and his refusal to pay the bridewealth for their marriages.
One of Lochor's sons was a great raider, but each time he brought cattle
home, Lochor took them away and used them for himself to marry
more wives. The invocation of the image of the rabbit during the performance was partly because of Lochor's unacceptable attitude. He
was in many ways like the rabbit who gathered resources unto himself,
using his traditional rights, exploiting not only his community, but also
members of his own family.

Familiar with the circumstances of the dry, hot summer, they knew
that he needed to water his cattle using the wells in the Longiro River,
but they also knew that Lochor was lazy and he wanted something for

which he had not labored. By bringing about the image of the rabbit, the members of the audience clearly communicated the fact that Lochor was not an ideal member, yet the community still had the responsibility to help him survive the long dry summer.

The image of the rabbit troubled the audience, as well as Longoli, the storyteller, who had tried his best to assist Lochor through his performance of the historical tradition, but they all knew that Lochor really did not deserve assistance. The intrinsically impersonal and ambiguous tradition, in this context, allowed Lochor and the people with whom he was in dispute to glimpse at how the ideal social relationship ought to be. The insight this performance afforded these men was to understand and appreciate the aesthetic and internal poetic of their tradition as well as their unique place when dealing with difficult and troubling social situations.

The numerous performances in which I participated, such as this one in Lokatap Rock and the one which took place in Nangalol Apolon, made it clear to me that, indeed, most historical traditions have little impact in their mere narrative forms. Context is crucial, not only for appreciation but also for understanding the meaning of the oral tradition. The Jie people whom I came to know during my stay in Najie had a difficult time interpreting the meaning of the historical traditions or stories without contextual information. In the above mentioned performances, it became clear that the contextual information surrounding the broader cultural scenes in which the performances take place itself forms the greater narrative without narrating a particular historical tradition. It would be a mistake to assume that narration of pastness can be determined by presence solely of the verbal text. On the contrary, the verbal text images can be hinted at and expanded on through body language and through the mood of the performance situation. The skillful storytellers powerfully use formulaic anecdotal expressions and body language in their imaginative renditions to produce an acceptable past and future through nonverbal performance.

Performances in both cases were deeply embedded in the tradition itself. Through the rhythmic movement of the storytellers and the tonal qualities of their words, poetic expressions were enmeshed with images of historical tradition to create new themes and interpretations. The political language surrounding the images of historical tradition, with all of their touchstone associations, brought together the standards of ancestral social relationship, making of these ancient images master

symbols and mnemonic devices, where the images of the historical traditions and their multivalent, multivocal messages disclosed continuity
with the past. With his artistic manipulation of the images of Nayeche,
for example, Apamulele revealed the verbal icons and their associated
details thus etching the images into fanciful and germane interpretations for the audience members.

Through their poetic performances, the storytellers who were involved
in the dispute mediations unfolded the plot of the historical traditions
steadily, harmoniously juxtaposing the events of the contemporary tainted world with the ideal world of the ancestors, bringing them together.
For the moment of performance, the conflicting parties were unified according to the ancestral ideal, as the members of the audiences became
charged by the emotions woven into the metaphors of pastness. The dramatic performances captured the attention of their audience, guiding
their focus to the ideal past and demanding identification with the ancestors to cope with the vulnerability of living in a dry environment which
rendered them interdependent. With the artful and dramatic movements
of the storytellers and the fanciful engagement of the members of the
audience, the historical traditions were no longer mere tales but rather
were processes within tales recounting the deeds of the memorable ancestors, the creators of the Jie and the Turkana societies, respectively.

In this way the storytellers focused attention upon the centrality of
hereditary rights, handed down by the heroes, which threw religion and
authority and interpretation of the ancestral memories into question.
A discursive interpretation of the anecdotal references to historical tradition and poetic representation of pastness emerged as a decisive fac-
tor for understanding the ancient past. At the same time discursive
interpretation was a result of the storytellers' poetic recalling of past
event memories at the center of struggle, rather than their concern
with the significance of their performances within the larger political
context and experience.

At the heart of both dispute mediations was the storytellers' rendi-
tion of the trope of pastness, the core of mythic survivals on the waterless plateau that harnessed the emotions of the conflicting parties and
the members of the audiences with a promise of solace and survival
in the dry environment. The poetic representations of the pastness as-
sured the contemporary world a steady relationship between the past
and the present. Pastness, in this sense, was a device of the storytellers
to bridge the gap between the ancestors and the living, and, in the process, recalling the soul of the historical tradition.

It was for this reason that the varying interpretations and recalling of the memories of Lodiny and Orwakol evoked a moral reaction to ecological and political threats, and enabled Lochor to find solace in the performances of historical traditions. Similar to the Jie and the Turkana predicament, people everywhere in this region share the problem of ecological crisis, warfare, and raiding. Thus, we see that the popular historical traditions presented in the previous chapter carry the messages of an effective moral response to the problems created by pastoralism; motifs of historical traditions revolve around feasts and famines and survivals. The patterns of historical tradition in this region engender the rhetoric of political alliances. Historical traditions describe people's afflictions with ecological and political crisis. Understanding of the themes and motifs of the oral traditions explain the discourses of life among these people.

The problem of subsistence for the Jie involves the exploitation of various natural resources scattered within and beyond their territories, which they share with their neighbors. The Jie people must maintain the integrity of these natural resources and their herds against attacks from outside. These problems present themselves to individual heads of the family who are responsible for the maintenance of family resources, particularly the herd, against the external threats. But these threats cannot be resolved without collective action at the local level. The everyday Jie social and political lives of people involve public gatherings concerned with the day-to-day organization of collective action and dispute mediations. Such gatherings usually attract men who are good orators and storytellers, who have good knowledge of their tradition and past and present political strife. These storytellers usually lead discussions involving the resolution of conflict situations arising from the problems of living in dry environment and the need to share natural resources, such as water wells and grazing land and to protect the family herd, as well as a host of other issues.

Appeals to the historical traditions summarize the expected generic social relations between the storytellers and their audience. The link between the present situation and the mythical one gives meaning to the discourse in question by framing the problem with powerful conventional sentiments, thus creatively managing to resolve the conflict during dispute mediation. Individuals protect themselves from the unpredictable environment and prevent possible disasters by linking their situation with the ancestral world in which sharing resources and cooperation is the standard practice. Anecdotal references to the historical traditions celebrate survival through sharing and cooperating and condemn refusal to share, which is understood as threatening the social system. Dispersals and adventures for water and food, especially during times of ecological crises, is the theme of most Jie historical traditions, which are recounted as true stories of the distant past. In some of these stories when some powerful kin refuses to share resources, the weak person wanders in the bush and survives on wild fruits and game. In some cases stories end happily with the rejected person finding a place with abundance of food and water. Such stories are not only the themes of the historical traditions but also themes of popular biographies, as I have shown in previous chapters.

The construction of historical tradition involves persuasive oratorical performances. This reenacted past involves the persuasive manipulation of the discourse with an intention to resolve the present conflict through rhetorical references to Nayeche's voice reflected in various historical traditions. Storytellers, such Apamulele, use their poetic skills to create a past that is so political in its form and so pleasing to contemporary audiences that it enables the storytellers to control the discourse of pastness and persuade their audiences to accept their interpretation of the past as legitimate, thus acquiring for it the power of discourse. The audience accepts a certain past because it is persuasive, artful, and poetic. The more poetic the memory images of past events, the more powerful they become, and hence they have a more lasting impact on the audience. When an image of a historical tradition is constructed artfully for political ends, then the art of persuasion becomes part of the historical tradition.

PART THREE

6 The Return of Nayeche and the Gray Bull Engiro

In this chapter, I examine the implicit meaning[1] of the Nayeche and the gray bull Engiro historical tradition, as a remembered memory and a repeated event. The contents of the remembrance of the past event contained in the Nayeche and the gray bull Engiro oral tradition are reproduced through storytellers' representations of them. These representations are not simple fixed historical messages, expressed explicitly, but are actively interconnected with present situations and are a part of the society's habitual actions. The memory of Nayeche and the gray bull Engiro's journey from the plateau to the plains is symbolically embodied in the Jie and Turkana landscapes. This poetic journey is metaphorically repeated during the annual movement of the Jie cattle from the Karamoja Plateau to the Turkana plains, as well as in the movement of the sorghum grain from the granary of the firemaker to the gardens of the Jie women. As in the poetics of return imbued in the oral tradition of the journey of Nayeche and the gray bull Engiro, Jie harvest ritual intimately portrays the theme of return, which is analogous to *awatoun*, an episode of the Jie marriage ceremony in which the bride returns to her natal home.

The participation of the Turkana women in the harvest ritual in this sense is an eloquent depiction of the implicit meaning of the oral tradition, which underpins the Jie and Turkana cultural discourses. The Nayeche and the gray bull Engiro oral tradition occur in salient aspects of the Jie and Turkana cultures, such as the Jie polity, marriage ceremony, and harvest ritual, transforming the oral tradition into a strong emotional image, and revealing its implicit meaning. This emotional image orders the discourse structure of the historical theme that explains how and why the Jie and the Turkana are related to one another. The

Figure 6.1: Moru a Nayeche (the hill of Nayeche). Note the grave of Nayeche in front of the hill. Author photo (Turkana land, northern Kenya)

Figure 6.2: A Turkana woman who has brought wild fruits to her Jie friend from the upper Tarash River region. Author photo (Nakapelimoru)

Figure 6.3: The anthropologist, returning with the Jie cattle from upper Tarash River to Najie. Author photo (Nakapelimoru)

historical theme contained in the tradition, however, is fluid and changing, not predictable and orderly.

The memory images contained in the Nayeche and the gray bull oral tradition vary in each locality, mainly according to the political economy of each ecological zone, but also according to many other factors. The memory images contained in the Nayeche and the gray bull Engiro oral tradition in each of these disparate localities are shaped by subsistence activities and by various other patterns of cultural and political ecology. These provide the Jie and the Turkana with discourses to construct their world and to engage in interethnic relationships. In these local traditions, Nayeche travels with ease from one locality to another, sometimes gathering wild fruits, and at other times fishing or planting local crops. Sometimes, Nayeche follows herds of bulls rather than the gray bull Engiro, and at other times, she pursues wild hippos, thus forming an integral part of the local cultural discourse and figuratively connecting the conceptual realms of the local people with their day-to-day empirical existence.

The Nayeche and the gray bull Engiro oral tradition is often "interlocked" with various other local traditions, linking salient social interactions and providing the plot for the local social dramas. This interlocking reveals the Nayeche and the gray bull Engiro oral tradition's "implicit meaning" (Vansina 1985, 143–4) in each locality. As Vansina points out, the implicit meaning of a tradition elucidates how the original memory images come to be depicted the way they are in the oral tradition involved.

Therefore, the point of exploring the implicit meaning of the Nayeche oral tradition is to move beyond its "explicit meaning" (Vansina 1985, 143) to understand how and why people tell a particular version of the Nayeche and the gray bull Engiro oral tradition. Through the implicit meaning, we can better understand the local meaning of the Nayeche and the gray bull Engiro oral tradition and the memory images it contains, as well as the way in which the local people represent the memory images of a given past contained in the tradition to represent their past to themselves. Investigation of the implicit meaning of a tradition itself requires one to understand how the local people's experiences are framed and filtered through the images of oral tradition.

This chapter focuses on the Nayeche and the gray bull Engiro oral tradition around the upper Tarash region in Turkana land and around Jimos village and the Nakapelimoru area in Najie. The analysis of the Nayeche and the gray bull Engiro oral tradition within these localities provides a unique opportunity to examine how it is interlocked with the significant local cultural memory scripts about the origin of the Jie polity and of the harvest ritual. This interlocking provides unique pathways for the local construction of identities and interethnic relationships both for the Jie of the Jimos village and Nakapelimoru village area and for the Turkana of the upper Tarash River region.

According to some Jie storytellers, Orwakol instituted the harvest ritual just before Nayeche went to the upper Tarash region. When Orwakol first arrived in Najie, he gave some sorghum to his eldest wife, Losilang, for her to cultivate on the banks of the Longiro River. The same night, Losilang kindled a new fire and slept with Orwakol on the cowskin. In the morning, Losilang shared the seeds with her co-wives, and they all settled on the different parts of the banks of the Longiro River to cultivate sorghum, except Nakapelimoru, the youngest wife of Orwakol, who went east and settled about thirty miles from the Koteen Hill. Nakapelimoru wanted to be where there was an abundance of wild

fruits in case of crop failure during the dry seasons and to be near her
natal family, who lived around the Koteen Hill. Orwakol built granaries
for all his wives, and, when all the wives harvested sorghum from their
fields, they returned the original sorghum seeds to Orwakol. Losilang
stored the seeds in her granary, which later became the master granary
of the Jie. As the wives of Orwakol expanded their gardens, Orwakol
named each of the settlements after their names. It was during this
time, the Jie storytellers say, that Nayeche, the daughter of Orwakol,
disappeared, and she was last seen in Nakapelimoru. "This is why,"
maintain the Jie storytellers, "the Jie people offer sorghum grain to the
firemaker during the harvest ritual, and this is why they call the seven
territorial divisions of the Lokorwakol section as Losilang, Kotyang,
Kanawat, Kotido, Panyangara, Komukunyu, and Nakapelimoru.
This is why all the Jie men build new granaries for their wives just before the harvest ritual. This is also why the Turkana women arrive in
Nakapelimoru during the harvest ritual, and this is why they call the
village through which the Turkana women enter Najie, Wotakau (the
place of return). This is why the Jie people say that the Turkana people
are the children of their daughter, and this is why the Jie firemaker encourages Jie women to share their sorghum with the Turkana women"
(Interview with Lodoch, Jimos village, September 1997).

In addition, this is why I argue that Nayeche, the daughter of
Orwakol, metaphorically returns to Najie during the dramas of the
harvest ritual, which coincide with the annual return of the Jie cattle
from the grazing lands in the upper Tarash region in the Turkana plains.
During this time, the Turkana women follow the Jie cattle to Najie and,
to receive some sorghum, they help the Jie women in the harvesting of
their fields. The harvest ritual refreshes the Jie people's memory of the
original polygamous family to which Nayeche belonged. The harvest
ritual, therefore, is a cosmic rejuvenation of kinship through the offering and receiving of sorghum between, on the one hand, the Jie firemaker and the Jie people and, on the other, between the Jie women and
the Turkana women. The coming together of the families and their communal tasting and eating of the new crops of sorghum grain are central
acts in the harvest ritual. Commensality of sorghum in the harvest
ritual is an important institution, in which the metaphoric return of
Nayeche is celebrated, in the model of the returning bride. During the
harvest ritual, the implicit meaning of the Nayeche oral tradition becomes apparent, providing a framework for the cycle of gift exchange,

on the model of kinship between the Jie and the Turkana, which facili-
tates the flow of sorghum to the Turkana.

The Nayeche oral tradition encapsulates, in my opinion, the "implicit
meaning" of local "salient social interactions" which are "repeated" as
"traditional dramas" (Boyer 1990). Seeing oral tradition from this point
of view enables one to embrace Elizabeth Tonkin's (1992) epistemological exploration of the "dialectical interlocking" of "memory" and "social
action" which "re-enact, modify, deny, and conserve 'pastness' as both
lived experience and mode of understanding" (1992, 111). The Nayeche
and the gray bull Engiro oral tradition as "genres of language" is a part
of the "habitus"; it is in line with Tonkin's historical explorations (1992,
108), and it is reproduced, transformed, and inductively modified by
skillful storytellers and competent members of the audience. My ethnographic participation in the performance of the Nayeche and the gray
bull Engiro oral tradition provided insights on the fluidity of its images,
which enables the storytellers to manipulate them to narrate a socially
acceptable past. As I elaborated in previous chapters, the past becomes
a point of view rather than a fixed moment in history during the performances of historical traditions. In this chapter, the works of Karin Barber
(1991, 2007), Steven Feierman (1974), and Ian Cunnison (1951) as well as
the recent work of John Tosh (2000) have been informative.

When concentrating on the images of the Nayeche oral tradition, I use
semiotic vocabularies and make extensive use of the works of Ohnuki-
Tierney (1993), Fernandez (1986), and Bloch (1986) to emphasize the
symbolic relationship between the Jie and the Turkana. The symbols
of the Nayeche and the gray bull Engiro oral tradition have multiple
referents, linking the symbols with myriad tropes and metaphors within both the Jie and the Turkana society. Some of these symbols, such as
sorghum grain, cattle, and the wild landscape, can be defined as "dominant metaphors" (Ohnuki-Tierney 1993). Metaphors used in everyday
practice, or "metaphors we live by," as an oft-cited phrase articulates,
link the figurative and the conceptual realms with everyday empirical
practices. In this sense, the metaphors contained in the Nayeche and
the gray bull Engiro oral tradition inform the Jie's and the Turkana's
understanding of their past interethnic relationships and provide them
with the necessary discourse to negotiate their present situations.

This chapter explores one central point, namely the implicit meaning
of the Nayeche oral tradition as expressed in the interlock between
the Nayeche and the gray bull Engiro oral tradition and the Jie harvest

ritual. This interlock connects the metaphoric return of Nayeche with the hidden dimensions of sorghum as a gift in the Nayeche oral tradition. Sorghum as a gift constitutes the central point in the Jie/Turkana historical discourse. It is from this point that the Jie and the Turkana women regulate the political economy between the two communities, on the model of marriage, in such a way that cultural models of historical traditions are revealed.

The Jie and the Turkana's traditional thought, expressed in giving and receiving sorghum grain during the harvest rituals, express a theoretical understanding of ethnicity, clan, and lineage politics between these two communities. This understanding is essentially comparable to Gulliver's sociological theorizing of "agnatic bond" (1955), achieved through the exchange of cattle and in the sharing of grazing lands and water sources among the Jie and the Turkana men. The implicit meaning of the traditional dramas, such as the ones encapsulated in the Nayeche and the gray bull Engiro oral tradition and in the Jie harvest ritual, lies in the fact of the "repeated events" (Boyer 1990), which are integrated into wider local causalities. In these local traditional dramas, sharing food and resources between ethnic communities and clans who occupy different ecological zones unites people, and refusing to share food fragments inhabitants through a push and pull type of causality, linking or dispersing communities on the model of family (Mirzeler 1999). These traditional dramas produce sets of beliefs that are integrated with local knowledge, and they are consistent and explanatory, similar to Neville Dyson-Hudson's theorizing of local politics (1966).

The Nayeche and the gray bull Engiro oral tradition reflects history but it does not refer to a fixed historical moment, which purportedly took place sometime in the 1720s. The logic of the historicity of the Nayeche and the gray bull Engiro oral tradition's origin is related to the phases of the harvest ritual and to the phases of the Jie marriage ceremony. Hence, there are complex interplays between the fragments of history, the phases of the harvest ritual, and the individual life cycle. Both the harvest ritual and the marriage ceremonies are repeated traditional events (Mirzeler 2004), which orient the world of the Jie, making their interethnic relationship with the Turkana comprehensible. The journey of Nayeche and the gray bull Engiro is not a fixed historical moment. Rather, it is a repeated event that is repeated discursively and metaphorically during the annual movement of the Jie cattle from the Karamoja Plateau to the plains and vice versa. In addition, this repeated event is also interlocked with the movement of sorghum grain from the granary of the Jie firemaker to the gardens of the Jie women, which constitutes another traditionally repeated event. The Jie semantic memory data contained in the Nayeche oral tradition is memorable, because it is drawn from the aggregate experiences of the people, which are repeated in the individual lifecycles as in marriage ceremonies, and in the phases of the Jie harvest rituals.

The Jie harvest rituals produce conditions that encourage marriages between the Jie and the Turkana because marriage is practically important for the exchange of resources. The memory of the journey of Nayeche and the gray bull Engiro provocatively and poetically triggers the implicit meaning of the tradition, fully expressed in the tradition of offering sorghum grain as a gift by the Jie women to the Turkana women during the performance of the harvest ritual. The implicit meaning of the memory of this journey is discursive as well as institutionalized in referring to the original event that created the complex interaction of practices between these two communities. The storytellers constantly modify the memory of Nayeche's journey to construct a pastness as a differently lived experience for both the Jie and the Turkana. The memory of Nayeche's journey provides these two communities with knowledge as to how their respective societies evolved and how splintering and realignments occurred and will continue to do so as a process.

The interlock between the Nayeche tradition and the Jie harvest ritual is the central puzzle of the Jie and the Turkana interethnic relationship, as represented in the local transactional strategies between these two communities. The Jie are the transhumant pastoralists and cultivators of sorghum, and the Turkana are the pastoralists, the gatherers of wild fruits, and the guardians of the Jie cattle in the annual grazing lands. In this locally enacted relationship, the Turkana depend on the Jie for sorghum grain, while the Jie depend on the Turkana for the safety of their cattle in the grazing lands. This interdependence is embedded in the discourses of the Nayeche and the gray bull Engiro oral tradition, as well as in the Jie harvest rituals. The Jie harvest rituals distinctively feature the role of women in the political thought of the Jie and the Turkana interethnic relationship, which is clearly linked to the Nayeche oral tradition. The placing of the "implicit meaning" within the Nayeche oral tradition therefore enables one to examine the participation of women in identity politics. The linkages between the Nayeche and the gray bull Engiro oral tradition, the harvest ritual, and

the marriage ceremonies, indeed, create a powerful space for women in
the Jie and the Turkana interethnic discourses.

While the Turkana around the upper Tarash River area practice rudimentary agriculture and grow a variety of sorghum along the river,
they depend mainly on livestock for their subsistence. They live on milk
and blood, and they supplement their diet with wild berries and nuts,
which are prolific in this part of the Turkana land. Sorghum grain, however, is scarce, and it is almost considered a delicacy (Gulliver and
Gulliver 1953, 63; Mirzeler 1999, 2009). During the harvest season, most
Turkana women from around the upper Tarash River go to Najie for
sorghum grain.
    The Turkana, who live around the upper Tarash River near the es-
carpment, sharing many cultural practices with the Jie, have similar rituals and botanical knowledge. The cultural similarities between these
communities are intensified by intermarriages and by the grain and iron
trade (Pamela and P.H. Gulliver 1953; Lamphear 1976; Mirzeler 2009).
It is common for the Jie women, particularly those who live in
Nakapelimoru area, to wander down the plateau to the Koteen Hill
area where the seasonal Turkana kraals are located as they gather wild
fruits. Likewise, while in the Koteen Hill area, the Turkana women go to
Nakapelimoru to get sorghum grain from the Jie women. When I interviewed some women in the upper Tarash River region, many of them
claimed to have come from Najie, particularly from Nakapelimoru, and
there are many Turkana women who are married to the Jie men in
Nakapelimoru, the nearest Jie village to the Turkana land.
    The Jie and the Turkana ecology around the upper Tarash River area
symbolizes the contrast between the plateau and the plain environment, encompassing a sense of the complementary geography, which
contains harmonious yet separate communities. For the Turkana, the
plateau where the Jie live is a major source of their subsistence, not
only because their rivers flow from the rain floods of the plateau, but
also because they get their sorghum from the plateau. For the Turkana
women around the upper Tarash River region, the Jie land represents
their maternal home, abundance of food, security, and a land for refuge from famine. Likewise, for the Jie women, the wild fruits of the
upper Tarash River region offer relief from famines. In this ecological
dyad, sorghum, cattle, and wild fruits are equally valuable to both the
Turkana and the Jie, and the need for these resources creates regular

transactions between the two communities. The journey of Nayeche and the gray bull Engiro in the oral tradition makes these transactions between the communities habitual, linking memory and action, and producing history.

In the absence of documentary evidence, it is difficult to know when the Jie polity evolved, as depicted in their oral traditions. However, the Jie oral traditions support the notion that the Jie society comes from one polygamous family; all their cattle come from one bull, and their grain comes from one granary. According to the Jie storytellers, Orwakol was like a village elder but he was much more powerful. The family of Orwakol was and still is the representation of all the Jie. While the settlement of Lodiny, in the Lokatap Rock region, divided the Jie into north and south, the departure of Nayeche and her subsequent settlement in the upper Tarash region extended the Jie to the east, creating an interdependent relationship between the Jie in the plateau and the Turkana in the plains.

According to some Jie storytellers, Orwakol subsisted on the meat of his cattle and on the sorghum grain of his wives, cultivated in the seven territorial divisions and stored in the master granary, that of his eldest wife. Only in the event of famine did Orwakol eat solely meat. Orwakol and his eldest wife were alone permitted to eat grain from the master granary, which is said to contain the power and the pure wealth of the Jie. By eating the grain from the master granary, Orwakol and his eldest wife metaphorically ate the power and the pure wealth of the Jie (Mirzeler 1999).

The metaphor of the master granary is comparable to that of the gray bull Engiro. For the Jie, just as all the sorghum comes from the granary of the eldest wife of the first firemaker, all the cattle come from the gray bull Engiro, as Engiro went to different parts of the Karamoja Plateau and to the plains of Turkana impregnating the cows. Hence, all the cattle in Najie and in the surrounding regions are ultimately the offspring of the gray bull Engiro, and therefore, they all belong to the Jie. This is why, I was told, Jie people raid the cattle of their neighbors. Consequently, the activity of raiding cattle is not seen as stealing, but rather as taking something that originally belonged to them. Likewise, the offering of the sorghum grain to the Turkana women during the harvest ritual is seen as giving something due to them since Nayeche, the daughter of the Jie, is the mother of the Turkana.

Nayeche bridges the Turkana and the Jie on the model of marriage. Marriages in Jie society are based not only on the exchange of cattle, but also on the exchange of grain. Through marriage, men have access to the gardens of women, and women have access to the cattle of men (Pamela and P.H. Gulliver 1953; Mirzeler 1999, 2009). In the Jie marriage custom, before the payment of bridewealth, the bride remains with her mother and cultivates her mother's garden, storing the grain in the granary of her mother. After a significant payment of bridewealth, the bride moves to the home of her husband and her husband builds a granary for her in her new home. After seven days, the bride returns to her parental home, taking the final payment of her husband's bride-wealth, in the form of cattle, to her father. This phase of the marriage ceremony is known as *awatoun*. During this part of the marriage cere-mony, the bride spends the night in her maiden hut with her husband. That night she kindles a fire and sleeps with her husband on the cow-skin. In the morning her mother gives her sorghum grain and allocates to her a piece of land to cultivate. The custom of kindling of a new fire, sleeping on the cowskin, and receiving sorghum grain and a piece of land from one's mother are the themes embedded in the oral traditions of Orwakol and his seven wives (Mirzeler 1999).

Marriage is the most important institution tying together separate villages and creating cohesive networks of friendships within the Jie society, between the Jie and the Turkana, and between the Jie and their other neighbors. The obligation to share land and grain, created through marriage between groups, shows that the marriage relationship is not a mere transfer of cattle between men as bridewealth payment, but an establishment of permanent ties and social obligations to share the grain of women and other agricultural food and wild fruits between groups.

Similar to the cattle metaphor, the granary metaphor informs the Jie conceptual understanding of their world in a significant way. The Jie use the metaphor of grain and granary when they talk about human growth. This is why, as Lodoch once pointed out to me, if you ask the Jie children where they come from, they would say, "I come from the granary of my mother. When my father put his seeds in the granary of my mother, my mother's blood got mixed with the seed of my father, and I was conceived."

The literature on food as self is extensive, emerging from various key theorists who have defined the field and the semiotics of food (Karp

1980; Galaty 1986; Ohnuki-Tierney 1993; Parry 1985; Raheja 1988; Willis 2002). These scholars are keenly aware of the symbolic utility of food as constitutive features of self-identity, and they have examined the interplay between self, food, and tropes. For Emiko Ohnuki-Tierney, for instance, food and food production, and their associations with metaphors, define and produce meaning. Her interpretation of rice grain as one of the foundational categories of the Japanese traditional polity explicates the role the commensality of rice plays in defining boundaries between the people who share the commensal food and those who do not. As each member of the community consumes the food, the food becomes a part of his or her body. The food embodied in each individual "operates as a metonym by being part of the self" (Ohnuki-Tierney 1993, 130).

Since sorghum is a gift from Akuj (God) to Orwakol, the first firemaker of the Jie, its production and consumption are not mere activities, but rather cosmological acts, which require a proper production to make sorghum appropriate for human consumption. When the first rains drop to the ground, the Jie women perform a ritual called *asulany*, in which each woman picks up her hoe (*emeleku*) very early in the morning, goes to the path that takes her to her garden, scoops up a handful of soil (*ngalup*) from it, and brings it to her home and puts it under her granaries. After the scooping of the soil, each woman offers sorghum beer to Akuj and to the ancestors in the shrines in the bush, and then she returns to the cattle enclosure (*arii*) of her home, where she drinks sorghum beer collectively with other women.

Just before the sowing of the seeds begins, the women collectively perform another ritual called *ngikawo*, in which women from each village boil a calabash full of sorghum at the entrance of the cattle enclosure (*ekidor*) in the evening after which they summon everybody to come and gather at the cattle enclosure to eat the boiled sorghum seeds and bless the hoes. After eating the boiled seeds, the women pour some boiled seeds on the threshold of the cattle enclosure as offerings to Akuj. This ritual is also performed to appease the sun, to prevent it from destroying the gardens with its heat. That is why this particular ritual is performed in the evening, during the cool period of the day.

Women help each other to weed their gardens until the sorghum plants grow knee high. At the end of the weeding period, women collectively sacrifice a black ram in one of the gardens, and perform a ritual called, *akiwos ngimomwa a emesek kirionon* (the sacrifice of the black ram for smearing the sorghum plants). The black ram is speared near a water pool (*atapar*). The undigested food inside the intestines (*ngikujit*) is mixed with water and is distributed among all the women who culti-vate together for them to sprinkle on their sorghum plants. This ritual is done to protect the sorghum plants from sickness and insects. After the sprinkling of the water, the women eat the roasted meat together as a sign of commensality.

After the sorghum ripens, all the women of Najie go to their respective gardens and collect the best heads of the sorghum, bring them home, and boil them together with the roots of *esaal* (a small climbing plant with gray leaves) to perform a ritual called *ngingarot*. After eating the boiled sorghum together with the members of their families, one woman in each family saves one sorghum head and the water from the boiled sorghum, sprinkles her garden with this water, and, in the following manner, offers the seeds to the women ancestors who grew sorghum in abundance in the past:

> *Akimuju na ekimuji esuwa na*
> *Talalau kingenyar*
> *Akuj, keena, Nairanabwo, keena, ngakosikiro nguna ekilipit iyong*

> (This food which we are eating now
> Let it be more and more
> God, hear us, Nairanabowo,[2] hear us, what we are asking you for)

During the harvest time, all the women, children, and men go to their gardens to harvest their sorghum and thresh it in their villages. The fire-maker then sends messages to the heads of each clan to bring the sor-ghum seeds and to put them in the granary of his eldest wife. Upon hearing this message, the head of each clan goes with a calabash full of new sorghum seeds to the home of the firemaker and offers it to his el-dest wife. After everybody has brought the sorghum seeds, the eldest wife of the firemaker then pounds the seeds in the Ebur (the public sor-ghum pounding hollow in Jimos village) near her home, and the fire-maker pours the chaffed grains into his eldest wife's granary at night.

The eldest wife of the firemaker brews beer from the mixed grains, which were collected from each clan. The firemaker summons the head of each clan and, in his cattle enclosure (*arii*), offers them this beer. This episode of the harvest ritual is known as *apoka*. During *apoka*, all the families brew beer from the newly harvested grains and drink it in their own cattle enclosure almost simultaneously with the firemaker and the clan heads.

Sorghum grain and sorghum agriculture play an important role not only in the Jie polity, but also in the identity politics of the Jie women (Gulliver 1971; Mirzeler 1999). Some Jie storytellers suggest that the original sorghum grains were brown (*enoryana*), and reddish (*arenger*). These were the colors of the sorghum from which the wives of Orwakol made the original beer and bread during the first harvest ritual. The custom of mixing the brown and the reddish sorghum seed in their ceremonial beer and bread in the contemporary harvest rituals may have come from this tradition.

Each woman keeps her favorite type of sorghum seed within the household, with the original seeds given to her by the firemaker each year, and she stores them above the kitchen fire. This tradition of mixing the seeds of the family with the seeds of the firemaker both maintains the genetic variety of the sorghum of the ancestors and ties each family symbolically to the firemaker as the head of the Jie polity and the supreme leader of the harvest rituals. Thus, the production of sorghum has always been a sacred political activity for the Jie (Mirzeler 1999, 164–78).

Jie sorghum farming practices have undergone tremendous transformations since the British occupation. The British officers' efforts to encourage agricultural developments continued intermittently until the 1950s, during which decade they introduced ox plowing, which attracted the men to become involved in agriculture as well (P.H. Gulliver 1971, 65–70; Pamela and P.H. Gulliver 1953). In the same decade, they also developed various agricultural schemes and programs to encourage farming. The British efforts were embraced by the postcolonial states, and, in the 1960s and 1970s, the agricultural development reached its peak, especially after the introduction of the serena sorghum, and has remained steady ever since.[3]

With the introduction of serena sorghum, Jie agriculture improved tremendously, and their fields yielded opulent crops, filling their granaries when adequate rain is available. Even though the Jie people show appreciation for the abundance of food that they enjoy as a result of the introduction of the serena sorghum, they nevertheless make the distinction between their indigenous sorghum, or *nyimumwa a ta papaa* (sorghum of the ancestors), and the sorghum introduced to them by

Europeans, or *nyimumwa a ngikakwang* (sorghum of the white people). The differences between the two sorghum types lie, according to the Jie, in their origin. Whereas the Jie sorghum comes directly from Orwakol, their firemaker, the serena type of sorghum comes from a *mzumgu* (Swahili word for foreigners, mainly used to indicate a white person from Europe or America), about whom they know very little. With its origin mysterious, serena sorghum can be obtained simply by purchase from a local shop. Thus, the origin of the serena sorghum cannot be traced to any particular human being. The Jie people do not see the serena sorghum as superior to their traditional sorghum seeds. On the contrary, the symbolic significance of their traditional seeds as a gift from their ancestors remains remarkably strong, giving additional value to their traditional seeds.

When various missionaries and development agencies introduced the serena type of sorghum, they are said to have polluted the granaries of the Jie. It was not long after the introduction of the serena type of sorghum in Najie that the Jie seriously considered reviving their traditional polity, which had not been practiced since the time of Lotum, who was a firemaker in the 1940s and 1950s. That is why, I was told, the Jie selected Nakapor as a firemaker.

In the Jie culture, time is not precise and the year is divided into wet (*akiporo*) and dry (*akamu*) seasons, which are marked by the movement of cattle from the east (*kide*) to the west (*to*). The year is also marked by the traditional tasks of plowing and sowing, which are carried out by the women, while grazing the cattle is the responsibility of the men. The year starts with the wet season during Lodunge, the first month of the year, during which people start clearing and digging their gardens. It is also during Lodunge that the Jie cattle set off from the west, from the Labwor hills and from the Acholi land, to the banks of the Longiro River in Najie. Toward the end of the second month of the wet season, a little rain begins to fall and patches of green grass flourish. The strong whirling winds begin to subside as occasional clouds form in the sky, and the people start clearing their gardens, while those in the kraals begin driving their cattle back to the villages to help their wives, sisters, and mothers in clearing and digging the gardens. It is also during this month that the firemaker sends messages to the seven clans of the Orwakol territorial divisions, for them to come, get the seeds, and begin to plant their gardens.

When all the cattle arrive in Najie and begin grazing on the banks of the Longiro River, the people gather in the cattle enclosure (*arii*) with their empty calabashes to receive their seeds from the firemaker. The firemaker mixes his saliva with the sacred clay (*emunyen*) from the Longiro River in the Ebur (the hollow rock where people pound their grain), and he smears it on the people, before distributing the sorghum seeds to the heads of the seven clans for them to plant in their gardens.

During the third month of the wet season, heavy rains fall, the rivers start flowing, and the people continue to till their gardens and to plant their seeds. In the fourth and fifth months of the wet season, both the men and the women weed their gardens, the cattle begin to disperse from the banks of the Longiro River near the Jimos village, where Orwakol is said to have captured the gray bull Engiro. They then proceed to the east and settle in the main grazing lands in the plateau near Nangalol Apolon (the great river), Koteen Hill, Kanakosim, and other places. During the sixth and the last month of the wet season, sorghum bushes are full of grain and have many different colors as the grain begins to ripen. The sorghum fields rustle as the occasional wind blows amidst the chirping sounds of the birds. At this time, some people begin to harvest certain sections of their fields. It is also during this time that the older men, who remain in the villages when the cattle go to the grazing land, start going to the riverbeds and to the hills to collect *ngatetelei* branches, and they begin building new granaries for their wives.

During Lopoo, the first month of the dry season, actual harvesting begins, continuing until the end of the second month of the dry season, during which time the cattle camps settle at the edges of the plateau in the east near the Turkana plains. If the dry season is prolonged and the wells dry out, the cattle proceed farther down to the upper Tarash River region in the Turkana plains, passing through the wild landscape, the same way Nayeche and the gray bull Engiro are said to have done, and return to the Koteen Hill on the plateau.[4]

While in the Koteen Hill area, the Turkana people bring their cattle and combine them with the Jie cattle. The Jie women from the Nakapelimoru area bring some sorghum grains for their husbands and brothers, and they make butter and sour milk for the people in the villages in Najie. When the Jie women are in the Koteen Hill area, the Turkana women visit the Jie cattle camps to inquire about their friends and relatives in Najie. When the Jie cattle begin moving toward Najie, the Turkana women follow them with their donkeys. Some Turkana women bring along a few goats to exchange for sorghum on arrival in Najie. The Turkana women gather wild fruits that are abundant in the wild landscape at this time of the year. In the process, they almost reverse the journey of Nayeche as depicted in the Nayeche oral tradition. Upon reaching Wotakau, the last village on the eastern periphery of Nakapelimoru, which literally means the place of return, the Turkana women begin visiting various homesteads in different villages. Carrying goat skin sacks (*ngichwe*) full of wild fruits on their heads, the Turkana women continue to walk behind the cattle toward Jimos village, coinciding with the performance of the harvest rituals in Najie. This practice reenacts the drama of the return of Nayeche and the gray bull Engiro from the upper Tarash River region, as depicted in the oral tradition of origin. Such dramas are not conscious actions; rather, they are habitual and traditional practices.[5]

The discourse structure embedded in the narrative and in the ritual performance event works together to facilitate such actions and dramas. The journey of the Turkana women to Najie on the plateau during the harvest ritual is the unplanned and unscheduled drama through which historical knowledge is expressed and through which the implicit meaning of the evoked messages of memory, contained in the Nayeche oral tradition, is revealed. The dramatic movement of the Jie cattle going through the harvested fields, eating sorghum stalks and wild cucumbers with the Turkana women behind them, enables the Jie and the Turkana people to emphasize the ideal ties.

As the Jie men who return from the grazing land meet with their wives in their cattle enclosures and drink beer made from the newly harvested sorghum grain, the Turkana women join and drink with them. The Turkana women's drinking of the sorghum beer with the Jie men and women legitimizes a social order and completes the annual calendar. It secures the integration of the men and the women, the ethnic communities, and the cattle and the sorghum. At this stage of the ritual performance, the practices of pastoralism and agriculture become synchronized. When the Turkana women offer wild fruits to the Jie women as gifts, as well as help them to harvest their fields, they reveal their assumptions about their interethnic relations and cultural identities in relation to the Jie people. These assumptions are important means through which the members of both communities understand, evaluate, and experience their changing social relations as they go through periods of war and peace with one another. The friendly relationships between the women help the people to forget about past conflicts over cattle, demonstrating that the Turkana people are able to secure the safety of the Jie cattle, and the Turkana women can, as their "sisters," trust the young Jie men to walk along with them to Najie.

Drinking sorghum beer and eating sorghum grain are not only dominant social actions of the harvest ritual. They are also a part of the contextualization of the interethnic relationships between these two communities, on the model of the "host-guest relations," as in marriage, similar to Kratz's exploration of the Okiek women's circumcision ritual performances (1994). For instance, following the footprints of the cattle, bringing the wild fruits, offering help in harvesting the fields, drinking sorghum beer in the cattle enclosure, and receiving sorghum grain weave together the themes of the Nayeche oral tradition with the practices of the Jie polity and the marriage ceremony (Mirzeler 1999). This interweaving of cultural themes enables the ritual participants to recall past intermarriages and to strategically discuss past memories that reproduce the conditions that have made the present relations possible.

The harvest rituals generate a warm hospitality response from the Jie women, as is expected of women when they welcome the returning bride during the *awatoun* phase of the marriage rituals. This gives the harvest ritual the aura of a marriage ceremony, which suggests the notion of ethnic unity between the Jie and the Turkana people on the model of family and lineage. Simultaneously, the giving and receiving of the sorghum and the wild fruits emphasizes the relationship between the Jie women and the Turkana women, based on "matrimonial strategies" (1977, 48, 58–71), which provide "practical mastery" (Bourdieu 1977, 2, 88–9) over the interethnic dependency through marriage. In fact, when in Najie, the Turkana women make the marriage arrangements, negotiate the transfer of cattle as bridewealth, and establish kin ties. Through marriage, the Turkana women convert their mythic kin ties, as expressed in the Nayeche and the gray bull Engiro oral tradition, into genealogical ones. Through genealogical kinship, the Turkana women make their exchange relationship with the Jie women official, thus securing their access to sorghum.

The arrival of the Turkana women in the Jie villages during the harvest time is an "unscheduled but expected" (Kratz's phrase 1994, 214) part of the ritual event, commemorating the annual return of Nayeche and the gray bull Engiro. It is natural for the Turkana women to come to Najie during the harvest time, when there is peace between these communities, because there is plenty of sorghum grain available. Many

Turkana women also come to help their friends or relatives to harvest the grain. The arrival of the Turkana women to Najie, bringing wild fruits as a gift to the Jie women, is neither necessary nor important to the performance of the official harvest ritual, in which the firemaker plays the central role. It is natural for the Turkana women to pick wild fruits, which are abundantly available in the wild landscape on the way. I was told that the harvest ritual can continue without the presence of the Turkana women, but that the Jie people also remember the presence of the Turkana women during the past harvest rituals.

When the Turkana women wander in the villages, waiting anxiously to receive sorghum grain during the harvests, no one questions why they gather outside the cattle enclosures of the Jie people. The presence of the Turkana women is, therefore, patterned as if it were "scheduled" to take part in the performance of the ritual. The sound of the women coming from the harvested fields and from the cattle enclosures invokes themes of generosity toward the Turkana women, enhancing the performance of the ritual. The Jie and the Turkana women invoke their relationship and talk about their memories of past famines and the gathering of wild fruits in the wild landscape, as well as harvesting together in years past.

The women's emotional expressions about past events, combined with helping one another and the encouragement of visiting one another again in the future, as well as the making of marriage arrangements, are the unscheduled parts of the performance of the harvest rituals. The Jie and the Turkana women understand that such emotional displays are also expressed during the *awatoun* phase of the marriage ceremony, when a bride returns to her natal home. I was once told that the arrival of the Turkana women from the plains along with the Jie cattle during the harvest rituals parallels the bringing of the last cattle payment of the bride-price by the bride during the *awatoun*.

The harvest rituals end when the firemaker offers some sorghum beer in his cattle enclosure, made from the newly harvested grain, to the heads of the seven territorial divisions. The offering of the sorghum beer by the firemaker evokes, in multiple ways, the symbolism associated with the original event of the distribution of the sorghum grain by Orwakol to his seven wives in the oral tradition. The offering of the sorghum beer by the contemporary firemaker is therefore a reenactment of the enduring memory images of the event of the gift exchange by the original polygamous family. This repetition of the memory enhances the Jie and Turkana relations, and it provides a pathway for the members of these two communities to discuss sorghum as the gift of the ancestors to both the Jie and the Turkana people.

Since sorghum is a gift from the ancestors, it is the precious inalienable possession of the ancestral family, which has been given to the Jie mothers and passed down to their daughters upon their marriages. This is why the Jie mothers offer sorghum from their granaries to their daughters when they bring the cattle as the last payment of their bridewealth to their fathers and brothers during the *awatoun* phase of the marriage ceremony, invoking the memory of the original distribution of sorghum grain and cattle by their ancestors. During the *awatoun* ritual, the bride kindles a new fire and sleeps with her husband in her maiden hut on a cowskin, which evokes the complex images of the oral tradition in which Losilang initially received the sorghum grain from Orwakol. It is in this sense that the arrival of the Turkana women during the harvest rituals is analogous to the *awatoun* phase of the marriage ceremony. This interweaving of the images of the oral tradition with the marriage ceremony and with the harvest ritual extends sorghum into a cycle of gift exchange between the Jie and the Turkana women, on the model of offering sorghum as a gift to married daughters by their mothers, thus uniting the Jie and the Turkana people on the model of marriage. Thus, at the core of the Nayeche oral tradition lies the sorghum grain as one of the key foundational categories with effective functions in Jie historical tradition. The cattle metaphor has long been the main object of the academic conceptualization of pastoralist communities in East Africa since the time of Evans-Pritchard, whose model of the agnatic politic has influenced most anthropological endeavors. However, the role of sorghum grain has yet to be incorporated into these debates. The academic privileging of cattle and its association with human and cultural reproduction among African pastoralist communities denotes cattle as inalienable possessions, but the implicit meaning of the Nayeche oral tradition demonstrates that cattle is not the only inalienable possession.

7 A Jie Storyteller's Autobiography: The Significance of Nayeche and the Gray Bull Engiro Oral Tradition

This chapter explores the relationship between oral tradition and autobiography. In doing so, it examines how Lodoch, the Jie storyteller, frames his life experiences according to his imaginative tradition and how he transforms his enduring memories into oral tradition when he talks about himself and his society. Although it is his own creation and necessarily interpretive and probably partly fictionalized, Lodoch's autobiography reveals vital truths about the Jie oral tradition. He often frames his experiences around the images of his tradition and fuses the moments of crisis in his life with the crises of his society. I address the fusion of Lodoch's memories into oral tradition and vice versa through analyses of his autobiographical narratives and his tales. I compare both the oral tradition and autobiography of Lodoch against the backdrop of basic cultural notions that the Jie hold about their society – the cultural representation of the world and the social relationships within it, in short, their world view. As told here, both the autobiography and oral traditions are products of Lodoch and my own ethnographic presence.

In any autobiographical analysis, the discussion of how widely the contextual net is thrown raises crucial questions. How can we compare idiosyncratic autobiographical materials, full of significant details of personal memories and experiences, with larger oral traditions? How can we show the influence of the personal memories on the oral tradition and vice versa?

Autobiographical studies, albeit useful to situating an individual within the culture, have certain weaknesses. They are weighted toward the individual, with little regard for the individual interacting within the wider scope of culture (Brumble 1988). My own solution to situate Lodoch's autobiography within the larger culture sets his

Figure 7.1: Lodoch in 2009. Courtesy of Sister Camilla Roach (Moruongor village)

personal memories in a wider context of oral tradition. For me, situating Lodoch's autobiography within a larger context is important, since I look to his autobiography for something other than facts about his life or facts about a particular historical period. I look at Lodoch's autobiography for odd bits of information that are not available to me elsewhere. I am interested in the phenomena of: (1) the art of framing one's autobiography in the model of oral tradition and (2) the transformation of personal memory images into a larger oral tradition.

I am convinced that we must learn about the relationship between autobiography and oral tradition to understand the Nayeche and the gray bull Engiro oral tradition. Although worries about as-told-to autobiographies are numerous, with careful collaboration and with enough knowledge about the subject's motivations and culture, along with meticulous recording and editing, a researcher can capture accurate as-told-to autobiographies (Brumble 1988; Dweyer 1982; Shostak 2000). I hope this chapter will aid anthropologists, folklorists, and historians insofar as it analyzes particular autobiographical narratives in the light of oral traditions. What I offer in this chapter is no more than experimentation of the study of oral tradition.

When I asked Lodoch to tell me about his life, I did not ask him to participate in something entirely foreign to him. In fact, Lodoch responded to me according to his own autobiographical narrative conventions. Lodoch's response is not unique. Various scholars encountered similar situations when they tried to record autobiographies (for example, Crapanzano 1980; Dweyer 1982; Kennedy 1977; Kratz 2001; Shostak 2000). In my view, it is important to pay attention to the Jie autobiographical conventions to better understand the Jie oral tradition. Lodoch's autobiography often merges with oral tradition. His skillful molding of his personal memory images with the oral traditions of his society implies processes of transformation of personal memories into oral tradition. These processes illuminate the relationships that exist between individual memory, myth, and oral tradition, showing how oral traditions such as Nayeche and the gray bull Engiro are not only about events, but also about possible relations in the life of the storytellers. These autobiographical images are not always immanent in the oral traditions themselves – they are often added to the oral traditions by skillful storytellers.

Autobiography and biography, as creative writing, often generate contentious debates over what constitutes autobiography, biography, and life history (Brumble 1988). Whatever their differences, the use of each of these terms by scholars affects the representation of the actual context of production of life history as to where it begins as an ethnographic exchange (Kratz 2001; Shostak 2000). As a scholarly genre, autobiography refers to life history as it is told; but autobiography can also be called biography, since the interest of the researcher inevitably directs the life history narrative (Brumble 1988). Because of this, some scholars have given up making any distinction between autobiography and biography. As De Maille (1985), Krupat (1985), and Shostak (2000) demonstrate, with careful fieldwork methodologies the researcher can avoid directing the narrator's tales of their life histories. However, as these scholars also demonstrate, no matter how careful a researcher is with his or her methodology, the question of which parts of self are taken as a part of life and what experiences should be edited becomes critical.

The question of methodology in the studies of life histories inspired many anthropologists who have produced important autobiographical and biographical materials since the early 1930s, and giving birth to sophisticated use of life histories for the study of culture and personality (Brumble 1988; Krupat 1985; Kennedy 1977; Langness 1965). Since then, life histories have been taken up by anthropology and folklore. Some examples of biographical studies and examples of this method in the field of anthropology and folklore are John G. Kennedy's *Struggle for Change in a Nubian Village* (1977); Scheub's "And So I Grew Up" in Patricia W. Romero's *Life Histories of African Women* (1988); and Basgoz's "Life History of Mudami, the Poet of Poshof" in *Folklore Writings* (1986).

In *Struggle for Change in a Nubian Community*, Kennedy attempts to understand the individual and the individual's impact on culture and society. The autobiography begins with Kennedy's arrival with his family in Kanuba, a Nubian village, on the banks of the Nile, and his encounter with Shatr, a forty-year-old dark-skinned Nubian man. After introducing Shatr, Kennedy disappears from the ethnographic setting completely, only to reappear after Shatr stops talking. Speaking without stopping, Shatr seems to delight in confessing his most private experiences. He shares with Kennedy his experiences of growing up and his first intercourse with his wife. Reading Shatr's confessions, one cannot help but to imagine a patient talking to a psychoanalyst about his deep fears and sexual desires. Kennedy reappears at the end of the book, only to offer his psychoanalytical insights about the autobiography of Shatr.

Shatr, born in Kanuba, lived with his grandmother during his formative years. He later went to Cairo to live with his somewhat westernized father. While in Cairo, Shatr became conscious of his dark skin. He often remembered the tales his grandmother told about the dark waters of Nile and its creeping monster that ravaged the date palm fruits at night. Images of darkness reminded Shatr of his skin, which distinguished him from his lighter skinned, westernized Egyptian stepmother, who disdained Shatr for his dark skin.

When Shatr returned to Kanuba as a young man, he became a village leader and sought to eradicate the memories of the dark images and spirits of the ancient Nile traditions, which had haunted him in Cairo. In Kanuba, he remembered Cairo's narrow streets, his cold room there, and the white mosque across from which he lived. Later, Shatr wove these new images from his memory into Kanuba traditions. However, the more Shatr tried to eradicate dark images of Nile traditions and replace them with white images of Cairo, the more he feared darkness, which reminded him of the deep, dark waters of the Nile and the ancient spirits of his grandmother's tales. One night, Shatr passed an abandoned house and saw a dark image standing still behind the house and shining under the moonlight. Paralyzed by the sight of this dark mass, Shatr fired his gun. People came running and saw Shatr shaking in fear, gun in hand. The dark image, which frightened Shatr so much that he almost shot it, was his neighbor, who had gone out to defecate.

Kennedy makes few comments about his editorial work on the life history of Shatr. Without adequate information about his editorial work, we do not know how Shatr's voice was channeled in such a way that he spoke using language so infused with psychoanalytic terminology.[1]

In "And So I Grew Up," Scheub offers the personal narrative of Nongenile Masithathu Zenani, an eighty-year-old South African storyteller and an accomplished traditional doctor. The autobiography of Zenani differs from Shatr's in the sense that Zenani's autobiography looks back to the ancestral world, the world of the Xhosa before colonialism and apartheid. Zenani's autobiography has to do with her tradition and the old ways, the ways of the ancestors.

The autobiography was recorded in a lemon grove near Zenani's home in front of a small audience. Scheub publishes the translated version of the tape-recorded autobiography in the order in which Zenani tells it. Although Scheub does not tell us about his editorial work, from his translation it seems that Scheub has cut nothing and that the range of what Zenani tells was her own choice. Moreover, Scheub does not give us the reasons that Zenani tells her life history and why he recorded it.

Zenani chooses the material for her autobiography. She begins with an account of her growing up and her marriage, but Zenani recounts more than that, including other things like her struggle with colonial powers and the apartheid system. We do not know what Scheub's expectations were in recording this life history; however, it seems that Zenani was encouraged to include her feelings toward the colonial presence and to talk about understandings of her culture prior to colonial contact. This is a window through which we may glimpse a precontact conception of autobiography and tradition in this far-flung South African community.

Zenani depicts her ancient traditions, her family, and her people. The images of her fanciful tales are quite distinct from the images of white people in whose mines her husband worked as a young man. When Zenani tells about her husband's short visits from the mines, she tells of his deeds as a traditional man. It is in this spirit, too, that Zenani gives Scheub an extended account of her family relations. She mixes the images of her tales and the rites of passage with her own life history, because of who she is in relation to her people, her tales, and her traditions.

Sabit Ataman was a renowned storyteller and a performer of *hikaye* (Anatolian love stories) in Ankara, Turkey. Sabit recited his life history to Basgoz in 1967, a year before Sabit's death. Sabit's narration of his personal history is close to Zenani's in its themes in oral tradition. Basgoz gives us the personal narrative in conversational order, and it seems nothing has been cut out (if so Basgoz does not mention it). However, the flow of dialogical engagement between Basgoz and Sabit is ordered around the kinds of things that Sabit wants to say about his life and his art. Basgoz interjects periodically and asks for clarification about the things that Sabit tells him.

The personal narratives of Sabit open with his birth in a remote eastern Anatolian village, during the late Ottoman period. Sabit tells Basgoz about a dream that he had when he was seven years old while he was herding sheep in a grazing land near a river. Like Zenani, after talking very briefly about this childhood memory, Sabit jumps to his puberty years and talks about an episode in which he experienced a recurrent dream, which caused him to become a gifted *ashik* (mystical lover) like Kerem (a heroic character in Turkish *hikaye* tradition), a Muslim *ashik* who fell in love with Asli, the daughter of an Armenian *keshish* (priest of an Ancient Anatolian religion). According to Basgoz, Sabit's dream about Kerem, the traditional hero, opens a framework for Sabit to identify himself with Kerem, the popular character of Anatolian oral tradition.

With this background I turn to Lodoch's autobiographical tales with the goal of enhancing understanding of the historical traditions of Jie society. Before I recorded his autobiography, Lodoch had recounted some autobiographical narratives during our journeys to different villages and kraals to meet storytellers. Those narratives were part of our dialogues and exchanges about our lives, as I also shared with him my experiences in Turkey and in the United States. We delivered our narratives to each other in natural conversations, sometimes in English and sometimes in Jie. During these dialogical exchanges, I realized that Lodoch's autobiographical tales paralleled the oral traditions of his society. Most of Lodoch's autobiographical tales were episodic. Listening to these episodic narratives revealed sufficient fragments of oral tradition to encourage me to record his narratives shortly before my departure from the field.

Lodoch's willingness for me to record aspects of his autobiography/ biography was because I was a *"lopaya kang,"* his friend. However at the same time, the recording of his autobiography created tremendous pressure between us, stemming mainly from my over concern about completing the project before my departure (Mirzeler 1999). At times, I lost all hope of completion of the project, because Lodoch was away visiting friends or doing various other things. I probably would have not become anxious in recording Lodoch's autobiography had I started the project earlier in my fieldwork. Because of the pressures of time, recording the life history interviews created the most intense moments both for me and for Lodoch. However, recording Lodoch's autobiography proved to be productive as it provided me with the deepest insights about Jie life and oral tradition. The life history interviews I conducted with Lodoch tallied almost thirty hours in the Jie language. The typewritten transcriptions are hundreds of pages. I translated the transcriptions with the help of Lodoch and a few friends. In the translations, I retained many Jie expressions that reflected nuances unique to Jie. Part of Lodoch's autobiography/biography appeared in my dissertation, "Veiled Histories and the Childhood Memories of a Storyteller" (1999), used in my following analysis.

It is illuminating to examine closely and to compare Jie oral tradition with the autobiography of Lodoch, not just to the composite perspective of the many biographies, as I have done in chapter 3. In doing this, we can come to understand the reciprocity of influence between individual autobiography and oral tradition, and how each mutually informs the other.

Because oral traditions are produced by individual storytellers, they reflect the complex process of fashioning experience into narrative. In this sense, oral traditions contain culturally specific experiences. As the critiques of the culture and personality schools of thought have shown (Brumble 1988, 21, 95, 97), we may not be able to understand the

specific thought patterns of another culture, but we may have less difficulty understanding the life history of an individual from another culture, however exotic that individual and his or her culture may appear.

In this chapter, I examine the autobiography of Lodoch, to explore
how themes and motifs within autobiography correspond to images
within oral traditions. More specifically, I am looking at experiences and
their expressions within the historical tradition, and vice versa. I am
aware of the problem of conflicting motivations and autobiographical
assumptions of both the person whose autobiography is recorded, and
the recorder of the autobiography (Mirzeler 1999). As Brumble (1988),
Dweyer (1982), Glassie (2010), Kratz (2001), and Shostak (2000) delineate, recording autobiography involves multiple problems of inference
such as the narrative conventions of the subject's own culture and tradition and certain philological and translation problems involved in
writing autobiography.

It was in this critical spirit that I earlier approached Lodoch's autobiography (Mirzeler 1999). Lodoch's autobiography often merges with his
use of oral tradition. His skillful molding of his personal memories with
the historical tradition of his society illuminates how personal memories
and accounts relate to historical traditions. Close attention to the interrelationship between historical tradition and the autobiographical narrative of a person like Lodoch shows how his identity and status derive
from his connection to his community and history. As Ogot (2001, 32)
aptly points out, in the case of the Luo society, oral traditions record the
interconnections between history and individual life history

Of all the stories in Jie historical tradition, the narrative of Nayeche
and the gray bull Engiro most resembles Lodoch's autobiography. The
Nayeche story illuminates more than one episode in Lodoch's life. The
story of Nayeche and the gray bull is largely concerned with basic
Jie cultural foundations, and, as such, these narratives provide the basic
means by which Lodoch can draw connections between historical and
autobiographical events.

The story of Nayeche and the gray bull Engiro is heuristic. As we
can see from Lodoch's autobiography, the story of Nayeche prepared
Lodoch for his adult role, teaching him his interethnic social obligation
to the Turkana, who depend on the Jie, and vice versa. It also informed
him of the taboos of his society that he should obey. For example, in
his autobiography we learn how, as a child, Lodoch kicked a gourd in
which Atoot, a Turkana woman, was churning milk while the cattle

were entering an *arii* (a cattle enclosure). The gourd broke and the milk spilled. Atoot was upset at what Lodoch did and called Lodoch's mother. Lodoch's mother chased him in anger until his father came and asked her to clarify what had happened, and why she was chasing the child so frantically. Lodoch's mother replied, "He has broken the gourd in which Atoot was churning milk, after the cattle had already entered the cattle enclosure." (Mirzeler 1999, 277).

Lodoch then goes on and says:

> I then said to my father, "Atoot was churning milk after the cattle had already entered the cattle enclosure." My father then said to my mother, "Yes, Lodoch is right. You go back and tell Atoot not to churn the milk after the cattle have already entered the cattle enclosure. Lodoch had just followed the *etal* (observances, plural *ngitalia*) of our forefathers." So my mother went back silently inside the house. (Mirzeler 1999, 290)

Any Jie child of at that time, witnessing Lodoch's heated exchange with Atoot, would clearly understand that Atoot was behaving in a manner suggestive of a bad omen, one that could place a curse on the cattle during their annual return from the plains of Turkana to the plateau. Such observances, as Lodoch remembers, must have been important during the harvest rituals when the Turkana women would come to get sorghum grain from the Jie women.

According to Lodoch, his mother told his sisters not to let any Turkana women help them churn milk, harvest grain, or fetch water while the cattle were entering the cattle enclosure, when these women would come for sorghum during the harvest. They also should be careful to whom they offered sorghum or from whom they received wild fruits. They must be careful, as the Turkana women might poison the wild fruits, drop bewitched grains in the granaries, or spy on their cattle.

It is illuminating to get an individual perspective on the practices of the Jie from their traditions, rather than only a composite account from many people. Lodoch remembers the firemaker going around after the harvest "and knocking on the granaries of the houses and telling the women to be generous to the daughters of Nayeche when they come to beg for sorghum grain."

Lodoch also remembers helping Atoot fetch water as a child. He recalls Atoot and other Turkana women telling the stories of Nayeche and Napeikisina as they harvested in the fields. "The Turkana women always came and helped their Jie friends harvest, and assisted with other hard work as well." One day Lodoch told me how the Turkana women watched the firemaker offering beer made from the grain of his eldest wife to the heads of the seven territorial divisions. Lodoch said that, after the ceremony, the Turkana women always scrambled in the cattle enclosure of the firemaker and fought with each other for the last bit of leftover beer in the calabashes.

Most Jie women had Turkana friends who came annually, as Atoot did, to ask for sorghum grain from the Jie women in the name of Nayeche. Lodoch also told me that the Jie women used to bring dried wild fruits, which "tasted so good," and sacred clay from Moru Apolon, which "cured illnesses." The Turkana women helped the Jie women to harvest the fields and thresh the grain. At the end of the harvest, the Jie women would offer full sacks of grain to the Turkana women, who would load them onto their donkeys and returned to the plains. But they would always come back during the harvest to help the Jie women thresh the grain. When these women came, they also made marriage arrangements, which would result in festive marriage ceremonies where they would consume much sorghum beer and much meat.

As we can see from Lodoch's childhood memories, the images of the Nayeche stories are interconnected with the harvest ritual. This particular childhood memory not only lets us see the interconnection of the Nayeche story with the harvest rituals, but also shows how Orwakol's distribution of sorghum grain from the granary of his eldest wife to his seven wives metaphorically united the seven territorial divisions of the Orwakol clan in the past as the head of the original family.

As we remember, after Orwakol's wives dispersed and settled on the banks of the Longiro River, he made a fire from wet branches, offered the grain to his wives, and said to them:

> When the sorghum ripens in your gardens, I want you to bring half of it to my granary. When the rainy season comes, wait for the cattle to return from the east; from the land of Nayeche and Tarash. When the cattle reach Koteen or Nangalol Apolon you should start bringing your sorghum and pour it in my granary here in Losilang. (Mirzeler 1999, 234)

Lodoch concludes by traditionalizing the current political situation in Najie and says,

> That is why the people of Losilang are in charge of making fire and distribute sorghum grain from the granary during the harvest ritual and why the

people of Najie start making a lot of beer after the harvest and drink it in the cattle enclosure of the firemakers in Losilang. This is why we make a lot of beer when the cattle return from east, from the land of Turkana, and settle in Koteen and Nangalol Apolon. (Mirzeler 1999, 234)

From this we can see an instance of the Jie people using their histori- cal traditions to justify the present politico-ritual status quo. There is nothing new in Lodoch's statements about the past; but the Jie people place great emphasis on them. Moreover, these political relations not only involve the Jie, but also the Turkana.

Also, as we remember from the stories of Nayeche, she was from Najie. She left long ago and never returned. But again we remember that, according to Lodoch, the firemaker went around and rapped on the granaries of the Jie women saying "be generous to the daughters of Nayeche." This in a sense commemorates Nayeche metaphorically re- turning to her parental home during the harvest rituals.

Again, the harvest ritual coincides with the return of the cattle from the Turkana plains. With the cattle motif, we see reflected here the return of the gray bull Engiro along with Nayeche. When the cattle return, they pass through the harvested fields and eat the sorghum stalks while the Turkana women drink beer with Jie women. With this we see unity and commensality, not only within the family and two ethnic communities, but also between the cattle and the grain, as well as between men and women who return from the grazing land along with the cattle to rejoin their spouses. The cattle metaphor demarcates divisions within family and society, with grain having an integrat- ing role.

The story of Nayeche is integrated not only with the harvest ritual, but also with other important rites of passage, such as marriage. We learn from Lodoch's autobiography that his wife, Napiyo, returned to her natal home a week after her marriage. She and Lodoch drove forty fat cows before them as a payment of Napiyo's bride-price to her par- ents. When they reached her natal home, her parents took the cows and gave their blessings for her to wear the *abuo* (a skirt made of cowskin which is worn by a newly married woman). Let us hear how Lodoch relates this occasion:

After Napiyo's parents took the cows, Napiyo stayed with us for a week, wore the *abuo*, and then went for *awatar* (the first return of the bride to her parental home). Napiyo stayed with her parents for a week while she prepared beer from the grains of her mother's granary for my family. I went there on the sixth day, entered Napiyo's *aloket* (maiden hut) and spent the night with her. That night, Napiyo made a new fire, took off the *abuo* that my mother made for her, and exchanged it with the one her mother had made for her. We consummated our marriage that night. (Mirzeler 1999, 325)

Lodoch tells how, in the morning, Napiyo offered beer to the guests in the cattle enclosure. They drank the beer, carrying the remaining beer home. As they were leaving, Napiyo's mother gave her a sack of sorghum as gift. Lodoch continues,

When we reached home [Lodoch's parental home], we passed through the *ekidor*, gathered in the *arii*, and set the calabashes and the sacks full of sorghum on the ground. Napiyo poured all of the beer in a big pot that stood in front of my mother's house. After she poured the beer, she began to distribute beer to all of the visitors. I slaughtered a ram for everyone and Napiyo boiled the sorghum. We ate the meat and grains in the *arii* and drank beer all night. (Mirzeler 1999, 325–6)

As we can see, the theme expressed in the marriage ceremony and the harvest rituals are parallel; they both contain images of the daughter's return to the parents' home, and the eating of grain given by the mother in the cattle enclosure. The sexual act, food consumption, and the exchange of cattle and grain are the main elements in both of these ceremonies. As I have shown in my earlier work (Mirzeler 1999, 2004), the sexual act is seen as similar to food consumption. In Jie society, food production and reproduction, seen as similar processes, both conceptualize identities.

The Nayeche stories contain certain elements of ritual initiation. Upon leaving her parental home in Najie, Nayeche moves into a dry landscape and survives a succession of trials. The gray bull Engiro leads her, with its footprints from the plateau to the plains. "She followed the footprints of the bull and said, 'Oh, it is true, it is true, the bull must know where there is water. I am thirsty.'"[2] In the plains she discovered wild fruits, so she was able to survive the famine.

As I have pointed out earlier (Mirzeler 1999), oral traditions among the Jie are instruments of socialization. Lodoch states that the images of grain and granary are discussed among Jie children. Consider, for instance, Lodoch's childhood memory in which he and other children discuss the subject of parental love and where children come from.

When I was a young boy, some children said, "Ehh, I came from the seeds of my father. My mother is just a granary, the place where my father puts his seeds." But some other children said, "Ehh, my mother is more important. She is the one, who cared for me and brought me up." Then the other children would say, "But whose blood have you come from? Didn't you come from the blood of your father? Didn't the blood of your father give you life?" The children would then say, "Look, when your father put his seed into the stomach of your mother, the blood of your mother nurtured the seed, and the seed swelled and you formed." We then would say, "Oh yes, we came from both of our parents, and we love both of them. If it were not for the granaries of our mothers, the seeds of our fathers would dry up and die. Let us love both of our parents." (Mirzeler 1999, 297)

These childhood conversations are in many ways a self-examination so immediately understandable, so universally human, that they allow us to accept the autobiographical nature of historical traditions. The images of Lodoch's childhood self-examination are clearly distilled from historical tradition of Orwakol and his seven wives in which Orwakol's wives nourish his seeds in their fields and store them in their granaries after the harvest.

I am convinced that historical traditions are autobiographical, and the stories and childhood memories of Lodoch support this conviction. His autobiography is inseparably connected with the historical traditions of his society, however innovative and singular it may have been to have his autobiography recorded by an anthropologist.

We now see that other storytellers who told me their historical traditions might also have been motivated to examine themselves and talk autobiographically about themselves and the history of their society. In that sense, anyone who reads Lodoch's account of the death of his brother Achila can come to a clear sense of how the Jie might experience the loss of gray bull Engiro. The death of Achila recalls the death of Engiro.

In that cold morgue, Lodoch shed abundant tears, and many months later he had to marry Locheng (Achila's wife), to keep the family herd together, as required by their society. The scene Lodoch describes is complex, and illustrates the autobiographical and biographical nature of the story of Engiro.

Lodoch initially wanted to bury Achila under the tree in front of his home in Moruongor, but did not have enough money to transport the corpse. He then decided to bury him under a tree in the Labwor hills of Abim. After the burial, Lodoch went to Kacheri to inform Locheng,

Achila's wife, of the death of her husband. Here is how Lodoch describes the scene:

> Napiyo, the children, and I set off under the heat of the sun and walked to Kacheri. It was windy, and dust was blowing. It was the end of the dry season; death and hunger were sweeping the plains of Najie and Kacheri. There was no water and no food. At Kacheri, Locheng, and my sister, who was living with Achila, saw us from a distance. They started running towards us. I crouched down and covered my face to conceal my tears. Locheng knew that Achila had died. She burst into tears and cried out loud, "Emanic a kang! Emanic a kang! (My bull! My bull!)." (Mirzeler 1999, 328–9)

Again the cry of Locheng, "My bull! My bull!" is so universally human that it gives sufficient reason to accept the story of gray bull Engiro as autobiographical tradition. Once we sense how autobiographical the historical traditions are, it is easier to trace the episodes of the variants of the gray bull Engiro stories to the lived experience of the Jie.

The thematic images of historical traditions are projected into the autobiography of Lodoch at all levels of his experience. One of the most explicit statements about the assumed backdrop of historical tradition can be illustrated with an episode, which transpired about a year after the death of Achila, after he received the summons from his maternal uncle Yongotum and went to Kacheri:

> When I reached Kacheri, Yongotum, the brother of my mother, and a few other elders were sitting in the etem (man's resting place usually built next to the cattle enclosure) of Achila. (Mirzeler 1999, 329)

We should keep in mind that Locheng was listening to the old men talking to Lodoch, with her ear pressed against the fence of the etem:

> Yongotum called me and said, "You will marry the wife of your dead brother, and keep the amachar. The family herd should not be divided."
> I replied, "If that is the case, I will marry her and keep the herd together."
> I left the etem, got a ram and put it in the anuk of Locheng. When the evening came, I went to Locheng's house and sat in her ekal (yard). After some time, I got my courage up and entered her house.
> She knew that I was going to enter into her house and become her husband. She had a new fire flaming in the fireplace and she was curled up

in the corner, waiting for me, silently. There was no conversation between
us for a while.

Finally, she said, "You have entered my house without my knowledge."

I said, "I thought you had heard everything we talked about at the *etem*.
There is no problem. I have already entered your house and you have made
the new fire." Locheng remained silent as she spread the cowskin on the
ground near the fire. Then she lay down on it. I lay down next to her
and did not say anything. My thoughts took me to my childhood years:
I remembered Locheng washing me as a child, putting oil on my body
and cuddling me. I chased those thoughts away immediately, and began
to think about our herd, the family herd, and the *amachar*, the cattle of
my father and the father of my father. I mounted Locheng and she did not
refuse. She was submissive without emotion. The fire died near morning
and she did not replenish it. (Mirzeler 1999, 330)

We should remember the historical tradition regarding the sacrifice
of the gray bull Engiro,[3] and juxtapose the images of that tradition with
this episode of Lodoch's autobiography. We will recognize the similarities between the scene of Lodoch's consummation with Locheng and
the consummation of Orwakol with Losilang in the historical tradition.
The images of the new fire, the *amachar*, and the ensuing consummation
episode are immediately recognizable to us, illustrating Lodoch's skillful use of the images of tradition to frame his life experiences. Making
fire and keeping the fire going are important images for continuity of
life. We should remember that Locheng did not replenish the fire that
night after Lodoch consummated the marriage.

Let us compare, for instance, that autobiographical episode, with the
episode of the historical tradition:

[a]fter Orwakol branded the offspring of Engiro and distributed the *amachar* to his seven sons . . . Losilang kindled a new fire in her hut and slept
with Orwakol on the cowskin. (Mirzeler 1999, 400)

Lodoch admired his father's skill as a storyteller, and he learned the
art of storytelling from him. We can see from his autobiographical narrative how his personality was formed as he listened to his father telling him stories.

"When my father told us the story of gray bull Engiro and how the bull
drank the water at the well in the Longiro River, I wanted to have a bull

just like that, a gray bull with a beautiful hump. I also became fascinated with the story of Nayeche, and her struggle over cattle in Koteen Hill. Whenever the Turkana women came to get sorghum from us, I would ask them, "Is it true that you are the grandchildren of Nayeche? Do you come from the Tarash River?" (Mirzeler 1999, 299)

Lodoch was impressed not only by his father's stories, but also by his father's experiences of hunting and raiding. His father recounted stories such as, "When I was this or that old, I killed a lion or an elephant. I went raiding and brought so many cattle home and married so and so." Lodoch seemed to be fascinated by his father's personal experiences and he connected these experiences to his own. For instance, a lion tore out one of his father's eyes when he was a young shepherd. Later Lodoch's father speared the lion that did this to him and gave its skin to his father, Lodoch's grandfather, as a gift. The deeds of Lodoch's father very much define his father's identity, and people talked about his father's one eye as a sign of his bravery in single-handedly killing a lion.

When he was a boy, Lodoch's father ordered him to form the horns of the ox. As we remember, the shaping of the horn is an important activity for a Jie boy coming of age. The boy shapes the horns of his personal ox as he sees fit, and people give the boy a new name according to the shape of his ox's horns. Instead of shaping the horns of his ox, Lodoch cut off one of the horns, leaving the other one intact. He did not shape the remaining horn. He just let it grow. The people called Lodoch "Lokori Wala" (the red and white one with one horn). It is perhaps not an accident that Lodoch cut off one of the horns of his personal ox. He perhaps chose to do this as a way of commemorating his one-eyed father's bravery.

Lodoch kept his one-horned ox "until the Toposa came to Najie for the sacred clay of Longiro for their *asapan* initiation" (Mirzeler 1999, 302). According to Lodoch,

"The Toposa always come to Najie to get clay from the Longiro River. And whenever they come, they also ask for food. People are always generous to Toposa whenever they ask for food. When the Toposa came again that year to get the sacred clay of Longiro River, some of them stayed in *arii* (cattle enclosure) of my father. They begged me to give them my one-horned bull. My father then said, "If the Toposa ask you to give them your bull, you should give it to them otherwise they can curse us and our cattle can be wiped out completely. The Toposa are our brothers. The reason they separated and became different people is that Orwakol refused to give

them the right thigh meat of the gray bull Engiro. So we must give the meat
to appease them." After hearing what my father had said, I gave my bull to
Toposa, and they slaughtered it and ate its meat. (Mirzeler 1999, 302)

The memory Lodoch describes is interwoven with the historical
memory of his society. Lodoch's offering of his ox to the Toposa illuminates how historical traditions are used to justify the present politico-
ritual practices. Let us juxtapose this particular memory of Lodoch with
the images of a crucially distinctive historical episode in the story of
gray bull Engiro – the sacrifice of the gray bull on the rock of Daidai,
which led to the separation of the Toposa from the original Jie family.
While Orwakol and his sons were eating the flesh of Engiro, "The people of Toposa wanted to have the right thigh of the bull, but Orwakol
refused to give that portion of the meat to the Toposa people, who then
got upset and left Daidai" (Mirzeler 1999, 244). We also remember it
was during this time that a young girl called Nayeche left Daidai in
search of wild fruits and water, never to return home.

We should recall, when traditionally the Toposa people come during
the *asapan* ritual performance to receive sacred clay from the Longiro
River, they ask for meat from the Jie, paralleling the annual return of the
Turkana women to ask for sorghum grain from the Jie women with the
model of the returning Nayeche. While this return of the Toposa people
indicates the commensality of meat, the return of Nayeche involves the
commensality of grain. Commensality of meat and grain appears to involve a system of gift exchange – the original gift of meat and grain
from the ancestors in the past and the counter gift of the meat and grain
in the present (Mirzeler 1999, 2004).

We find similarities between historical tradition and the personal
memories of Lodoch so frequently that we can be fairly certain that the
images of historical traditions and personal memory are so connected
and mutually influential as to form the foundation of Jie historical
knowledge.

To reiterate, let us again compare the image of commensality of the
exchange of meat and grain in historical traditions with an interesting
memory of Lodoch, which transpired the night after he consummated
his marriage with Locheng:

In the morning I went to *anuk* (goat enclosure), got the ram, and sacrificed
it. Since I had slept with the wife of my dead brother, the old women came
and smeared both Locheng and me with the *ngikujit* of the sacrificial ram

and the clay of Longiro River. Locheng then went and got sorghum from her granary and boiled it. We sat and tasted the sorghum and the meat and then offered the meat and the grains to people in the *arii*. Locheng had become my wife. (Mirzeler 1999, 330–1)

This particular memory image gives us a clear sense of how historical knowledge forms the basis of not only interethnic relationships, but also family relationships in Jie society. Both the personal memory images and those of historical traditions articulate the symbolic equivalence of agropastoral production and human reproduction. Furthermore, meat and grain are considered the only food for commensality following the exchange. This commensality is essentially an act of communion between a man and a woman, between the ancestors and the living, between families, and between different ethnic communities. This exchange, however, is not an economic exchange or generalized exchange based on trust. It is a generalized exchange of bodies in Mauss's sense of gift exchange (1967). One keeps the gift while giving it away.

Almost everything that Lodoch tells us about his life is explicitly or implicitly related to the oral traditions of his society. However, this interrelationship is not confined to stories of Nayeche and the gray bull Engiro. When listening to Lodoch's stories, the first thing one notices about them is that they are connected and unified by his autobiography. Even his folktales contain elaborately detailed images drawn from personal memory. The details of the images in his folktales seem to be as important as they are in the historical traditions of his society. Often they concern his emotional experiences, attachments, and identifications.

As I have pointed out, Lodoch was fascinated with the one-eye image of his father. Lodoch also connected the one-eye motif with the one breast of Napeikisina, the famous villain of Jie folktales, which he was so fond of telling. It is interesting that Lodoch frequently used this particular motif as an analogy to describe the inadequate nature of the Najie's soil to justify the dependence of Jie people on meat and milk. He also used a similar analogy to describe his mother mocking his father. Lodoch told me how one day, when one of the baby goats had disappeared, his mother looked around to find it. When his father saw his mother running around frantically looking for the missing goat, he asked her what she was doing going around the *arii* so frantically. She told him she was looking for the newborn goat. His father told her that he had just seen the little goat pass through the left side of the fence. Upon hearing this, his mother mocked him and said to him, "Ehh, how could you see the goat pass through the left side of the fence, when you are blind in your left eye?"

Lodoch, it appears, has skillfully transformed this personal memory image into an interesting episode in the story of the Fox and the Elephant, in which the wives of the elephant were looking for the fox who had killed their husband. When "the vulture with one eye saw the fox running, and leaving behind a cloud of dust," he told the wives of the elephant, "The fox has just came out and he is running this way."[4] All the other vultures who were devouring the carcass of the elephant looked at this one-eyed vulture and said to him, "Ehh, how can you see where the fox went in this cloud of dust with only one eye."[5]

Another interesting story told by Lodoch about a man called Ebongo, further demonstrates how Lodoch transforms his personal memory images into the images of his stories. Lodoch frequently mentioned his admiration of Ebongo who killed a lion all by himself. Lodoch's admiration for Ebongo is closely related to his admiration for his father, who also struggled with a lion, and the circumstances led to the loss of one of his eyes. The image of the lion appears again and again in the Angu stories, which he is so fond of telling, and in his childhood memories. On an occasion, when Lodoch was a young shepherd, a lion devoured one of the cows Lodoch was herding. The death of that cow devastated Lodoch's father. He hit Lodoch until he became unconscious, calling him a hyena.

For his father, Lodoch was the son, and, as a son, he should be a successful herder, a worthy warrior, a sought-after child. But what his father saw was another side of Lodoch, one that he considered a disturbing side of his character. He saw that Lodoch was not a good herder, but was only pretending to be one. He was a shepherd in disguise, who sought to become the head of the home, but was only masquerading as a loyal shepherd of the family herd. Because of Lodoch's selfishness, his father thought, the family herd was in danger. He was an ungrateful hyena in disguise, like the hyena in the folktales.

Another personal memory image that Lodoch frequently transformed into historical memories is the tamarind tree in front of Lodoch's home under which his father and Achila lay before Achila's death. It was this same tree where Lodoch saw his sister Lokui for the last time, early in the morning before her death. Lodoch recalls this poignant moment in his life and remembers Lokui with her hoe on her back, standing under the tree. It is not surprising that Lodoch buried Achila under a tree in Labwor, which resembled the tamarind tree in front of his home. The image of the tamarind tree corresponds to more than a single episode in Lodoch's life.

Because the tamarind tree is so closely connected with Lodoch's deeply felt personal experiences, he frequently fuses the image of the tamarind tree in front of his home with his performances of oral tradition. This artful transformation of his personal memories of the tamarind tree is richly detailed. The following passages from the historical tradition about the war between the Jie and the Acholi people, and the fictional tale, A Bat and His Friends Who Went Raiding, give a good sense of this.

In the historical tradition about the war between the Jie and the Acholi (Mirzeler 1999, 270–3), after a lengthy discussion, the Acholi people decided to raid the Jie cattle. They set off toward Najie with their guns until they reached a huge tamarind tree near the Dopeth River. The Acholi decided to settle their wives and their war provisions under the tree, and then went to attack the Jie villages. When the Acholi soldiers approached Lokatap Rock, the Jie soldiers defended their cattle and chased away the Acholi soldiers. The defeated Acholi soldiers hastily retreated toward the tamarind tree, under which they had left their wives and provisions. As they ran toward the tree, dark clouds engulfed the whole plain and the tree became invisible.

The Acholi could not see where the tree was and began to run toward Maaru. The Jie people continued to follow them and, catching up with them before they reached Maaru, killed many of them in a valley, which is now called Naokot (literally, blood), which became flooded with the blood of the Acholi people. After slaughtering all the Acholi men, the Jie warriors went to the Dopeth River and found the Acholi women, still waiting under the tree, and brought them to Lokatap (Mirzeler 1999, 273).

Detail by detail, Lodoch transforms the images and the themes of this historical episode into an episode from the well-known folktale of the bat and his friends that go raiding in a faraway place. In the folktale, after they raided the cattle, they found a tree in the middle of a plain. It started to rain and the animals took refuge under this tree.

As the heavy rain drops pounded on the ground, the place grew dark, and the cattle could no longer be seen. When the wind blew during the heavy rain, the cattle became frightened and ran away. The whole plain was flooded and the rivers began to flow.[6] After the rain stopped and the dark clouds disappeared, the animals searched for the cattle but they could not find them and they cursed the tree (see part 4).

In the historical memory we see women being left under the tree, whereas in the folktale, we see cattle. In Jie culture, cattle are used as the bride-price for women. In the first case, the Acholi lost the women as a result of their intention to steal, in the latter case we see the bat and his friends lost the cattle, which they had stolen. In both instances the storyteller gives an implied message that stealing will result in loss of wealth. We also see Lodoch losing his father, sister, and his brother under the tree. In each of these cases the image of the tree is associated with important losses.

In one of Lodoch's memories of a peace-making ceremony in Moru a Nayeche, the dark clouds descended and a turtle emerged from the surrounding bush. It stood on its hind legs and stretched his head out (Mirzeler 1999, 351–3). That turtle is understood in many ways to be like the turtle that betrayed Jie society in the folktale Lodoch was so fond of narrating, "The Rabbit Who Did Not Drink Water." It is interesting that Lodoch should fuse the image of the turtle, which betrayed society with the images of dark clouds and rain in Moru a Nayeche. That turtle, in many ways, symbolizes Nayeche who, in some variants of the story, refuses to give cattle to the elders in the village, and also betrays her society by taking the fire of Orwakol and the gray bull Engiro and refusing to return home.

The above analyses have shown the relationship between oral tradition and autobiography. Oral tradition is a product of personal memory, folktales, and historical traditions. Skillful storytellers, like Lodoch, transform their personal reminiscences into oral tradition. What the storytellers bring to the oral traditions are their personal memories and experiences that can be recognized. Neither the biographical nor the historical events have intrinsic meaning built into them. The story and meaning therein are entirely dependent on the artistic ability of the storyteller. Through the infusion of biographical memory images into the plots of oral traditions, storytellers make sense of both their personal and collective pasts. They transform their biographical memory images and their emotional experiences into appropriate historical traditions. In doing so, the storytellers transmit the knowledge and meaning of past events to the next generation. Historical events such as famines and droughts during the time of Nayeche and the lost gray bull Engiro continue to happen in the contemporary time and place, and how they were dealt with in the past continues to be relevant to current Jie society. From this perspective, historical traditions are not only the stories of actual events that are reported, remembered, and transmitted, but they also justify the structure of those events in everyday life. Differences and similarities between Jie and Turkana and between the people of Orwakol and Lodiny are kept alive through performances of historical traditions. History explains differences between people. This is why historical traditions are so important and why they are told as they are and contain the episodes they do. The biographical contexts of the historical traditions that I describe here are themselves products of the storytellers' unique memory images. The images of historical traditions are no less opaque than biographical memory images, and vice versa. Each biographical memory adds a number of possible narratives that need interpretation if we are to fully understand a given historical tradition. The relationship between the historical tradition to be analyzed and the biographical material is a paradoxical one, and needs further research.

Conclusion

By way of conclusion, based on the analysis in the preceding chapters, I restate that Nayeche and the gray bull Engiro story, as a master narrative, does not refer to one particular episode in history. Rather, it is one of the key tokens in imagining the past by both the Jie and the Turkana people. The historical and cultural particularities of Nayeche and the gray bull Engiro story follow a general pattern, which is common in oral tradition in the region spanning Karamoja Plateau and the shores of Lake Turkana. To fully come to terms with Nayeche and the gray bull Engiro as a master narrative, I have shown the importance of remembering and meaning making in a general way. In my discussion of Nayeche and the gray bull Engiro story, I postulated its discursive specificity in relation to its remembering during various performance contexts.

As noted in chapter 4, the ancestral spatial organization of Moru a Nayeche and its physical relationship to the Tarash River and the plateau express interdependence and complementarity. The spatial dichotomy between the plateau and the plain serves an anticipatory discursive and ideological role. Recall that the spatial arrangements of the early 1700s were concomitant with splintering and fissioning of the ancestral family, including its ethnic elements in the region. It is easy to see how discursive ideologies of oral tradition serve to explain contemporary people's interethnic relations and access to land, water, and other resources based on oral traditions referring to their ancestors. The spatial organization between the Longiro River and the Dopeth River area works the same way. Beside reproducing discursive images of interdependency, the story of Nayeche and the gray bull Engiro produces kinship ties and moral responsibility to share natural resources, between two communities, both on the plateau, and in the plains around the

Tarash River region. One can affirm this understanding by examining the harvest rituals and marriage rituals and by examining the interethnic relationships between people living around the upper Tarash River in the plains and in Nakapelimoru on the plateau.

The Turkana and the Jie identities are marked by the respatialization of tribal territories and access to resources. While the memory of Nayeche has become a part of the oral tradition, the right to share resources between the two communities is continuously debated by storytellers. It is for this reason that during the respatialization of resources the storytellers manipulate the memory of where Nayeche and the gray bull Engiro traveled in the landscape, which rivers they crossed and where they drank water. In this respect, Moru a Nayeche serves as a tangible reminder of the Jie and the Turkana communities' kinship ties. The presentation of Moru a Nayeche during performances has little to do with the knowledge about the past. Rather it is about the revisioning of it for the present social order. References to Moru a Nayeche as a memory of a place during performances serve the two communities as a resource for imagining the past, as they attempt to solidify, through memory of events, their hold on the local resources. Here the storytellers render the memory of Nayeche and the gray bull Engiro tangible in the landscape.

The storytellers and the members of the audiences dialogically remember the memory of Nayeche and the gray bull Engiro's journey that transpired on the ancestral geographical sites, engaging the historical tradition with memory and place. Walking along the banks of the Longiro River and of the upper Tarash River and participating in the performances of historical traditions have shown me how the storytellers bring together the aura of tradition, the specificity of place, and collective memory as they poetically unfold the narrative of the capturing of the gray bull Engiro on the banks of the Longiro River and the journey of Nayeche on the waterless plateau. The dry courses of the rivers engender memory, evoking the poetics of pastness. Culturally specific memories of Nayeche and the gray bull Engiro, disguised and entangled in the workings of the performances, are spatially embedded in the waterless plateau and in the magnificent sites of Moru a Nayeche and of the Tarash River.

The ancestral geography of the Longiro River, Moru a Nayeche, and the Tarash River are instructive of the way the storytellers construct their historical images. Orwakol's capturing of the gray bull Engiro while drinking the muddy water from the well of the Longiro River and Nayeche's arrival to the Tarash River readily filter the image of Nayeche and Engiro into historical discourse, marking places as sanctified. The journey of Nayeche and the gray bull Engiro on the plateau, recounted during performances, produces its own authority, making the journey a sacred moment and transforming the sites of historical tradition into the "centers of creation" (Eliade 1960). While the performative particularities of the Longiro River, Moru a Nayeche, and the Tarash River in historical traditions may be unique to the ancient Jie and the Turkana geography, they follow a general pattern that is endemic to all the other traditions I have collected in the surrounding area.

By the 1720s, Moru a Nayeche perhaps emerged as a place of memory in its parochial setting, and the story of Nayeche and the gray bull Engiro was told and retold by countless storytellers to incorporate their symbolic journey, from the plateau to the plains, as a new social order through the dynamic processes of performances, meaning making, memorializing, and identity creation. The effect of telling versions of Nayeche and the gray bull Engiro stories was the making of identity – or the fashioning of the vulnerable Jie self – over the Turkana other within a structured relationship of kinship ties. My suggestion is that such an aspect of oral tradition emerges within the regional discourse of ideology, as I have shown in chapter 5. On one hand the discourse of vulnerable dependent self and on the other the construction of the moral responsibility to share meager resources serve the social, political, and economic imagination of the communities in this vast, dry land.

Stories like Nayeche and the gray bull Engiro provide moral discourses that encourage communities to see their vulnerable lives in a perceptively distinct light. We must take into account the fact that images and symbols of tradition produced during the performances are relevant to present contexts and hence the memories of the past are not totalized and fixed. However, Moru a Nayeche as a place of memory shapes and informs a wide range of social experiences laden with meanings that have not been noticed and explored by Lamphear or Gulliver.

Like Moru a Nayeche, other places of memories work in tandem with other processes, such as those constructed around kinship ties and tribal affinities. Stories such as Nayeche and gray bull Engiro, therefore, order human relations between communities, as well as underscore the impact of present predicaments. They serve as signs through which processes of remembering inform social and political relations between social and political actors. Moru a Nayeche is a place of memory precisely because the memory of ancestral experiences and the current

predicaments coalesce around these articulations during various performances. Inflections of memory symbolism of Moru a Nayeche serve
as semiotics of place in informing and shaping social relations between
social actors and their histories.

The semiotics of Nayeche and the gray bull Engiro's journey on the
waterless plateau and in the plain, therefore, mimetically connect local struggles with the movement of Nayeche. Nayeche's pursuit of the
gray bull Engiro to the upper Tarash River and her settlement around
the hill serves to anchor the meaning of her journey to foundational
and mythical past, binding social actors in the present with the sense
of history and subjectivity. The Moru a Nayeche as a place of memory
and its connection with the Longiro River and with Daidai in Najie
serves as a critical map for the Jie and the Turkana to imagine their
present relationships.

As I have shown in chapter 5, anecdotal reference to Moru a Nayeche
during various meetings demonstrates how events from the past serve
to advance various plots in the present, endowing them with a sense of
history. It is through this master narrative that Moru a Nayeche as a
place of memory must be read. The journey of Nayeche and the gray
bull Engiro on the waterless plateau, then, serves as a fragment of discursive memory that advances a plot of social and political relations
between the Jie and the Turkana with a myth of origin.

The story of Nayeche and the gray bull Engiro is educational and biographical. The story of Nayeche and the gray bull Engiro prepared
Lodoch for his adult role, teaching him his interethnic social obligation
to the Turkana people around the Tarash River region, who depend on
the grains of the Jie. It informed him of taboos of his society. As we have
seen, the theme of marriage ceremony and the harvest rituals are synonymous with the thematic images of Nayeche and the gray bull Engiro's
journey in the story. It is thus not necessary to talk about fixed chrono-
logically ordered historical messages in any meaningful sense of the
word in the story. As the foregoing analysis has shown, oral traditions
such as Nayeche are continually reinterpreted and endlessly debated as
people imagine their personal and collective identities. Historians who
put their faith in the clear historical messages and chronologies of oral
traditions, are missing a layer of narrative and are uncritical in crediting academic versions of African histories. In this respect, historical messages and chronologies attributed to oral traditions such as Nayeche
and the gray bull Engiro are not the result of the interpretations of local

African communities, but rather of the impact of western academic trends and forms (Hanretta 2009).

The memory images found in traditional discourses and customs have their own cultural contexts and are subject to the interpretations of their bearers in response to popular issues and predicaments. The images of oral traditions are more flexible and permeable, yet less predictable in meaning, than Africanist historians have thought (Barber 1991; Tonkin 1992). What gives Nayeche and the gray bull Engiro tradition its coherence and power is the fact that it lays deep in people's collective consciousness, informing them of who they are and how they should behave. Yet, as a discourse, Nayeche oral tradition is continually reinterpreted and reconstructed for its continued legitimacy. Precisely because oral traditions are so embedded in local discourses and so emotionally compelling, they are readily evoked. Therefore historicity of oral traditions is limited. Historians should perhaps focus on the meaning and significance of oral traditions, and their dynamic interpretations between the storytellers and the members of the audiences in various contexts. People debate contemporary issues in terms of ideas and beliefs drawn from their oral traditions, reformulating them and revising them in the context of the present, as I have shown here (Mirzeler 1999 and 2004).

Thus, oral traditions and their attendant discourses are more fluid than the Africanist historians imagined. Seeing oral traditions with fixed historical messages might give historians a chance to develop Africa's past, yet it would cause them not to see the ongoing negotiations and compromises between the storytellers and their audiences over the meanings of their traditions and their shared moral ideologies.

Here, the issues of shared moral ideology lead into the meanings of oral traditions and their competing interpretations. Harnessing ancestral moral ideology for survival and sharing resources embodied in the stories enable the storytellers to create a stable political relationship, which is appealing to the Jie and the Turkana's own values and institutions. To invoke the shared images of oral traditions, both the storytellers and the members of their audiences have to appeal to both the past and the future, to affirm to themselves what they had been as well what they imagine themselves to become in the future. For this reason the storytellers mold the images of their traditions to express their predicaments in the broader context of modernity and more specifically in their conflict with the Ugandan nation-state. A good example of this, as described in chapter 1, is Nacham's reconfiguration of the vision of his society's future by deploying the images of oral tradition and fusing them with the sentimentally informed images of the Jimos village and its destruction by the Ugandan army in 2007.

Recall Nacham's narrative of his return to his village from exile, a story imbued with the images of the gray bull Engiro's return from the kraals in his tradition. In making the destroyed village a place of history, Nacham's storytelling has allowed us to witness the looming task of the Jie storytellers' imagining their culture and society at a time of violent state intervention and expanding globalization, which is instrumental to the Jie's modernization. And instrumental in keeping the Jie identity during these violent escalations is the collective icons of oral tradition, such as Nayeche and the gray bull Engiro, Orwakol, and Lodiny, whose images yield places of memory. Such collective past images of oral tradition bind ideological sources of meanings, giving the displaced Jie in Kampala the markers of their new social order.

During such crisis, as in disarmament, the storytellers like Nacham search for places of memory that embody particular images and identities. Such searches for these places from the collective past enable individuals to attach themselves to the ideological sources of meaning, in the process of converting their experiences of displacement from the places of memory. Nowhere have these historical detachments been experienced more profoundly than during the first decade of the twenty-first century among the displaced Jie people in Kampala. The disarmament dispersed a large number of people and brought them to Kampala. The sheer diversity and magnitude of the cosmopolitan city seems to have allowed the displaced storytellers to reproduce their traditional heroes in the city in new and powerful ways.

With the disarmament, the creation of new pastoralist grazing land, and the new modern economy, the patterns of traditions are profoundly disrupted. The changes in the traditional patterns produce new memories and new social orders with their attendant discourses that underscore the modern nation-state project itself. Here the storytellers' creative use of oral tradition is not only one of the arts of resistance, but also one of the responses to the "logic of modernity," as suggested by Richard Flores in the context of Alamo's emergence as a place of memory (Flores 2002).

What I am suggesting by the logic of modernity is the power of modernity to break, dislocate, or remove social relations from their original locus and then to relocate and represent them in distinct spatial and temporal domains. For Flores (2002, 153–5), rapid cultural changes and novel experiences forced by modernity ruptures social life and a sense of belonging to a tradition. From this perspective, I take the introduction of the AK-47 into Jie culture and the subsequent violent disarmament project launched by the modern state to be a transformational process through which Jie tradition is dislocated from its origins. Jie storytellers have sought to come to terms with modernity by manipulating both symbolic and social worlds as Jie society has been transforming.

In this context, while the cultural contents of new oral traditions may be distinct, their symbolism emerges from the same motifs that order patterns of the Jie cultural experiences. In this respect, the pastness of oral tradition is as important as its future, and any interpretation focusing exclusively on the historicity of oral tradition is bound to fail. Historians therefore need to see how storytellers and audiences jointly lead the people into the future while attaching them to the past in endless processes of becoming, while synthesizing both the old and the new images of their traditions (Spear 2003).

The main argument of this book has to do with "partials truths" of the Nayeche and gray bull Engiro story with various aspects of Jie culture, history, collective memory, and individual memory. My own theoretical matrix has led me to explore the way in which images of the past are embedded in oral traditions along with their clusters of symbols, then are deployed by individual actors to render the present world and human actions meaningful. Looking at oral tradition's "partial connections" pragmatically but not reductively provides a way of linking rhetorical aspects of oral tradition with multiple discourses. From this perspective, the story of Nayeche and the gray bull Engiro provides glimpses inside historical traditions, one of the most poorly understood genres of African oral tradition.

When popular biographies, autobiographies of storytellers, and performances are considered together, they challenge the scholarly interpretative framework that connects historical traditions to particular moments in history. Nayeche and gray bull Engiro is embedded in the landscape, collective memory, and biography, orienting and naturalizing social relations around the images and plots of the story. This enables the members of the society to construct an identity for themselves and to create a meaningful past. Interpretations of the past become institutionalized by means of ritual reiterations, such as the harvest and the marriage ceremonies. Through Nayeche's story, people tell themselves and others about the present, drawing creatively on memories of ancestral families to form new collective and individual identities. It is insufficient, then, to treat such stories as material that can be mined to reconstruct history.

At this point, I return to Strathern's notion of "partial connections" and I suggest that "contradictions" arise in the forms of historical interpretation when we consider the use of oral tradition's historicity in Jie culture, simply because the past is differently valued and differently understood in Jie society. Nayeche's story is a form of historical discourse and its partial connections with the present may elicit a sense of pastness, but to use this sense to craft a particular past is poor historical reasoning. There are no clear correspondences between the elements of the Nayeche oral tradition and the events of the 1720s. Identifying correspondences between historical processes and oral traditions favors academic historians over Africans' use of their own history (Hanretta 2009). The images of Nayeche and gray bull Engiro enable the Jie and the Turkana to imagine and experience their pastness with their attendant partial connections and partial truths. Academic Africanist historians therefore would benefit from Strathern's suggestion that they examine their historical representations and consider the compatibility of information regarding historicity of oral tradition across cultures in light of the contextually informed partial connections between the images of the past and competing representation of pastness. Such an approach can provoke rethinking the standard baseline for analogy in the way past is represented across cultures. Historical reasoning is not universal, and not all societies rely on chronology in their understanding of history. The present study encourages historians to understand that their sources may include historical accounts that were never intended to be factually accurate but rather had other purposes in their context.

Lamphear, influenced by the Africanist historians of 1960s and 1970s, attempted to reconstruct Africa's past using oral tradition as historical evidence. The intense interest in reconstructing Africa's past was almost as strong as in the years from the mid-nineteenth to the mid-twentieth centuries, when the colonization processes were taking place and eroding African traditions and customs. Scholars of African history gathered a detailed corpus of oral tradition and reconstructed the African history using the very stuff of conventional historiography. Their arguments regarding the reliability of oral tradition as historical evidence were based on some of the centralized societies' use of memorized traditions, which were recited by trained specialists. Lamphear's approach to the Jie and the Turkana oral tradition belongs to this generation of research, and his reconstruction of the Jie's past was pathbreaking for its time. Although his work preceded the critical study of oral tradition, he has not taken the opportunity to revise his work in light of this. An Africanist historian, John Tosh (2006, 330), who uses oral tradition to reconstruct the Lango people's history, one of the communities living near Najie, maintains that, "Unlike primary documentary sources, oral tradition does not convey the original words and images from which the historian may be able to re-create the mental world of the past." I agree.

Lamphear's methodological convention was based on widely shared theories of oral tradition as history as formulated by Jan Vansina (1965). J.B. Webster et al. (1973) was one of the first to lay out the model of the historical study of oral tradition in northern Uganda and in the surrounding regions. Although Webster's book did not become the prototype for later works, other Africanist historians, such as Cohen (1977), Tosh (1978), Lamphear (1976), and Sobania (1980), followed his reconstructionist model, producing comparative data on various aspects of political systems in the broader region in various articles and books. Indeed, all these works used the Durkheimian model of segmentary lineage system, along with a model of emerging political communities.

Lamphear's chronological presentation of the Jie people, based on generation and age-set analyses dating back to the early 1700s, is replete with difficulties, particularly in the reconstruction of Africa's chronological history from oral tradition, as is elsewhere well documented and explored (for example, D. Henige 1974, 1982, 1986, and 2005; R. Reid 1997; M. Twaddle 1975; J. Tosh 2000; E. Tonkin 1986; J. Vansina 1971). Henige's comparison of orally transmitted knowledge around the world, detailing genealogies from various places and times, indicates patterns of chronological distortions emerging mainly from telescoping and lengthening of the past (Henige 1974). The unreliability of oral tradition's uncertain chronology, as delineated by Henige, is widely accepted by numerous anthropologists and historians (for example, Ocan 1994; Reid 1997; Twaddle 1975; Tonkin 1986; Vansina 1971, 1989; Varadarajan 1979; Warren 1976). My research findings on the use of oral tradition in reconstructing the past of the Jie people are congruent with these scholars' criticisms. For example, when I interviewed Jie elders regarding the succession of the firemakers and various events, they presented them in different sequences at each interview. As the selection of the Jie and of the Turkana historical traditions presented in part 4 of this book clearly indicates, historical traditions do not contain sequences of events connected to time periods and hence are unusable in chronological constructions.

According to Paul Spencer (1978, 134), Lamphear's reconstruction of Jie chronology assumes a predictable continuity of time and the "unbreakability" of the Jie generations, which contain "anomalies" and "cumulative mismatch" between age and generation-set. Spencer (1978, 148) maintains that the observations of both Gulliver, the principal anthropologist of the Jie community, and Lamphear are based on limited points of the total time continuum, and both lack sufficient regional contextualization, demographic data, and longitudinal observations of age span and developmental cycles, without which one cannot produce a conclusive estimate of intervals between successive generations. In addition, there are vast durational differences between Gulliver and Lamphear's work in the calculation of the interval between successive Jie generations. For example, while Gulliver (1953, 148) estimates the interval between successive Jie generations at twenty to thirty years, Lamphear estimates it at forty years. We see discrepancies in the interval elsewhere: Spencer's more sophisticated analysis estimates the generation intervals at about fifty-five years. Yet E. Stites et al. (2012) (see also Stites 2013) estimate the intervals of the Jie generation-set at about twenty-five years, demonstrating the major disruptions in the developmental cycles of generation-set during the last few decades caused by the ongoing violence in the region.

Perhaps the work of Lamphear would have been more compelling if he had adequately considered the developmental cycles of generations and had better contextualized them and if he had had alternate sources of information. So it is difficult to determine whether Lamphear's historical reconstruction of Jie chronology reflects the actual unfolding of the past history. I nevertheless, for the presentation of Jie history, accept his reconstruction of Jie history, with reservations and with some risk. I will therefore assume all the historical events suggested by Lamphear, going back to 1700, including the successions of the firemakers and the rise of Loriang as a unifying war-leader, are among the key events in the Jie's history.

Lamphear correlates the stories of the early Najie settlement that are embedded in Jie oral tradition with the complex problem of identifying Nilotic origin and migration, with particular reference to events that took place around the Koteen Hill area on the Karamoja Plateau. His argument regarding the association of the Jie's origins with Nilotic migration is at best a hypothesis in East African historiography; hence one cannot say with any certainty from where these immigrants came, beyond what typological and linguistic comparisons suggest (Twaddle 1975). The result is a conjectural history rich with the complexities of the early Nilotic immigration and settlement patterns in central Karamoja.

Lamphear's reconstruction of the Jie and the Turkana clan histories and political institutions going back to the early 1700s is too distant to survive in oral tradition in the absence of memorization. Without independent corroborating evidence, details of how the Jie emerged through clan segmentation and then expanded by ethnic assimilation, based on oral tradition are impossible to determine. The oral traditions I collected in their contexts (see part 4 for examples) strongly suggest multiple possibilities of how clan leaders might have emerged, and they support his overall interpretation of the Jie histories of the firemaking clans. However they do not support the chronological sequences of the historical events and the succession of the firemakers, as delineated by Lamphear. In my view, Lamphear's findings demonstrate how oral tradition can enable one to see some of the ways in which political offices can be established and mythical sources manipulated for political purposes.

From about the 1720s, the Jie people of Karamoja Plateau and the Turkana people of the upper Tarash River region perhaps shared a common view of the universe and ideology, as delineated by Lamphear. This includes the assumption about the origin, economic and political interdependence, rituals, values, traditional authority and symbols of these two communities. Among the symbols connected directly with their common ideology was the gray bull Engiro that fathered their cattle, and the wild fruits of Nayeche, which flourish abundantly in the bushes, enabling them to survive. In addition, they perhaps inherited the sorghum from Orwakol (Mirzeler 2004), the original Jie firemaker, and the iron from the Labworian smelters who forged hoes and spears from the soil of Mount Toror.

The constellation of oral traditions, including the story of Nayeche and the gray bull Engiro, embodies the ideology surrounding their resources and their way of life. In each story, the ideology is expressed slightly differently, reflecting the art of remembering showing how the ancestors shared their resources to survive. The common theme of these stories, namely moral responsibility for sharing of resources and political cooperation for survival, is the same throughout the vast dry region.

As I have shown in chapter 3, the morality of these stories encompassing a wide region can be baffling. How did these diverse traditions with
common themes form in this vast dry zone? Did these stories with similar core images emerge independently in each of the various political
communities living in distinct ecological zones in the region?

PART FOUR

The Stories

Introductory Note

In the 1990s and in the early 2000s, I made a number of research trips to Karamoja Plateau, the Turkana land, and environs. During my trips, I tape recorded many of the discussions and performances of the storytellers. I walked more than 1,000 miles conducting research, working with storytellers and collecting myths, epics, and poetry. My collection consists of over two hundred transcriptions, translated from the Jie and Turkana languages into English. The transcriptions range from one to ten pages, double spaced. All of the stories I collected are tagged with the name of the storyteller, the date and place of performance, the nature of the audience, and brief comments about the stories. Moreover, I cataloged the performances and discussions and wrote field notes.

In this section, I provide some of these stories not only because the analysis in the preceding chapters draws significantly from these stories, but also because these transcribed oral materials constitute a rich resource for anthropologists, folklorists, and historians. Anthropological and historical studies of East African oral traditions have often provided fragments of the stories, using them for historical reconstruction as well as the socioeconomic and political implications of oral traditions. No written corpus of oral tradition exists among the Jie and Turkana people. Of all the existing studies of oral tradition of the East African hunter-gatherers, pastoralists, farmers, and fishing communities, very few provide a corpus of oral tradition as a particular folkloric genre and performing art. Thus, this section will be an important contribution to the scholarly literature on oral tradition of the East African hunter-gatherers, pastoralists, farmers, and fishing communities. The stories given here were recorded in one of two ways: on tape and in dictation. All stories listed were tape recorded except when dictation by hand is explicitly indicated. In each case, the stories were told in Jie or Turkana and later translated with the help of my research assistance. I have given relevant information regarding the collection and translation of the stories in the introduction to the book. I group the stories in three sections: historical traditions, folktales, and popular biographies.

I have tried to translate all the stories relatively literally to preserve the flavor of the original narratives, while at the same time rendering them intelligible to readers. Jie and Turkana stories were sometimes narrated in abrupt ways rather than in flowing sentences and paragraphs. This I have tried to smooth by making relevant transitions between sentences as well as between paragraphs. I have included one story (of the gray bull Engiro) with a nearly literal translation in the Historical Traditions section to show the interested readers how I translated the oral sources.

Based on Jie and Turkana friends' suggestion, I used the Latin alphabet (as did earlier scholars) in my transcription of the original sources. In all, I recorded over two hundred stories, although I heard more. In making the selection for the present book I have tried to include versions of folktales, historical traditions, and biographies that I used in my analysis in this volume. However, the selections in the volume should not be considered as the ideal versions of the stories. Titles of the stories are my own, as the storytellers do not give the stories titles. Rather they identify them by their themes. Consequently, in citing a story I do not place its descriptor in quotation marks although to an Anglophone reader it appears that a title is given. Repetitions often used in oral narratives are not included here except a few phrases emphasizing the movements of the characters in the dry landscape such as Nayeche's pursuit of the gray bull Engiro or young men's search for pasture and water. I sometimes compressed lengthy repetitions in some segments of narratives to allow in the present book publication of a number of short and medium-length transcriptions instead of merely a few longer ones. This decision to abridge the transcriptions was made with the awareness that repetitions in the oral tradition do articulate meaning and are important tools helping the audience to comprehend the performance. Otherwise, all stories are presented here as closely as possible to their original recording. I have not paraphrased or improved any of the historical traditions except a few of the folktales to make them accessible to Anglophone readers. I have indicated the place of recording rather than the birthplace or the residence of the storytellers. Finally, all ages given as descriptors of the storytellers were approximations I made at the time of the performance.

List of Stories

These stories represent a part of the data on which my research and analyses are based.

An asterisk (*) in front of a descriptor indicates the inclusion in full in part 4; these stories are cited in the endnotes for the chapters with a descriptor, a number, and "part 4." When a story appears simply with a descriptor and a number, the story cited was collected and transcribed and remains in my collection but is not published here.

The following abbreviations are used in citations: JHT (Jie Historical Traditions), JFT (Jie Folktales), THT (Turkana Historical Traditions), JTHT (Jie and Turkana Historical Traditions), EHT (Elmolo Historical Traditions), and PB (Popular Biographies).

Jie and Turkana Historical Traditions

*1 **The Story of the Gray Bull Engiro and Longiro River**
Storyteller: Lochoro (a 50-year-old Ngikuliak man)
Place: Kotido

*2 **The Gray Bull Engiro**
Storyteller: Lotiang (a 50-year-old Jie man)
Place: Kotido, near the edge of a sorghum field where people were threshing their sorghum

3 **The Death of Engiro**
Storyteller: Longok (a 50-year-old man) (dictated)
Place: Rengen, under the tree on the side of a village path

4 **Daidai Rock**
Storyteller: Lodoch (a 65-year old man)
Place: Jimos village, under a tree near the homestead of Rianaro

5 **The Original Ancestral Conflict**
Storyteller: Logwee (a 50-year-old man) (dictated)
Place: Under a tree near the Longiro river, Kotido, Kotido District

*6 **The Original Ancestral Conflict**
Storyteller: Lokapelan (a 50-year-old Jie man)
Place: Under a tree near the road between Kotiyang and Rengen (Najie)

*7 **The Original Ancestral Raiding**
Storyteller: Lodoch (a 65-year-old man)
Place: Kalakuruk Rock

8 **The Arrival of Lodiny to Daidai**
Storyteller: Urien (a 40-year-old man)
Place: In front of Urien's home, in the Jimos village

22 **Ngolengiro, the Bull of Lokolong**
Storyteller: Ekitoi (a 50-year-old woman)
Place: Komukunyu

*23 **The Original Ancestral Fire**
Storyteller: Napeyo (a 65-year-old Jie woman)
Place: Kotyang village

24 **Orwakol and His Seven Wives**
Storyteller: Lodoch (a 65-year-old man)
Place: Kotido, under a tree near a dusty road

25 **Dongiro, the Cradle Land**
Storyteller: Lodoch (a 65-year-old man)
Place: Kotido

26 **Kanakosim**
Storyteller: Michael Lodio (a 50-year-old man)
Place: Kotido

*27 **Nakadanya, the Cradle Land of Long Ago**
Storyteller: Akiru (a 75-year-old Matheniko woman)
Place: Moroto

28 **The Memory of Maaru Hill**
Storyteller: Lokui (a 50-year-old Ngikuliak woman)
Place: Under a tree at the foot of Maaru Hill

29 **Nayeche**
Storyteller: Boiboi (a 30-year-old man)
Place: Mustafa Mirzeler's home in Jimos village

30 **Nayeche**
Storyteller: Lodoch (a 65-year-old man)
Place: Mustafa Mirzeler's home in Losilang near Jimos village

*31 **Nayeche**
Storyteller: Koriang (a 50-year-old Jie man)
Place: Under a tree near the Lokatap Rock

32 **The Great Sacrifice of Long Ago**
Storyteller: Lodoch (a 65-year-old man)
Place: Jimos village

33 **The Origin of Sorghum**
Storyteller: Tongon Apachulumo (a 40-year-old man)
Place: Jimos village

34 **The Story of Anyuli**
Storyteller: Lodoch (a 65-year-old man)
Place: Jimos village

35 **The Katap War**
Storyteller: Lokware (a 60-year-old man) (dictated)
Place: Kotido

36 **The Legend of Mount Toror**
Storyteller: Nakapor, the Jie Firemaker
Place: Jimos village

37 **Ceremonies of Long Ago**
Storyteller: Nakapor, the Jie Firemaker
Place: Jimos village

38 **The Original Ancestral Conflict**
Storyteller: Lokapelan (a 50-year old man)
Place: Kotiyang village

39 **The Story of Lokerio**
Storyteller: Achuka (a 55-year-old Turkana woman)
Place: Lapur Hill

40 **The Story of Apatepes**
Storyteller: Erukudi (a 65-year-old Elmolo man)
Place: Kalakol (Turkana land)

41 **Nayeche**
Storyteller: Chegem (a 70-year-old Turkana woman)
Place: Moru Apolon (Turkana land)

*42 **Nayeche**
Storyteller: Napau (a 50-year-old Turkana woman)
Place: Lodwarr (Turkana land)

*43 **Nayeche**
Storyteller: Napedo (a 50-year-old Turkana woman)
Place: Moru Apolon (Turkana land)

44 **Nayeche**
Storyteller: Lomorukai (a 74-year-old Turkana man)
Place: Lodwarr (Turkana land)

45 **Nayeche**
Storyteller: Tapuka (a 60-year-old man)
Place: Lokuchar Village (Turkana land)

46 **The Story of Lokorijam**
Storyteller: Lomuria (a 75-year-old Turkana woman)
Place: Moru Apolon (Turkana land)

47 **The Story of Lokorijam**
Storyteller: Akoru (a 60-year-old man)
Place: Lokuchar Village (Turkana land)

48 **The Story of Apatepes**
Storyteller: Akoru (a 60-year-old Emachar man)
Place: Lokuchar Village (Turkana land)

49 **The Story of the Vulture**
Storyteller: Kwuya (a 65-year-old man)
Place: Kakuma (Turkana Land)

Elmolo and Other Historical Traditions

1 **The Story of Sepenya**
Storyteller: Kimeron (a 50-year-old Elmolo man)
Place: Arapal, Mount Kulal

*2 **The Story of Sepenya**
Storyteller: Akimat (a 50-year-old Elmolo-Turkana woman)
Place: Arapal, Mount Kulal

3 **The Story of Sepenya**
Storyteller: Sebastian (a 45-year-old Elmolo man)
Place: Loiyangalani

*4 **The Story of Sepenya**
Storyteller: Sebastian (a 45-year-old Elmolo man)
Place: Loiyangalani

5 **The Story of Sepenya**
Storyteller: Kayo (an 80-year-old Elmolo man)
Place: Komote village

*6 **The Story of the Pregnant Camel**
Storyteller: Lessas (a 50-year-old Rendille man)
Place: Chalbi Desert, near a spring

7 **The Story of the Woman and the Well**
Storyteller: Sebastian (a 45-year-old Elmolo man)
Place: Loiyangalani

8 **The Story of Moite Hill**
Storyteller: Napau (a 65-year-old Elmolo-Changille woman)
Place: Layeene village

9 **Sepenya, the Pregnant Gabra Woman**
Storyteller: Kayo (an 80-year-old Elmolo man)
Place: Komote village

10. **The Story of Elwak (the South Island)**
Storyteller: Lengutuk (a 55-year-old Elmolo man)
Place: Komote village

Popular Biographies

*1 **The Memory of Nacham**
Storyteller: Lodoch (a 65-year-old man)
Place: Jimos village

*2 **The Memory of Aony**ot
Storyteller: Lodoch (a 65-year-old man)
Place: Moruongor village

3 **The Memory of Ebongo**
Storyteller: Lodoch (a 65-year-old man)
Place: Jimos village

4 **The Memory of Lojukar**
Storyteller: Lodoch (a 65-year-old man)
Place: Jimos village

*5 **The Memory of Nakol and His Father**
Storyteller: Lodoch (a 65-year-old Jie man)
Place: Moruongor village

6 **The Memory of Koryang**
Storyteller: Lodoch (a 65-year-old man)
Place: Moruongor village

7 **The Memory of Apese-Arengan and his Brother Nakadon**
Storyteller: Lodoch (a 65-year-old man)
Place: Jimos village

8 **The Great Hunger**
Storyteller: Lodoch (a 65-year-old man)
Place: Kotido

9 **The Memory of Nakapor's Granary**
Storyteller: Lodoch (a 65-year-old man)
Place: Kotido

11 **The Angola and Akiturutur Performances**
Storyteller: Rianaro (a 50-year-old man)
Place: Jimos village

11 **The Story of Adapal**
Storyteller: Ebei (a 50-year-old Turkana man)
Place: Kalakol, Turkana land

12 **The Story of Ewat**
Storyteller: Ebei (a 50-year-old Elmolo man)
Place: Komote village

13 **The Story of Loolel**
Storyteller: Ekale (a 60-year-old Elmolo man)

Place: Layene village
14 **The Story of Lenapir**
Storyteller: Napapu (a 65-year-old woman)
Place: Kalakol, Turkana land
15 **The Story of Lesiipo**
Storyteller: Joseph Leusin (a 35-year-old Elmolo-Rendille man)
Place: Layene Village

Jie Folktales

1 **The Honey-Badger**
Storyteller: Logwee (a 40-year-old woman)
Place: Jimos village
*2 **The Elephant and the Fox**
Storyteller: Lodoch (a 65-year-old Jie man)
Place: Jimos village
*3 **A Bat and His Friends Who Went Raiding**
Storyteller: Lodoch (a 65-year-old Jie man)
Place: Moruongor village
*4 **The Hyena Who Ate Baby Goats**
Storyteller: Nangorin (a 30-year-old Jie man)
Place: Nayese village
*5 **The Man Whose Child Was Eaten by the Hyena**
Storyteller: Longoli (a 30-year-old Jie man from Nayese village)
Place: Nayese village
*6 **The Rabbit Who Did Not Drink Water**
Storyteller: Lodoch (a 65-year-old Jie man)
Place: Losilang in Mustafa Mirzeler's home in Jimos village
*7 **The Rabbit and the Baboon**
Storyteller: Lodoch (a 65-year-old Jie man)
Place: Kotido
*8 **The Story of the Rabbit Who Was Caught Stealing Food**
Storyteller: Logwee (a 40-year-old Jie woman)
Place: Jimos/Kotido village
*9 **The Hyena and the Bell**
Storyteller: Logwee (a 40-year-old Jie woman)
Place: Jimos village
*10 **The Hyena and the Calf**
Storyteller: Logwee (a 40-year-old Jie woman)
Place: Jimos village

*11   **The Story of a Monkey Who Was Caught Stealing Food**
      Storyteller: Napedo (a 50-year-old Jie woman)
      Place: Jimos village
 12   **The Quail and His Wife**
      Storyteller: Ekeno (a 50-year-old woman)
      Place: Nakapelimoru
*13   **The Story of Napeikisina**
      Storyteller: Napeyo (a 50-year-old Turkana woman)
      Place: Oyokwara village in Moru Apolon area in Turkana land
*14   **The Story of Napeikisina**
      Storyteller: Lodoch (a 65-year-old Jie man)
      Place: Behind the cracked wall of a mud-plastered shop in Kotido

Jie and Turkana Historical Traditions

1 The Story of the Gray Bull Engiro and Longiro River

Storyteller: Lochoro (a 50-year-old Ngikuliak man)
Place: Kotido
   (1) Kolong apotu ngitunga tonyout alo Koteen potu arai ngikogorok ngigaron ka ngikaarak ngityang. (2) Ani epote edolunete nangolol Longiro namoni ngina enyaritae Nakeru a Ngijie neni Daidai toriamut ngityan ngulu adedengak aneni. (3) Toriamut ngakipit a nakinding enyaritae Nachuur. (4) Toleke angolol torwoo tabala ruu-uu, kiirame eruye a nakiding elwana. (5) Ani epote ngitunga lugu erai ngakamijak toriamut emanik eyai neni emasi angolol ngina anakiding enyaritae Nachur, achuur ngina eleleyala ngakipi. (6) Aleleunito ngache kip alo Daidai anyepewae nyameni. (7) Ekau apotu ngitunga totama epite ngo-lo kiritaret ngityang ngulu dedeng anakiding anaga. (8) Ani nakware kinkokis ngitunga lugu akim ngina alalan ani epote ngityang ngulu dedeng ngikomolo, ngikwei, ngilobai, ngirisae, ngingatungo, apotu kimasa anyasarae kiritasi anawat kech. (9) Ekau kiyarasi ngityan ngulu dedeng apotu ngitunga kiboikinas nangolol na. (10) Tolimokis angolol na Longiro ani erai ariamunio emani ngolo ngiro emasi ngakipi aneni. (11) Taraunai Longiro, Longiro tar napakana dang enyaritae Longiro. (12) Apotu ngitunga lugu temasi, "Ikiboinin tokana akooyan arau ere yok, "Tolimokis cho ikes amoni ngina Akerru a Ngijie. (13) Alokiding amoni na ayai ataaba ngina apolon ngina aloseneneete ngitunga aki-booyoo angina taparach. (14) Etemonokin Ngijie daadang nataaba

imadana kim losimakunyuk. (15) Tolimokinoe ekiro ataaba ana be Daidai ani erai etemonokin Ngijie daadang nataaba iborete. (16) Inges cho enyaritere ataaba na be Daidai tar napakana.

TRANSLATION

(1) Long ago people left Koteen and came to the west as hunters of wild animals and gatherers of fruits. (2) When they reached Longiro River near the bush named Nakeru a Ngijie (ground of the Jie), where Daidai is located, they found wild animals there. (3) They found water in a place named Nachuur (a place where there is a waterfall). (4) The river was flowing ruu-uu (sound of river flowing), and its sound could be heard from faraway. (5) When these people came in search of pasture, they found a bull drinking water in the river in Nachuur, where the water falls. (6) Some water was flowing from Daidai beside the bush. (7) Later people wondered how they could chase the wild animals from this place. (8) At night the people made great fires and when the wild animals like hyena, leopards, lions, hartebeest, and jackal came, they threw burning logs at them and the animals ran away. (9) After they chased wild animals, people settled around the river. (10) They named the river Longiro because they found a gray bull drinking water there. (11) The river is called Longiro up to today. (12) Afterward, the people said, "We have stayed in this bush for a long time and it has become our home." They decided to name this place Nakeru a Ngijie. (13) There was a big rock in the middle of the bush and people went and sat on it every morning. (14) All the Jie people fitted on this rock when they sat there to receive the sunshine in the morning. (15) They named the rock Daidai because all the Jie people fitted when they sat on it. (16) That is why that rock is called Daidai up to today.

2 The Gray Bull Engiro

Storyteller: Lotiang (a 50-year-old Jie man)
Place: Kotido, near the edge of a sorghum field where people were thrashing their sorghum

Long ago, a bull was swept here. Perhaps it was Akuj who brought the bull Engiro, or perhaps it was the river that swept the bull here. When the people went to the river after it had rained, they found the bull in the river and they asked, "Where did this bull come from? What color is it?"

Someone replied, "The bull is a gray color with white patches." Someone else said, "Yes, since we have found the bull here, we should name this river Longiro." Akuj may have brought this bull, or perhaps the river swept it to the land of Orwakol.

When all the people went to the river, they found the bull in the river, near Karabokol,[1] in Daidai. When they went to their sacred place, they found the bull there.

The people of Orwakol and Lodiny had two *emunyen* (sacred clay) wells there. The *emunyen* of Lodiny is in the north, and the *emunyen* of Orwakol is in a gully. Both of them are alike; they are not different. They brought a cow and blew air into its vagina and killed it. Then they speared the gray bull there in Daidai, after which they prayed and said, "This rock (Daidai), this river (Longiro River), and *emunyen* belong to Akuj. It was Akuj who put them there in Loonei (a sacred place in Kotyang).

Long ago, the Toposa left Daidai because they did not get any of the meat from the thigh of the bull (the gray bull). The Toposa people left from here (Daidai), like Nayeche did. They went beyond the Dodos land up to a place now called Topos. Nayeche was a woman who fought with her mother and left. But on that day (the day they captured and sacrificed the gray bull), all the Jie people were at that sacred place called Daidai.

6 The Original Ancestral Conflict

Storyteller: Lokapelan (a 50-year-old Jie man)
Place: Under a tree near the road between Kotiyang and Rengen (Najie)

When Orwakol was in Kanakosim, his niece gave birth to a baby boy and they named him Lodiny. Because Lodiny's father never paid the bride-price for Lodiny's mother, he stayed in Orwakol's home as a herder. While Lodiny's mother was a good farmer who grew a lot of sorghum, Lodiny grew up and became a good herder and took care of all the goats of Kanakosim by himself. Lodiny was very much loved by the old men and women of Kanakosim. When Orwakol took all the cattle to the grazing land in Nyanga, Lodiny became the leader of Kanakosim who cared for the elderly and the women.

Lodiny loved his uncle Orwakol and admired him. Still, Orwakol was very critical of Lodiny and he often told him, "You are the son of a woman whose bride-price has not been paid. Your mother's bride-price has not been paid. I have not yet eaten the meat of any cattle from your mother. You are the son of a woman whose bride-price has not yet been paid."

In spite of Orwakol's cruelty, Lodiny continued to love his uncle and admired him as a great leader. Because of Orwakol's hatred toward Lodiny and Lodiny's innocent love for his uncle, Akuj (God) blessed Lodiny, and he became more powerful and rich than his uncle. Akuj gave Lodiny the power to dream about places where there was water and pasture, while other people's cattle died of hunger and thirst Lodiny was blessed by Akuj to become a wealthy cattle owner and a successful raider.

When Lodiny became rich and successful, he went to Koteen with his cattle. Orwakol heard about Lodiny's success and his cattle. He sent him a message asking him to come and join him in Daidai. Lodiny went to Daidai and settled there. Everybody in Daidai loved Lodiny including the Ngikuliak people. Lodiny taught the Ngikuliak how to care for animals and the Ngikuliak taught him how to hunt and kill wild animals. While in Daidai Lodiny's cattle increased and they became many. Orwakol grew angry at Lodiny's success and started to take the cattle away from him. But Lodiny never grew angry at his uncle. He said, "Let him take as many cattle as he wants. I can always go and get more cattle."

Lodiny went and captured more and more cattle. Daidai became full of cattle. There were more cattle than there was grass and water to support them.

While in Daidai, Lodiny took many wives from the Dodos and Ngikuliak people, and became friends with these people. Orwakol did not approve Lodiny's relations with the Ngikuliak and the Dodos people. One day he took all of Lodiny's cattle and told him to go and live with the Ngikuliak and the Dodos people. Lodiny gathered his wives and went from Daidai and settled in Namoja, a bush in Rengen near the Lokatap Rock. From there he went raiding with the Dodos people and brought many cattle. Lodiny became rich in cattle again. He became so rich that he made Orwakol look very poor.

After Lodiny became so rich in cattle and settled in Rengen, Orwakol realized that Lodiny had separated himself from him and his family had become a different people. He heard the children of Lodiny sing a song, which went:

We have won. We have defeated Orwakol
We defeated Orwakol, who claimed to be so great
We have won. We have defeated Orwakol

Orwakol became angry at these songs. He went to Rengen and gathered all of Lodiny's cattle, and said to Lodiny, "Your mother's bride-price has not yet been paid. You are the son of a woman whose bride-price has not yet been paid. Let me have all these cattle. These cattle belong to me. They are not enough to pay your mother's bride-price."

One day Lodiny stood up and said to Orwakol, "Uncle, my uncle Orwakol, I have paid you my mother's bride-price many times over. All those cattle in Daidai belong to me. I went and raided cattle from Bokora, from Matheniko, and from the Pian and I gave all to you. You have taken enough cattle from me in the name of my mother's bride-price. You don't touch these cattle. They belong to me. They are my cattle."

When the people saw Lodiny and Orwakol arguing over cattle in front of the cattle enclosure, they gathered together and told Orwakol, "We are the people of Rengen. This land belongs to us, and the Namoja bush is our shrine."

Orwakol replied, "If that is indeed so, I let you become different people. But I want you to remember that the Longiro River is mine and it belongs to my people. You cannot water your cattle in that river, and you cannot use the *emunyen* there. Daidai is also mine, and you cannot sacrifice there." After this, Orwakol left and went back to Daidai empty handed without taking a cow with him.

After Orwakol had left, Lodiny gathered his people and told them, "My people, the wells in Longiro River belong to my uncle Orwakol so don't water your cattle there. You dig your wells in the Dopeth River and get your *emunyen* (sacred clay) from there. Sacrifice your cattle in this bush here in Namoja. In Namoja, you pray for rain and curse sicknesses. There is a plant called *amoja* with sharp and pointed tips, growing in this bush. Don't cut this plant. Let it grow wild. That plant brings clouds and makes rain."

After Orwakol and Lodiny separated in this way, they began to make their fire facing different directions. Orwakol made his fire facing south and Lodiny made his fire facing north. Many years passed. Both Orwakol and Lodiny grew old and they never spoke to one another. They sacrificed separately and they never shared the meat. Whenever Orwakol cooked meat in Daidai, Lodiny and his people smelled the meat and sighed with resentment. Whenever Lodiny sacrificed, Orwakol did the same.

One day, when Orwakol had become very old and was not able to walk, he asked his people to take him to Namoja where Lodiny lived.

When he reached Namoja, Lodiny ordered his people to sacrifice seven cattle for his uncle and his people. Lodiny's people immediately sacrificed seven cattle and they ate the meat in Namoja.

Orwakol said to his people and the people of Lodiny, "My people and the people of my nephew Lodiny, we are one. We are uncle and nephew. Lodiny had already paid his mother's bride-price. From now on, whenever Lodiny sacrifices, he will make his fire facing north, and he will share the meat with my people. In the same way, whenever my people sacrifice, they will make their fire facing south and share the meat with the people of Lodiny."

This is all about the story of Orwakol and Lodiny. This is why the Rengen people face north when they sacrifice and cook their meat, and the people of Orwakol face south when they cook their sacrificial animals, and they always share meat with each other whenever they sacrifice.

7 The Original Ancestral Raiding

Storyteller: Lodoch (a 65-year-old Jie man)
Place: Kalakuruk Rock (Najie)
When Orwakol came, when people came from the east from Moru Apolon, they settled in a place called Kanakosim at a rock, which is now called Karimojong. Long ago, they settled their villages around Kanakosim Rock, which is in between the Lokwakiel and the Apule rivers.

One day Orwakol stood up and said to his people, "This place has become dry. The last time we checked in Nyanga, we found water there. We found a great deal of water there. Even the pasture there was green. Let us migrate with these cattle to that pasture." He set off for that pasture along with those people who wanted to migrate with him. They set off at once to Nyanga, and settled there. They drank water from there for the whole dry season.

When the rainy season began, some people came from home, from Kanakosim, to the Orwakol's kraals in Nyanga. When they reached the kraals, they said to the people in the kraals, "You drive the cattle home. It is rainy season already. There is plenty of grass for the cattle in the villages. We need milk and blood."

The people in the kraal said, "The cattle cannot be driven home. They are still grazing here." The people from the villages then went back home.

When they reached home, the old men said to them, "What is wrong again?" The people replied, "Nothing. The people in the kraal said they do not want to send cattle home. They are still grazing." The old men then said, "No, you get *ngalita*[2] and beat the people in the kraal and drive the cattle this way."

The young men (*ngikarachuna*) went back to the kraals. Because they were the people of village, and because there was no food in the villages, these young men were very thin. But the people in the kraal were very fat and strong. The people from home said to the people in the kraals that the old men in the villages had told them to bring some cattle home. But the people in the kraals once again said no. When the people in the kraals noticed the young men from the village were carrying *ngalita*, they asked, "Is this why you are handling those sticks? Are they for fighting with us?"

The home people said, "Yes, if you refuse to give us cattle, we will beat you." The people of the kraal told them they would not give them the cattle. Then they began struggling and fighting for cattle. Since the people of home were very weak, the men in the kraals threw them down and bit them and chased them away.

When the young men from the villages returned home, they said, "*Okoe*, those people have become bad. They have become very strong fighters; they defeated us; what can we do? They refused to give us cattle." The old men in the village told the young men to go back to the kraal and tell the people there that the old men in the village wish to know why they refuse to give them their cattle.

This time a large number of old men accompanied the young men, handling *ngalita* and clubs (*ngibelai*), and went to the kraal. When they reached there, they fought and said, "Why are you refusing to give us the cattle? Why are you refusing to give us the cattle?" The people from other kraals surrounded an old man from home and beat him to death.

The people of the home then said, "Aa, these people killed a person. Those people have become wild and strong fighters. What can we do?" They dispersed and went back home and told people what happened in the kraal. The old men in the village then said, "Eeeh, if it is like that, let us curse, let us curse those people in the kraal, so that the diseases may finish them." The old men were the only ones who talked.

One of the old men said, "Let us gather together and kill those people. After all, we are many." But one of the old men said, "No, we should not kill those people, they are our children and brothers. If we kill them, *ekuron* (a curse) will come amidst us and finish us." The people then said, "It is really true. It is really true. Truly, a curse will come and finish us. How can we kill our children and brothers? They are our own blood, which came from our bodies."

As hunger and sickness continued in the village, the elders became annoyed once again and said, "Aa, how can a curse come upon us, and yet they have our cattle, and they have made them theirs alone. I am going to drive those cattle to home."

So the old men in the village gathered together and went as a group to the kraal. They went and went. They hid and watched the *ngikeyokok* (young shepherds). When they saw the young shepherds together, they hid. When they saw a young shepherd who was alone, they beat and beat him and killed him.

When some of the shepherds saw that the old men from home are killing young shepherds, they shouted and shouted to alarm people in the kraal. The men in the kraals came together and followed and followed the old men until they caught them while they were crossing Nangalol Apolon (the great river). They fought and fought with them and wrested half of the cattle from them and drove them to Nyanga. After the struggle at Nangalol Apolon, the old men in the village were able to drive half of the cattle away, and when they reached their village in Kanakosim, they said to people, "What can we do? What can we do? Those people in the kraal have become different from us completely. They have become strong fighters. What can we do?"

One of the elders in the village said, "You people, let us leave those other people alone. Let them graze the cattle like that. Since they are looking after our cattle, when we need cattle, we will go to the kraal and steal cattle from there." Other old men then said, "Let them graze our cattle. When we need cattle we will go and steal more cattle from them." Another old man said, "Let us organize a big raiding group (*ajoree*), and drive the cattle from Nyanga to our home in Kanakosim." They truly gathered and went to Nyanga and surrounded the kraal there. They beat the people in the kraals with clubs, and they fought and fought. Since the people in the village were not well fed and they were weak, they did not have enough strength to defeat the people of the kraal. So, the people in the kraal beat them (the people of village) and chased them. During this fight, some people from the village were clubbed to death. The people from home were chased and driven back home empty handed.

One day Orwakol gathered his people in the kraal again and said, "You people, what can we do? These people (the people in the home village) steal and run away with our cattle. Is this not because we are near to them? I think we should move farther away. Let us migrate to another place. Let us go to the northwestern side of Mount Toror so that we will be far away from them and hence they cannot come and steal our cattle. If they still come to steal our cattle, we can follow them and grab our cattle from them."

The people accepted these words and they migrated to a place called Loreria Ngorok, near Lokibuwa River, and settled there. When Orwakol's kraal settled around the Lokibuwa River, the conflict between the people in the village became intense. When the people from the village came and stole cattle from the kraal, the people in the kraal did the same and went to the village in Kanakosim and stole the cattle back and brought them back to the kraal.

As the fight and raiding and counter-raiding increased, the people in kraal migrated from Loreria Ngorok, to a place called Daidai, where they found the gray bull Engiro on the banks of Longiro River. The gray bull was wild and it was living with many other wild animals, and drank water from Longiro River. Orwakol settled his kraal there and that place became their home forever.

19 The Memory of the Ngipalajam

Storyteller: Lokui (a 60-year-old Jie woman)
Place: Kotyang village

Ngipalajam was the generation that punished the *ngikeikokou* (children) when they disobeyed them and refused to share their cattle with people at home. The elders of the Ngipalajam generation had great mystical power and they could predict the future. When they said something was going to happen, it did happen. If they told people to migrate away from one well to another in a drier place with no grass, people migrated. No one ever questioned them.

They were so powerful that if they said someone would die, it happened. They foresaw the coming of the rains and famines and their predictions never failed. The elders of that age were named Ngipalajam because they had only a few cattle and gave only goats for the bride-price. Since there were not enough cattle, these people did not have enough cow skins to sleep on. Only a few people had them. So people slept on the grass. This is why these people were called the Ngipalajam.

During their era there was only one bull, Ngolengiro, the bull of Lokolong.

The men of Ngipalajam were not only harsh to children, but they were also very harsh to women. For example, when these men had gathered in their *etem* (men's gathering place), they made the women wait on them, making beer for them and filling their *amot* (pots), washing their calabashes, and preparing their sleeping places. When the men gathered in their homes, they sent the women off to grind sorghum seeds for them, preparing bread and brewing beer, and filling their tobacco containers. The men's gatherings usually lasted all night long and they consumed much beer. If a woman refused to do the work and disobeyed the men, the Ngipalajam ordered *ameto* (a traditional punishment), and they tied her to a tree infested by *ngikadengero* (black insects with sharp claws), and they banged the tree to awake the ants which came out of their holes and bit the woman. They punished the woman in this manner until she promised never again to disobey the men.

Some of the elders of the Ngipalajam generation were great rainmakers. The men of the Ngipalajam generation usually gathered in a place called Nakirwakaret Looya to pray for the rain to come. Nobody disobeyed the Ngipalajam, except Nayeche who was chased away from Nakapelimoru. Nayeche later joined a group of young men who were bitter toward men of the Ngipalajam for their cruel treatment of young people and women. These young men had a few emaciated cattle in Koteen Hill, and Nayeche gathered wild fruits for them and they ate together. One day, when the men of Ngipalajam came to get some cattle from Koteen, the young men there refused and a fight ensued.

Some people said that Ngipalajam lived during the time of Orwakol, but others said they lived during the time of Lobeyekuri, a great kraal leader who had many wives, but only a few cattle. The cattle were few at this time, because the cattle of Najie were afflicted with *aburr*, a disease that caused the cattle to lose their fur, leaving them bald and ultimately killing them.

23 The Original Ancestral Fire

Storyteller: Napeyo (a 65-year-old Jie woman)
Place: Kotyang village

The people said that the story of Orwakol goes back to ages past when he came to Daidai with his seven wives and made a new fire. When Orwakol made the fire, he started new *ngitalia* (traditions) and established new taboos. They put the master granary in the *ekal* (yard) of Losilang, the eldest wife of Orwakol, and gave her the first fire. After this fire, they gave fire to Kotyang, the second eldest wife, followed by the third wife, Kotido, followed by Kanawat, and so on, until all seven wives had received the new fire.

The seven clans then gathered together at Kalakuruk Rock (the Rock of the Cows) and told the rest of the clans to remove all the ashes and made a new fire from the fire of Orwakol. All the people in Najie then removed the old ashes and made new fires in their hearths.

After all the fire was distributed, Orwakol gathered the seven clans once again in Daidai where he sacrificed an unblemished black *ikale* (a baby goat) and divided the meat into seven parts, and put them into an *akuit* (calabash) that did not have any cracks or broken parts. The eldest women from each clan then took some *ngikujit* (undigested food) from the intestines of the sacrificial animal and put them in their calabashes, mixing them with the *emunyen* (sacred clay) of Karabokol from the Longiro River. They mixed the clay and the *ngikujit* thoroughly, making a paste, and smeared themselves with it, and then smeared their children. They then sprinkled the leftover mixture of clay and *ngikujit* in their gardens.

A few days after sprinkling this in their gardens, Orwakol called the eldest males of the clans to gather together in Daidai. When they gathered there, Orwakol sacrificed the gray bull Engiro, and each clan head sacrificed a bull. Altogether they sacrificed seven bulls.

After the sacrifice of the bulls, Orwakol turned south and made a new fire from the wet branches of the essegessege tree, and cooked meat with the newly made fire. The men feasted together all day and through the night. In this ceremony, the clan elders declared Orwakol the creator and head of the Orwakol clan.

After this ceremony Orwakol returned to his home in Jimos village along with the seven elders. When the people reached Jimos village, the elders told Orwakol never to eat the meat of a dead animal and never to eat sorghum from the fields of other people outside of Najie, even the sorghum of the Rengen people. They told him to sit under a tree and watch the cattle coming and going from the grazing land. They also told him that he should hold his *akapet* (a small piece of cow skin) as he sat under the tree watching the cattle go grazing and return. The *akapet*, they said, should be from a cow that was speared, not from an already dead cow.

Orwakol remained the Jie firemaker until his death. When he died, the heads of the seven clans gathered together in the *arii* (cattle enclosure), and Lowatomoe, the eldest son of Orwakol, killed an *emesek* (a black ram) before they buried the dead body of Orwakol.

27 Nakadanya, the Cradle Land of Long Ago

Storyteller: Akiru (a 75-year-old Matheniko woman)
Place: Moroto

Longo ago, when all the people of Karimojong were one, before they had dispersed to become the Jie, the Dodos, the Matheniko, the Bokora, and the Teuso, they lived in place called Nakadanya. Nakadanya was a sacred place and it was named after a great leader named Kadanya. This was before the time of Orwakol, Lodiny, and Nayeche.

After a long dry season, there was a deadly famine in Dongiro, and Kadanya, the father of the Karimojong people migrated from there with his wives and sons in search of food and water. When Kadanya and his family reached the headwaters of the Apule River, he had only a few emaciated cattle. One day, while Kadanya was sleeping under a tree near the river, he had a dream in which Akuj told him to take his wives and sons to a rock in the bush near the Apule River. Akuj told Kadanya that the rock had seven gates, and that all the gates were closed. He told him to build a home for each of his wives in front of each of the gates, and that he must guard the gates and never open them.

After the dream, Kadanya led his people to the rock, and settled there. He named the rock Nakadanya and warned his wives and sons about the gates and told them never to open the gates.

In the bush around Nakadanya were many wild animals, and wild fruits grew in abundance. The people of Kadanya lived in Nakadanya for many years, hunting and gathering. One day, Kadanya and his sons went hunting at the foot of Mount Moroto and caught a black and white spotted bull with beautiful horns and brought it to Nakadanya. Here, the bull mounted the cattle of Kadanya and the herds multiplied and became many. Kadanya gave milking cows to each of his wives.

The people in Nakadanya prospered, and their herds grew large. The kraals that settled around the Nakadanya Rock increased and grew into large villages. In time, however, the people began to fight over the cattle and began to break away from one another, calling themselves the Jie, the Turkana, the Dodos, the Matheniko, the Bokora, the Pian, the Toposa, and the Teuso.

As they named themselves in this way, they also began to say, "*Ooitokoi*, the people of Pian have better land, and the Jie have more cattle than the Matheniko. What can we do? The Jie are richer than all of us. Let us go and open some of these gates to see what will happen. Maybe Akuj will give us more cattle and we will also be rich." They opened one of the gates. Akuj then cursed the people with diseases, droughts, famine, and hunger. People began raiding one another.

As the people continued raiding one another, the son of Lokolimoe, a Jie man, was killed. Lokolimoe cried and mourned for his son and told the Matheniko and the Bokora people, "Look, you have killed my son. Are we not brothers? Are we not the sons of Kadanya? Did we not all live in peace in Nakadanya? Who told you to open the gate? Don't you know that our father told us never to open the gates of Nakadanya? Because you did this, my child is dead. But since you have already opened one of the gates, let us open the other gates and continue to fight."

In response, a man from the Turkana said, "My people, my brothers, let us not open any more gates. Let us close the one already opened and offer sacrifices. Then we will have peace." Other people from the Jie, the Turkana, the Dodos, the Matheniko, the Bokora, the Pian, and the Toposa agreed: "Eeah! Let us close the opened gates and let us sacrifice a bull on the Nakadanya rock for our ancestors. If we do not make peace, only the ashes and the *ngikeaal* (three-stone hearths for cooking) will be left." They then sacrificed a bull and broke their spears and buried them.

This is the story of Nakadanya.

31 Nayeche

Storyteller: Koriang (a 50-year-old Jie man)
Place: Under a tree near the Lokatap Rock

We don't know why Nayeche went away from Najie. Some people say she left from here because of hunger, other people say that she left because her brothers chased her away. One morning Nayeche walked away from Daidai and started her journey toward the east. She passed through Nakapelimoru and went and went through the bush and over rivers. Nayeche cried as she walked, "It is all right if my people don't want me. I will go and settle in faraway places."

At that time, there was also a big famine and all the cattle of Najie died of hunger. Nayeche walked and walked and crossed Nangalol Apolon. The great river was dry. She continued her journey until she reached Koteen Hill. When she reached Koteen Hill she said, "Let me continue my journey; this is the place where the people of Najie graze their cattle."

Nayeche walked and walked until she reached the Tarash River at the base of the escarpment. When she reached the Tarash River, she drank water from Lokipoto Well near the escarpment. She then saw a hill near the banks of the river and said, "This hill will be my home." She climbed up the hill, and slept there. When she woke up, she gathered wild fruits on that hill and ate them. There were many wild fruits on the hill. She gathered and gathered wild fruits and spread them on the ground to dry.

That hill later became Nayeche's home. One evening, Nayeche made a fire before she went to sleep. A gray bull, which was roaming around the river, smelled the fire and climbed the hill. When Nayeche saw this bull she recognized him and said, "Ehh this is the gray bull of Orwakol which had disappeared long ago." She made a place for the gray bull next to her and they slept together that night.

In the morning, the gray bull went to Tarash River to graze, while Nayeche gathered wild fruits. The bull came back and slept with Nayeche next to her fire again. This went on for a long time.

One day, the people of Orwakol started looking for the lost gray bull and followed his footprints. They followed and followed the footprints of the gray bull until they reached the hill where Nayeche stayed. When they reached the hill, they saw the gray bull sleeping with Nayeche. They said, "Ehh this is the gray bull. Ehh this is Nayeche who was chased away."

Nayeche also recognized these young men, and she offered them some wild fruits. The young men stayed on the hill with Nayeche for a few days. They said, "Why don't we come and settle here with our cattle too?" They set off to go back to Najie to bring families and their cattle.

When they reached Najie, they told Orwakol and his people that they had found the gray bull sleeping with Nayeche, who was chased away from Najie long ago. They said that the place where they found the bull had green grass and plenty of water. When these people wanted to take their cattle to that place, the people of Najie refused, and said, "Go and bring the gray bull here. If he refuses to come you sacrifice him there and bring his meat here for us to eat all together."

The young men didn't listen to what the people of Najie said. They gathered all their cattle together before the sun rose and they set off for Moru a Nayeche. When they reached Moru a Nayeche, the gray bull mounted all the cattle and the cattle multiplied. After many years, the old men of Najie sent a message to the young men to send some cattle back home. The young men in Moru a Nayeche refused. The old men and women in Najie gathered together and went to Moru a Nayeche and demanded the cattle. The young men refused to return the cattle. The people of Najie attacked Moru a Nayeche, but the young men were more powerful and they chased the people of Najie away.

When the people of Najie were defeated, the old men gathered together and cursed the people of Moru a Nayeche saying, "Go and you will never find home for yourselves, and may your stomachs never become full. May you always depend on the people of Najie!" These people left cursing Nayeche, the gray bull, and all the cattle and the young men there in Moru a Nayeche.

After the people of Najie left, the sun became hot, burned all the grasses in Moru a Nayeche, and dried the water in Tarash River. The people migrated toward the lake. When they reached the lake, some of these people became fishermen and some of them returned and settled around the Tarash River again.

42 Nayeche

Storyteller: Napau (a 50-year-old Turkana woman)
Place: Lodwarr (Turkana land)

Long ago, when the Ngipalajam age group chased Nayeche from Najie, she went to join the kraals in Koteen Hill area. Nayeche was one of the young people who ran away from the Ngipalajam age group. She first went to Nangalol Apolon, but the kraals of the Ngipalajam were there. She then went to Koteen Hill, and there she stayed with other young kraal leaders and survived on wild fruits. The people in the village in Najie sent a message to the kraal in Koteen Hill and asked them to drive some cattle home, but the people in the kraal refused. When the people in the kraal refused to send the cattle, the people in the villages went to the kraal in Koteen Hill area, and there they fought with the young people who refused to give them some cattle. They fought and fought those who refused to give them some cattle. Nayeche was one of the persons who refused to give cattle to people in the villages. They fought and fought using *ngibilae* (sticks).

The people of the village then said, "Let us go back to our villages. These young people refused to give us cattle." The young people then followed Nayeche and migrated to the Tarash River and they found a hill there teeming with wild fruits. Nayeche and those who followed her became Turkana. Some years later, a gray bull followed the footprints of Nayeche to the Tarash River and became the bull of the Turkana people.

The old people in Najie then cursed Nayeche and those who became Turkana saying, "You will never have a village and never have a home. You will roam and suffer from hunger and thirst and never have enough to eat."

This is why the Turkana are nomads and always on the move. That is why even now in Turkana land near the Tarash River, there are some Jie villages.

43 Nayeche

Storyteller: Napedo (a 75-year-old Turkana woman)
Place: Moru Apolon (Turkana land)

This is the story of the origin of the Turkana people. I will tell you now how the Turkana tribe was born. The Turkana people were once Ngijie. Then came a time when drought and famine swept through the Jie land, killing animals and the people. It is during this time people say, Nayeche wandered in the bush around the hills and in the dry riverbeds until she reached the Tarash River. Nayeche was old and she was from the Ngiduya clan. When she came here, she found many wild fruits.

Nayeche decided to settle here. She built a home with a strong fence like the ones in Najie. Soon, two bulls strayed from the Jie herd in Koteen Hill area, and they followed and followed the footprints of Nayeche and came to Tarash River, where Moru a Nayeche is.

The bulls wandered in the bush until they smelled the fire of Nayeche. They went toward it and found Nayeche there, and they stayed with Nayeche. They stayed with Nayeche.

During the day, the bulls grazed in the bush and in the evening they slept by the fire of Nayeche. They (the bulls) became inured to Nayeche. Later, ten Jie men followed the footprints of the lost bulls. They followed the footprints of the lost bulls. They followed and followed until they reached Moru a Nayeche. When these Jie men saw Nayeche, they recognized her. Nayeche offered the young men wild fruits and they ate them. When they were satisfied, she told them that the lost bulls were with her. She told them that the bulls return to her home every evening.

The young men saw that this place had plenty of rainfall and an abundance of green grass. The men then decided that they should go to Najie, the Jie land and bring their families and cattle from there and settle here. When they reached Jie land, they told people about Nayeche, the lost bulls, Nayeche's fire, and the teeming wild fruits there.

Upon hearing this, many Jie families came down and settled around the hill. The people built large, well-fenced villages around Moru a Nayeche. They made several gates in these fenced villages where several families could live with their cattle. People and their cattle could enter and exit from west, east, south, or north. These people lived here and their cattle produced plenty of milk, blood, and meat. The people became very happy and began their traditional dances. Since people were well fed and happy, they went dancing every night. Life returned to its usual merriness, and the people danced.

One day, the old men from Najie came to get some cattle from people who settled around Moru a Nayeche, but the people and Nayeche refused to give them the cattle.

After this, they sent other people from Najie to Moru a Nayeche, but they too failed to get the cattle. This went on, until the old men decided that they should go themselves. But the people in Moru a Nayeche refused to abide by the authority of the fathers, and fighting began.

At first, the people fought with sticks. Then they reverted to spears until the old men gave up and returned to Najie. The young people remained around Moru a Nayeche, and changed their name to Ngiturkana. The name Turkana comes from the name of the caves where the cattle hid to protect themselves from the rain. These caves were called Ngiturkanin, which was later changed to Ngiturkana. When the people came from Najie to Moru a Nayeche, there were Maasai people living in that area. There were some Maasai villages remaining and other Maasai people moved to the Mount Elgon area. Some Maasai remained in Moru a Nayeche region.

When the Turkana people came to Moru a Nayeche, they mixed with the Maasai. Those Turkana are now known as the Ngisigir. They can be easily recognized, because they put red ochre on their heads and beads. The ochre that the Maasai smear on their bodies today is the same ochre that the Ngisiger use today.

The people who came from the Jie land belong to the Nginya generation. These people lived in Moru a Nayeche for a long time and later they gave birth to another generation known as the Ngisugur. The generation that Nayeche belonged to was the Ngidewa. The Ngidewa later migrated to the shores of Lake Turkana.

There once was a man known as Tepes, who practiced witchcraft, transformed himself into a baboon, and sometimes, into a human. It was during this time that Lokerio was born. Lokerio belonged to the generation of Ngipei and he is the son of Tepes.

While living around the lake, the long dry season wiped out the cattle. These people remained without cattle for a long time. Some people say that their cattle were decimated because of the curse of their elders from whom they seized the cattle in Najie. These people who migrated to the shores of the lake remained without cattle. They survived on fish alone. And these people fished and ate fish, and some continued to die. The people lived like this for a long time. One day, Lokerio, who became the leader of these wandering people, had a dream about camels living across the lake. He told the people that he'd had a dream about camels across the lake. He said, "Our people should go raiding to that land and bring the camels back from across the lake."

Lokerio struck the lake with his stick, the water parted, and a path appeared in the middle of the water. People went to raid the Ngiratele (the Rendille people) and the Borana people from across the lake. They seized camels, cattle, and many other animals. There were many camels. After the people returned with the captured animals, Lokerio made the water come together again and closed its path.

Lokerio belonged to the Ngimonia clan, also known as Ngisigir. When these people brought their animals, the Turkana clans scrambled and fought for them. The Ngichurro clan took many animals, leaving the Ngikamatak clan with very few. The Ngisigir clan took the other animals. There were a lot of conflicts between clans and the people began to disperse.

Lokerio's people settled in the Lapur and Lomogol areas. The Ngichurro clan migrated and settled on the banks of the Turkwell River. They were attacked by the tsetse fly, which killed all their animals. The Ngikamatak had no animals. They were very poor. The Ngisigir clan who settled around Lapur, unlike the Ngikamatak, became very rich. This was how the Turkana originated. They (the Turkana) came originally from the Jie land. When they came here, they also brought with them the tradition of making fire. Nayeche was the first person to make fire in Turkana land. That is why when the Turkana people perform their ceremonies, the Ngiduya clan makes fire from sticks. They are known to have received their knowledge of making fire from Nayeche.

Elmolo and Other Historical Traditions

2 The Story of Sepenya

Storyteller: Akimat (a 50-year-old Elmolo-Turkana woman)
Place: Arapal, Mount Kulal

During the time when the sons of Loiborkineji were circumcised in Otto, the sun became very hot and dried all the wells and burned all the grass. People died like flies and they began to disperse in all directions. Some went to the Lmarle, some went to the Pelekech, some went to Mount Kulal and some went to Mount Nyiro. They said that this drought was the worst one they had ever experienced. It was during that time that Loiborkineji led his people from Otto and came to the Moite Hill area and settled there. While at Moite Hill, Loiborkineji slept under an acacia tree and had a dream in which flocks of birds came from the direction of Mount Kulal, with green grass in their beaks and perched on the branches of the tree. In the morning when Loiborkineji shared his dream with Lmasula, his eldest wife, she suggested to him that God has shown him the vision that there was grass in Mount Kulal. "Let us migrate there," she told him.

When Loiborkineji gathered his people and told them about his dream, some people said, "Eh, this place is good for us. We will stay here. It is true there is not enough grass here, but we do not have any cattle. We will fish, and those of you with cattle can migrate there. We will still be brothers."

The next day Loiborkineji indeed set off for Mount Kulal. Those people with a few cattle and goats followed him, and those who did not have any cattle stayed in Moite and they became the Elmolo. Loiborkineji and his people walked and walked until they reached Komote, a little oasis with some freshwater wells and trees, where they stopped and rested. They got fish from the lake and ate together.

After settling Komote, Loiborkineji sent some young men to search for pastures in Mount Kulal. The warriors went in search of the pastures on the slopes of Mount Kulal and there they found Arapal, a bushy place with green pastures and water on the slopes of Mount Kulal overlooking Mpasso (Lake Turkana). The place was teeming with wild fruits.

When the young men returned to Komote and told Loiborkineji about the place, some people said "This place is good for us. There is also a freshwater well here. There is enough fish in the lake. We do not have goats or cattle and hence we do not need green pasture. We will stay here and survive on fish. We will not migrate to Mount Kulal." And when Loiborkineji and his people continued their journeys, these people stayed in Komote and lived on fish.

The people set off to migrate to Arapal. As they were walking toward Arapal, a young woman named Sepenya became pregnant out of wedlock and her father and her brothers chased her away accusing her, saying that she was sleeping around with warriors. They told her, "Go to those warriors who impregnated you. You give birth to your child there." Sepenya went to the bush and wandered in the desert in search of food. She came to the Sarima well and from there she descended to the shores of the lake and looked at the Elwak (the south island). She implored, "The island of my ancestors, open the water and let me come to you." Elwak responded to Sepenya and the water of the lake was parted and Sepenya walked to the island.

On the island Sepenya gave birth to a boy who she named Merisiya. She lived in Elwak with her son surviving on fish. Many years later when her son grew up and became a man, Sepenya told her son, "Merisiya, my son. I am becoming old and approaching the age of *katunge* (the age that a woman can no longer give birth). When I die who will keep you company? Who will continue our lineage?" The same night Merisiya slept with his mother and Sepenya became pregnant with twins, a boy and a girl.

One day Sepenya told Merisiya the story of their migration and the dispersal of people to Komote and Mount Kulal. Merisiya was a good swimmer and a good fisher. He could go in the water and catch fish with his bare hands without using a net or harpoon. One day Merisiya decided to swim to the shores of the mainland and he did. Upon reaching the shores, he met some men catching fish using harpoons. Merisiya asked them who they were and these people told him, "We are Elmolo." Merisiya then told them about his mother and his family living on the island. People remembered Sepenya who was pregnant and chased away by her father and her brothers.

After staying with the people in Komote for some time, Merisiya dove into the water to swim back to the island. The Elmolo people called him to come back, but Merisiya became like a fish and disappeared into the deep water.

4 *The Story of Sepenya*

Storyteller: Sebastian (a 45-year-old Elmolo man)
Place: Loiyangalani

Long ago, there was a famine and there was no food or water. People died like flies as they fought with one another for food. People dispersed in search of food and water. The Samburu went south and the Rendille followed them. Among the Samburu there was a pregnant woman whose brothers chased her away for being pregnant out of wedlock. This woman was Sepenya. Sepenya wandered forlornly in the desert until she came to the shores of the lake and saw an island there. This was the South Island. She then took her necklace and prayed to God to open a path for her so that she could cross the water and go to the island. Sepenya lived on the island and later she gave birth to a baby boy. When her son grew up she married him. Together they had children and their children later married one another and thus the Elmolo evolved.

6 The Story of the Pregnant Camel

Storyteller: Lessas (a 50-year-old Rendille man)
Place: Chalbi Desert, near a spring

Long ago, there were two Rendille brothers who always fought for water. One day, during a long dry season, a pregnant camel belonging to the youngest brother drank the water from the camel trough of the older brother. The older brother then demanded the younger brother to return the water which the camel had drunk. Since it was at the height of the dry season and all the wells were dry, the older brother did not have any water and hence he did not know what to do. When the older brother became obstinate and insisted on his younger brother returning the water which the camel had drunk, the younger brother did not know what to do to appease his irate brother. He finally resolved the situation by slaughtering the pregnant camel which had drunk the water to get the water from its stomach and return it to his brother.

Jie Popular Biographies

1 The Memory of Nacham

Storyteller: Lodoch (a 65-year-old man)
Place: Jimos village

Nacham was from Choichoan. Some people say that he was a Ngikuliak and others say he was just from one of the clans of the Lodiny people in Rengen. In any event, Nacham was a good hunter, and he was good friends with the Ngikuliak people. He used to hunt elephants with Ngikuliaks for the white people. The white people gave Nacham a gun. He was the only man in the whole of Najie who had a gun. While growing up I used to hear a lot about Nacham. People used to say,

Nacham killed ferocious lions and angry elephants all by himself. I admired Nacham and I wanted to be like him when I grew up.

One year in the1950s, the sun became very hot and scorched the plane of Najie. It dried the rivers and ponds, burned the sorghum, and parched the land. That year, famine hit the whole of Najie and people began to die of hunger. People dispersed all over the place. Some people went to Turkana gathering wild fruit, others went to Labwor and Acholi begging for grains, and still others went to the Mount Moroto and started living with the Tepes people, hunting wild animals there.

They said that Nacham disappeared during that long hot summer and went with his gun all the way to Mount Maaru where he slept in a cave and hunted wild animals. He hunted and hunted and dried the meat which he brought to his family in Choichoan. The next day Nacham left to do the same thing, following the footprints of the wild animals all the way to a river called Lomuton in Kacheri. The river was flowing. Nacham drank the water from the river and rested under an *ebobore* (wild fig tree) tree that cast thick long shadows. Nacham spent the night under the *ebobore* tree and made a big fire. The wild animals smelled Nacham's fire and slept next to him under the tree.

When morning came, Nacham went again looking for wild animals in the bush called Lopetei, near the Lomutan River. That day, Nacham killed an elephant. He cut its meat and spread it out near the wild fig tree where he spent the night. He wanted to wait there until the meat was dry so he could take it to his family in Choichoan.

One day, as Nacham was drinking water from the Lomutan River he tasted the soil and he thought to himself and said, "This soil is good. Why don't I grow sorghum here?" Nacham planted the sorghum grains on the banks of the river. They grew very fast. Nacham then thought and said, "If I go back to Chaichoan now, the wild animals will ruin the sorghum. Why don't I wait until I harvest the sorghum and then go back home?"

Nacham stayed there and stayed there until the sorghum became ripe. The people in Choichoan began to wonder about him. Some people thought, wild animals might have killed him, and others thought he probably died of thirst and hunger while he was searching for wild animals. The people of Lodiny started looking for Nacham. They went this way and that way looking for Nacham. They were wondering what might have happened to him.

One day, they saw the footprints of Nacham in Longem River, mixed with the footprints of wild animals. They followed and followed the footprints until they came to Lopetei bush and found Nacham sleeping under the wild fig tree, and said, "Ehh, this is Nacham. Look at him, he has grown so fat and healthy, yet we thought he might have died of hunger and been eaten by wild animals."

Nacham saw these people and said to them, "Oh, you have found me. Come and have some dried meat and sorghum." Nacham offered them dried wild animal meat and gave them sorghum grain to eat. These people stayed with Nacham for a long time and they helped him to harvest his sorghum. Nacham gave them sacks full of sorghum and dried meat to take to his family in Choichoan and he also gave some for the people in Rengen.

When the people returned to Rengen, they said, "There are a lot of wild animals and sorghum in Kacheri. Nacham has grown much sorghum there and it has ripened."

People said, "Ehh, why don't we go over there now. We have nothing here. The famine has killed most of us already. Let us go to Kacheri, where Nacham is."

When the news of Nacham's success reached the land of Najie, the Ngikuliak people became very happy and they all said, "Our son Nacham has grown sorghum and he has dried much meat there. Let us all migrate there. Ehh, Nacham is our son. His father and mother were from Kodokei. He is our son, let us all migrate there and grow sorghum." So all the Ngikuliak people migrated and settled near Mount Maaru, and became farmers.

After all the Ngikuliak went to Kacheri, a large number of people from Lodiny and Orwakol clans also migrated to Kacheri. Even Nakapor, the firemaker and his family from the Jimos village migrated there. They all stayed there and stayed there and became the people of the Kacheri. The people who migrated there grew much sorghum. When the government people heard the success of Nacham, they sent an expert farmer named Jim Rowland, to introduce new crops and train people to become expert farmers.

The people who went there became different than the people of Najie. They started to call themselves the people of Kacheri, but they were still brothers of the Jie people who remained in Najie. Later they made the wild fig tree where Nacham first settled into a sacred shrine. Now the people of Kacheri do their sacrifices under that tree.

Nakapor took the fire of the Orwakol clan there. Whenever the people of Jie have a conflict with the people of Kacheri, they kill bulls and make their fires there. When the people in Kacheri harvest their sorghum, the people of Jie help them. The people in Kacheri give them sacks full of sorghum.

Sometimes, when the rains are late in Najie and the crops fail, we go to Kacheri and ask people to give us sorghum. The people of Kacheri are related to the people of Najie. They even share the same fire. The sorghum which grows in Kacheri originally came from the fields of Najie. Nacham took the original seeds from the granaries of the Najie.

2 *The Memory of Aonyot*

Storyteller: Lodoch (a 65-year-old Jie man)
Place: Moruongor village

Long ago there was a man named Aonyot, who later became a rich man in Wotakau. When Aonyot grew up, hunger struck, and hatred arose between him and his brothers. His brothers were married, but he was not. One day Aonyot quarreled with his older brother and his older brother told him. "You should not come to disturb my children and you should not eat the food which I find for my children. Why don't you go and look for food like everybody else, instead of sitting down and doing nothing." So, Aonyot's older brother chased him away. But, since there was a big famine then, Aonyot kept going to his older brother's house trying to find whatever was left over to eat. The famine continued for a long time. People were mixing green vegetables with blood and trying to make *atap* (bread) from it. There was no sorghum grown that year. People gathered fruit from *ekadoline* (a thorny climbing tree).

One day, Aonyot went to the home of his older brother and asked his wife for food. "Mother, what can I do? Hunger is almost killing me. Would you please help me with some vegetables to eat? Yesterday I slept without any food."

The wife of his older brother told him, "Your brother is bad. If he sees you here he will quarrel with you and with me. Come back at night, and I will put some vegetables and blood for you on top of the firewood." Aonyot got food from the wife of his oldest brother in this way for a long time.

One day, Aonyot thought and said, "The vegetables and the blood this woman has been giving me is not enough; I am going to die from hunger. Let me steal some goats and eat meat." Aonyot stole a goat, but he was caught after he ate it and beaten very badly by the people who caught him. The goat's owner dragged Aonyot to his older brother's home and demanded that Aonyot's older brother pay for the bad behavior of his younger brother.

After that, Aonyot went to a remote village and asked a girl in one of the houses for some vegetables. The girl felt sorry for Aonyot and gave him some vegetables to eat. He went back and asked for more vegetables and the girl gave him more vegetables again. The following night Aonyot went to that girl's home again asked her to give him a ram. The girl gave him the ram and told him to take it to a very faraway place to slaughter it. Aonyot took the ram far away to a bush near a hill called Madang near Dodos.

He killed the ram with a spear and ate some of it on the spot. He put the rest of the meat in his bag and went to the hills in Loyoro. He stayed there for three days watching the cattle grazing there. He saw what the herders were doing and where they were sleeping. As Aonyot was spying on the cattle, he saw a very large herd and said, "Ehh, this will be enough for me."

Aonyot kept his eye on this particular herd, and followed the herder around. When the herder went to defecate he caught him and told him that he was going to take the cattle away from him. If he screamed he would kill him, but if he kept quite he would let him survive.

The herder agreed, and they both started driving the cattle to Najie. They drove the cattle together until they reached Madang hill. At Madang hill, Aonyet let the boy go. After the herder went away, Aonyot drove the cattle up to Nakapelimoru and put the cattle in the kraal of his friend and told him, "You watch after my cattle and let me go to Rengen. I will be back soon." His friend agreed to take care of the cattle.

Aonyot went to Loyoro to spy for more cattle, instead of going to Rengen as he said he would.

In Loyoro, Aonyot went to a place called Kopotto and started spying for cattle again, until he found another big herd and followed the herder around. When he saw the herder in the bush by himself, Aonyot jumped with his spear and told the herder to keep quiet and drive the cattle with him. The herder and Aonyot drove the cattle to Madang. When they reached Madang, Aonyot told the herder to follow the same road back to where he came from. After the herder left, Aonyot drove the cattle to the kraal of his friend in Nakapelimoru.

When he reached the kraal of his friend, he told him, "You have helped me when I needed help. Now I am a rich man with a lot of cattle.

I want to use these cattle to marry the girl who helped me when I was really hungry. She gave me vegetables and then she let me take a goat from her father's herds. Let us go and talk with the father of that girl."

Aonyot and his friend arrived at the home of the girl who gave Aonyot a goat to eat. They went to the *etem* inside the fence, where the father of the girl was sitting. When the girl's father saw Aonyot and his friend he got up and said, "Ehh, visitors have come to my home. What message have you brought for me?" Aonyot told the father that he came to ask for permission to marry his daughter. The father of the girl responded, "You have come for marriage." Aonyot and his friend answered, "Yes."

The father of the girl said, "If you have enough cattle you may marry my daughter." The father of the girl said to himself, "Ehh, is it Aonyot or the other one who wants to marry my daughter? If it is Aonyot, he is a thief. He has nothing. Just the other day, they beat him for stealing a goat. Where could he have gotten enough cattle to marry my daughter?"

The father of the girl said, "Okay, which one of you wants to marry my daughter?" Aonyot's friend replied, "Aonyot is the one who is going to marry your daughter." The father of the girl said doubtfully, "Aa, if you have enough cattle you can bring them."

Aonyot said, "I do. Now you tell me, have any of your rams disappeared recently?" The father of the girl replied, "Yes, thieves have been stealing my goats every now and then. Even the other day, one of my rams disappeared; and we could not find out who stole it."

Aonyot said, "I was the one who stole your ram. One day I was very hungry and I needed to eat meat. I came here and I asked your daughter if I could steal a ram from the *anuk* and she kindly allowed me to do that." The father of the girl got upset and said, "Ehh, you are the one who stole my ram?" Aonyot replied, "Yes, I did, and I will give you a cow in place of that ram. I want to marry that daughter of yours."

The father of the girl was very happy to hear that he was going to get a cow for his stolen ram. The father of the girl then said, "Okay, how many cattle will you give for my daughter?" Aonyot replied, "You decide how many I should give you."

The father of the girl said, "How about forty cows?" Aonyot replied, "Okay, let me drive the cattle here."

Aonyot and his friend went and brought forty cows for the father of the girl and put them in his *arii*. Aonyot took the girl with him to his friend's house and stayed there until they built their own home.

Later Aonyot had many children from this woman, and he also continued to raid cattle from herders. When Aonyot's older brother heard about his brother's success he said to himself, "Iiii, why did I chase my brother when he came to beg food from me. Now he is so rich and I cannot go and ask him for some cattle." The older brother of Aonyot was very ashamed, and he regretted what he did to his brother.

In a few years Aonyot became one of the richest men in Najie. He married nine more women, and had many children. Aonyot continued to be successful, but his older brother got very sick from jealousy and died.

5 The Memory of Nakol and His Father

Storyteller: Lodoch (a 65-year-old Jie man)
Place: Moruongor village

Nakol was a young man from the Orwakol clan who lived with his father in Rengen. He used to go raiding in the Turkana land and brought a lot of cattle home. But, his father used these cattle to marry many wives. One day, Nakol quarreled with his father and said, "You use my cattle for your marriages, and yet I have not been married and I have no cattle."

His father said, "Aa, what do you expect me to use to pay for my marriages? All these cattle here bear my cattle brand."

Nakol replied, "I got these cattle with my own sweat, risking my own life, and now you are saying that all these cattle bear your cattle brand."

Nakol's father responded, "Don't you know that you came to be this age by drinking the milk and blood of my own cattle. How about my cattle, the cattle that you ate long ago while you were still young. Do you know how much I cared for you from the day you were born. Who protected you from the wild animals and disease?"

Nakol replied, "Even if it is like that, you have used my cattle to marry so many wives. You have taken enough cattle from me to compensate for all that you have done for me, and even more. I want to take these remaining cattle and go away and separate myself from you. I will settle somewhere else."

"Nakol, are you saying that you want to separate from me?"

"Yes."

"If it is like that, I cannot force you to live with me. You can separate from me, but I want you to remember, if you separate from me you cannot use my cattle brand, and when your sisters marry, I will never give you the cattle, which I will receive from their husbands. If you are going to be a different person, you cannot come and use our shrine when you are sick. You cannot ask my ancestors for assistance. You will no longer be my relative. When you marry, your wives will not be able to use the *ngitalio* (traditions) of my ancestors."

Nakol replied, "I will not use your cattle brand and I will not pray in your shrines to your ancestors. My wives will not adopt your family traditions. I will go away and become a different person."

Nakol left his father's home, settled with one of his friends in Kacheri, and became a person of that place. He started to use the cattle brand of his friend, and later when he got married, his wife used the customs and traditions of his friend's family. That is all about Nakol.

Folktales

2 *The Elephant and the Fox*

Storyteller: Lodoch (a 65-year-old Jie man)
Place: Jimos village

Long ago, a fox left his den to hunt. He walked and walked until he found a bull. He drove the bull and drove the bull until he met an antelope. The antelope asked the fox, "Can I come with you? We can drive the bull together."

The fox replied, "Eei, my uncle told me that if I met an antelope with a reddish-yellow color, kill him, skin him, and bring the skin so we can make a *ngicheleta* (skins sown together for women to use as a dress)."

The antelope replied, "Okay, you go ahead and drive your bull by yourself."

The fox drove and drove the bull until he met an eland. The eland asked, "Fox, can I come with you? We can drive the bull together."

The fox replied, "My uncle told me that if I met an eland, kill him and bring the skin so we can make *ngarakanes* (a long rope-like skin, which is used for tying fire-wood).

The eland said, "Okay, you go ahead and drive the bull all by yourself."

The fox continued his journey and drove and drove the bull until he met a rhino. The rhino asked, "Fox, can I drive the bull with you?"

The fox replied, "My uncle told me that if I met a rhino with long horns and short legs, kill him and bring his skin so that we can make shoes for ourselves."

The rhino said, "Okay, you go ahead and drive your bull all by yourself."

The fox continued his journey driving the bull until he met a giraffe. The giraffe asked, "Hey fox, can I come with you? We can drive the bull together."

The fox replied, "No, my uncle told me that if I saw a giraffe with a spotted skin, cut his tail so we can put it on during marriage ceremonies."

The giraffe replied, "You go ahead. You drive the bull all by yourself." The fox drove and drove the bull until he met an elephant. The elephant asked, "Fox, can I drive the bull with you?"

The fox replied, "Eei, my uncle told me, if I met an elephant, kill him and let people know that I had killed an elephant."

The elephant replied, "Hey fox, what are you saying? I can't hear you."

The fox said, "You come with me and we will drive the bull together."

The fox and the elephant drove and drove the bull together until they reached the house of an old woman. The old woman opened the door of the cattle enclosure where they killed the bull and skinned it. The fox got the fatty meat of the bull and threw it into the old woman's house.

When the elephant saw what the fox was doing, he asked, "What is that you are doing? *Ooitokoi*! You cannot throw the fatty part like that."

The fox continued to skin the bull and throw the fatty meat inside the old woman's house.

The elephant asked again, "Why are you throwing the fatty meat into the house of that old woman?"

The fox said, "It is not the fatty meat that I am throwing, it is the pus which I am throwing away." The fox continued to throw the fatty meat inside the house of the old woman.

After skinning the bull, they both became thirsty. The elephant told the fox to go and collect some water. The fox stood and went up to the water pond. He drank some of the water and then he stirred it. He brought the muddy water for the elephant. The elephant asked him, "Why did you bring me muddy water? What has spoiled the water at the pond?"

The fox replied, "My uncle's bulls – the black ones, the red-and-white spotted ones, and the gray ones – they all spoiled the water." The elephant told him to pour out the water and bring clean water.

The fox poured the water out and went again for water. As before, the fox drank the clean water and brought muddy water for the elephant.

The elephant again told him to go and bring back clean water. The fox went away, but again came back with muddy water.

The elephant became annoyed and said, "I'll go and get water for myself." The elephant went to the pond, drank clean water, and came back to finish skinning the bull. But, while the elephant had been gone, the fox put all the meat behind a rock in this old woman's yard.

The elephant came back and called for the fox. "Fox, where are you?" The fox replied, "I am here – behind the rock. Come over here." The elephant saw the fox's fingers between two rocks.

The fox said, "You see my fingers? Knock on this rock to open it and I can come out with all the meat. The elephant knocked the rock with his head, "*tur, tur*" (the sound of elephant's head knocking against the rock).

The fox said, "Keep knocking against this rock until it opens, so that I can come out with all the meat."

The elephant knocked and knocked against the rock. The fox continued to encourage him. The fox showed his fingers from the crack of the rock again and said, "Here elephant, you see my fingers coming out now. Knock harder and harder."

The elephant knocked, "*tur, tur,*" again and again. The fox told the elephant "Go a little ways and run and hit the rock. It is about to open." The elephant went a little distance away and ran toward the rock. He knocked his head against the rock so hard that he broke his head. The fox told the elephant to do it again, but the elephant did not respond. The fox said the same thing again, but the elephant remained silent.

The fox sent an *asiling* (a small black ant) to see what happened to the elephant. The *asiling* found that the elephant had died and he told the fox. The fox didn't believe the ant and said, "This ant is lying."

He sent an *asuna* (a large black ant) to see what happened to the elephant. The *asuna* came back and said, "The elephant's head is broken and he is lying dead near the rock."

The fox didn't believe the *asuna* either and said, "Ehh, this *asuna* is lying to me too." He sent an *emukunye* (a medium-sized black ant) to find out what happened to the elephant.

The *emukunye* hurriedly went and came back and told the fox, "The elephant is lying dead with his head broken."

The fox said again, "Ehh, you are lying to me."

The fox sent a *lokolongo* (a black dung beetle) to see what happened to the elephant. The *lokolongo* went and came back rolling a piece of the elephant's brain.

When the fox saw the *lokolongo* rolling the piece of the elephant's brain, he said, "Eii, this is the brain of the elephant. He is really dead."

The fox went to see the elephant's dead body. When he reached the rock, he found the elephant lying in front of the rock with his head broken. The fox began to sing:

Lokolongo, you the short one,
You work hard.
You work hard, but you have been despised.
Lokolongo, the short one,
You work hard.
You work hard, but you have been despised.

The fox began to skin the elephant as he sang. He skinned and skinned and took all the meat into the house. As he was skinning and skinning, the wives of the elephants saw the fox and said, "We are looking for our husband. We don't know where he went."

The fox replied, "I don't know where he is either. I have not seen him."

The elephant's wives said, "What are you doing there?"

The fox said, "I am skinning the bull."

The wives of the elephant asked him, "Can you turn the thing that you are skinning over so we can also see?"

The fox turned over the thing he was skinning and showed it to the elephant's wives. The wives of the elephant said, "Ehh, this is our husband."

The fox started to run and run and dove into a pond, "*chakulum*" (the sound of water). The wives of the elephant did the same, "*chakulum, chakulum, chakulum,*" looking for the fox.

Finally, the wives of the elephant caught the fox by the leg. The fox said, "Ehh, you caught a root."

The wives of the elephant said, "Ehh, this is a root we caught." Because the women thought the leg of the fox was a root, they let it go. The fox ran away at once. He ran and ran until he entered an anthill.

The elephant's wives said, "It is good he entered there." As the wives of the elephant ran toward the anthill, vultures hovered over the elephant's carcass. Among these vultures was a vulture with one eye.

The elephant's wives told the vultures, "We will give you the ants to eat, if you help us catch the fox." The vultures agreed to this and they all started to dig the anthill. As they were digging the anthill, the fox got out and threw a handful of *ngikok* (reddish-brown ants with claws) at the vultures and the elephant's wives. The *ngikok* attacked the eyes of the vultures and the fox got away.

The one-eyed vulture saw the fox leaving behind a cloud of dust. He told the others, "The fox just came out and he is running this way."

All the vultures said, "Ehh, how can you see where the fox went in this cloud of dust with only one eye?"

The one-eyed vulture said, "Aa, he has already gone." While the vultures were arguing among themselves, the wives of the elephant continued to dig the anthill with a piece of wood, "*kwer, kwer, kwer*" (the sound of wood while digging).

While the wives of the elephant were digging, "*kwer, kwer, kwer*," the fox changed his form and went back to the anthill. He said, "Wives of the elephant, what are you digging here?"

The wives of the elephant replied, "The fox that killed our husband is hiding in this hole. We are trying to dig the hole so we can catch him and kill him."

The fox in his changed form replied, "Let me help you. Give me that stick and I will dig the hole for you."

The fox took the stick and started to dig the hole, "*togelele, togelele*" (the deep sound made by digging).

While the fox was digging the hole, the one-eyed vulture recognized the fox and said, "This looks like the fox we have been looking for."

The wives of the elephant and the rest of the vultures said, "Ehh, what is wrong with you? Why do you accuse people for nothing? How can you see with that one eye?" They continued to dig the hole.

The fox at this point ran away and when he reached a far enough distance, he laughed and said, "Ha, ha, ha, foolish women, I am here." The herd of elephant women ran after the fox, but he disappeared in a cloud of dust.

3 A Bat and His Friends Who Went Raiding

Storyteller: Lodoch (a 65-year-old Jie man)
Place: Moruongor village

Long ago, a bat (*lamenua*) gathered many birds and animals together and said to them, "What can we do to get some cattle?"

They all said, "First let us send somebody to find where the cattle are, and then we can decide how to get them." The crowd sent two birds to go.

The birds flew and flew, looking for cattle everywhere but they could not find any. The birds continued to fly to a very far land. They saw many cattle grazing in green pastures near a huge river next to a hill. The birds said, "Ehh, there are many cattle, there are many cattle. Let us go and tell those people to come and get them, get them all."

The birds hurriedly flew back to the place they came from. When they reached there, they summoned all the birds and animals and said, "Come and gather together again."

When they all had gathered together, these birds said, "We have found cattle. They are very many. They are very many. They are near a hill next to a huge river."

The birds and the animals said, "Let's go to steal (akole) those cattle." Some animals objected to this and said, "If we go as thieves (ngikokolak), we cannot steal the cattle, because that place is too far away."

Other animals said, "We are all young and brave animals. We can walk for many days and nights. We can raid (ajore) and fight if we have to. Let's bring those cattle back here." After some discussion, all the animals and birds decided to go cattle raiding in that place.

The next morning all the animals and the birds set off to that place to raid the cattle. After sleeping for four nights on the road, they reached that land and raided the cattle on the fifth day. They drove the cattle, they drove the cattle, and slept with them on the way. On the fourth day, on their way home, the rain began to fall as they reached a barren, flat land with a huge tree on it.

When the animals came near the tree they said, "Let's take shelter under that tree." A heavy rain fell and all the animals and birds gathered under the tree. They left the cattle in the open place. As the heavy raindrops pounded on the ground, the place grew dark, and the cattle could no longer be seen. When the wind blew the heavy rain, the cattle became frightened and ran away. The whole plain was flooded and the rivers began to flow.

When the rain stopped, the animals and the birds began searching for their lost cattle saying, "Where did those cattle go? Where did those cattle go?" They went one way and they found that the river was swollen high so they could not pass. They went another way and found that the river was flowing so heavily they could not pass. The rainwater washed away the footprints of the cattle. The cattle had disappeared completely.

They slept on that plain for two days and searched for the lost cattle as the flooded rivers subsided, but they could not find them. They said to themselves, "We crossed the rivers and searched for the cattle and we could not find them. Now the water has gone and the rain has stopped. Let's go back to the tree where our cattle got lost. Let's go there and find out if it was the tree that chased away our cattle. Let's go and ask that tree about all these things. If it is the tree who caused our cattle to disappear, we will curse that tree."

All the birds and the animals gathered together and went to that tree. When they arrived, they assembled under it and began to swear. The birds perched on the branches of the tree one by one and swore, "If it was this tree that caused our cattle to disappear we shall never perch on it again. Let us cut off one of our toes so that we do not step on the ground on four toes."

The birds each cut off one of their toes and stepped on the ground on three toes. Even today, you will not find a bird, which steps on four toes.

After all the birds swore and cursed the tree, the bat who organized the raid said, "If it was the rain that came from the sky that caused our cattle to get lost, I will never look up to the sky any more." The bat held on to the branch of the tree and hung upside down, looking at the ground.

The elephants (*ngitome*), buffalo (*ngikasowa*), rhino (*ngamosingo*) and zebra (*ngitukoi*) said, "If it was this tree who caused our cattle to get lost, we shall never climb on it any more. We shall walk on the ground and we shall not climb on this tree again."

The leopards (*ngirisae*) came to the tree and swore, "I will climb on this tree. I will climb on this tree, because I don't know if it was this tree that caused our cattle to disappear. I shall look up and I shall look down. I will climb on the tree and walk on the ground. I don't know whether it was the people who own the cattle who came and took the cattle away, or if it was Akuj (God) who became upset and took them. Akuj doesn't approve of raiding."

This is why the leopards climb on the trees and walk on the ground. This is why Akuj curses the raiders, and never blesses them.

4 The Hyena Who Ate Baby Goats

Storyteller: Nangorin (a 30-year-old Jie man)
Place: Nayese village

Long ago, a certain kraal migrated and settled in a bushy place. The people of this kraal found an *atapar* (pond) in that place. They put pieces of *ngakape* (hides) in the water to make *ngasaja* (saddles for donkeys). The hyena came and ate all the *ngakape*. When the woman of the kraal sent her son to bring the *ngakape* from the pond, the boy found that the *ngakape* were not there.

The boy told his mother the *ngakape* had disappeared from the pond. The woman said, "There is nothing that can eat the *ngakape*. Check if they might have been stuck in the mud."

When the boy looked to see if the *ngakape* had become stuck in the mud, he saw footprints near the pond and went back to tell his mother.

The people went to the pond to see what kind of footprints they were. When they reached the pond, they realized that the footprints belonged to a hyena. That same day, the hyena told people that he had lost one of his calves and had been looking for it all over the bush, but couldn't find it. Since it was already becoming dark, he asked if it would be okay for him to spend the night with them.

The people said, "There is no place for you to sleep here, but you can sleep at the *anuk* (baby goat enclosure)." The hyena entered the *anuk* and slept there. At night, the hyena ate the baby goats as the goats shrieked, "*ngwee, ngwee, ngwee.*"

The people of the kraal said to the hyena "What is happening to the baby goats? Are you pinching them?"

The hyena said, "It is the *ngikachere* (a brown-colored bird with a sharp red beak, which sucks blood from cattle and goats) who are disturbing the baby goats."

The people said to him, "Chase the *ngikachere* away from the baby goats." The hyena continued to strangle and eat the baby goats all night, and afterwards, ran away before the morning light.

5 The Man Whose Child Was Eaten by the Hyena

Storyteller: Longoli (a 30-year-old Jie man from Nayese village)
Place: Nayese village

Long ago, the child of a certain man did not listen to his father's advice and got lost in the bush. A hyena found the child and ate it. After eating the child, the hyena left and a fox came to that place. He saw the blood stains on the bush and the leftover intestines lying on the ground. The fox ate the left over intestines and licked the blood.

The father of the child began to search for him. When he reached the bush where the hyena ate the child, he found the bloodstains and said to himself, "This must be the blood of my child. An animal must have eaten my child."

The father of the child called all the animals to find out who ate him. All the animals gathered together and the man told all of them, "Tell me who has eaten my child. If you don't tell me, I will kill all of you."

The man gathered firewood and made a big bonfire and said to the animals, "Whoever has eaten my child will not be able to jump over this fire."

He told the animals to begin jumping over the fire, one by one. He called the elephant first. "Elephant, you jump first. If you have not eaten my child, you will not fall in this fire."

The elephant replied, "If I am the one who ate your child, I will fall in this fire." The elephant jumped over the fire without falling.

The man called the giraffe, which came forward and said, "If I am the one who ate your child, I will fall in this fire." The giraffe also jumped over the fire.

The buffalo came next and said, "If I am the one who ate your child, I will fall into this fire." The buffalo also jumped over the fire.

The man called the hyena to jump over the fire. The hyena said, "If I am the one who ate your child I will fall into this fire. When the hyena tried to jump over the fire, he fell in and was burned.

Finally, the fox came and said, "If I am the one who ate your child, I will fall in this fire." The fox jumped, but only his tail was burned.

The fox said to the man, "The hyena ate your child, but I only licked the blood."

The man, who was upset with his son for ignoring his advice, gathered the bones of the hyena and the bones of his child from the fire and put them together in a gourd. The man churned the gourd in the morning and said, "Nacham, my child, how big are you?"

Nacham replied, "I am as big as an *emukunyo* (a small black ant)."

The following morning, the man churned the gourd again and said, "My child Nacham, how big are you now?"

Nacham replied, "I am as big as an *esuma* (a big black ant)."

The following morning the man churned the gourd again, and said, "My child Nacham, how big are you now?"

Nacham replied, "I am as big as a toe."

The next morning the man churned the gourd and asked again, "Nacham, my child, how big are you now?"

The child replied, "I am as big as a puppy."

The next morning, the man churned the gourd and asked again, "Nacham, how big are you now?"

Nacham replied, "I am as big as I was before." The man broke open the gourd and Nacham came out as he was before.

6 The Rabbit Who Did Not Drink Water

Storyteller: Lodoch (a 65-year-old Jie man)
Place: Losilang in Mustafa Mirzeler's home in Jimos village

One day during the dry season, all the animals gathered together and said, "We are thirsty (*akure*). Let's go and look for a place where there is water. Let's go and search for water in the river and dig a well in the bed." All the animals went together to dig a well. The animals also called for rabbit (*apoe*) to go with them.

The rabbit said, "Aaa, I don't want to dig a well because I don't drink water, and I don't want my hands to get dirty."

The rabbit lay in the bush while all the animals went to dig the well in the riverbed. They dug until the water came out. All the animals came and drank water from this well. But one day, they found no water in the well and wondered who had drunk it all. They said to themselves, "Someone must have come at night and drank all the water."

It was the rabbit who fetched the water at night, and took it to his home. The rabbit continued to fetch water at night, and take it to his home. But one day, the animals found the footprints of the rabbit near the well and said, "These are the footprints of the rabbit. The other day he said he doesn't drink water, but he comes at night and takes the water to his home."

Someone went to rabbit's home and found water there. He asked rabbit, "What is this?" The rabbit replied, "Akuj (God) gave me this water and it has been with me for a long time."

One day, the birds hid and watched over the well. When night fell, they saw the rabbit coming to fetch water. As the rabbit climbed down into the well, the birds made noise, "*chiwi, chiwi, chiwi,*" and chased the rabbit away. But later that same night, when the birds fell asleep, the rabbit came back again and fetched the water from the well.

The next day when the animals came to drink water, they saw the footprints of the rabbit and found the well dry again. The animals said to the birds, "Why did you let the rabbit drink water from our well?"

The birds protested, "No, the rabbit did not come."

The animals said to the birds, "No, the rabbit came when you were asleep."

This time they asked the *abook* (turtle) to watch over the well at night, and catch the rabbit when he came to steal the water. The *abook* watched over the well and waited all night to see if the rabbit would come, but the rabbit did not come.

But one night the rabbit came to drink. When he stretched out his hand, the turtle caught it. The rabbit implored and said, "Release my hand! Release my hand! Let me go and I will give you a cow." The turtle let go of the rabbit's hand and the rabbit went back to his home without drinking the water.

The next night, when the rabbit felt thirsty again, he went back to the well to drink water. When he stretched his hand to get the water, the turtle caught his hand again.

The rabbit and the turtle got into a fight. When the rabbit wanted to hit the turtle, the turtle withdrew his head, along with the rabbit's hand, into his shell. The turtle's shoulders squeezed the rabbit's hand and the rabbit said, "*Ooitokoi*, please let me go. Please let me go, you are breaking my hand. Leave my hand alone and let me go. I will give you a cow."

The turtle said to the rabbit, "You have not given me the cow that you promised the last time."

The turtle and the rabbit wrestled and struggled all night until morning. When the animals came in the morning, they found the turtle and the rabbit wrestling, and they caught the rabbit. The animals said, "Let's kill the rabbit. The other day he said he doesn't drink and he doesn't steal water. Let's beat him up and kill him."

The rabbit begged, "Don't beat me. Just kill me."

The animals said, "How can we kill you? Do you want us to kill you with sticks or with stones?"

The rabbit said, "No, no, not with sticks or with stones. If you want me to die quickly, get some banana leaves. Cut the soft parts of the leaves and remove all the hard parts; wrap me in them, and put me under the sun. I will die very quickly."

The animals gathered banana leaves and cut the hard parts out. They wrapped the rabbit with the soft parts and put him under the sun. They sat under the tree and waited for the rabbit to die under the heat of the sun. At midday the animals said, "The banana leaves are dry, he must be dead by now. Let's go and check."

When the animals came to check to see if the rabbit had died, they picked him up and carried him to the tree. While they were carrying the rabbit, all the dried out banana leaves crumbled and fell down. As the banana leaves fell, the rabbit jumped down and ran away quickly. The animals shouted after the rabbit, "Stop, stop, stop . . ." The rabbit never stopped, but kept on running.

The animals started chasing the rabbit. The rabbit ran, and entered a bush and disappeared. The animals could not find the rabbit. They became angry and said, "We hate you rabbit. You are a thief (*erai iyong ekakolan*). We will kill you, when we catch you."

That is why today, animals like the fox chase and chase rabbits. That is why the rabbits don't walk around freely when other animals are present. That is also why the rabbits eat and drink at night and hide in the bush during the day.

The reason that the rabbit is a dark gray color is because he stole clay (*emunyen*) and smeared it on himself to make the people think that he is sacred, and thus, feel afraid when they see him. The gray color is similar to the earth and it is sacred. When he is in the bush, other animals cannot see him because of his color. When the rabbit sleeps, his eyes remain wide open as if he were awake. When he is awake, his eyes are half closed as if he were asleep.

7 The Rabbit and the Baboon

Storyteller: Lodoch (a 65-year-old Jie man)
Place: Kotido
One day the wild animals gathered together and said, "Who should we elect to become our leader, a leader who will govern all of us. Let us elect the elephant!"

But the baboon protested against this decision and said, "The elephant walks on fat round legs. I, the baboon, should be elected. I use my hands and I look like a human. I pick up things with my hands and I put them in my mouth."

The rabbit said, "No, I should be elected, because I know everything. When I see people crossing, I salute them and I greet them. I even know how to greet people when I run."

The baboon said, "I also know how to greet people like that."

A crowd of animals disagreed with both and said, "No, why do you say that? You are both young."

Some animals said, "The baboon should become the leader."

The rabbit protested and said, "No, I should become the leader."

The baboon disagreed, "No, I don't want the rabbit to become the leader."

The rabbit said to the baboon, "If you want, let us fight and whoever wins should become the leader." Both the rabbit and the baboon went to prepare for their fight the next day.

While the baboon went to find a strong club, the rabbit brought some water and poured it into a gourd. He got another gourd and poured blood in it, and still a third gourd and poured in sour milk mixed with blood.

When they met the next day for the fight, the rabbit came with his gourds and the baboon came with his club. The rabbit put down his gourds and told the baboon to beat him with his club. As the baboon beat the rabbit with his club, the rabbit banged the water gourd on the baboon. The gourd broke and water poured over the baboon's face.

The baboon beat the rabbit again, but the rabbit caught his club and banged the baboon on his face with the gourd full of blood. The gourd broke and the blood poured down on baboon's face.

The rabbit screamed, "Blood, blood is coming down."

The rabbit immediately picked up the last gourd filled with sour milk mixed with blood and banged it on baboon's face and said, "Your brain is coming out of your head."

When the baboon saw the mixture of blood and sour milk dripping from his head, he said, "Ehh! This really is my brain."

When the rest of the animals saw this, they ran away and said, "Ehh, his brain is really coming out. The rabbit is really tough."

The animals scattered and ran away in fear. They said, "The rabbit should become the leader."

After the animals said the rabbit should become the leader, they went away. The baboon ran away and climbed up the mountain and the rabbit went into the bush. When the baboon reached the top of the mountain, he said to himself, "Ehh, I cannot fight with the rabbit. Let me stay here, up on the mountain. If I go down there, the rabbit will kill me."

From then on when the baboon came down to eat wild fruit, he watched for the rabbit and ate his fruit timidly. He ran to the mountain quickly saying, "If the rabbit gets me, he will beat me and my brain will come out of my head." This is why the baboons stay on top of the mountains even now. This is why whenever a baboon sees a rabbit on the plain, he runs to the top of the mountain, and the rabbit runs into the bush.

8 The Story of the Rabbit Who Was Caught Stealing Food

Storyteller: Logwee (a 40-year-old Jie woman)
Place: Jimos village

Long ago, there was a man who grew millet near a river. The rabbit found the garden and saw that the millet was yellow and had ripened. The rabbit went around and around the garden and realized that it was well fenced. "Where can I pass through to eat the millet?" thought the rabbit. The rabbit then went around and around the fence again, looking for a hole to pass through until he found a place where the bush around the fence was sparse. After the rabbit tore down the bush and thorns that covered that part of the fence, he slipped through into the garden and ate until he was satisfied.

The following morning the rabbit came back again, and ate and ate until he was overly satisfied, and then he passed through the hole to the outside. The rabbit continued with his habit of eating the millet in the garden while no one was around.

One day, when the man came to inspect his garden, he realized that someone ate his millet again. He said, "*Ooitokoi*, it seems like someone has harvested my millet before I could." The man found footprints around the garden and said, "*Ooitokoi*, these are the footprints of the rabbit. The rabbit is the one who ate my millet."

The next day, when the man came back to his garden, he noticed that some more millet had been eaten and he saw the footprints of the rabbit again. The man went around and around and said, "Eeehh, where was the rabbit when I worked so hard in my garden?"

The next day, the man put a trap in his garden with the hope of catching the rabbit. After a while, a bird became trapped. When he came back to his garden he saw the bird hanging from the trap and killed him, saying, "You are the one who has been eating my millet."

The man took the bird and set many more traps. He went to his home and gave the dead bird to his wife and said, "Cook this bird and we will eat it as it ate our millet."

The following day when the rabbit came back to eat the millet, he saw many traps being set and said, "*Ooitokoi*, he set many more traps now." But the rabbit was able to jump over the traps very carefully and ate more millet and ran away.

When the man came back to his garden, he found that all the traps were empty. More millet had been eaten and the footprints of the rabbit were on the ground again.

The man went to rabbit's home and said, "Rabbit, why are you eating my food?"

The rabbit became defensive. "I am not the one who ate your food. I don't need to eat other people's food. I have plenty of food in my home."

The man said, "Rabbit, tell me the truth, that you are not the one who has been eating my food."

The rabbit swore and said, "Look, if you don't believe me, we can go to an *emuron* (prophet) and ask him. He will be able to tell you the truth. I am not the one who ate your food. I don't need your food." At this point, the rabbit was very firm and demonstrated anger toward the man who accused him of stealing his millet. The man shook his head in disbelief and went away.

The next day, the man gathered wax from all the hives and heaped and pounded and pounded it, until it became sticky. He used wood to make a scarecrow (*eketen*), which he shaped into a human form. He smeared the sticky wax all over it and put the scarecrow in the middle of his garden and left.

The rabbit came back late in the evening, as usual, and found that all the traps had been removed from the garden. He quietly passed through the hole and went inside.

When the rabbit entered the garden, he saw the scarecrow. Thinking that it was a person, he said, "Who are you? What are you doing in my friend's garden? You are the one who has been eating my friend's millet." The scarecrow remained quiet.

The rabbit called again, "You! Who are you?" The scarecrow remained quiet still. The rabbit pressed, asking, "Are you a human being or what?" The scarecrow said not one word.

The rabbit then said to the scarecrow, "Now you are keeping quiet. This is my friend's garden and I am looking after it. Who are you to come and stand in the middle of my friend's garden so quietly like that?" At this point, the rabbit was trembling with anger.

"Now," said the rabbit, "if you still keep quiet like that, I will slap you hard. Tell me who you are before I slap you." The rabbit thought, "If I slap this person, he will be afraid and run away and then I will eat the millet again." The rabbit asked again, "Who are you?"

When the scarecrow continued its silence, the rabbit became angrier and slapped it. The rabbit's hand got stuck. He tried to pull his hand away to no avail. As the rabbit struggled, he yelled at the scarecrow, "This is my brother's garden. You leave my hand. Now if you don't leave my hand, I will slap you with the other hand. Do you think I have only one hand? Move, MOVE NOW," said the rabbit furiously. But, the scarecrow remained quiet.

The rabbit slapped the scarecrow again, very hard, and his other hand became stuck. The rabbit then screamed and said, "Leave my hands now. I will kick you if you don't!" Then the rabbit started kicking and this time his feet got stuck in the sticky wax.

The rabbit said, "Leave me! Leave me! Let me go. If you don't, I will bite you. Do you know that I have very sharp teeth?" The scarecrow remained quiet and still did not say a word. The rabbit then bit the scarecrow very hard and his teeth went deep inside the sticky wax. The rabbit was completely stuck. He could not move or utter a word.

The next day the man came back to his garden and went around and around his garden and he found that the rabbit was stuck on the scarecrow.

He came nearer and said to the rabbit, "The other day when I asked whether you were the one who ate my millet you swore and said you are not the one. You even wanted me to go to the prophet if I did not believe you. When you escaped the other day, you thought that I was a fool, but now you are caught."

The rabbit was so scared at that point that it began to defecate and urinate. The urine of the rabbit poured on the ground, "*chuurr*" (sound of pouring urine) and its feces dropped on the ground, "*dach, dach, dach*" (sound of dropping feces).

The man said, "Oh, I've got you. There is nothing to do but kill you. You started harvesting my millet before I did. You ate my food before I tasted it. Today is the end of you." The man hit the rabbit with his club, "*bubb, bubb, bubb*" (sound of beating with a club) until it died.

The man forcefully plucked the rabbit off the sticky wax and took him to his wife and told her that the rabbit was the one who ate the food. "Now we will eat the rabbit," he said.

9 The Hyena and the Bell

Storyteller: Logwee (a 40-year-old Jie woman)
Place: Jimos village

One day, a hyena began to eat baby goats in a kraal that was settled near a mountain. The owner of the kraal became upset, but he could not catch the hyena so he decided to move his kraal before the hyena finished eating all his goats. The owner pulled up stakes very early in the morning before dawn, while the hyena was still going after the baby goats.

When the man left with his livestock, the hyena said, "Oh, the kraal is migrating now." The hyena moved around in search of food and went to the goat enclosure where the baby goats were kept. He smelled the goat fat that was smeared on the *ngarubae* (collar, made out of skin, with a bell, tied to the neck of cattle), which was left hanging on a branch of a tree. The smell of the fat smeared on the *ngarubae* attracted the hyena and he became impatient.

After he looked around the abandoned kraal, making sure that there was no one around, he started to jump desperately to catch the *ngarubae* that smelled of animal fat, which drove the hyena crazy. He jumped higher and higher until the *ngarubae* came down and slipped onto his neck. As the hyena made efforts to get the collar off his neck, the bell sounded, "*dolong, dolong, dolong*" (the bell's sound). When the hyena heard the sound of the bell, he became frightened and ran away. He ran and ran. As he ran faster and faster the sound of the bell became louder and louder.

When the hyena fled into the bush and knocked against the trees, the bell sounded still louder. The hyena ran and ran, to escape the sound of the bell, but it continued to follow him. The frightened hyena defecated as it ran and ran. As the bell chased the hyena, the feces of the hyena turned the color black. But the bell continued to ring and chase the hyena until he dropped dead.

In the meantime, the man who migrated his kraal realized that he had forgotten the collar with the bell and he returned to his old kraal only to find the dead hyena with the bell around his neck. When he saw the dead body of hyena with the collar on its neck, he said, "The hyena ate my baby goats, but he could not eat the bell." The man than took the bell from the neck of the dead hyena and left, saying, "You ate my baby goats, now the vultures will eat you."

10 The Hyena and the Calf

Storyteller: Logwee (a 40-year-old Jie woman)
Place: Jimos village

During a particularly dry season, a certain man moved his kraal to settle on the banks of a river where there is plentiful water. Since the man had set off very early in the morning before the sunrise, he did not know that during the night, one of his cows had given birth to a calf. Because it was still dark, the man did not see the calf sleeping in the corner of the *arii* (cattle enclosure) either. And so the man drove his cattle, including the mother, leaving the sleeping calf behind.

After the kraal had migrated, a hyena came to the abandoned kraal, and smelled around in search of food. The hyena searched and searched and by morning, passed through the entrance of the *arii* where the calf was. When the abandoned calf saw the hyena he ran toward him thinking he was his mother. The hyena said, "Aaa, the thing which I thought was food is now trying to eat me!" The hyena ran and the calf followed it while bleating, "*Beee, beee, beeeee, beeeeeeee.*"

Seeing the calf coming after him the hyena became terrified and he ran and ran until he defecated out of fear. The frightened hyena ran until it found a hole that he tried to go down. He was so terrified that he dropped dead in the entrance of the hole, half of his body inside the hole and the other half outside the hole. The calf stood by the body of the hyena wondering whether it was its mother.

In the meantime, the man who moved his kraal realized that one of his cows had given birth and the calf must have been left in the old kraal. The man hurriedly returned to the old kraal looking for the calf. When he reached the kraal, he saw the footprints of the hyena and his feces. Following the footprints, he found the body of the hyena sticking out of a hole and the calf standing beside it. When the calf saw the man, he ran to the man thinking that he was his mother. The man drove the calf to his mother and when the calf saw her, he became so happy, he jumped, and jumped.

11 The Story of a Monkey Who Was Caught Stealing Food

Storyteller: Napedo (a 50-year-old Jie woman)
Place: Jimos village

Once there was a man who grew sorghum near the foot of a hill. One day the monkeys from the hill came down and ate the sorghum in the garden. When the man noticed that some animals had eaten part of his crop, he put a very thick fence around his garden. When the monkeys came back, they noticed the thick fence, but they jumped over it and plundered the crops. The next day the man noticed that the animals had come back to plunder his garden again.

He decided to put *ngatawatai* (traps made of thick branches and ropes) on all sides of the garden. The next day, when the monkeys came back they jumped over the fence, and one of the monkeys got caught in *ngatawatai*. It cried and kicked as it tried to free itself from the trap. The rest of the monkeys, upon seeing their friend trapped, became frightened and dispersed back up the hill.

The next morning, when the man came back to his garden, he saw the monkey struggling to free itself from the trap. He said, "The *ngatawatai* caught him. I've got him."

The man got a big rope and began to tie the monkey down very firmly as he said to him, "You! You have been eating my food. Food that you did not work for." The man tied one leg of the monkey to one tree and the other leg to another. He tied the hands of the monkey in the same way. After the monkey was firmly tied down, the man started to skin him. He skinned the monkey and skinned the monkey.

When the monkey was skinned completely, he set him free telling him, "You go now. I have removed your skin in the same manner you have removed the sorghum from my garden. You tell your friends who came to eat my food that you paid with your skin for the food that you have stolen. You go and bring back my food and I will give your skin back to you."

The skinless monkey ran up to the hill where his friends were. When his friends saw him without a skin and bleeding, they were frightened and ran away from him. Each time the skinless monkey went to his friends, they ran away in horror and scattered in the mountains.

The skinless monkey floundered in the mountains alone until it dropped dead. Witnessing what happened to their friend, the monkeys swore never to go the people's garden and never to steal food that they did not work for.

13 The Story of Napeikisina

Storyteller: Napeyo (a 50-year-old Turkana woman)
Place: Oyokwara village in Moru Apolon area in Turkana land

Long ago, in another age, there was a woman called Napeikisina who was a cannibal. She slaughtered people and ate them. One day she went to the villages and inquired about young girls to help her weed her gardens. Four girls agreed to help her and they went to Napeikisina's home the next day. Napeikisina told her daughter to watch these girls and show where they needed to weed. When it reached midday, Napeikisina's daughter came and told these young girls that her mother would bring them two calabashes full of milk. One of the calabashes would be dirty and old. The other one will be new and clean. Napeikisina's daughter told them that the milk in the clean calabash would be her mother's milk, but the milk in the dirty calabash would be a cow's milk. She told them, "My mother is a cannibal and she is going to slaughter you all tonight."

When the sun reached its zenith, Napeikisina came with two calabashes of milk and put them in the corner of the field. One of the calabashes was dirty and broken; the other one was clean and new. The clean calabash contained the milk of Napeikisina and the other calabash contained the cow's milk. After putting the calabashes down, Napeikisina told the young girls to drink the milk when they felt thirsty and hungry. After putting the calabashes in the corner of the garden, she left. After Napeikisina left, the children dug a hole in the ground, and into it they poured the milk from the clean calabash, and they drank the milk from the dirty calabash.

After some time had passed, Napeikisina came to check on the girls and said to them, "My nieces." The children replied, "Yes, our aunt."

"Have you drunk your milk?" Napeikisina asked. "Yes, our aunt, we have drunk the milk," replied the girls. Napeikisina responded, "Oo, you continue to weed. I will go back home and prepare your dinner."

So Napeikisina went back to her homestead and the young girls continued to weed the gardens until the evening. Napeikisina then sent her child to summon the young girls to come home for dinner. When the young girls came, Napeikisina told them to come in. The children entered the home and sat on the cow skin, which Napeikisina had laid on the ground for them to sit on. Napeikisina then went back outside and continued to cook food for the girls. After the food was ready, Napeikisina brought the food and served them. As the girls ate their food, Napeikisina went outside to urinate and her daughter came inside and told the girls "You will be slaughtered. My mother has sharpened her knife and she will slaughter you tonight." After saying this, she left.

When Napeikisina came back from urinating, she told the girls, "You, my nieces, you sleep at my home tonight and you will finish weeding tomorrow."

The children replied, "Indeed, we will sleep in here tonight and we will finish weeding tomorrow."

When the time came to sleep, Napeikisina went outside and lay down near the threshold of the house and fell asleep. When she was sound asleep, the girls pinched one another and said, "One of us should remain here and the rest of us must run away. The one who remains here must make noise on the cow skin so that Napeikisina will think that we are still inside the house. After we reach some distance the one who is left inside should run away."

After this conversation, one of the girls said she was a fast runner, so she decided to stay in the house while the other girls ran away. So one by one the girls tiptoed and jumped over Napeikisina and went outside. After some time had passed, the girl who remained inside the house said to herself, "They must by now have gone some distance away. So I too should run and escape; but when she tried to jump over Napeikisina, she stepped on Napeikisina's breast. Napeikisina woke up and picked up her big knife and began to chase the girl. The girl ran faster and faster, but so did Napeikisina. Eventually Napeikisina could not keep up with the young girl. When the young girl reached a certain river, she saw her friends had already crossed the river and they were standing on the opposite riverbank. When the young girl reached the river she said, "River of our ancestors, divide so that I can cross." The river divided and the young girl crossed the river. Once the girl crossed the river, she said, "River of our ancestors, come together and flow." The river then came together and began to flow. When Napeikisina reached the river, she said to the girls, "Oh, the river is flowing. My nieces, show me where you crossed the river" One of the girls then threw an *amorok* (a long wooden stick used for repairing spears) in the middle of the flowing water and said to Napeikisina, "If you want you can come directly up to where *amorok* is standing. That is where we crossed the river." When Napeikisina went toward the *amorok*, she was carried away by the water and drowned.

Napeikisina's body dragged in the water until it became stuck at a bend in the river. It remained there for a long time and it transformed into an *ekaale* (a tall thorny tree with small leaves, which bears yellow sweet fruit).

This tree bore plenty of fruit, and when people from the villages found out that the *ekaale* tree had much ripe fruit and that some had already fallen down, they said, "Oh, this tree has so much fruit. Let us gather these fruits." They gathered the fruits, and put them in their sacks, and took their fruit-filled sacks back to their homes.

In the village, when people put the fruits in their mouths, the fruits perforated and fell through their mouths to the ground. The people then put the fruits into big sacks and took them back to where the tree was. The fruits penetrated the bags and fell out. The people then said, "What is wrong with this tree? This tree must be cursed. Why is it that when we want to eat its fruits they penetrate our mouths and fall to the ground, and when we try to put them in the bags, they do the same and fall out of the bags?"

Some people said, "Let us leave these fruits. These fruits must be from Akuj (God)." They then took the fruits back to the tree and left them there, and returned to their village. After the people left, the tree transformed into a pumpkin bush and had many pumpkins on its vines. Some people who were passing by saw the pumpkins and said to themselves, "Oh, these pumpkins are ripe and they are the perfect shape to be gourds. Let us pick them." After these people brought the pumpkins to their village, they designed each pumpkin into a beautiful gourd and used them to hold milk, butter, and water. When the people in the village went to look after their cattle and weed their gardens during the day, the gourds gathered together inside the cattle enclosure and danced.

One day, an old woman, who was too old to go to the fields, saw how the gourds danced in the cattle enclosure, and she told people about this. The people did not believe her and told her that she was a liar. The woman kept quiet and the gourds continued to gather and dance in the cattle enclosure when the people went to work. One day, as the gourds were dancing, an old man came back early and saw the gourds were dancing and singing in the cattle enclosure. The man then ran to the people's gardens and told them, "My people, return all the gourds to the place where you got them. What that old woman said to you is true. Indeed, I saw these gourds dancing with my own eyes."

The people then returned to their village and collected all the gourds and returned them to the place where they got them. When the people left, the gourds turned into a cow and gave birth to a calf. A man who was passing by saw the cow with a big udder feeding her calf, and said, "Oh, this must be somebody's cow. Ay, this calf is big. The cow must have given birth to the calf a long time ago."

After making sure there was no one around watching him, the man drove the cow and its calf stealthily to his home. He entrusted them to his wife and told her to keep her mouth shut. The woman took the cow to the *arii* (cattle enclosures) and tied the calf down and began to milk the cow. So as the woman milked the cow, *churr, churr, churr* (the sound made during milking as the milk pours into the calabash), the cow said to the woman, "Ayyy, Nachurruchurro (the nickname it gave to the woman who milked it), you milk and milk. How about my calf? Don't you want to leave some milk for it?"

The woman was frightened and said, "*Ooitokoi*! Is this cow talking to me? What is happening?" She poured the milk from the calabash into a big gourd and continued to milk the cow making the sound *churr, churr, churr*.

The cow said again, "You, Nachurruchurro, you milk and milk. Don't you want to leave some milk for my calf?"

The woman stood up and said, "Aaa! This cow is bad." She then untied the calf and let it suckle its mother. She poured the milk into a big gourd again and went to her home and told her husband, "This cow talks. It told me, 'You milk and milk. Don't you want to leave some milk for my calf?'" The man told his wife, "Aaah, you stupid, woman! How can a cow speak? What is wrong with you? Are you cursed?"

The next morning, the man sent his daughter to milk the cow. When the girl went and milked the cow, *churr, churr, churr*, the cow said, "You, Nachurruchurro, you milk and milk. Don't you want to leave some milk for my calf?"

The girl became frightened and ran back home and told her father, "What my mother said is true. This cow talks."

The man became upset and told his daughter, "*Ooitokoi*! Have you and your mother lost your minds?" The man did not believe his daughter either.

So days went on and the same thing continued each time the mother or the daughter milked the cow, and they continued to report the situation to the man, but the man continued to disbelieve his wife and daughter. But one day, he decided to hide in the cattle enclosure and see what happened when his daughter milked the cow. That morning when the daughter milked the cow, it talked again and said, "Nachurruchurro, don't you want to leave some milk for my calf?" Upon hearing this, the man became frightened and immediately drove the cow and the calf back to the river where he had found them.

When the man left the river, the cow and the calf turned into a ram. When the people who were passing by the river saw the ram grazing, they said, "*Ooitokoi*! There is a ram here." Some people said, "Let's go and slaughter it and eat it." Some other people said, "Let's not kill it. If the owner of the ram finds out, he will be angry." Other people said, "Let us kill the ram and eat it. Nobody will see what we do. Nobody is around here but us." They then slaughtered the ram, built a big fire, and started to cook it in a very big pot. They cooked and cooked but the meat remained raw. They stoked the fire and they cooked and cooked more, but the meat still remained bloody and raw. They then said, "*Ooitokoi*, the pot is refusing to boil. Let us build more fire." They made a bigger fire and they cooked the meat until the morning. But when the morning came, they realized that the meat was still raw and the pot was still cold.

The people then said, "*Ooitokoi*! What should we do?" One of the people then said, "Is this not the thing that people said turned into a cow that spoke? How did it become a ram?" Another one then said, "*Ooiii*, isn't the place where we got the ram the place where they said they had found the cow that speaks?" All the people then said, "Aaah, this thing is bad. Let us return it back to the place where we found it." They then put the meat in the skin of the ram and took it back to the place where they had found it. They left it there and returned to their villages.

After the people left, the meat of the ram and its skin turned into an *elebulebwoit* tree (a tree that bears a type of red juicy fruit, which is called *ngalebulebwo*). Some days later, when some young girls came to the place gathering green vegetables and wild fruit, they saw the *elebuleb-woit* tree with a lot of ripe fruit hanging from it, and said, "*Ooitoikoi*, the *elebulebwoit* tree. Look, its fruits are ripe, red, and juicy. Look, some of them have even fallen on the ground." The girls then climbed the tree and picked the fruits. As they were picking the fruits, some girls said, "Let us close our eyes and see who will pick the most ripe fruit." While they picked the fruits, all the girls opened their eyes except one. That one girl picked a lot of unripe fruit, while the rest of the girls picked only ripe fruit. After they came down, all the girls said, "Let us open our eyes." Except for the one girl who had kept her eyes closed and who had picked both ripe and unripe fruits, their eyes were already open. When they pretended to open their eyes, the one who truly had closed her eyes also opened her eyes, and they found that everyone picked ripe fruits except the girl who had indeed closed her eyes. They then said to the innocent girl, "Eehh, you have picked many unripe fruits. How did you pick these unripe fruits? Your hands were not selective in picking the ripe fruits."

The girl who had truly closed her eyes said, "Aah, how can I go home when I have only a few ripe fruits and a lot of unripe ones?"

The other girls told her, "Eeh, why don't you climb back up the tree and pick some ripe fruits while we wait for you here under the tree?" The girl then climbed up the tree and began to pick ripe fruits. The girls who waited for her under the tree defecated there and ran away.

While the innocent girl was picking fruits, she told the girls under the tree who she thought were waiting for her, "My sisters, wait for me. I am coming down with my fruits. Please wait for me."

The feces of the girls then responded, "*Oooi*, we are waiting for you. Hurry so that we can go home together." When the girl came down, she looked around and saw the feces of the girls and realized the girls were already gone.

The girl then said, "*Ooitokoi*, my friends have deceived me. It was their feces who responded to me when I was up on the tree." She then put her *ngalebulebwo* in her sack and walked home.

As she was walking, she saw a certain woman weeding her garden and eating *ngikachukuem* (soft watery root). The girl said to the woman, "Oh, woman, are you eating *ngikachukuem*?" The woman replied, "Yes." The girl then said to the woman, "Are these watery roots satisfying to you? You can only suck the water out of them. Here take some of my *ngalebulebwo* to satisfy your hunger."

The woman took the *ngalebulebwo* and ate them, and the girl sat under the tree and watched the woman eating. After she had finished eating, the woman resumed her work, but the girl continued to sit under the tree watching her. When the evening came, the woman prepared to return home, and the girl under the tree said to her, "Oh, give me back my *ngalebulebwo*. I also want to go home."

The woman said, "Aaah, how can I give you back your *ngalebulebwo*. They are already in my stomach. You gave them to me and told me to eat them. What can I do now?"

The young girl began to cry:

Ooi yaa icheberu, icheberu erikan
Nyake lelebulebwo, ngakalebulebwo
Eiyata ngachim a ngidwe katokang a lokitoe kayee

(*Ooi yaa* a woman, a woman finished my *ngalebulebwo*
My *ngalebulebwo*, the ones from the tree, where the feces of my sisters
    responded to me
My sisters responded to me from that tree.)

The woman, bewildered by the actions of this young girl, said, "Aah, if you are going to curse me, come with me and I will give you something else." They then walked together and when they reached the home of the woman, the woman churned some milk and gathered some butter and put them into a gourd. She gave them to the girl and told her to go home. The girl got the milk-filled gourd and walked and walked. When she reached a certain river she stopped and put the gourd down on the river's bank, and went to the river to wash her hands and drink some water. While she was still washing her hands, the bank of the river collapsed and the gourd that was filled with milk fell into the river and was carried away by the water. The girl began to cry again:

Ooiiyaa iche ngolol, iche ngolol ngakakilen abukori ngakakile
Ngakakile kaini ichebur, icheburu erikari ngakalebulebwo
Ngakabulebwo eiyata ngachin ngachin a ngidwe katokang aloitoe kaye

(*Ooiiyaa* a certain river, a certain river spilled my milk
My milk, which I was given by a certain woman, a certain woman who
    finished my *ngalebulebwo*
My *ngalebulebwo* from the tree where the feces of my sisters responded to me)

. The river then told the girl, "If you are going to curse me like this, I want you to stop. Take this fish in place of your milk and go." The girl took the fish and walked away. She walked and walked and when she reached a very faraway place, an eagle came down and grabbed her fish from her head and flew away. The girl began to cry again:

Ooiiyaa ichulili, ichulili akopori eka koliya
Eka koliya kainin iche ngolol, iche ngolol abukori ngakakile
Ngakakile kaini icheberu, icheburu erikari ngakalebulebwo
Ngakabelebulebwo eiyata ngachin a ngidwe katokang alokitoe kaye

(*Ooiiyaa* eagle, eagle grabbed my fish
My fish, which was given to me by a certain river, a certain river, which
    spilled my milk
My milk, which I was given by a certain woman, a certain woman who
    finished my *ngalebulebwo*
My *ngalebulebwo* from the tree where the feces of my sisters responded to me)

Seeing the girl crying like this, the eagle gave her a feather. The girl took the feather and walked and walked until she reached a certain faraway place where some people were dancing and celebrating a wedding with grass on their heads instead of feathers. She said to these people, "Ayyy, you people, you are dancing without feathers. You have donned your heads with grass? Here take this feather and don your head with it." These people took the feather and donned their heads with it and continued to dance. While they were dancing the feather fell and broke. The girl began crying again:

Ooiiyaa, iche kimwomwor iche kimwomwor abili aka kopiro aka kopiro
kaini ichulili
Ichulili akapori eka koliya, eka koliya kaini iche ngolol iche ngolol abukori
    ngakakile
Eka koliya kainin iche ngolol, iche ngolol abukori ngakakile
Ngakakile kaini icheberu, icheburu erikari ngakalebulebwo
Ngakabelebulebwo eiyata ngachin a ngidwe katokang alokitoe kaye

(*Ooiiyaa*, a certain dance, a certain dance broke my feather, my feather that
was given to me by an eagle
An eagle grabbed my fish, my fish, which was given to me by a certain
    river, a certain river, which spilled my milk

My fish, which was given to me by a certain river, a certain river, which
   spilled my milk
My milk, which I was given by a certain woman, a certain woman who
   finished my *ngalebulebwo*
My *ngalebulebwo* from the tree, where the feces of my sisters responded
   to me)

Seeing the girl crying in this way, the people said, "Eee, if it is like
that, you wait and we will give you this good shepherd stick."
   The girl took the stick and walked and walked until she reached a
very faraway place, and saw a shepherd looking after his cattle using a
broken branch. She said to the shepherd, "You, shepherd, what are you
doing with that broken stick? Don't you have a shepherd stick? I can
give this shepherd staff to you if you'd like."
   The shepherd said, "Okay, bring me the stick." The shepherd took
the stick and began to use it in gathering and herding his cattle. When
a cow ran away the shepherd went after it and beat it with the stick, but
the stick broke. When the girl saw her stick broken, she began to cry:

Ooiiyaa iche keyokon, iche keyokon abili eka bela kaini iche kimwomwar
Iche kimwomwar abili aka kopi, akakopir kaini ichulili, ichulili akapori eka
   koliya
Eka koliya kainin iche ngolol, iche ngolol abukori ngakakile
Ngakakile kaini icheberu, icheburu erikari ngakalebulebwo
Ngakabelebulebwo eiyata ngachin a ngidwe katokang alokitoe kaye

(*Ooiiyaa*, a certain shepherd, a certain shepherd broke my staff, my staff that
was given to me by a certain dancer
A certain dancer who broke my feather, my feather that was given to me
   by an eagle, which grabbed my fish
My fish, which was given to me by a certain river, a certain river, which
   spilled my milk
My milk, which I was given by a certain woman, a certain woman who
   finished my *ngalebulebwo*
My *ngalebulebwo* from the tree, where the feces of my sisters responded
   to me)

The shepherd, who was puzzled by all this, said to the girl, "What
can I give you? Can I give you a cow? Can I give you a ram? If you cannot drive the cow, you can certainly drive the ram home." So the

shepherd gave her a ram and she drove it and drove it until she reached a very faraway place and saw a woman sacrificing a dog for her dead husband. The girl said to the woman, "*Eei*, you, woman, I have never seen people sacrificing a dog for their dead relatives. Can I give you this ram so you can sacrifice it for your dead husband?"

The woman replied, "You can give me that ram." The woman took the ram and slaughtered it and cooked the meat and offered it to her guests. After people ate and finished the meat, the girl began to cry again.

The woman then said, "*Ooitokoi*, what can I do now? You gave me the ram and I sacrificed it for my dead husband, and we all ate the meat and finished it. Now you are crying. I have nothing to give you. But I can give you one of my children." The girl took the child and walked away. She walked, walked, and walked until she reached a very far-away place where she found a certain kraal, and she slept there with the child given to her. The next day she decided to stay in the kraal with her child and she stayed there for a long time.

After some time passed, the girl said to the people in the kraal, "I want to go and visit my family." The people replied to her, "If it is like this, why don't you leave this child to help us in fetching water and gathering firewood. We will take care of him until you return." In the morning, she decided to leave the child with the elder people to help in carrying water and firewood.

The girl then told the people, "Okay, you keep my child and let him help you until I come back from visiting my family." The girl then went back to her home. Time passed and she returned and found that the people in the kraal had moved away. She looked for the footprints of the people to determine where the kraal had moved. She looked, looked, and looked but could not find any trace of footprints. She than began to follow a certain path, but the path at a certain point divided into several different paths, and she did not know which path to take. This conjunction is the place where the story of Napeikisina ended.

14 The Story of Napeikisina

Lodoch (a 65 year old Jie man)
Place: Behind the cracked wall of a mud-plastered shop in Kotido

Some children went to weed the garden of their aunt, Napeikisina. While the children were weeding, Napeikisina's blind child was also there. Even though her child was blind, Napeikisina told her to watch

the other children so that they would not go anywhere and she then
went away to weed another garden.

While these children were weeding the garden, some other children
were softening goat skins at Napeikisina's home. The blind child said
to the children who were softening the goat skins, "My mother told me
to watch you."

Napeikisina slaughtered people who visited her. She slaughtered
many people. Slaughtered, slaughtered, and slaughtered. When these
children came to weed the garden, Napeikisina's child said to them,
"You weed now, but you will be slaughtered later." Napeikisina's child
again said to the children, "When my mother comes, you will all be
slaughtered."

The children were frightened and said, "What can we do? What can
we do?"

When they were finished weeding, the children returned to
Napeikisina's house. Napeikisina returned from the garden, lay at the
threshold of the house, and fell asleep. One child started to soften
the goat skin, while another began to make a hole in the back wall of the
house.

As these children continued to soften the skin, it made noise, *kuk, kuk,
kuk*, while the other child opened up the back wall. As this child was
digging through the back wall, the children who were softening the
skin sang a song:

> Our puppy with a spotted nose!
> Do it quickly and we go.
> Our puppy with spotted nose!
> Do it quickly and we go.

This child continued to soften the skin, making the noise, "*kok, kok,
kok,*" while the other child went on widening the hole in the back wall
of the house so that the children could escape. Finally, the hole was
made and the children went out one by one, except for one child. This
child would not go through the hole and she remained inside. She wondered, "What can I do now? Napeikisina has blocked the threshold
with her one breast which is as long as my arm." But this child was a
fast runner, so she told the other children to meet her at a certain place.

The children left and the last child, who remained inside, jumped
over the threshold and went out *pup! pup!* (sound of footsteps), but she
stepped on Napeikisina's long breast. Napeikisina was lying there with

her knife, which she used to kill people.

Napeikisina woke up and ran after the child. The child ran and ran. When the child jumped over a tree, Napeikisina also jumped. When the child went into the bush, Napeikisina also went into the bush, and chased her saying, "I must taste her. I must taste her."

The child ran and Napeikisina followed her until they reached a place where the children who ran through the hole were waiting to meet the child who had remained inside the house. Napeikisina found the children while they were crossing the river. The children beat on the water and the water parted.

Napeikisina's single breast was too heavy and she couldn't run fast enough to catch the child. When the child reached the river, the river had already closed and was flowing. The child beat on the water and said, "River, of my ancestors say *pee*. (the sound of reverse water flow), so that your child may cross." The water divided and the child crossed the river to the place where the other children were waiting. The river started flowing again.

Napeikisina reached the river. She saw the children on the other side of the river and impatiently (*kibunyakin*) tried to cross the river. Napeikisina said to the children, "Children of my mother, tell your river to say *pee* so that your aunt may cross."

The children said, "River of our ancestors say *pee*, so that our aunt may cross." The water divided again. When the water divided, Napeikisina climbed down into the river bed. When she reached the middle of the river, the children said, "Flow river of our ancestors."

The river said, "*Bruuchhh*! (sound of the river flowing suddenly)."

The river drowned (*tonyam*) Napeikisina and swept her away and turned her into water. The children went home. The river carried Napeikisina away and she became *ngikolya* (fish). People caught these fish without knowing that they were Napeikisina and dried them. After being dried, the fish gathered in the *arii* (cattle enclosure) and started to talk to each other. The people were horrified and returned the fish to the river.

In the river, the fish turned into gourds. People fetched these gourds and made calabashes from them. When the people went to work in their gardens, the calabashes gathered in the cattle enclosure and began to dance and sing.

Tutur, tutur, tutur! (sound made by gourds when they dance)
We have become *ngikaripio*

Tutur, tutur, tutur!
We are now *ngaderakai*
Tutur, tutur, tutur!
We have become *ngitwool*
Tutur, tutur, tutur!
We have become *ngabolokoi*
Tutur, tutur, tutur!
We have become *ngikeretin*

When people were away, the children in the villages saw the gourds dancing every day and they told this to their parents. People paid no attention to what the children said, but one day they hid themselves and watched to find out if what their children said was true. They found that what the children had said about the gourds was indeed true and returned the gourds back to the river. The gourds in the water turned into a fish. People caught this fish split it in half and spread it out to dry it in the sun.

An *echuli* (eagle) flew down and took the fish away. The voice of Napeikisina cried out, "Eagle, why did you take my fish, which the river had given me."

The eagle offered its feather as a gift and said, "Take this *totach* (payment) for your fish, since I have eaten your fish and it is in my stomach."

Napeikisina sang:

It is the eagle who took away my fish
My fish, which the river had given me
The river had spilled my milk
My milk a woman had given me
This woman ate my *ngalebulebwo*
My *ngalebulebwo*, which I picked from the tree
The tree where the feces of my sisters responded to me

Napeikisina went on and found people eating at a wedding without a feather. Napeikisina said to these people, "Ehh, you are eating at the wedding without a feather. Here, take my feather." People took the feather and continued their wedding feast with the feather, but the feather broke. Napeikisina cried for her feather and the people here gave her an *ebela* (a herder's stick).

Napeikisina took the *ebela* and gave it to the young herders (*ngikeyokok*) and they broke it. Napeikisina began to sing again.

Some shepherds, some shepherds broke my *ebela*.
My *ebela* was given to me by somebody
Somebody broke my feather
My feather was given to me by an eagle
The eagle took my fish
My fish was given to me by the river
The river spilled my milk
My milk was given to me by a woman

The shepherd gave Napeikisina a cow in payment. Napeikisina took the cow and walked away. On the road, she saw people using *ngingok-wo* (dogs) to pay a bride-price. Napeikisina said to these people, "Are you using dogs to pay a bride-price? Why don't you use my cow instead? Take this cow and use it for the bride-price and return it to me later. "

The following day, Napeikisina came back again and found that her cow had been used for bride-price, and she began to sing a song.

Ooiiyaa (sorrowful expression), the bride, the bride took away my cow
My cow was given to me by a man
My cow was given to me by a man
The man broke my *ebela*
My *ebela* was given to me by shepherds
The shepherds took my feather
My feather was given to me by an eagle
The eagle took my fish
My fish was given to me by the river
The woman destroyed my *ngalebulebwo*
I got my *ngalebulebwo* from a tree
where the feces of my sisters responded to me.

Napeikisina became a *miini* (a sticky thing) and people named her Mini-Ikwaparwata. After some time, Napeikisina changed again and became a beautiful baby. This baby lay in a ravine in the bush. A woman with an ugly baby came and found Napeikisina in the shape of a baby lying in the ravine. The woman picked Napeikisina and left her own baby in the ravine. This woman took Napeikisina to her home. People in the village said, "This child is so beautiful, but your baby was not this beautiful before." The woman said, "Ehh, this is the one, which was my baby."

After some time, whenever this woman went to the gardens, this baby changed into an adult and started grinding and cooking. But just before the woman came back home, Napeikisina became a child again and started crying. The woman's older children told her, "Our baby sister became an adult and started cooking and grinding."

The woman told her children, "You are stupid. How can a baby cook?"

This situation went on for some time. The woman's older children kept telling their mother how Napeikisina transformed herself into an adult when the woman left her home to go to the gardens. The woman became suspicious and said, "Ehh, let me see whether this thing is true."

This woman hid herself in the *arii* and watched. She saw how the baby transformed herself into an adult and started grinding and cooking. The woman became frightened and said, "*Ooi*, I threw away my own baby for this one." The woman took Napeikisina in the form of a baby and tried to take her back to the ravine where she picked her up, but she couldn't. The woman looked for help from people to get rid of Napeikisina in the form of a baby.

People tried to help this woman and took the baby back to the ravine. But the baby came back again, like a piece of gum that sticks. Some people said, "Let us migrate away from here." Other people panicked and said, "Let us slaughter a fat ram and eat it."

When they slaughtered a fat ram, Napeikisina, in the form of a baby, took the fatty parts of the ram and ate them all. After eating, she became drowsy and fell asleep. As soon as Napeikisina slept, people left immediately and said, "Let's move and leave her in the *awii* (kraal)."

After the people left, a man came and found the abandoned kraal and saw Napeikisina in the form of a baby lying on the thorny fence. The man said, "Ehh, these people migrated and left this child here." When the man picked Napeikisina up, she attached herself to the man's *lomedot* (headdress). When the man tried to pluck Napeikisina off his headdress, she struggled with the man. The man could not get rid of Napeikisina.

Napeikisina told the man, "Let's stay in this abandoned kraal." The man accepted and stayed there with Napeikisina for a long time until they became very hungry.

When Napeikisina became very hungry, she told the man, "Let's migrate from here. Let's go somewhere else where we can find food."

Napeikisina and the man walked and walked until they reached another kraal. Napeikisina told the man, "Let's steal a fat ram from this kraal and eat it."

The man said, "Okay, let me go and steal a ram."

When the man reached the *anuk* (goat enclosure), Napeikisina barked like a dog and said, "People of this kraal, people of this kraal, someone is stealing your ram." The man ran away before he could steal the ram.

Napeikisina and the man continued to walk and walk until they became very hungry again. Again, Napeikisina told the man, "Let's steal something today."

The man stole a ram and roasted its meat. Whenever the man tried to put the meat in his mouth, Napeikisina grabbed it and ate it until the whole ram was finished. After Napeikisina ate the fatty ram meat, she got drowsy and slept on the man's headdress. As Napeikisina slept, her hands became loosened from the headdress. The man stood up and felt that his head had become light again. He went away and disappeared.

When Napeikisina woke up, she wondered where the man had gone. She looked for the man, but could not find his footsteps. The next day, the hyena (*nakamol*) smelled the aroma of the ram, which Napeikisina and the man had roasted. The hyena came in search of the ram's meat. When the hyena came in, Napeikisina attached herself to the hyena's neck. The hyena tried to throw Napeikisina from his neck, but could not. He began to run and run. It ran through the bush, rivers, and hills with Napeikisina on its back. The hyena was frightened by Napeikisina and started to defecate. The hyena defecated and defecated as it ran until it fell dead.

Notes

Introduction

1 The term oral tradition is susceptible to various interpretations. For the purpose of this study, oral tradition refers to orally transmitted narratives that recount past events that purportedly took place beyond the limits of personal testimony and experience. These events are remembered without dates and chronologies and they usually refer to past epochs, such as the time of the creation and development of polity, and they may involve archetypal figures or ancestral families. These traditions are made of fragmentarily preserved memory images about tribal and clan migrations and conflicts. Sometimes these memories reconcile ancient genealogical times with present concerns, blending fantastic and realistic images.

2 Rural Uganda and rural Kenya have been affected by two powers that have attempted to absorb the hinterlands into a larger political entity: the British colonial state and the Ugandan and Kenyan centralizing states. The effects of these efforts have been felt in many ways: agricultural, demographic, economic, medical, religious. I sometimes describe these effects in sum as "modernization," although no one word can accurately capture all the changes that occur in a rural society when it becomes the focus of a strong political power with assimilationist aims.

3 Becoming an apprentice to a storyteller in the Karamoja Plateau and Lake Turkana region is not assuming a highly specialized role. Nearly all members of society have an opportunity to function as storytellers. In other contexts, such as those involving production of material culture, an apprenticeship is instruction in a highly specialized craft. See R.M. Dilley (1989).

4 In following general anthropological guidelines, I informed the individuals about the nature of my research and established working relationships

that were beneficial to all parties. While conducting research and publishing my research results, I made sure that I did not harm the safety, dignity,
or privacy of the people with whom I worked. I appropriately obtained
in advance the informed consent of persons who were involved in my
research. Throughout my research, I carefully and respectfully negotiated
the limits of my relationships with the people with whom I collaborated in
the field. The 2009 American Anthropological Association research guidelines are available at: http://www.aaanet.org/issues/
policy-advocacy/upload/AAA-Ethics-Code-2009.pdf
5 *Awatoun* is the marriage ceremony component during which the bride
   returns to her natal home.
6 This is congruent with Scheub's analysis of Zenani's autobiographical
   tales against the backdrop of the oral tradition of her society. Zenani was
   a Xhosa storyteller (Scheub 1988).
7 I am grateful to the anonymous reader for pointing out the work of
   Strathern's *Partial Connection*. I am also thankful to C. Kratz for engaging
   in email conversation with me regarding the use of partial truth as illumi-
   nated by Strathern.

1 Jie Past and Present

1 Pamela Gulliver coined the term "Karimojong Cluster" to refer to the common origin of the Nilotic-speaking communities on the Karamoja Plateau
   and beyond (interview with Pamela Gulliver, London, 15 June 2002).
2 The preceding four paragraphs are drawn from Mirzeler 2004 as well as
   from my predoctoral and postdoctoral research conducted between 1996
   and 2011.
3 These terms are reversed among the Bokora, Matheniko, and Pian communities, with *anyamet* generally referring to a generation-set, and *asapanu*
   to an age-set (also see Lamphear 1976, 38). The sociopolitical organization
   revolving around generation-set systems of the Jie displayed considerable
   variation in comparison to the rest of Karimojong Cluster, yet they all
   share several features of the system in common (Muller 1989, 88).
4 Tufnell's Report, 11 September 1911, E.A. 2119.
5 Parts of the preceding fews paragraphs appeared in *Anthropology News*
   (Mirzeler 2012).
6 See part 4 for the rabbit stories. See also chapter 3.
7 See, for example, Lamphear's discussion of Loriang (1976, 232).
8 Slyomovics (1998) describes how the displaced Palestinians render tangible the memories of their lost villages and homes by drawing maps of
   them. I have found similar responses among the Azeri storytellers when

they talk about their villages destroyed by the Armenians in Nagorno Karabagh, Azerbaijan (Mirzeler and Jafarov 2012).

9 See part 4, Jie Folktales (JFT): The Rabbit Who Did Not Drink Water (no. 6).

10 See part 4, JFT: The Story of Rabbit Who Was Caught Stealing Food (no. 8).

2 Ethnography of Storytelling

1 The storytellers create their images not only with their words but also with the movement of their bodies and rhythm of their voices. With the dance-like movement of their bodies and hands, they elicit and control the emotional elements important to the organization of narrative plot (Scheub 1998, 128–31). Most analyses of performances include only general descriptions of the use of body; however, the nonverbal aspects of the performances are key to the contextualization process. For Bauman (1977, 8), the meaning of performance is lost if equal weight is not accorded to the nonverbal aspect of the performance, so as to analyze how verbal and nonverbal performative modes intermingle and complement each another. However, as Briggs (1988, 17) points out, folklorists and anthropologists have not yet developed adequate means to capture the nonverbal aspects of performances and, thus, this component of oral performances continues to be "fuzzy."

3 Patterns and Images of Historical Tradition

1 Here I use Vansina's (1986, 106) exploration of "culture hero." According to Vansina, the art of storytellers and the dynamic of memory favor the idealization of certain historical personages, crediting them with being creators of cultures. Consequently, the storytellers use these heroic characters as models to show how society should function in the present.

2 See, for example, part 4, Jie and Turkana Historical Traditions (JTHT): The Original Ancestral Conflict (no. 6), The Original Ancestral Raiding (no. 7), Nayeche (no. 31). See also JTHT: The Original Ancestral Conflict (no.5).

3 Part 4, JTHT: Nayeche (no. 31) illustrates this point very well, as does JTHT, Nayeche (nos. 29 and 30); Elmolo Historical Tradition (EHT): Sepenya (nos. 1, 2, 3, 4, and 5).

4 Other examples include the journey of Orwakol from Dongiro to Daidai on the banks of the Longiro River, in The Great Journey from Dongiro to Nakadanya (Mirzeler 1999, 214–20); Kadanya's search for a new cradle land around Moru Apolon (the Great Hill), Mount Moroto, and the Apule River, in part 4, JTHT: Nakadanya, the Cradle Land of Long Ago (no. 27); and Lodiny's search for new cradle lands and water sources on the plateau as depicted in JTHT: The Memory of Rivers (nos. 11 and 12).

5 Nayeche (Mirzeler 1999, 253–9).
6 Orwakol, for example, is seen as the original initiator of the existential conflicts between the people in the villages and the kraals: the conflict between Orwakol and Lodiny over resources, see part 4, JTHT: The Original Ancestral Conflict (no. 6); Kadanya's irresistible compulsion to stop raiding and waging war, see part 4, Nakadanya (no. 27); Orwakol's ritual offering of sorghum and cattle brand to his wives and sons, respectively, see Orwakol and His Seven Wives (Mirzeler 1999, 231–4).
7 The Death of Engiro (Mirzeler 1999, 245–8).
8 Napeikisina (Mirzeler 1999, 179–87); part 4, JFT: The Story of Napeikisina (no. 13).
9 A key part of my analysis of folktales in this book derives from Scheub's (1969, 1996, and 2002) interpretive frame as well as local (Jie and Turkana) storytellers' interpretation.
10 Part 4, JTHT: The Gray Bull Engiro (no. 2), The Original Ancestral Conflict (no. 6). Similar motifs are found in Jie biographical narratives, part 4, Popular Biographies (PB): The Memory of Nacham (no. 1), The Memory of Aonyot (no. 2), The Memory of Nakol and His Father (no. 5); also see Memory of Ebongo, The Memory of Lojukar, The Memory of a Long Dry Summer, The Memory of Koryang, The Memory of Apese-Arengan and His Brother Nakdon (Mirzeler 1999, 363–4, 365–7, 372–3, 379–80, 381–3).
11 JTHT: The Original Ancestral Conflict (no. 5), The Arrival of Lodiny to Daidai (no. 8).
12 Part 4, JTHT: Nàyeche (no. 31).
13 Part 4, JTHT: The Original Ancestral Conflict (no. 6).
14 Part 4, PB: Nacham (no. 1).
15 Part 4, JTHT: The Original Ancestral Raiding (no. 6).
16 JTHT: The Legend of Mount Toror (no. 36).
17 JTHT: Nairanabwo (nos. 16, 17, 18); Nakadanya (no. 27).
18 THT, Lokorijam and the Vulture (Mirzeler 1999, 279–82).
19 Historical traditions differ from folktales in that they report events, and hence they are historical in Lutz Rohrich's sense (1991, 10–12). For Rohrich, historical legends are histories as much as folktales are stories. This point is also made by Pekka Hakamies (2010, 10).
20 JHT, Orwakol and his Seven Wives (Mirzeler 1999, 231–4).
21 Part 4, JTHT: The Original Ancestral Conflict (no. 7).
22 Lamphear establishes the date for this generation as being circa the early 1720s (1976, 110).
23 Part 4, JTHT: The Memory of the Ngipalajam (no. 19). In JTHT: 19, Lokui, the storyteller, states that during the Ngipalajam era "there was only one bull, Ngolengiro, the bull of Lokolong, the original bull of the entire

Najie." Lamphear corroborates the Ngipalajam age set to circa the 1720s (Lamphear 1976, 110).

24 In JTHT: Ngolengiro, the Hornless Bull of Lokolong (no. 20), Logwee, an 80-year-old storyteller, told the members of the audience that the bull of Lokolong lived when he was growing up. If Lokolong's bull lived while Logwee, "was growing up," the time period, which the bull of Lokolong lived would correspond to roughly to mid-1920s or early 1930s. If so, this eyewitness account contradicts Lamphear's dating of the historical tradition, to the 1890s.

25 JTHT: Nairanabwo (no. 18).

26 JTHT: Nairanabwo (no. 17).

27 Part 4, JTHT: Nayeche (no 42); also see The Bulls of Nayeche and the Camels of Lokerio (Mirzeler 1999, 274–8).

28 Part 4, JTHT: The Original Ancestral Conflict (no. 6); The Conflict Between Orwakol and Lodiny (Mirzeler 1999, 235–41).

29 Part 4, JTHT: The Original Ancestral Conflict (no. 6).

30 JHT, The Death of Engiro (Mirzeler 1999, 243–4).

31 JTHT: Nayeche (no. 30); The Death of Engiro (Mirzeler 1999, 263–6)

32 The heroes and heroines of some of these survival stories elicited curiosity in the early explorers who traversed the region or carried out scientific expeditions. In the late 1800s, Cavendish (1898) a British explorer, recorded a version of the story. It recounts a natural tragedy in Lake Turkana, which transformed a hill at the southern tip of the lake into an island and thus separated the people who lived on the hill from the mainland. Nearly half a century later, when Sir Vivian Fuchs visited South Island in 1934, he found the remains and patterns of the ancient settlement, and domestic goats, even though there was no trace of human life. This suggests the historicity of the myth, which was first recorded by Cavendish. In 1990s, I recorded variants of the Sepenya historical traditions both among the Elmolo, the Rendille, and the Samburu people and visited the South Island where Sepenya undertook the dangerous journey and visited the now extinct pastoralist and aquatic settlements.

The contemporary Elmolo people connect this particular geological disaster, which transformed the hill into an island, with the journey of Sepenya, the Elmolo ancestral heroine of Samburu pastoralist descent who was the victim of a violent storm. Comparing Elmolo with Sepenya as victims of lake tragedies is the organizing principle in Elmolo tradition. In this way, the Elmolo historical tradition reveals its strong ties with various aspects of the Jie and Turkana historical tradition, which underpin the profound ideological implications of the memory of Nayeche's journey.

33 Part 4, EHT: Sepenya (no. 2).

34 Here I refer to the Changille people who live near Ileret in northeastern tip of Lake Turkana.
35 Part 4, PB: Nacham (no. 1).
36 PB: Koryang (Mirzeler 1999, 379–80).
37 PB: Apese Arengan and His Brother Nakadon (Mirzeler 1999, 381–2).
38 Part 4, PB: The Memory of Nakol and His Father (no. 5).
39 PB: The Story of Lesiipo (no. 15).
40 PB: The Story of Adapal (no. 11).
41 Part 4, PB: The Memory of Aonyot (no. 2).
42 Part 4, JFT: Napeikisina (no. 13); Napeikisina (Mirzeler 1999, 179–87).
43 JFT: Napeikisina (nos. 13 and 14).
44 Part 4, JFT: The Man Whose Child Was Eaten by the Hyena (no. 5).
45 Part 4, JFT: The Rabbit Who Did Not Drink Water (no. 6).
46 Part 4, JFT: The Hyena Who Ate the Baby Goat, The Hyena and the Bell, The Hyena and the Calf (nos. 4, 9, and 10).
47 JFT: Napeikisina (Mirzeler 1999, 179–87).
48 Part 4, JFT: The Man Whose Child Was Eaten by the Hyena (no. 5).
49 Part 4, JFT: Napeikisina (no. 13); JFT: Napeikisina (Mirzeler 1999, 179–87).
50 Part 4, JFT: The Elephant and the Fox (no. 2).
51 Part 4, JFT: A Bat and His Friends Who Went Raiding (no. 3).
52 Part 4, JFT: The Story of the Rabbit Who Was Caught Stealing Food, The Story of a Monkey Who Was Caught Stealing Food (nos. 8 and 11).
53 JFT: The Honey-Badger and the Baboon (no.1).

4 The Jie Landscape, Memory, and Historical Tradition

1 Part 4, JTHT: Original Ancestral Fire (no. 23); also see Orwakol and His Seven Wives (Mirzeler 1999, 231–4).
2 According to some storytellers, one of the important functions of the *anyuli* image in Daidai is to forewarn the Jie people about the coming of famines and sicknesses. When the Jie original family first settled in Daidai, Orwakol performed a ritual entitled Angola to chase away sickness and various other calamities. After the performance, the storytellers posit, Orwakol thrust the *anyuli*, into the ground in Daidai in remembrance of that original performance of the Angola ritual and told the people:

   "'Whenever hunger strikes and you experience hardship and disease, come here and sacrifice your cows and bulls. Before you disperse, I want you to remember that there will be calamities. I will warn you with the sign of this *anyuli* (metal bar) that you see out of these gathered stones. When the *anyuli* appears from the stones you must sacrifice your animals here. The iron bar will go down by itself after you do that.'" JHT: The Story of Anyuli (Mirzeler 1999, 226–7).

According to the Jie storytellers, the *anyuli*, resting on the eastern frame of the granite mass immersed in the ground, testifies to Orwakol's sacrifice of the gray bull Engiro, his offering of the *amachar* (cattle brand) to his sons, and the original offering of sorghum grains to his wives. As I elaborate, the *anyuli* appeared in 2002, and Nakapor, the then Jie firemaker, performed an Angola ritual in Daidai. According to Lamphear's (1976, 97) research, anywil (*anyuli*), as a symbol, is used in the Bari ritual to exorcise illness from the villages. He finds the parallel usage of the iron-bar symbol among the Jie, Dodos, and Lotuko people.

3 According Agole Aldos, a great Labworian storyteller, the first iron maker in Labwor was Omongo. Omongo was the first person who built the iron furnace and melted the *elelo*, the iron ore of Mount Toror. It was also Omongo who forged the spear that ruptured the body of Engiro (Interview with Agole Aldo, Abim, 14 March 1997).

4 JTHT: The Great Sacrifice of Long Ago (no. 32); also see The Death of Engiro (Mirzeler 1999, 243–4, 245–8).

5 According to Lamphear (1972, 504) there is a small site around Koteen that contains "very thin shards of 'deep-grooved' pottery and microliths." During my several visit in the area, I was unable to locate this small site. I was, however, able to locate large shallow-basin grinding stones on the northeastern part of the hill that attest to the presence of the ancient agricultural settlements of the area.

6 JTHT: Dongiro, the Cradle Land (no. 25).

7 Lodoch drew upon this description elsewhere in another historical tradition, a typical scene in the dry course of Nangalol Apolon, the great river, which characterizes the rivers of the plateau and plain as being full of the footprints of the ancestors. When talking about Nangalol Apolon, the storyteller always says something about an important river named Lotirr River that flows parallel to Nangalol Apolon and is near Katarot, a rock which resembles Daidai, an ancient ancestral settlement, where the Jie and Turkana occasionally gather for peacemaking ceremonies and to offer sacrifices. During these ceremonies they pour water of the Lotirr River over one another to cool themselves and become calm (*akitililim*). During these ceremonies the Jie and the Turkana also make fire and exchange it. They call this place Katarot, which literally means cold, not only because it is cold, however, but because there are not enough trees with which to make fire.

5 Historical Tradition and Poetic Persuasion of Pastness

1 Because of the political sensitivity of this performance case study, I use pseudonyms for names of people and places, and I have altered the nature of the conflict in order to protect the identity of the participants in the performance event.
2 Koromwai is an unpopulated place near Rengen. Koromwai derives its name from ngikoroma, which means thorny tall trees.
3 Nyakwai is a place east of Labwor. According to oral traditions, people from Bokoro settled in a place called Rogom. Later people from Panyangara also went and settled in Nyakwai in a place called Loopongo. Later the people from Panyangara and the people from Bokora who settled in Nyakwai joined together and resettled in a place called Pupu. Tradition also indicates that some Labwor people from Morulem also joined the Bokora and the Panyangara people in Pupu, and, as a result, the Pupu became a mixed community.

6 The Return of Nayeche and the Gray Bull Engiro

1 I borrow the term "implicit meaning" from J. Vansina (1985). For Vansina, implicit meaning of oral tradition refers to how the original memory images come to be depicted the way they are in a particular tradition. The point of exploring implicit meanings of oral traditions is to move beyond their "explicit meaning" (143) and to understand how and why people recount oral traditions. Also see Mirzeler (2004).
2 As mentioned earlier, Nairanabwo was a prophet remembered for preventing famines and ensuring good harvests.
3 Also see the debate on this issue between Mirzeler (2007a, 2007b) and Knighton (2005, 2007).
4 According to Pamela Gulliver, the Jie women often talked about young people going to the Tarash River region and never returning. For Pamela Gulliver, the story of Nayeche indeed is the story of the young people who refuse to return to Najie from the Turkana land once they are in the plains of the Turkana (Interview with Pamela Gulliver, London, July 2002).
5 The Turkana women do not consciously plan to go to participate in the Jie harvest ritual. Rather they go to Najie during the harvest to help their Jie relatives and friends in harvesting their gardens and to receive some grain in return for their help.

7 A Jie Storyteller's Autobiography

1 In a similar work, Crapanzano examines the autobiography of Tuhami, a
   Moroccan from Meknes in a work entitled, *Tuhami: Portrait of a Moroccan*. This
   work can hardly be called an autobiography or life history, since all we see in
   the book are Tuhami's reactions to Crapanzano, a psychoanalytically oriented
   American anthropologist. We find Crapanzano at the center of his book that
   is supposed to be about Tuhami. In fact, the book reads like Crapanzano's
   autobiography, rather than someone else's. In this respect, Crapanzano's
   work differs from Kennedy's. Crapanzano gives the reader a full account of
   how he met Tuhami and how he interviewed him and recorded his life history step by step. However, we rarely hear Tuhami speak. Crapanzano places
   his voice in the foreground and keeps Tuhami, and Lhacen, the translator, in
   the background thus creating a distance between himself and Tuhami. This
   distancing is compounded with the presence of Lhacen, who not only trans-
   lates, but also makes sure that Tuhami tells the truth. In *Moroccan Dialogues:
   Anthropology in Question*, Dweyer is critical of Crapanzano's psychoanalytical
   approach, and he tries to distinguish systematically between ethnographic
   dialogue and autobiographical dialogue, or what he calls the Moroccan
   dialogue. In Dweyer's view, Crapanzano's portrait of Tuhami is not autobiographical, asserting that the psychoanalytical genre interfered with his
   dialogue with Tuhami. This interference involves the conflicting motivations
   and autobiographical assumptions of both Crapanzano and Tuhami. To
   avoid the problems of interference, Dweyer considers Moroccan narrative
   and philological conventions in his dialogues with Faqir, the person with
   whom Dweyer worked. In recording and translating the dialogues, steeped
   in Moroccan narrative convention, the full meaning of Faqir's growing up
   experiences emerge full of symbolism, illuminating self and other relations,
   which shed light on anthropology's key concerns at the time.
2 JTHT: Nayeche (no. 30).
3 JTHT: The Great Sacrifice of Long Ago (no. 32).
4 Part 4, JFT: The Elephant and the Fox (no. 2).
5 Part 4, JFT: The Elephant and the Fox (no. 2).
6 Part 4, JFT: A Bat and His Friends Who Went Raiding (no. 3).

The Stories

1 A source of sacred clay, located on the northern bank of Longiro River,
   next to Daidai.
2 A branch of a particular tree called *ngalita*, which grows in Karamoja.

Glossary of Places and Selected Words

Abim	small town in Labwor county
Acholi	one of the communities west of the Jie people
akimwaar	harvest rituals
Akuj	God
Alerek Hill	sacred hill in Abim, Labwor County
amachar	cattle brand
apolon	big, important
Apule River	one of the main rivers in Karamoja
arii	cattle enclosure
asapan	age-class
atap	bread
awatoun	part of marriage ceremony during which the bride returns her natal home, taking the last part of the cattle as a bride-price
eteran	bride
Daidai	Jie cradle land and a sacred grove on the banks of Longiro River
dhuka	shop or store
Dongiro	Jie ancestral cradle land in southeastern Ethiopia near the Omo River
Dopeth River	main seasonal river in northern Najie
ebela	stick
echula	bridewealth
edula	granary
edunyet	neighborhood
eemut	story (*ngiemuto*, plural)
eepit	fire stick

ekal	yard
ekapilan	witch, evil person
ekapolon	important person, mostly referring to kraal leaders or chiefs
ekasukout	elders
ekeworon	firemaker
ekerujan	dreamer
ekicholong	stool
ekile	male
ekipe	water spirit, symbolic representation of female spirit associated with thunder, rain, moon (*ngipian*, plural)
ekisil	peace
ekitoi	tree, wood, or branches; medicine or poison
ekor	honey-badger
ekoworan	prophet
ejamu	ox hide
ejie	fight
elope	self
emesek	ram
emoit	enemy, stranger
emon	ox
emunyen	sacred ritual clay
emuron	traditional doctor, prophet, diviner
eparait	ancestor, an ancestral spirit
epiding	small door
etaaba	rock
etal	tradition, custom (*ngitalia*, plural)
etau	spirit, soul, life force
etem	sitting and gathering place for men in or outside the homestead
eteran	bridegroom
Jimos	village in Najie
Kaabong	small town in Dodos, formerly known as Tshudi Tshudi
Kacheri	small Jie community in northern Najie
Kalakuruk	sacred rock in Losilang section of the Orwakol clan
Kanawat	one of the territorial sections of the Orwakol clan
Karamoja	northeastern district of Uganda
Karimojong Cluster	seven tribes, speaking dialects of Niloitic language, all offshoots of one another

Kiru	village near Abim, Labwor
Komukunyu	one of the territorial sections of the Orwakol clan
Koteen Hill	hill in Karamoja Plateau
Kotido	one of the territorial sections of the Orwakol clan
Kotyang	one of the territorial sections of the Orwakol clan
lara	dry-season month, more or less corresponding to November
Lokalodiny	territorial division belonging to the Lodiny clan
Lokatap Rock	rocky hill in the Rengen division of the Lodiny clan. Lokatap Rock, cradle land for the Lodiny clan, located in the Lokalodiny section in Najie
lokijuka	literally, pushing; used by the Karimojong people to denote the coming of the British Protectorate of Uganda, pushing north into Karamoja
Longiro River	one of the major rivers in the Lokorwakol territorial division in Najie
Losilang	one of the territorial sections of the Orwakol clan
Lokibuwa	water wells near Panyangara, at the foot of Mount Toror
Loyoro	small town in northern Dodoth
Magos	low-lying hills southeast of Nakapelimoru
Moroto	town in Karamoja
Moru A Nayeche	hill on the headwaters of *Tarash River*, where Nayeche, the Turkana heroine of origin, settled; named for Nayeche
Moru a Eker	sacred rock near Jimos village
Mount Toror	one of the mountains in southwestern Najie
Mount Moroto	one of the largest mountains in Karamoja
Moru Apolon	mountain in Turkana land
Moruongor	village in near Jimos village
Mzumgu	Swahili word referring to foreigner, used mainly to refer to the foreigners of European descent
Muhindi	Swahili word, referring to people of Indian origin
Nadul	Nakapor's wife
Najie	Jie land in the central Karamoja Plateau
Nakapelimoru	largest territorial section of the Orwakol clan
Nangalol Apolon	one of the main rivers in Karamoja Plateau
Napau	Turkana storyteller from Kalobeyei, northern Kenya
ngaatuk	cattle
Ngijie	Jie people in plural, also warriors

ngikujit	chyme, undigested foodstuff in the intestines of cows and goat
ngimumwa	sorghum
Nyanga	one of the Jie cradle lands
Ngipalajam	Jie generation set, which, according to Lamphear (1976, 119), was initiated in the early 1700s
Panyangara	one of the territorial sections of the Orwakol clan
Poet clan	Jie clan that makes the granary for the firemaker
Teuso	one of the Karimojong Cluster people, living south of the Karamoja community
Toposa	one of the Karimojong Clusters, living in southern Sudan
Toroi	village in Losilang
Turkana	one of the largest Karimojong Cluster tribes, living in the Rift Valley in a semidesert zone in northern Kenya

References

Abu-Lughod, L. (1986). *Veiled Sentiments: Honor and Poetry in a Bedouin Society*. Berkley: University of California Press.

Amadiume, I., and A. An-Na'im. (2000). "Introduction: Facing Truth, Voicing Justice." In I. Amadiume and A. An-Na'im (Eds.), *The Politics of Memory: Truth, Healing and Social Justice*, 1–19. London: Zed Books.

Anttonen, P.J. (2005). *Tradition through Modernity: Postmodernism and the Nation-State in Folklore Scholarship*. Helsinki: Finnish Literature Society.

Bakhtin, M.M. (1981). *The Dialogic Imagination*. Austin: University of Texas Press.

Barber, J. (1962). "The Karamoja District of Uganda: A Pastoral People under Colonial Rule." *Journal of African History*, 3(01), 111–24. http://dx.doi.org/10.1017/S0021853700002760

Barber, J. (1968). *Imperial Frontier*. Nairobi, Kenya: East Africa Publishing House.

Barber, K. (1991). *I Could Speak until Tomorrow: Oriki, Women, and the Past in a Yoruba Town*. Washington, DC: Smithsonian Press.

Barber, K. (2007). *The Anthropology of Texts, Persons and Publics: Oral and Written Culture in Africa and Beyond*. Cambridge: Cambridge University Press.

Basgoz, I. (1986). *Folklor yazilari (tr. Writings in Folklore)*. Istanbul: Anadolu Yayinlari.

Basgoz, I. (2008). *Hikaye: Turkish Folk Romance as Performance Art*. Bloomington: Indiana University Press.

Basso, E.B. (1995). *The Last Cannibals: A South American Oral History*. Austin: University of Texas Press.

Bauman, R. (1977). *Verbal Art as Performance*. Illinois: Waveland Press.

Bauman, R. (1986). *Story, Performance and Event: Contextual Studies of Oral Narrative*. Cambridge: Cambridge University Press. http://dx.doi.org/10.1017/CBO9780511620935

Behrend, Heike. (1999). *Alice Lakwena and the Holy Spirits: War in Northern Uganda 1986–1997*. Oxford: James Currey.

Bell, W.D.M. (1925 [1958]). *The Wanderings of an Elephant Hunter*. London: Neville Spearman and the Holland Press.

Bivins, M.W. (2007). *Telling Stories, Making Histories: Women, Words, and Islam in Nineteenth-Century Hausaland and the Sokoto Caliphate*. Portsmouth: Heinemann.

Bloch, M. (1977). "The Past and the Present in the Present." *Man*, *12*(2), 278–92. http://dx.doi.org/10.2307/2800799

Bloch, M. (1986). *From Blessing to Violence*. Cambridge: Cambridge University Press.

Bohannon, P. (1953). "Concepts of Time among the Tiv of Nigeria." *Southwestern Journal of Anthropology*, *9*, 251–62.

Bourdieu, P. (1977). *Outline of a Theory of Practice*. Cambridge: Cambridge University Press. http://dx.doi.org/10.1017/CBO9780511812507

Boyer, P. (1990). *Tradition as Truth and Communication: A Cognitive Description of Traditional Discourse*. Cambridge: Cambridge University Press. http://dx.doi.org/10.1017/CBO9780511521058

Briggs, C. (1988). *Competence in Performance: Creativity of Tradition in Mexicano Verbal Art*. Philadelphia: University of Pennsylvania Press.

Brumble, D. (1988). *American Indian Autobiography*. Berkeley: University of California Press.

Campbell, J. (1972). *The Hero with a Thousand Faces*. Princeton: Princeton University Press.

Cashman, R. (2008). *Storytelling on the Northern Irish Border: Characters and Community*. Bloomington: Indiana University Press.

Caton, S. (1990). *Peaks of Yemen I Summon: Poetry as Cultural Practice in a North Yemeni Tribe*. Berkley: University of California Press.

Cavendish, H.S.H. (1898). "Through Somaliland and around the South of Lake Rudolf." *Geographical Journal*, *11*(4), 372–96. http://dx.doi.org/10.2307/1774709

Cisternino, M. (1979). *Karamoja the Human Zoo: The History of Planning for Karamoja with Some Tentative Counter Planning*. University of Wales Swansea: Center for Development Studies.

Cisterino, M. (1981). *Some Socio-Economic Evaluation of Famine and Relief in Karamoja: What Next?* Moroto: Moroto Diocese. Office of Social Services and Development.

Cohen, D. (1977). *Womunafu's Bunafu: A Study of Authority in a Nineteenth-Century African Community*. Princeton: Princeton University Press.

Cohen, D. (2001). "Introduction: Voices, Words, and African History."
In L. White, S. Miescher, and D. Cohen (Eds.), *African Words, African Voices: Critical Practices in Oral History*, 1–21. Bloomington: Indiana University Press.

Cunnison, I. (1951). *History of the Luapula: An Essay on the Historical Notions of a Central African Tribe*. Lusaka, Zambia: Rhodes-Livingston Papers.

Collins, R.O. (2006). "The Turkana Patrol of 1918 Reconsidered." In special issue, M.K. Mirzeler (Ed.), "Lake Rudolf (Turkana) as Colonial Icon in East Africa," *Ethnohistory (Columbus, Ohio)*, 53(2), 95–119. http://dx.doi.org/10.1215/00141801-53-1-95

Connerton, P. (1989). *How Societies Remember*. Cambridge: Cambridge University Press. http://dx.doi.org/10.1017/CBO9780511628061

Crapanzano, V. (1980). *Tuhami: Portrait of a Moraccan*. Chicago: The University of Chicago Press.

Darley, H. (1935). *Slaves and Ivory*. New York: Robert M. McBride and Co.

De Maille, R. (1985). *The Sixth Grandfather: Black Elk's Teachings Given to John G. Neihardt*. Lincoln: University of Nebraska Press.

Dilley, R.M. (1989). "Secrets and Skills: Apprenticeship among Tukolor." Michael Coy (Ed.), *Apprenticeship: From Theory to Method and Back Again*. 181–9. New York: State University of New York Press.

Dorson, R.M. (1972). *Introduction. African Folklore*. Bloomington: Indiana University Press.

Dweyer, K. (1982). *Moroccan Dialogues: Anthropology in Question*. Baltimore: The Johns Hopkins University Press.

Dyson-Hudson, N. (1966). *Karimojong Politics*. Oxford: Clarendon Press.

Eaton, D. (2010). "The Rise of the 'Traider': The Commercialization of Raiding in Karamoja." *Nomadic Peoples*, 14(2), 106–22. http://dx.doi.org/10.3167/np.2010.140207

Eliade, M. (1960). *Myths, Dreams, and Mysteries*. London: Harvill.

Feierman, S. (1974). *The Shambaa Kingdom: A History*. Madison: University of Wisconsin Press.

Fernandez, J.W. (1986). *Persuasions and Performances: The Play of Tropes in Culture*. Bloomington: Indiana University Press.

Flores, R. (1995). *Los Pastores: History of Performance in the Mexican Shepherd's Play of South Texas*. Washington: Smithsonian Institution Press.

Flores, R. (2002). *Remembering the Alamo: Memory, Modernity, and the Master Symbol*. Austin: University of Texas Press.

Galaty, J. (1986). "East African Hunters and Pastoralists in Regional Perspective: An 'Ethnoanthropological' Approach." *Sprache und Geschichte in Afrika*, 7(1), 105–31.

Geertz, Clifford. (1973). *The Interpretation of Culture*. New York: Basic Books.

Glassie, H. (2010). *Prince Twins Seven-Seven: His Art, His Life in Nigeria, His Exile in America*. Bloomington: Indiana University Press.

Gray, S. (2010). "'Someone Dies in Your Lap': Structural, Ecological and Political Effects on Child and Maternal Health Care Decisions, Moroto District, Uganga, 2004." *Nomadic Peoples*, 14(2), 44–71. http://dx.doi.org/10.3167/np.2010.140204

Gray, S. (2000). "A Memory of Loss: Ecological Politics, Local History, and the Evolution of Karimojong Violence." *Human Organization*, 59(4), 401–18.

Guiomar, J. (1989). "Vidal de la Blache's Geography of France." In P. Nora (Ed.), *Realms of Memory*, 187–209. New York: Columbia University Press.

Gulliver, P., and P.H. Gulliver (Eds.). (1953). *The Central Nilo-Hamites*. London: International African Institute.

Gulliver, P.H. (1951). *A Preliminary Survey of Turkana*. Cape Town: University of Cape Town.

Gulliver, P.H. (1952a). "The Karamojong Cluster." *Africa: Journal of the International Africa Institute*, 22(1), 1–22. http://dx.doi.org/10.2307/1157083

Gulliver, P.H. (1952b). "Bell-Oxen and Ox-Names among the Jie." *Uganda Journal*, 16, 73–5.

Gulliver, P.H. (1953). "The Population of Karamoja." *Uganda Journal*, 17, 68–185.

Gulliver, P.H. (1955). *The Family Herd*. London: Routeldge and Kegan Paul.

Gulliver, P.H. (1971). "Jie Agriculture." *Uganda Journal*, 35, 65–70.

Hakamies, P. (2010). "Story and Reality in Folkloristics." *Folklore Fellows' Network*, 39, 9–11.

Halbwachs, M. (1950). *The Collective Memory*. New York: Harper-Colophon Books.

Hanretta, S. (2009). Islam and Social Change in French West Africa: History of an Emancipatory Community. Cambridge: Cambridge University Press.

Henige, D. (1974). *The Chronology of Oral Tradition: Quest for Chimera*. Oxford: Clarendon Press.

Henige, D. (1982). *Oral Historiography*. London: Longman.

Henige, D. (1986). "African History and the Rule of Evidence: Is Declaring Victory Enough?" In B. Jewsiewicki and D. Newbury (Eds.), *African Historiographies: What History for Which Africa?* 91–104. London: Sage Publications.

Henige, D. (2005). *Historical Evidence and Argument*. Madison: University of Wisconsin Press.

Herring, R. (1974). "A History of the Labwor Hills." Unpublished doctoral dissertation. University of California, Santa Barbara.

Herzfeld, M. (1991). *A Place in History: Social and Monumental Time in a Cretan Town*. Princeton: Princeton University Press.

Herzfeld, M. (1982). *Ours Once More: Folklore, Ideology, and the Making of Modern Greece*. Austin: University of Texas Press.

Hobsbawm, R, and Terence Ranger eds. 1983. *The Invention of Tradition*. Cambridge: Cambridge University Press.

Hofmeyr, I. (1993). *"We Spent Our Years as a Tale That Is Told": Oral Historical Narrative in a South African Chiefdom*. London: James Currey.

Jackson, M. (2006). *The Politics of Storytelling: Violence, Transgression, and Intersubjectivity*. Copenhagen: University of Copenhagen.

Karp, I. (1980). "Beer Drinking and Social Experience in an African Society: An Essay in Formal Sociology." In I. Karp and C. Bird (Eds.), *Explorations in African Systems of Thought*, 83–119. Bloomington: Indiana University Press.

Karp, I. (1978). *Fields of Change among the Iteso of Kenya*. London: Routledge and Kegan.

Kassam, A. (2006). "The People of the Five 'Drums': Gabra Ethnohistorical Origins." *Ethnohistory (Columbus, Ohio)*, 53(1), 173–94. http://dx.doi.org/10.1215/00141801-53-1-173

Kennedy, J. (1977). *Struggle for Change in a Nubian Community*. Palo Alto: Mayfield Publishing Company.

Knighton, B. (2005). *The Vitality of Karamojong Religion: Dying Tradition or Living Faith*. Hants, UK: Ashgate Publishing Ltd.

Knighton, B. (2007). "Of War-Leader and Firemakers: A Rejoinder." *History in Africa*, 34(1), 411–20. http://dx.doi.org/10.1353/hia.2007.0009

Kratz, C. (1993). "We've Always Done It Like This... Except a Few Details: Tradition and 'Innovation' in Okiek Ceremonies." *Comparative Studies in Society and History*, 35(1), 30–65. http://dx.doi.org/10.1017/S0010417500018259

Kratz, C. (1994). *Affecting Performance: Meaning, Movement, and Experience in Okiek Women's Initiation*. Washington: Smithsonian Institution Press.

Kratz, C. (2001). "Conversations and Lives." In L. White, D. Miescher, and D. Cohen (Eds.), *African Words, African Voices: Critical Practices in Oral History*, 127–61. Bloomington: Indiana University Press.

Krupat, A. (1998). "America's Histories." *American Literary History*, 10(1), 124–46. http://dx.doi.org/10.1093/alh/10.1.124

Krupat, A. (1985). *For Those Who Come After: A Study of American Indian Autobiography*. Berkeley: University of California Press.

Lamphear, J. (1972). "The Oral History of the Jie of Uganda." Unpublished doctoral dissertation. University of London, England.

Lamphear, J. (1976). *The Traditional History of the Jie of Uganda*. Oxford: Clarendon Press.

Lamphear, J. (1986). "The Persistence of Hunting and Gathering in a Pastoral World." *Sprache und Geschichte in Afrika, 7*(2), 227–65.

Lamphear, J. (1988). "The People of the Grey Bull: The Origin and Expansion of the Turkana." *Journal of African History, 29*, 27–39.

Lamphear, J., and Webster, J.B. (1971). "The Jie-Acholi War: Oral Evidence from Two Sides of the Battle Front." *Uganda Journal, 35*, 23–42.

Langness, L. (1965). *The Life History in Anthropological Science*. New York: Holt Reinhart.

Lefebvre, H. (1974 [1984]). *The Production of Space*. Malden: Blackwell Publishing.

Levi-Strauss, C. (1967). "The Story of Asdiwal." In E. Leach (Ed.), *The Structural Study of Myth and Totemism*, 1–48. London: Tavistock Publications Limited.

Lokuruka, M., and Lokuruka, P. (2006). "Ramifications of the 1918 Turkana Patrol: Narratives by Nguturkana." In M.K. Mirzeler (Ed.), *Lake Rudolf (Turkana) as Colonial Icon in East Africa*, a special issue of *Ethnohistory, 53*(2), 121–41. http://dx.doi.org/10.1215/00141801-53-1-121

Mauss, M. (1967). *The Gift*. New York: Free Press. [1925].

Mburu, N. (2001). "The Proliferation of Guns and Rustling in Karamoja and the Turkana districts: The Case of Appropriate Disarmament Strategies." http://www.journalogy.net/Author/34519926/nene-mburu

Meeker, M. (1979). *Literature and Violence in North Arabia*. Cambridge: Cambridge University Press.

Mills, M. (1990). *Oral Narrative in Afghanistan: The Individual in Tradition*. New York: Garland Press.

Mirzeler, M. (1999). "Veiled Histories and the Childhood Memories of a Jie Storyteller." (Unpublished doctoral dissertation). University of Wisconsin, Madison.

Mirzeler, M. (2004). "Oral Tradition of Origin as a Remembered Memory and Repeated Event: Sorghum as a Gift in Jie and Turkana Historical Consciousness." *Ethnohistory (Columbus, Ohio), 51*(2), 223–56. http://dx.doi.org/10.1215/00141801-51-2-223

Mirzeler, M. (2006a). "The Embodiment of the Voyage of Sir Vivian Fuchs to the South Island in the Elmolo Oral Tradition." *Ethnohistory (Columbus, Ohio), 53*(1), 195–220. http://dx.doi.org/10.1215/00141801-53-1-195

Mirzeler, M. (2006b). "The Journey of Major Rayne on the Banks of Turkwell River: Silent Political Assignment and Travel Writing." *History in Africa*,

33(1), 271–86. http://dx.doi.org/10.1353/hia.2006.0018

Mirzeler, M. (2007a). "The Importance of Being Honest: Verifying Citations, Rereading Historical Sources, and Establishing Authority in the Great Karamoja Debate." *History in Africa, 34,* 383–409. http://dx.doi.org/ 10.1353/hia.2007.0014

Mirzeler, M. (2007b). "The Trickster of Karamoja." *History in Africa, 34,* 421–6. http://dx.doi.org/10.1353/hia.2007.0015

Mirzeler, M. (2009). "Sorghum as a Gift of Self: The Jie Oral Tradition as Memory." *History in Africa, 36,* 390–415.

Mirzeler, M., and Young, C. (2000). "Pastoral Politics in the Northeast Periphery in Uganda: AK-47 as a Change Agent." *Journal of Modern African Studies, 38*(3), 407–29. http://dx.doi.org/10.1017/S0022278X00003402

Mirzeler, M., and Jafarov, A. (2012). "The Memory of Loss: Voices of Azeri Storytellers from Nagorno Karabakh." *Journal of Muslim Minority Affairs, 32*(2), 253–68. http://dx.doi.org/10.1080/13602004.2012.694669

Mirzeler, M.K. (2012). "Voices of Karimojong Storytellers." *Anthropology News.* http://www.anthropology-news.org/index.php/2012/09/14/voices-of-karimojong

Mkutu, K. (2010). "Complexities of Livestock Raiding in Karamoja." *Nomadic Peoples, 14*(2), 87–104. http://dx.doi.org/10.3167/np.2010.140206

Mkutu, K. (2003). *Pastoral Conflict and Small Arms: The Kenya-Uganda Border Region.* London: Safeworld.

Muller, H. (1989). *Changing Generations: Dynamics of Generation and Age-Sets in Southeastern Sudan (Toposa) and Northwestern Kenya (Turkana).* Saabrucken: Verlag Breitenbach Publisher.

Nagashima, N. (1968). *Historical Relations among the Central Nilo-Hamites: An Analysis of Historical Traditions.* University of East Africa Social Science Council Conference: Sociology Papers. 2. Makerere Institute of Social Research.

Narayan, K. (1989). *Storytellers, Saints, and Scoundrels: Folk Narrative in Hindu Religious Teaching.* Philadelphia: University of Pennsylvania Press.

Neumann, A. (1898 [1994]). *Elephant Hunting in East Equatorial Africa.* London: Rowland Ward.

Nora, P. (1989). "Between Memory and History: Les lieux de memoire." *Representations (Berkeley, Calif.), 26*(1), 7–25. http://dx.doi.org/10.1525/ rep.1989.26.1.99p0274v

Nora, P. (1989). Introduction to *Realms of Memory,* In P. Nora (Ed.), *Realms of memory (IX-XII).* New York: Columbia University Press.

Novelli, B. (1988). *Aspects of Karimojon Ethnosociology.* Italy: Novastampa di Verona.

Novelli, B. (1994). *The Karamojong: A 'Resistant' People*. Kampala, Uganda: Karamoja Diocese Publication.

Novelli, B. (1999). *Karimojong Traditional Religion*. Kampala, Uganda: Comboni Missionaries.

Ocan, C. (1994). "Pastoral Resources and Conflicts in North-Eastern Uganda: The Karimojong Case." *Nomadic Peoples Journal* 34/35, 97–142. http://cnp .nonuniv.ox.ac.uk/NP_journal/archive.shtml

Ogot, B.A. (1994). *The Jii-speakers: Economic Adaptation and Change*. Kisumu, Kenya: Ayange Press.

Ogot, B.A. (2001). "The Construction of Luo Identity and History." In L. White, S. Miescher, and D. Cohen (Eds.), *African Words, African Voices: Critical Practices in Oral History*, 31–52. Bloomington: Indiana University Press.

Ohnuki-Tierney, E. (1993). *Rice as Self: Japanese Identities through Time*. Princeton: Princeton University Press.

Parry, J. (1985). "Death and Digestion: The Symbolism of Food and Eating in North Indian Mortuary Rites." *Man*, 20(4), 612–30. http://dx.doi.org/ 10.2307/2802753

Pazzaglia, A. (1982). *The Karimojong: Some Aspects*. Bologna, Italy: E.M.I. della Coop.

Pratt, M. (1992). *Imperial Eyes: Travel Writing and Transculturation*. London: Routledge.

Raheja, G.G. (1988). *The Poison in the Gift: Ritual, Prestation, and the Dominant Caste in a North Indian Village*. Chicago: The University of Chicago Press.

Reid, R. (1997). "The Reign of Kabaka Nakibinge: Myth or Watershed?" *History in Africa*, 24, 287–97. http://dx.doi.org/10.2307/3172031

Schieffelin, E. (1976 [2005]). *The Sorrow of the Lonely and the Burning of the Dancers*. New York: Palgrave Macmillan. http://dx.doi.org/10.1057/ 9781403981790

Scheub, H. (1969). "The Ntsomi: A Xhosa Performing Art." (Unpublished doctoral dissertation.) University of Wisconsin, Madison.

Scheub, H. (1988). "And So I Grew Up." In P.W. Romero (Ed.), *Life Histories of African Women*. London: Ashfield Press.

Scheub, H. (1996). *The Tongue is Fire: South African Storytellers and Apartheid*. Madison: University of Wisconsin Press.

Scheub, H. (1998). *Story*. Madison: University of Wisconsin Press.

Scheub, H. (2002). *The Poem in the Story: Music, Poetry, and Narrative*. Madison: University of Wisconsin Press.

Schlee, G. (1989). *Identities on the Move: Clanship and Pastoralism in Northern Kenya*. Manchester: Manchester University Press.

Schneider, W. (2008). Introduction. In W. Scheneider (Ed.), *Living with Stories: Telling, Re-telling, and Remembering*, 1–17. Logan: Utah State University.

Schweitzer, G. (1898). *Emin Pasha: His Life and Work* (Vol. I). Westminster: Archibald Constable and Co.

Shostak, M. (2000). *Nisa: The Life and the Words of a !Kung Woman*. Cambridge: Harvard University Press. [1981].

Slyomovics, S. (1998). *The Object of Memory: Arab and Jew Narrate the Palestinian Village*. Philadelphia: University of Pennsylvania Press.

Sobania, N. (1980). "The historical tradition of the eastern Lake Turkana basin c. 1840–1925." (Unpublished doctoral dissertation.) University of London, England.

Sobania, N. (1988). "Fishermen Herders: Subsistence, Survival and Cultural Change in Northern Kenya." *Journal of African History*, 29(01), 41–56. http://dx.doi.org/10.1017/S0021853700035982

Spear, T. (2003). "Neo-traditionalism and the Limits of Invention in British Colonial Africa." *Journal of African History*, 44(01), 3–27. http://dx.doi.org/10.1017/S0021853702008320

Spencer, P. (1978). "The Jie generation paradox." In P.T.W. Baxter and U. Almagor (Eds.), *Age Generation and Time: Some Features of East African Age Organizations*, 133–49. London; C. Hurst and Company.

Stites, E. (2007). "Outmigration, Return, and Resettlement in Karamoja, Uganda: The Case of Kobulin, Bokora County." Feinstein International Center, Tufts University.

Stites, E. (2013). "Identity Reconfigured: Karimojong Male Youth, Violence and Livelihoods." (Unpublished Dissertation). The Fletcher School of Law and Diplomacy, Tufts University.

Stites, E., et al. (2012). "Tradition in Transition: Customary Authority in Karamoja, Uganda." (Draft presented at African Studies Association Conference in November.)

Strathern, M. (1991 [2005]). *Partial Connections*. New York: Rowman and Littlefield.

Sundal, M. (2010). "Nowhere to Go: Karimojong Displacement and Forced Settlement." *Nomadic Peoples*, 14(2), 72–86. http://dx.doi.org/10.3167/np.2010.140205

Tedlock, D., and Mannheim, B. (Eds.). (1995). Introduction, *The Dialogic Emergence of Culture*. Urbana: University of Illinois Press.

Thomas, E.M. (1965). *Warrior Herdsmen*. New York: Alfred A. Knopf.

Tonkin, E. (1986). "Investigation of Oral Tradition." *Journal of African History*, 27(02), 203–13. http://dx.doi.org/10.1017/S0021853700036641

Tonkin, E. (1988). "Historical Discourse: The Achievement of Sieh Jeto."
    History in Africa, 15, 467–491. http://dx.doi.org/10.2307/3171876
Tonkin, E. (1992). *Narrating Our Past: The Social Construction of Oral History*.
    Cambridge: Cambridge University Press. http://dx.doi.org/10.1017/
    CBO9780511621888
Tosh, J. (1978). *Clan Leaders and Colonial Chiefs in Lango: The Political History
    of an East African Stateless Society c. 1800–1939*. Oxford: Clarendon.
Tosh, J. (2000). *The Pursuit of History: Aims, Methods, and New Directions
    in the Study of Modern History*. 3rd rev ed. Harlow: Longman.
Tosh, J. (2006). *The Pursuit of History: Aims, Methods and New Directions
    in the Study of Modern History*. London: Longman.
Tripp, A. (2010). *Museveni's Uganda: Paradoxes of Power in Hybrid Regime*.
    Boulder, Co: Lynne Rienner.
Twaddle, M. (1975). "Towards an Early History of the East African Interior."
    History in Africa, 2, 147–84. http://dx.doi.org/10.2307/3171471
Vansina, J. (1965). *Oral Tradition: A Study in Historical Methodology*. Chicago:
    Aldine Publishing.
Vansina, J. (1971). "Once Upon a Time: Oral Traditions as History in Africa."
    History in Africa, 100(2), 442–68.
Vansina, J. (1985). *Oral Tradition as History*. Madison: University of Wisconsin
    Press.
Vansina, J. (1989). "Deep-down Time: Political Tradition in Central Africa."
    African Studies Association, 16, 341–62.
Varadarajan, L. (1979, June 16). "Oral Testimony as Historical Source Material
    for Traditional and Modern India." *Economic and Political Weekly*, 14(24),
    1009–14.
Warren, D. (1976). "The Use and Misuse of Ethnohistory Data in the
    Reconstruction of Techiman-Gono (Ghana)." *Ethnohistory (Columbus, Ohio)*,
    23(4), 365–85. http://dx.doi.org/10.2307/481652
Wayland, E.J. (1931). "Preliminary Studies of the Tribes of Karamoja." *Journal
    of the Royal Anthropological Institute*, 61, 187–230.
Webster, J.B., et al. (1973). *The Iteso during the Asonya*. Nairobi: East African
    Publishing House.
Were, G.S., and Wilson, D.A. (1968). *East Africa through a Thousand Years:
    A.D. 1000 to the Present day*. Ibadan: Evans Brothers Limited.
Whitehead, N. (2003). "Three Patamuna Trees: Landscape and History in the
    Guyana Highlands." In N. Whitehead (Ed.), *Histories and Historicities in
    Amazonia*, 59–77. Lincoln: University of Nebraska Press.
Willis, J. (2002). *Potent Brews: A Social History of Alcohol in East Africa 1850–1999*.
    Oxford: James Currey.

Wilson, J.G. (1970). "Preliminary Observations on the Oropom People of Karamoja." *Uganda Journal*, 34(2), 125–45.

Young, C. (1994). *The African Colonial State in Comparative Perspective.* New Haven: Yale University Press.

Young, C. (2012). *The Postcolonial State in Africa: Fifty Years of Independence, 1960–2010.* Madison: University of Wisconsin Press.

Index

among children, 230–1; Jimos village's survival, 61; landscape and memory, 143–4; as metaphor, 208–9; model of womb, 147–8; wife as keeper of, 77; as womb of mother (creation story), 117

Guiomar, J., 141–2, 160

Gulliver, Pamela, xxi, 207, 209, 212, 326n1, 332n4

Gulliver, P.H., xxi, 6–7, 36, 39, 40, 67, 159, 171, 205, 207, 209, 212, 243, 250

guns and gun trade, 74–7; AK-47, 49–57, 54–5, 57, 74, 160, 174–5, 180, 247; in colonial encounters (1910s), 46–7; disarmament in storytellers' narratives, 55–63; military disarmament of Jie, 52. *See also* disarmament

Halbwachs, M., 10–11, 142

harvest rituals: burial of the hoe, 53; details of, 211–12, 228; and historical traditions, 87; interlock with Nayeche and the gray bull Engiro story, 204–16; and marriage ceremony, 199, 230; Nayeche's story's connection to, 117; in storytelling, 23

Herring, R., 40, 42

Herzfeld, M., 12, 141–3, 150, 152, 160

historical traditions/oral traditions: appearance of cultural hero, 102; as autobiography, 231–4; biographical tales, compared, 130; collection of, 255–6; contradictory double images, 116–17; create moral topography, 62; as discourse, 22–3; Elmolo and others (list), 344–5; Elmolo and others (transcriptions), 281–4; extension of customs and traditions, 104; fantasy elements, 7; flexibility of memory in, 245–6; folktales, compared, 135–7; food and resource sharing, 118–19, 251–2; hunger and thirst themes, 101–4; Jie and Turkana (list), 336–44; Jie and Turkana (transcriptions), 264–81; and Lodoch's autobiography, 236; and Logwee's storytelling, 94; meaning in metaphors of, 53–5; in mediations, 188; narrated by men, 85; performance, and interpretation, 93; performance, importance, 192–5; performance, occasions for, 81–2; performance, act of recalling as, 13–14; P.H. Gulliver's interpretation, 6–7; plots and roles of, 21–3, 109–22; reference to time/dates in, 111; and socialization, 230–1, 233–4; terminology, 10; thematic images, 104–5; thematic images, shared, 107; themes, Nayeche story as common, 101, 120–3; themes images, 93–4; Turkish, 4–5; of war with Jie and A Bat story, 238–9. *See also* biographical tales; folktales; Nayeche and the gray bull Engiro; stories; storytelling and storytellers

history and historical experiences: in context of present, 7–11; historical consciousness, 18; partial connections, 247–8; and poetic discourses of vulnerability, 11–12; and project of survival, 11–12; reference to time/dates in historical traditions, 111–12

Hobsbawm, R., 141

in historical context, xxi, 40, 44–7, 250; in historical memory, 45, 109
Losilang, in Lokorwakol, 43, 337; fieldwork, 66–7; map, *xv–xvi*; wife of Orwakol, 37, 143, 147, 149, 153, 202–3; wife of Orwakol and grain, 218, 228–9, 274; wife of Orwakol and historical tradition, 233. *See also* Jimos village
Lotum (Jie firemaker), xxi, 72, 73, 213
Lowatomoe (pseud.) (Jie scholar), 59–60
Lowokor, Philip, xix

Maasai people, 280
Mannheim, B., 14, 181
marriage: among villages, 38; in Aonyot story, 128–30; ceremonies in storytelling, 23; and harvest rituals, 199, 216; of Lodoch to brother's wife, 231–2; and Nayeche story, 117, 229–30
Marshall Thomas, E., xxi, 36
Matheniko people: enemies of the Jie, 171–2, 268; and generation-set, 326n3; and Jie origins, 275–6; neighbors of the Jie, 35; peace ceremony, 54
Mauss, M., 236
Mburu, N., 50, 59
mediations: ceremonies, 331n7; cultural public performances, 172–3; disputes over resources, 94; elders in conflict resolution, 173–80, 184–6; of November 1996 conflict, 173–80; October 1997, Lokatap Rock, 184–5; peace ceremony, 54; process of, 187–8; and rhetoric of pastness, 164–5; and vulnerability from environment, 170–1

Meeker, M., 23, 24, 165–71
memory and remembering: Dadai as place of origin, 147–51, 152–3 (*see also* Daidai [Jie shrine]); in droughts and famines, 107–8; embedded in landscape, 11, 15–16, 241–4; embodied in landscape, 114; flexibility of oral traditions, 245; and historical traditions, 110, 236–7; Jimos village community of, 62; landscape as shrine, 151–2; and landscape in performance, 140–3; Lokatap Rock as place of origin, 155–6; of Loriang, 45; and modernization, 54–5, 159–63; in *ntsomi* oral tradition, 102–3; oral traditions and the present, 8–11; of original Jie family, 147; places of memory, 244; political and social relations, 11–18; and rhetoric of pastness, 164–5; stock memory images, 189; and storytellers in exile, 64; varying images of, 201. *See also* dreaming, dreams
Mills, M., 30
Mirzeler, Mustafa Kemal, *201*
Mkutu, K., 50, 59–60
modernization, 9–10, 49–52, 56–7, 139, 246; use of term, 325n2
Moroto, 48–9
Moru a Awor, 74; map, *xvi*
Moru a Eker (phallic rock), 43, 143, *145*, 145–9, 337
Moru a Nayeche, 184, *199*, 337; in creation story, 117–18; ecology, 37; landscape and historical traditions, 241–4; landscape's significance, 156–9; in mediations, 177–8; memories embedded in, 10–11; in Nayeche and the gray bull Engiro,

sacrifice: of Engiro the gray bull, 105, 117, 154, 235; of Engiro the gray bull and mediations, 177–80; historical tradition structure, 110; during mediations, 184–5; memory and origin story, 143; in sorghum tending, 210–11; in story of Nairanabwo, 96–7
Samburu people, 108, 122, 283, 286, 318, 329n32
Scheub, H., 4, 23, 50–1, 56, 62, 64, 102–3, 105, 109, 131–2, 135, 139, 222–4, 326(intro)n6, 327(ch2)n1, 328n9
Schieffelin, E., 9, 15
Schlee, G., 101, 108, 122, 171
Schneider, W., 62
Sepenya (heroine of Elmolo tradition), 120–3, 329n32; The Story of Sepenya, 281–4
Shostak, M., 221–2, 226
Slyomovics, S., 10, 64, 142–3, 160, 326n8
Sobania, N., 101–2, 108, 119–22, 171, 249
Somali, 45, 46, 48, 59, 80
sorghum, 36, 38, 95, 338; beer as gift, 217; drinking of beer, 215–16; and female fertility image of the Ebur, 145; firemakers' distribution of, 74–5, 109; and firemakers' rituals, 41; firemakers' role, 51; as gift of ancestors, 217–18; in harvest rituals, 87, 203, 227–30, 234–6; introduction of serena sorghum, 212–13; May planting, 78; and modernization, 161–2; in Nacham's biography, 125–6; nurturing of the Jie, 147–52; production rituals, 210–16; role of metaphors in historical traditions,

53; sowed by Orwakol wives, 154; in story of Nairanabwo, 96–7. See also beer (sorghum beer)
Spear, T., 141, 247
Stites, E., 56–7, 64, 250
stories: A Bat and His Friends Who Went Raiding, 238–9, 295–7; The Elephant and the Fox, 291–5; The Gray Bull Engiro, 265–6; The Hyena and the Bell, 306–7; The Hyena and the Calf, 307–8; The Hyena Who Ate Baby Goats, 297–8; The Man Whose Child Was Eaten by the Hyena, 298–9; The Memory of Aonyot, 287–90; The Memory of Nacham, 284–7; The Memory of Nakol and His Father, 290–1; The Memory of the Ngipalajam, 272–3; Nakadanya, the Cradle Land of Long Ago, 275–6; Nayeche, 276–8, 278–9, 279–81; The Original Ancestral Conflict, 266–9; The Original Ancestral Fire, 273–5; The Original Ancestral Raiding, 269–72; The Rabbit and the Baboon, 302–3; The Rabbit Who Did Not Drink Water, 239, 299–302; The Story of a Monkey Who Was Caught Stealing Food, 308–9; The Story of Napeikisina, 309–18, 318–24; The Story of Sepenya, 281–3, 283–4; The Story of the Gray Bull Engiro and Longiro River, 264–5; The Story of the Pregnant Camel, 284; The Story of the Rabbit Who Was Caught Stealing Food, 303–6. See also biographical tales; folktales; historical traditions/oral traditions

216; in mediations, 176; in
Nayeche and the gray bull Engiro,
5–6, 88–91; from Tarash River, *200*;
traded for sorghum at harvest, 87;
women gather, 207

Willis, 210
Wilson, D.A., 40
Wilson, J.G., 43

Young, C., ix, 48–54

ANTHROPOLOGICAL HORIZONS

Editor: Michael Lambek, University of Toronto

Published to date:

The Varieties of Sensory Experience: A Sourcebook in the Anthropology of the Senses / Edited by David Howes (1991)

Arctic Homeland: Kinship, Community, and Development in Northwest Greenland / Mark Nuttall (1992)

Knowledge and Practice in Mayotte: Local Discourses of Islam, Sorcery, and Spirit Possession / Michael Lambek (1993)

Deathly Waters and Hungry Mountains: Agrarian Ritual and Class Formation in an Andean Town / Peter Gose (1994)

Paradise: Class, Commuters, and Ethnicity in Rural Ontario / Stanley R. Barrett (1994)

The Cultural World in Beowulf / John M. Hill (1995)

Making It Their Own: Severn Ojibwe Communicative Practices / Lisa Philips Valentine (1995)

Merchants and Shopkeepers: A Historical Anthropology of an Irish Market Town, 1200–1991 / Philip Gulliver and Marilyn Silverman (1995)

Tournaments of Value: Sociability and Hierarchy in a Yemeni Town / Ann Meneley (1996)

Mal'uocchiu: Ambiguity, Evil Eye, and the Language of Distress / Sam Migliore (1997)

Between History and Histories: The Production of Silences and Commemorations / Edited by Gerald Sider and Gavin Smith (1997)

Eh, Paesan! Being Italian in Toronto / Nicholas DeMaria Harney (1998)

Theorizing the Americanist Tradition / Edited by Lisa Philips Valentine and Regna Darnell (1999)

Colonial 'Reformation' in the Highlands of Central Sulawesi, Indonesia, 1892–1995 / Albert Schrauwers (2000)

The Rock Where We Stand: An Ethnography of Women's Activism in Newfoundland / Glynis George (2000)

Being Alive Well: Health and the Politics of Cree Well-Being / Naomi Adelson (2000)

Irish Travellers: Racism and the Politics of Culture / Jane Helleiner (2001)

Of Property and Propriety: The Role of Gender and Class in Imperialism and Nationalism / Edited by Himani Bannerji, Shahrzad Mojab, and Judith Whitehead (2001)

People of Substance: An Ethnography of Morality in the Colombian Amazon / Carlos David Londoño Sulkin (2012)

'We Are Still Didene': Stories of Hunting and History from Northern British Columbia / Thomas McIlwraith (2012)

Being Māori in the City: Indigenous Everyday Life in Auckland / Natacha Gagné (2013)

The Hakkas of Sarawak: Sacrificial Gifts in Cold War Era Malaysia / Kee Howe Yong (2013)

Remembering Nayeche and the Gray Bull Engiro: African Storytellers of the Karamoja Plateau and the Plains of Turkana / Mustafa Kemal Mirzeler (2014)